Irish Literature
A Reader

Irish
Studies

Ireland

Irish Literature

A Reader

MAUREEN O'ROURKE MURPHY
and
JAMES MACKILLOP

SYRACUSE UNIVERSITY PRESS

First Edition 1987
95 96 97 98 99 00   8 7 6 5 4 3

The paper used in this publication meets the minimum requirements
of American National Standard for Information Sciences—Permanence
of Paper for Printed Library Materials, ANSI Z39.48-1984. ∞™

Library of Congress Cataloging-in-Publication Data

Irish literature: A Reader

(Irish studies)
Bibliography: p.
Includes index.
1. Irish literature—Translations into English.
2. English literature—Irish authors.   3. English
literature—Translations from Irish.   I. Murphy,
Maureen O'Rourke.   II. MacKillop, James.   III. Series:
Irish studies (Syracuse University Press)
I'B1421.I76   1987   891.6'2'08   87-6500
ISBN 0–8156–2405–0 (alk. paper)

For DON MURPHY
(1934–1986)

Do chodladh san gcillse thuas
dod charaid ní cuimse an cás;
do ré níor fionnadh a raon
do thaobh gur bioradh re bás.

MAUREEN O'ROURKE MURPHY is Dean of Students and Associate Professor of English at Hofstra University, President of the American Committee for Irish Studies, and author of *A Guide to Irish Studies in the United States,* as well as numerous articles and reviews on Irish literature.

JAMES MACKILLOP is Chairman and Professor of English, Onondaga Community College and the author of *Fionn Mac Cumhaill* (Syracuse University Press), *Speaking of Words,* and *The Copy Book.* He is currently preparing *A Dictionary of Celtic Myth, Legend, Saga, and Folklore.*

CONTENTS

PREFACE

This anthology is designed to give undergraduate students access to the immense variety and richness of literature written in Ireland. Writing in the native language of Ireland is part of a living tradition more than a thousand years old; writing in English by natives of Ireland includes some of the most widely admired literary masterpieces of the past one hundred years. In some instances, Irish writers have written in both the Irish language (or Gaelic) and in English; in any case, the two traditions are never very far apart. What we have sought to present here is a sampling of what there is to be known. Some of the greatest Irish writers—Yeats, Joyce, and O'Casey, among others—are not found here, as their works are readily available elsewhere. Instead, we have given more attention to certain important poems, stories, and plays that may be harder to find.

For each author, we have tried to explain how the work included here relates to a larger body of work. In addition, at the end of each entry we include a selective bibliography to guide the reader both to principal works and to appropriate biography and criticism. The selections we have made will mean more, in our judgment, when viewed as a part of an author's larger output, or as a contribution to a trend or movement in aesthetics, religion, or politics.

Someone has remarked that all anthologies are as interesting for what they leave out as for what they include. Our highest criteria were that the works be significant in themselves, be representative of the author (or of a style or movement), and be teachable. Consequently, our organization is not thematic, and such chronology as we do impose can easily be ignored. Some instructors may wish to make their own links within the text. Myles Dillon's summary of the "Tragedy of the Children of Lir" from early Ireland, for example, invites a comparison with Katharine Tynan Hinkson's treatment of the story at the beginning of the twentieth century. The discerning reader will find many common threads: nature, and the importance of land-scape; the use of Irish tradition; exile.

Sea Cliff and Syracuse   MO'RM
Spring 1987   JMK

ACKNOWLEDGMENTS

Behan, Brendan. "The Confirmation Suit." By Permission of O'Brien Press of Dublin.

Boland, Eavan. "Athene's Song," "Child of Our Time." By permission of the author. "After a Childhood Away from Ireland." From *Nightfeed*, Eavan Boland, published by Arlen House, The Women's Press, Kinnear Court, 16–20 Sth. Cumberland Street, Dublin 2, Ireland.

Clarke, Austin. "Aisling," "The Straying Student," "Irish-American Dignitary," "Burial of an Irish President." By permission of R. Dardis Clarke.

Colum, Padraic. "The Plougher." By Permission of Devin-Adair. "The Book of Kells," "St. Stephen's Green," and "Expecting No One." By the permission of Dolmen Press.

Corkery, Daniel. "Solace." From *A Munster Twilight*, published by The Mercier Press, 4 Bridge Street, Cork, Ireland.

Devlin, Denis. "Lough Derg." Copyright 1942 by Marie C. Figarolo di Gropello. Reprinted from *Selected Poems* by Denis Devlin, by permission of Henry Holt and Company, Inc.

Dillon, Éilis. Translation of "Caoineadh Airt Uí Laoghaire." By kind permission of the author.

Dillon, Myles. Summary/translation, *Táin Bó Cuailgne, The Exile of the Sons of Usneach, the Frenzy of Suibhne. Early Irish Literature* published by The University of Chicago Press. Copyright 1948 by The University of Chicago Press.

Flower, Robin. "He That Never Read a Line," "Pangur Ban." By kind permission of Pat Flower.

Gogarty, Oliver St. John. "The Crab Tree," "Ringsend." By permission of Devin-Adair and Oliver Duane Gogarty. Selection from *As I Was Going Down Sackville Street* by permission of Harcourt Brace Jovanovich and Oliver Duane Gogarty.

Heaney, Seamus. "Digging," "Traditions," "Mossbawn: Two Poems in Dedication," "Punishment," "Exposure" from *Selected Poems 1965–1975* by Seamus Heaney. Copyright 1966, 1969, 1972, 1975, 1980 by Seamus Heaney. Reprinted by permission of Farrar, Straus and Giroux, Inc. Also by permission of Faber and Faber.

Hewitt, John. "The Glens," "An Irishman in Coventry." By kind permission of the author.

Hyde. Douglas. "The Necessity for De-Anglicising Ireland," selections from *The Love*

Songs of Connacht by permission of Mrs. Christopher (Joan) Sealy of Co. Wicklow, Ireland.

Kavanagh, Patrick. "Shancoduff," "Epic," "Pegasus," "Canal Bank Walk," "Lines Written on a Seat on the Grand Canal, Dublin," "In Memory of My Mother." From the *Complete Poems of Patrick Kavanagh*, The Peter Kavanagh Hand Press, New York 1972. By permission of Mr. Peter Kavanagh and Mrs. Patrick Kavanagh. Courtesy of Mr. Peter Fallon, Gallery Press.

Keefe, Joan. Translations: "Valentine Browne," "Friend of My Heart," "Sean O'Dwyer of the Glen." By permission of Joan Keefe. From *Irish Poems from Cromwell to the Famine* published by Associated University Presses, 1977.

Kelleher, John V. "Cú Chuimne." By permission of Dolmen Press and by kind permission of the author.

Kinsella, Thomas. "Kilcash," "In the Ringwood," "The Poet Egan O'Rahilly, Homesick in Old Age," "Handclasp at Euston Station," "Sisters." By permission of the author and Wake Forest University Press.

Lavin, Mary. "Happiness." By kind permission of the author.

Longley, Michael. "Emily Dickinson," "The Linen Industry," "In Memoriam." By permission of Gallery Press.

McGuckian, Medhbh. "The Mast Year," "The Soil Map." By permission of Oxford University Press.

MacNeill, Máire. Translations: "Scribe in the Woods," "Blackbird by the Belfast Lough," "Liadan Tells of Her Love for Cuirithir," "News of Winter," "Eve." By kind permission of the author.

Mhac an tSaoi, Máire. "Inquisitio 1584," "For Sheila," "Finit." By kind permission of the author and Sairseal agus Ó Marcaigh. "Lament for Séamus Ennis" by permission of the author.

Mahon, Derek. "A Disused Shed in County Wicklow," "The Snow Party." By permission of Oxford University Press.

Montague, John. "Like Dolmens Round My Childhood, The Old People," "A Grafted Tongue," "Lament for the O'Neills." By permission of Dolmen Press and Wake Forest University Press.

Muldoon, Paul. "Mules," "The Boundary Commission." By permission of Wake Forest University Press.

Murphy, Gerard. Translations: "The Bird Crib," "Poem XLI, *Duanaire Finn*, II. By kind permission of the Irish Texts Society, 22 Whitehall, London. "A Blue Eye Will look Back," "The Three Best-Loved Places," "Derry," "My Hand is Weary with Writing." By permission of Oxford University Press.

Murphy, Richard. "Roof-Tree." Reprinted by permission of Faber and Faber Ltd. from *The Price of Stone* by Richard Murphy. "Slate." Reprinted by permission of Wake Forest University Press, from *The Battle of Aughrim* by Richard Murphy.

ní Chuilleanáin, Eiléan. "Waterfall," "The Second Voyage." By permission by the Gallery Press.

ní Dhomhnaill, Nuala. "Deep Freeze," "Inside Out." Reprinted by the kind permission of the Irish-American bilingual journal *An Droichead/The Bridge*.

O'Brien, Flann. Selection from *At Swim-Two-Birds*. By permission of Walker and Co. and by kind permission of the Estate of Flann O'Brien and Grafton Books.

"A Bash in the Tunnel." From *Stories and Plays by Flann O'Brien*. Copyright 1951 by Brian O'Nolan. All rights reserved. Reprinted by permission of Viking Penguin Inc.

O'Conaire, Pádraic. "Put to the Rack." Trans. Eamonn O'Neill in *The Woman at the Window*. By permission of the Educational Company of Ireland.

O'Connor, Frank. "The Long Road to Ummera." By permission of A. A. Knopf and Joan Daves. From the *Collected Stories of Frank O'Connor,* copyright 1981.

Ó Direáin, Máirtín. "Honesty," "The Dignity of Sorrow," "Memories." By permission of An Clóchomhar, Teo.

O'Faoláin, Seán. "A Broken World." Reprinted by kind permission of Curtis Brown Ltd. on behalf of Seán O'Faoláin. Copyright Seán O'Faoláin, 1937.

O'Flaherty, Liam. "Going into Exile." By permission of A. D. Peters & Co. Ltd. and the Devin-Adair Publishers.

O'Ríordáin, Seán. "Back of the House," "Reoite," "Adhlacadh no Mháthair," trans. Valentine Iremonger. By kind permission of Sairséal agus Ó Marcaigh, Teo (and Mr. Iremonger).

Rodgers, W. R. "An Irish Lake," "The Party." Copyright W. R. Rodgers 1941. By permission of Lucy Rodgers Cohen.

Stephens, James. Extracts from *Insurrection in Dublin* and *Irish Fairy Tales.* By permission of The Society for Authors (London) on behalf of the copyright owner, Mrs. Iris Wise.

Ussher, Arland. Translation of Part I of "The Midnight Court." By kind permission of Arland Ussher's daughter, Hetty Staples, and son, J. M. Keith.

Irish Literature
A Reader

PART I

EIGHTH CENTURY TO THE IRISH LITERARY RENAISSANCE

EARLY AND MEDIEVAL
IRISH LITERATURE

With a manuscript tradition dating to the sixth century, Irish literature—the oldest vernacular literature in Western Europe—is remarkable for its range: law texts, genealogies, scholarly treatises, devotional tracts, and especially imaginative literature. Battles and burnings, feasts and forays, amours and elopements, voyages and visions are some of the themes of the tales that scholars have organized into four great Cycles of stories:the Mythological, the Ulster, the Fenian, and the Historical. (We might say that cattle rustling is the theme of the *Táin Bó Cuailgne,* Ireland's *Aeneid!*) Ours is only a summary of the action, but there is a splendid modern translation by Thomas Kinsella.

The "Exile of the Children of Usnach," one of the *réamhscéalta* or preliminary stories to the *Táin,* is the tale of a young woman betrothed to an old man who elopes with a young lover. It introduced the Tristan and Iseult theme into European literature. One of the most popular sources for later Irish writers, Deirdre's story has appeared in a score of modern versions, notably those of John Millington Synge and W.B. Yeats.

"The Exile of the Children of Usnach" and "The Tragedy of the Children of Lir" are two of the *Trí Truaighe na Sgéalaigheachta* [The Three Sorrows of Storytelling), though "The Tragedy of the Children of Lir" is probably a later (15th or 16th century) composition. The motif of children enchanted by an evil stepmother is, of course, familiar from folklore; readers may also know the story through Thomas Moore's poem, "The Song of Fionnuala."

Early Irish poetry also speaks of the sorrow of exile: first, the self-imposed exile of such early monks as St. Columcille, who left

3

Ireland in the sixth century to found a monastery at Iona; later, involuntary political or economic exile. Love, too, is tragic, being variously unlucky, unrealized, or unfulfilled. Scholars have commented on the freshness, intensity, and compression of Early Irish poetry. Many of the little poems found in the margins of manuscripts were written by monks who looked up from copying scripture to celebrate their surroundings. Comparing them to *haiku*, Kuno Meyer, who translated many of the lyrics, said: "Like the Japanese, the Celts were always quick to take an artistic hint; they avoid the obvious and the commonplace; the half said thing to them is dearest." The importance of landscape, embracing at once nature, place, and mythology, is a theme that has come down from the old hermit poets to their medieval counterparts, and later to modern and contemporary Irish poetry. It is a special feature of Middle Irish tales, such as those told about Fionn mac Cumhaill.

Since the eleventh century, the name of Fionn mac Cumhaill (Finn mac Cool) has been preserved in manuscript as well as in oral tradition. Fionn is the most popular Irish mythological hero. Contemporary storytellers include tales of Fionn and his warrior band, the Fianna, in their repertoires, while placenames and field monuments further testify to his place in folk memory. Like all cultural heroes, Fionn performed precocious feats as a boy, while as a man he leads the Fianna in hunting, in feasting, and in warfare. However, a darker side is revealed in *Tóraidheacht Dhiarmada agus Ghráinne* [Pursuit of Diarmaid and Gráinne], the Fenian parallel to "The Exile of the Children of Usnach," where Fionn is the injured older man responsible for the death of Diarmaid. The interested reader is directed to James MacKillop's *Fionn mac Cumhaill. Celtic Myth in English Literature*, which traces the figure of Fionn from Macpherson's *Ossian* to Joyce's *Finnegans Wake*.

Buile Suibhne [The Madness of Sweeney], the Middle-Irish romance translated by J. G. O'Keeffe, is another important source for Irish writers. Dating back to the second half of the twelfth century, there are earlier references to Suibhne Geilt ("Mad Sweeney") at the Battle of Magh Rath (637). Some of the best poems in the text are those in praise of the trees of Ireland, Suibhne's leafy home as he wanders in his frenzy through the country.

Ferguson used Suibhne's story in *Congal*, and he became Yeats's King Goll; Flann O'Brien used Suibhne for the Mad Sweeney versus Jem Casey episode in *At Swim Two Birds*. Suibhne appears in the title poem of the Donegal poet Cathal O'Searcaigh's first collection, *Súile Shuibhne* [Sweeney's Eye], and Austin Clarke has translated part of the romance. Finally, Trevor Joyce published a translation called *The Poems of Sweeny Peregrine,* and Seamus Heaney's adaptation appeared under the title *Sweeney Astray.*

Old Irish Prose

TÁIN BÓ CUAILNGE

Once when their royal bed had been made ready for Ailill and Maeve they conversed as they lay on the pillows. "It is a true saying, girl," said Ailill, "that the wife of a good man is well off." "It is true," said the girl. "Why do you say so?" "Because," said Ailill, "you are better off today than the day I wed you." "I was well off without you," said Maeve. "I had not heard or known it," said Ailill, "but that you were an heiress and that your nearest neighbors were robbing and plundering you." "That was not so," said Maeve, "for my father, Eochu Feidlech son of Finn, was high king of Ireland." And she went on to boast of her riches, and he of his.

Their treasures were brought before them, and it appeared that Maeve had possessions equal to those of Ailill, save for a splendid bull, Whitehorn, which had belonged to Maeve's herd but had wandered into the herd of Ailill because it would not remain in a woman's possession. All her wealth seemed to Maeve not worth a penny, since she had no bull equal to that of Ailill. She learned that there was one as good in the province of Ulster in the cantred of Cuailnge, and she sent messengers to ask a loan of it for a year, promising a rich reward. If the reward was not enough, she would even grant the owner the enjoyment of her love. The messengers returned without the bull and reported the owner's refusal. "There is no need to smooth over difficulties," said Maeve, "for I knew that it would not be given freely until it was taken by force, and so it will be taken."

Maeve summoned the armies of Connacht and Cormac son of Conchobar and Fergus son of Roech, who were in exile from Ulster at the time, and set out to carry off the precious bull. Before the expedition started, she consulted her druid for a prophecy. He told her that she at least would return alive. Then she met a mysterious prophetess who rode on the shaft of a chariot, weaving a fringe with a gold staff, and she asked her to prophesy. The woman answered, "I see crimson upon them, I see red." Four times Maeve appealed against this oracle, but each time the answer was the same; and the prophetess then chanted a poem in which she foretold the deeds of Cuchulainn.

On the first day the army advanced from Cruachan as far as Cúil Silinni, and the tents were pitched. Ailill's tent was on the right wing of the army. The tent of Fergus was next, and beside it was the tent of Cormac son of Conchobar. To the left of Ailill was the tent of Maeve and next to hers that of Findabair, her daughter. Maeve drove through the camp to see which troops were most eager and which most negligent, and she observed that the Gálióin [Leinstermen] excelled all the others. She returned to Ailill with this report and proposed that the Gálióin should be massacred before they advanced further, lest they should turn against Connacht in the battle. But she was persuaded merely to distribute them among the other troops, so that they could not combine against her. Fergus was appointed to guide the army, for the expedition was a revenge for him. He had been king of Ulster for seven years and had gone into exile when the sons of Usnach were killed in violation of his guaranty and protection. And so he marched in front. But he felt a pang of longing for Ulster and led the army astray northward and southward while he sent warnings to the Ulstermen. But the Ulstermen had been stricken with a mysterious sickness which afflicted them in times of danger, the result of a curse laid upon them by Macha, a fairy whom they had wronged. Cuchulainn and his father, Sualtam, were exempt from the curse, and they set out to oppose the enemy. They arrived at Ard Cuillenn, and Cuchulainn told his father to go back and warn the Ulstermen to depart from the open plains into the woods and valleys. He cut an oak sapling with a single stroke, and, using one arm, one leg, and one eye, he made it into a hoop, wrote an ogam on it, and fixed it around a stone pillar. Then he departed to keep a tryst with a girl southward at Tara.

The Connacht army reached Ard Cuillenn and saw the ogam. Fergus interpreted it for them. [His interpretation is in verse.] Any man who advanced farther that night, unless he made a hoop in the same way, would be slain by Cuchulainn before morning. Ailill decided to turn aside into the forest for the night. In the morning Cuchulainn returned from his tryst and found the army at Turloch Caille Móire, north of Cnogba na Ríg. There he cut off the fork of a tree with a single stroke and cast it into the earth from his chariot, so that two-thirds of the stem was buried in the earth. He came upon two Connacht warriors and beheaded them and their charioteers. He set their heads upon branches of the tree-fork and turned their horses back toward the camp, the chariots bearing the headless bodies of the men. The Connachtmen decided that the army of Ulster must be before them, and they sent Cormac son of Conchobar to reconnoiter, for they knew that the Ulstermen would not harm the son of their own king. Cormac advanced with three thousand men, but he found only the tree-fork and the four bleeding heads. When the rest of the army came up, they wondered at the sight. [Fergus chants a poem in which he bids the druids explain this marvel, and they answer in verse.] Fergus declared that it was *geis* for them to cross the ford at which the tree-fork stood until some one of them had removed it with one arm, standing in a chariot, as it had been cast. Maeve bade him do it himself. Seventeen times Fergus tried, and each time the chariot broke asunder, until his own chariot was brought him and he drew the tree-fork out of the ground.

Ailill decided to camp in the forest, southwest of Kells, and ordered a feast to be prepared and music provided. And when they had feasted and listened to music, Ailill asked Fergus who it could be that had killed four men so suddenly, and he named many of the famous warriors of Ulster. Fergus answered that it was none of these, but the boy Cuchulainn, his own foster-son and foster-son also to Conchobar, king of Ulster. [Here follows a long account of the boyhood feats of Cuchulainn.]

On the next day the army moved eastward, and Cuchulainn went to meet them. He surprised Orlam son of Ailill and Maeve and killed him, and the next day he killed three more with their charioteers. The army advanced and devastated the plains of Bregia and Muirthemne, and Fergus warned them to beware of Cuchulainn's vengeance. [His warning is in verse.] They went on into Cuailnge and reached the river Glaiss Cruind, but it rose against them so that they could not cross. A hundred chariots were swept into the sea. Cuchulainn followed hard upon them seeking battle, and he killed a hundred men. Maeve called upon her people to oppose him in equal combat. "Not I, not I!" said each one from where he stood. "My people owe no victim, and if one were owing I would not go against Cuchulainn, for it is not easy to fight with him." That night a hundred warriors died of fright at the sound of Cuchulainn's weapons.

Maeve sent a messenger to summon Cuchulainn to a parley with her and Fergus, but he would accept no conditions; and for the next three nights the army lay without pitching their tents and without feasting or music, and Cuchulainn killed a hundred men each night. The messenger was sent again to ask for terms, and he refused all that were proposed. There was one condition that he would accept, but he would not himself declare it. Fergus was able to tell that Cuchulainn would agree to single combat with a warrior each day, if the army would advance only while the combat lasted and would halt when the warrior had been killed until another was found. Maeve decided to accept the proposal, because it would be better to lose one man every day than a hundred every night.

[There follows a long series of single combats at a ford, with Cuchulainn always the victor. Maeve sometimes breaks faith and sends many warriors together. Once she sends six, and he kills them, and another time she sends a hundred, but Cuchulainn overcomes them all.]

Meanwhile Maeve turned northward to Dún Sobairche, and Cuchulainn followed her. He turned back to protect his own territory and found Buide son of Bán Blai, with twenty-four followers, driving the Brown Bull of Cuailnge, which they had found in Glenn na Samaisce in Sliab Cuilinn. The bull was accompanied by twenty-four of his cows. Cuchulainn challenged Buide and killed him, but, while they were exchanging casts of their spears, the great bull was driven off, and that was the greatest grief and dismay and confusion that Cu chulainn suffered on that hosting. Maeve plundered Dún Sobairche, and then after six weeks the four provinces of Ireland with Ailill and Maeve and those who had captured the bull came into camp together.

Lugh then came to help Cuchulainn [for he was his father] and told him to sleep for three days and nights and that he would stand before the army. While Cuchulainn slept, Lugh put herbs into his wounds so that he was healed in his sleep. Meanwhile, the boys of Ulster came and fought three battles against the army. They killed three times their own number, but all the hundred and fifty boys were killed. Then Cuchulainn awoke, and his spirit was strong within him, and he could have gone to an assembly or a foray or a tryst or an ale-house or to one of the chief assemblies of Ireland. "How long have I slept now, warrior?" said Cuchulainn. "Three days and three nights," said the warrior. "Alas for that!" said Cuchulainn. "Why so?" said the warrior. "The hosts have been all that time without attack," said Cuchulainn. "Indeed they have not, said the warrior. "Who has at-tacked them?" said Cuchulainn. "The boys came south from Emain Macha, a hundred and fifty kings' sons of Ulster, and they fought three battles against the hosts in the three days and three nights that you have slept, and three times their number fell by them, and the boys fell."

[Now the story tells at length of the vengeance of Cuchulainn for the boys of Ulster. This is a rhetorical passage to which the "runs" of modern folk tales correspond. The dressing of the charioteer and the arming of the hero are described in many words. The distortion of Cuchulainn in his frenzy is presented in a long passage. His war-chariot is armed with scythes. A list of his victims is given.] Cuchulainn killed a hundred and thirty kings in the Great Slaughter of Mag Muirthemne, and great numbers of dogs and horses and women and children and lesser people and mere rabble, for not one man out of every three of the Men of Ireland escaped without an injury to his leg or his head or his eye, or some lasting blemish.

After his fury and his great distortion, Cuchulainn showed himself in all his beauty to the women and girls and poets, for he did not think honorable the frightful shape he had worn the night before. Beautiful was the lad who came then to show himself to the hosts, son of Sualtam. [Here his beauty is described in a long rhetorical passage.] Maeve hid her face behind a fence of shields lest he should cast at her, but the girls asked the Men of Ireland to raise them on their shields to their shoulders to see the beauty of Cuchulainn. At last Maeve called upon Fer Diad to oppose Cuchulainn. Fer Diad was foster-brother of the hero. [This is the climax of the series of single combats.] Fer Diad has been threatened with disgrace if he refuses and is offered rich rewards if he consents. He laments his misfortune but cannot suffer dishonor. Fergus goes out to warn Cuchulainn that the terrible Fer Diad is coming against him, and again the dialogue is in verse. Fer Diad bid his charioteer harness his chariot, and the charioteer begs him not to go. He sets out, and Cuchulainn goes to meet him. [The language here is highly rhetorical, and the dialogues are repeated in verse after the prose. The whole episode makes 1,200 lines of the text.]

For three days Fer Diad and Cuchulainn fought, and neither gained any advantage over the other. Each night Cuchulainn sent leeches and herbs to heal the wounds of Fer Diad, and Fer Diad sent a share of his food to Cuchulainn. On the fourth day the choice of weapons lay with Cuchulainn, and he chose the "play of the ford." Then Fer Diad was afraid, for he knew that it was in the ford that Cuchulainn used to defeat every enemy. For a long time they fought equally, and at last Cuchulainn called for the *gae bolga*, the mysterious weapon whose use he alone had learned from Scáthach, the woman-warrior. [It was a spear which entered the wound as one point but made thirty points within.] Loeg set the *gae bolga* on the water, and Cuchulainn sent it against Fer Diad, and so Fer Diad was killed. Cuchulainn lamented the death of his friend. [There is a fine poem here.] He was himself prostrate from his wounds.

While Cuchulainn lay exhausted, single champions from Ulster came out to oppose the Men of Ireland [the Connacht army]. But Sualtam, Cuchulainn's human father, had heard in the distance the clamor of battle and said, "Either the sky is bursting or the sea is ebbing away or the earth is breaking asunder, or it is the clamor of my son fighting against unequal odds." He came to where Cuchulainn was and began to lament and pity him. And Cuchulainn sent him to Emain Macha to arouse the Ulstermen. Sualtam came to the palace and cried out, "Men are being killed, women are being carried off, cattle are being driven away!" Three times he called, but there was no answer; for it was a *geis* for the Ulstermen to speak before their king, and it was a *geis* for the king to speak before his druids. At last Cathbad the druid asked who was killing men and carrying off women and driving cattle away, and Sualtam told the news of Cuchulainn's long defense of Ulster. The druid answered merely that the man who had so insulted the king by speaking unbidden deserved to die. As Sualtam went away in anger, his shield turned against him, and the edge of the shield cut off his head. Conchobar said that there was too much noise. "The sky is above us and the earth below and the sea all about us. Unless the firmament with its showers of stars falls down upon the earth or the earth bursts asunder in an earthquake or the blue-bordered furrowy sea flows over the hair of the earth, I shall bring back every cow to her byre and yard and every woman to her home and dwelling, after victory in the battle."

Then Conchobar sent out a summons to the Ulstermen, and they came from east and west and north and advanced that same night as far as Iraird Cuillenn. Conchobar went ahead and brought in a hundred and sixty heads and a hundred and sixty women whom he had rescued.

Meanwhile, Ailill announced that he had now plundered Ulster from Samhain until spring and that he would wait no longer for the Ulstermen. They must come to Mag Ai and fight him there if they would. But, before departing, he sent out a scout to see whether the Ulstermen were coming into the plain of Meath. [Now the story gives a description of the approaching enemy as reported by the observer, in the manner beloved to these sagas. It makes more than five hundred lines of prose.]

That night the Morrígu, daughter of Ernmass, came to incite the armies against each other. [Her incantation is in archaic alliterative verse, the sense of which is obscure. It is followed by exhortations by Loeg, Cuchulainn's charioteer, and by Sencha the druid, addressed to the Ulstermen.]

In the morning, when the sun was up, the Ulstermen attacked, and the Men of Ireland came to meet them. Three times the Men of Ireland broke through northward, and each time they were driven back. Then Conchobar himself went into the field, where the enemy had been advancing, and found Fergus opposed to him. They fought shield to shield, and Fergus struck three mighty blows upon the shield of Conchobar so that it screamed aloud. But, remembering that he was an Ulsterman, he turned his anger against the hills, and three hills were shorn of their tops by his sword.

Cuchulainn heard the scream of Conchobar's magic shield where he lay prostrate from his wounds. He rose up in a heroic frenzy and seized no mere weapons but his war-chariot, body and wheels, to wield against the enemy. Fergus had promised, if ever he and Cuchulainn should meet in the battle, that he would retreat before him. When Cuchulainn now came against him, he led his company out of the fight, and the Leinstermen and Munstermen followed them, so that only Ailill and Maeve and their sons with nine battalions remained in the field. At noon Cuchulainn came into the battle. At sunset he had defeated the last battalion, and of his chariot there remained a few ribs of the body and a few spokes of the wheels.

Meanwhile, Maeve had sent the Brown Bull of Cuailnge to Cruachan, so that he at least should come there, whoever else might fail to come. Then she appealed to Cuchulainn to spare her army until it should go westward past Áth Mór, and he consented.

Fergus watched the army as it went west from Áth Mór. When Maeve lamented the disaster, he said that a drove of horses led by a mare could have no luck.

When the Brown Bull came to Cruachan, he uttered three mighty bellows, and the Whitehorned Bull heard that and came to fight him. All who had returned from the battle came to watch the bull-fight. They watched until night fell, and when night fell they could only listen to the great noise of the fight. The bulls traveled all over Ireland during the night, and in the morning the Brown Bull was seen going past Cruachan with the Whitehorned Bull on his horns. He galloped back to Ulster, scattering fragments of the dead bull's flesh from his horns on the way, and when he came to the border of Cuailnge, his heart broke, and he died.

summary by Myles Dillon

THE EXILE OF THE SONS OF USNACH

The Ulaid feasted one day in the house of Fedlimid, the chronicler of King Conchobar, and as the feast came to an end, a girl-child was born to the wife of Fedlimid; and a druid prophesied about her future. [The prophecy is pronounced in two long poems, parts of which have not yet been satisfactorily explained. Most of the text is clear. Her name is to be Deirdre. The child will grow to be a woman of wonderful beauty and will cause enmity and trouble and will depart out of the kingdom. Many will die on account of her.]

The Ulaid proposed to kill the child at once and so avoid the curse. But Conchobar ordered that she be spared and reared apart, hidden from men's eyes; and that he himself would take her for his wife. So Deirdre was intrusted to foster-parents and was reared in a dwelling apart. A wise woman, Leborcham, was the only other person allowed to see her.

Once the girl's foster-father was flaying a calf outside in the snow in winter to cook it for her, and she saw a raven drinking the blood in the snow. Then she said to Leborcham, "Fair would be a man upon whom those three colors should be: his hair like the raven, and his cheek like the blood, and his body like the snow." "Grace and prosperity to you!" said Leborcham. "He is not far from you, inside close by: Naoisi the son of Usnach." "I shall not be well," said she, "until I see him."

Once that same Naoisi was on the rampart of the fort sounding his cry. And sweet was the cry of the sons of Usnach. Every cow and every beast that would hear it used to give two-thirds excess of milk. For every man who heard it, it was enough of peace and entertainment. Good was their valor too. Though the whole province of the Ulaid should be around them in one place, if the three of them stood back to back, they would not overcome them, for the excellence of their defense. They were as swift as hounds at the hunt. They used to kill deer by their speed.

When Naoisi was there outside, soon she went out to him, as

though to go past him, and did not recognize him. "Fair is the heifer that goes past me," said he. "Heifers must grow big where there are no bulls," said she. "You have the bull of the province," said he, "the king of the Ulaid." "I would choose between you," said she, "and I would take a young bull like you." "No!" said he. Then she sprang toward him and caught his ears. "Here are two ears of shame and mockery," said she, "unless you take me with you."

Naoisi sounded his cry, and the Ulstermen sprang up as they heard it, and the sons of Usnach, his two brothers, went out to restrain and warn him. But his honor was challenged. "We shall go into another country," said he. "There is not a king in Ireland that will not make us welcome." That night they set out with 150 warriors and 150 women and 150 hounds, and Deirdre was with them.

Conchobar pursued them with plots and treachery, and they fled to Scotland. And they took service with the king of Scotland and built a house around Deirdre so that they should not be killed on account of her. One day the steward saw her and told the king of her beauty, so that he demanded her for wife; and the sons of Usnach had to flee and take refuge on an island in the sea.

The Conchobar invited them back and sent Fergus as a surety; but when they came to Emain, Naoisi and his followers were killed, and Deirdre was brought to Conchobar, and her hands were bound behind her back.

When Fergus and Cormac heard of this treachery, they came and did great deeds: three hundred of the Ulaid were killed, and women were killed, and Emain was burnt by Fergus. And Fergus and Cormac went to the court of Ailill and Maeve, and for sixteen years the Ulaid had no peace.

But Deirdre was for a year with Chonchobar, and she never smiled or raised her head from her knee.

And when the musicians came to her, she used to say:

> Though you think the fierce warriors fair, who march proudly over Emain, more proudly used they to march to their house, the brave sons of Usnach.
>
> Sweet to Conchobar, your king, are the pipers and horn-blowers, sweeter to me the cry of the sons of Usnach.
>
> Dear was the gray eye which women loved. It was fierce against an enemy. After a visit to the woods, noble course, delightful was his cry through the black forest.
>
> I do not sleep; and I put no purple on my nails. Joy comes not into my mind, since the sons of Usnach do not come.

Joy is not for me in the assembly of Emain which nobles fill, nor peace nor happiness nor comfort, nor a big house nor fair ornament.

And when Conchobar was comforting her she used to say:

Conchobar, what are you doing? You have caused me sorrow and tears. As long as I live, I shall not love you.

What was dearest to me under heaven, and what was most beloved, you have taken him from me,—a great wrong—so that I shall not see him till I die.

Two bright cheeks, red lips, eyebrows black as a chafer, pearly teeth bright with the noble color of snow.

Do not break my heart. Soon I shall die. Grief is stronger than the sea, if you could understand it, Conchobar.

"What do you hate most of what you see?" said Conchobar. "You," she said, "and Eogan son of Dubhthach." "You shall be a year with Eogan," said Conchobar. He gave her to Eogan. They went next day to the assembly of Macha. She was behind Eogan in the chariot. She had prophesied that she would not see two husbands on earth together. "Well, Deirdre," said Conchobar. "You look like a sheep between two rams, between Eogan and me." There was a big rock in front of her. She thrust her head against the rock, so that it shattered her head, and she died.

That is the exile of the Sons of Usnach, and the exile of Fergus and the Tragic Death of the sons of Usnach and of Deirdre. Finit. Amen. Finit.

summary by Myles Dillon

THE TRAGEDY OF THE CHILDREN OF LIR

After the battle of Tailtiu in which the Tuatha Dé were defeated by the Milesians [the Irish of later times], they assembled in one place from every part of the five provinces of Ireland and decided to choose a king for they preferred to be subject to one king of their own people rather than to different kings of the Milesians throughout the country. Those who hoped for election were Bodb, son of the Dagda,

Ilbrec of Assaroe, Lir of Síd Finnanchaid, Midir of Brí Léith, and Angus Óg, son of the Dagda. But Oengus did not desire it greatly, for he preferred to be as he was than to be king of the Tuatha Dé. Bodb was elected on account of the virtue of his father and because of his own virtue and because he was the eldest son of the Dagda.

Lir was offended by this choice, and he left the assembly without taking his leave of the others. They proposed to follow him and burn his house as a punishment for this misbehavior, but Bodb dissuaded them. Lir's wife died, and he fell into despondency; and Bodb proposed a reconciliation by offering Lir one of his foster-children in marriage, for the three daughters of Oilioll Árann had been fostered at his house at Loch Deirgdeirc. Lir chose Aeb, the eldest of the three, and returned with her to his dwelling, where a wedding feast was held. Aeb bore him twins, a son and a daughter, Aed and Fionnuala ["Fire" and "Whiteshoulder"]. She became pregnant again, and again she bore twins, two sons, Fiachra and Conn, but she died at their birth. Lir was again despondent and found comfort only in his children. Bodb gave him Aoife, a sister of Aeb, and they were married, and Aoife honored and loved her sister's children.

Bodb often visited Lir for love of the children, and often they used to go to his palace. When the Feast of Age was held at Lir's dwelling, the four children were the delight and entertainment of all. They used to lie on couches beside their father, and he would get up early in the morning to be with his children.

Aoife grew jealous of Lir's love for the children, and she pretended sickness and lay for almost a year as though sick and she planned their destruction. One day she set out with them, as though to visit Bodb, and Fionnuala did not wish to go, for she had a foreboding of evil; but she could not escape her doom. When they had gone some way, Aoife said to her people, "Kill the children of Lir, because their father has ceased to love me. I shall reward you as you desire." "No," said they, "We will not kill them. It is evil to think of such a deed, and worse to speak of it." Then Aoife sought to kill herself with a sword, but her womanly nature prevented her. They came to Lake Derryvaragh, and she told the children to bathe in the lake. When they were in the water, she struck them with a magic wand and changed them into swans.

Fionnuala reproached Aoife and foretold her ruin. She asked her to fix a term to the curse that she had laid upon them, and Aoife said that it would last until a woman from the south should be joined to a man from the north, namely, Lairgrén son of Colmán, king of

Connacht, and Deoch daughter of Fíngein, king of Munster. Since Fionnuala had asked for a term, no power of the Tuatha Dé could lift the curse until they had spent three hundred years on Lake Derryvaragh and three hundred years by the Mull of Cantyre in Scotland and three hundred years in Erris and around Inishglory. But Aoife relented, and, since she could not undo the curse, she granted the swans certain qualities. They would have the power of speech and the gift of singing, so that no music in the world would be equal to it, and they should have their senses and faculties. They should suffer no anguish in being in the form of swans. She spoke a lay in which the curse was repeated, and she lamented the anger of Lir which she had now brought on herself.

Aoife went to Bodb's dwelling. He asked for the children, and she replied that Lir would no longer intrust them to Bodb. He sent messengers to Lir, and Aoife's treachery was discovered. Bodb changed her into a demon, and she must wander through the air in this form forever. He and the Tuatha Dé came to the shore of the lake and stayed listening to the music of the swans. And the Men of Ireland, too, came from every part to listen to the swans, so that for three hundred years the Tuatha Dé and the Men of Ireland were by Lake Derryvaragh; and the swans conversed with them during the day and sang them to sleep at night. And all who heard the music slept peacefully, though they were sick or in trouble. All were happy after hearing the music.

At the end of that time Fionnuala said that it was time to go. She said farewell to Bodb in a short poem, and the swans flew away to the Mull of Cantyre. That lonely sea was a place of hardship for them, and their sufferings are described. They were scattered by a storm in winter, and Fionnuala lamented in verse their misery and remembered the happiness of the past. All night she waited alone on the Rock of Seals, and in the morning she saw Conn approaching wet and weary. Then Fiachra came and she warmed him under her wing; and she said, "If only Aed would come, we should be without complaint."

By day they visited the shores of Ireland or Scotland and at night they returned to Mull. One day when they were in the mouth of the river Bann, they saw horsemen approaching. These were the two sons of Bodb with a third of the fairy host, who had been in search of them. They brought tidings of the Tuatha Dé. Lir and Bodb were well, and all were now assembled at Síd Finnachaid for the Feast of Age, peaceful and happy except for the sorrow because of the absence of the four children of Lir. Fionnuala replied in a poem lamenting their fate. The people of Lir were happy, but his children had a cold dwelling place. They had exchanged satin for the feathers of swans. The white sand and the sea water were their food instead of the mead of the hazel tree. Once they enjoyed the instruction of Manannán, the conversation of Bodb, the sweetness of the kiss of Angus.

At the appointed time Fionnuala said that they must go to Erris. They suffered great hardship there for a long time. One night was the worst of all, when the sea froze from Erris to Achill. Fionnuala lamented their misery:

> Sad is the cry of the swans tonight. It is an ebb or a drought that has caused it: no cool water beneath them, their bodies waste from thirst.
>
> No firm supporting water, no wave washes their sides. The pleasant sea has frozen so that it is smooth as a board.
>
> O God, who made heaven and earth and delivered the six hosts, save, too, this flock. Even the strong become weak through suffering.

"Brothers," said Fionnuala, "believe in the God of truth, who made the heaven with its clouds and the earth with its fruits and the sea with its wonders, and you shall have help and comfort from the Lord." And they believed and received comfort and suffered no more from storm or bad weather.

At the end of three hundred years they returned to Síd Finnachaid and found the site empty and deserted, without house or fire or dwelling. They uttered three cries of sorrow, and Fionnuala spoke a lay:

> Strange it is to see this place without house or shelter. My heart is sad from what I see.
>
> No dogs, no sporting hounds, no women, no stately kings, I never knew this place to be thus in my father's time.
>
> No drinking horns, no cups, no feasting within painted walls; no horsemen, no happy youths—
>
> . . . .
>
> Formerly this place was not left to grass and forest. All that we knew are dead, and we are here, It is strange.

They returned to Inishglory and remained there until St. Patrick came to Ireland and Mo Chaemóc to Inishglory. One morning they heard the bell for matins. When the singing of matins was over, they sang their lovely song, and Mo Chaemóc heard it and prayed that he might know who made such music. It was revealed to him. He took the swans, and he joined Fionnuala to Aed, and Conn to Fiachra with silver chains, and they stayed with him and were his delight, and they forgot all their suffering.

It was then that Lairgrén was king of Connacht, and Deoch, daughter of the king of Munster, was his wife. She heard the fame of the birds and desired them for herself, and Lairgrén came and seized them. But his violent act undid the magic which disguised them. They were changed back and appeared as three withered old men and an old woman.

Mo Chaemóc baptized them and they died; and they were buried, Conn on the right side of Fionnuala and Fiachra on her left, and Aed in front. And they went to heaven. And Mo Chaemóc was sad after they were gone.

summary by Miles Dillon

OLD IRISH POETRY

NEWS OF WINTER

Found in a late sixth century life of St. Columcille, this poem—a gloss on the word for "sea"—is attributed to Fionn.

> News for you:
> The stag roars,
> Winter pours,
> Summer's end.
>
> High cold wind,
> Low lies sun,
> Short its run,
> Sea waves pound.

Bracken browns,
Clumps are bare,
In grey air
Wild goose cries.

Cold has seized
Song bird's wing,
Ice is King.
This is my news.

trans. Máire MacNeill

THE BLACKBIRD BY BELFAST LOCH

In his edition of the poem, Gerard Murphy suggests the blackbird
was singing from a gorse bush. Loch Lee (Loch Loígh) is Belfast
Lough.

The small bird
lets a trill
from bright tip
of yellow bill.

The shrill chord
by Loch Lee
of blackbird
from yellow tree.

trans. Máire MacNeill

LÍADAN TELLS OF HER LOVE FOR CUIRITHIR

These early seventh century lovers were the subject of a ninth
century poem that describes how Líadan promised to marry Cuirithir
but became a nun instead. Cuirithir entered a monastery in the Déisi
(Waterford); Líadan followed him there, but he fled. The poem
attributed to Líadan is the earliest known of the Irish women's

laments. Líadan and Cuirithir anticipate a later fascinating and tragic clerical couple—Héloïse and Abelard.

Void of joy
what I have done:
the one I loved I crossed.

Crazed I was
to take that vow
and outlaw his desire.

Not pain he sought
but a quiet road
to Paradise.

For small cause
I hurt him most
whom I would hurt the least.

I Líadan
loved Cuirithir:
Nothing is more true.

A short time
we were together
Cuirithir and I.

Forest music
sang to us
and the sound of the sea.

I thought then
nothing I would do
could vex Cuirithir.

No secret now:
I loved him
as I loved no other.

A roar of fire
has split my heart;
without him I die.

trans. Máire MacNeill

THE SCRIBE IN THE WOODS

This ninth century lyric was found in the margin of Priscian's treatise
on Latin grammar in the monastery of St. Gall near Lake Constance,
Switzerland, a monastery famous for its library of Irish manuscripts.
The Irish St. Gall (d.645) is the Swiss patron saint.

Over me green branches hang
A blackbird leads the loud song;
Above my pen-lined booklet
I hear a fluting bird-throng

The cuckoo pipes a clear call
Its dun cloak hid in deep dell:
Praise to God for this goodness
That in woodland I write well.

trans. Máire MacNeill

THE VIKING TERROR

Another St. Gall manuscript poem mentions the Vikings, who began
to raid Ireland in the ninth century.

Bitter is the wind tonight,
It tosses the ocean's white hair:
Tonight I fear not the fierce warriors of Norway
Coursing on the Irish Sea.

trans. Kuno Meyer

PANGUR BAN

Another ninth century poem found in a miscellany of notes on grammar, astronomy, and Latin poetry in the monastery of St. Paul in Carinthia (southern Austria) suggests that the monk-poet must have been a kindred spirit to the monk-scribe whose playful white cats arrest their own mice on the Chi-Rho page of The Book of Kells. Pangur is a Welsh name. Ban (Ir. *bán, bawn*) means white.

I and Pangur Ban, my cat,
'Tis a like task we are at;
Hunting mice is his delight,
Hunting words I sit all night.

Better far than praise of men
'Tis to sit with book and pen;
Pangur bears me no ill will,
He too plies his simple skill.

'Tis a merry thing to see
At our tasks how glad are we,
When at home we sit and find
Entertainment to our mind.

Oftentimes a mouse will stray
In the hero Pangur's way;
Oftentimes my keen thought set
Takes a meaning in its net.

'Gainst the wall he sets his eye
Full and fierce and sharp and sly;
'Gainst the wall of knowledge I
All my little wisdom try.

When a mouse darts from its den,
O how glad is Pangur then!
O what gladness do I prove
When I solve the doubts I love!

So in peace our tasks we ply,
Pangur Ban, my cat, and I;

In our arts we find our bliss,
I have mine and he has his.

Practice every day has made
Pangur perfect in his trade;
I get wisdom day and night
Turning darkness into light.

trans. Robin Flower

THREE NINTH-CENTURY POEMS FOR STUDENTS AND PILGRIMS

HE THAT NEVER READ A LINE

"Son of learning" is a literal translation of *mac léinn* (pron. mac lay in), the Irish word for a student.

'Tis sad to see the Sons of learning
In everlasting Hellfire burning
While he that never read a line
Doth in eternal glory shine.

trans. Robin Flower

THE PILGRIM AT ROME

To go to Rome
Is much of trouble, little of profit:
The King whom thou seekest here,
Unless thou bring Him with thee, thou wilt not find.

trans. Kuno Meyer

CÚ CHUIMNE

A poem from the Annals of Ulster, A.D. 747

Cú Chuimne in youth
Read his way through half the Truth
He let the other half lie
While he gave women a try.

Well for him in old age,
He became a holy sage.
He gave women the laugh.
He read the other half.

trans. John V. Kelleher

From the Tenth or Eleventh Century

EVE

I am Eve, great Adam's wife;
I doomed Jesus from far off;
I lost Eden for my kind;
'Tis I should hang on the cross.

I had a king's house to rule.
Evil the choice that ruined me,
Evil the withering penalty.
Alas! my hand is foul.

'Twas I plucked the apple down,
Losing mastery to greed;
For that, women while they live
Will be captive to folly.

No ice would be anywhere,
No glistening windy winter,

No hell would be, no terror
Nor any sorrow but for me.

trans. Máire MacNeill

COLUMCILLE'S POEMS

These poems are attributed to St. Columcille—after St. Patrick, Ireland's most beloved saint. A member of the royal Uí Neill family, Columcille was born in Gartan, in Tír Luigdech, the modern parish of Kilmacrenan, County Donegal in 521 (d.597). He founded monasteries at Derry (546) and Durrow (551) before he left Ireland in 563 to establish a foundation at Iona. (From its summit he could still see Ireland.)

Adamnán's *Life of Columcille* describes Irish monastic life in the sixth century. Columcille's poems provide other insights: the identification with place, the loneliness of exile, and the tedium of the scribe's life. The *Cathach*, a manuscript of the Psalter believed to have been written by Columcille, is in the Royal Irish Academy.

THE THREE BEST-BELOVED PLACES

The three best-beloved places I have left in the
peopled world are Durrow, Derry (noble angel-haunted
     city),
and Tír Luigdech.

DERRY

Many wonders and miracles did God work for Columcille in Derry. And because he loved that city greatly Columcille said:

This is why I love Derry, it is so calm and bright;
for it is all full of white angels from one end to
the other.

A BLUE EYE WILL LOOK BACK

Columcille about to leave Ireland, A.D. 563:

> There is a blue eye which will look back at Ireland;
> never more shall it see the men of Ireland nor her women.

MY HAND IS WEARY WITH WRITING

My hand is weary with writing; my sharp great point is not thick; my slender-beaked pen juts forth a beetle-hued draught of bright blue ink.

A steady stream of wisdom springs from my well-coloured neat fair hand; on the page it pours its draught of ink of the green-skinned holly.

I send my little dripping pen unceasingly over an assemblage of books of great beauty, to enrich the possessions of men of art—whence my hand is weary with writing.

trans. Gerard Murphy

FROM *DUANAIRE FINN*

THE BIRD-CRIB

This poem about Fionn, one of a collection called the *Duanaire Finn* or the Poem Book of Fionn, was probably written in the fifteenth century. Gerard Murphy, who edited the poem, describes similar bird-cribs or bird-traps that were used in the Irish countryside when he was a boy. The question marks indicate unclear entries in the text.

> 1 "A hazel bird-crib: who made one, tell,
>   ancient men: and tell which of you first
>   played the jerking(?) trick upon birds."

2 "Dost thou hear, thou ancient man, the
question which the Táilgheann puts? Answer,
according to thy knowledge, the question
Patrick asks."

3 One day when Fionn was on Sliabh Luachra
of the full glens he chanced to be apart
from the Fian with three score willing
warriors.

4 Although we were strong we were uneasy
and ignorant, beneath a dark magic mist,
till we decided on a plan.

5 As Fionn, son of Cumhall, prince of the
Fianna, glanced out towards the west,
he sees
a tall roving warrior clad in a handsome
red suit.

6 On the big man's right hand was a beautifully coloured bird-crib of red gold: he
caught as he wished what birds went past
him.

7 The warrior came towards us on the fair-
sided heavy hill, and indeed greeted us in
polished pure words.

8 "If thou and all thy band come with me,
O Fionn of the truly brave Fianna, I shall
give you what is old in every drink and
what is new in every ancient food."

9 We, the people of Fionn of the unsheathed
weapons, rose up quickly: although no
good came of it to us, we were not slow
to rise.

10 The big man went before us: we followed
him (and it was sad) to the stronghold

of Inbhear dhá Shál where the crib was
prepared.

11 When the big man had gone out from
us beyond the gate of the stronghold,
without delay he closed a door of rough
iron upon us.

12 For seven days and nights we were in
the high-ditched earthen fortress without
food; and no one came to see us from far
or near.

13 In imitation of the jerking (?) crib, to secure
sufficient birdcatching for every man, Fionn
made a hazel crib (the lesson was not neglected[?] by us), that we might get from the
jerking (?) crib sufficient birdcatching
for every man of us.

14 At the end of seven days spent thus the
son of Troghan comes to see us: he thought
we were not alive, and came to behead us
all on one day.

15 We come from all sides about the son of
Troghan then: when we came round
him in fury his magic availed him nothing.

16 Fionn bore the red man away, though
our anger was great against him; and he
sent him safe to his house, although we did
not so will it, O cleric.

17 The best act of clemency ever done by
the good son of Cumhall, prince of the
Fiana, was to conduct the red man safe
and to ward us off.

18 There, O cleric of the jewelled croziers,
is an act of clemency done by Fionn,

the man who practised all valour: by
him was the crib prepared.

19 O Caoilte, although I am weak, do not let
it pass if I speak a lie: any person as good
as Fionn sawest thou ever in thy time?

20 "As regards his soul and his body (though
tonight my appearance is gloomy) no man
living in his age had nobility equal to
that of Fionn."

FROM *BUILE SUIBHNE* [THE MADNESS OF SWEENEY]

THE FRENZY OF SUIBHNE

Suibhne son of Colmán was king of Dál nAraide. One day St. Rónán
was marking the boundaries of a church in that country, and Suibhne
heard the sound of his bell. When his people told him that the saint
was establishing a church in his territory, he set out in anger to expel
the cleric. His wife Eorann sought to restrain him and caught the
border of his cloak, but he rushed naked from the house, leaving the
cloak in her hands. Rónán was chanting the Office when Suibhne
came up, and the king seized the psalter and threw it into the lake. He
then laid hands on the saint and was dragging him away, when a
messenger arrived from Congal Claen to summon him to the battle of
Moira. Suibhne departed with the messenger, leaving Rónán sorrowful. Next day an otter from the lake restored the psalter to the
saint unharmed. Rónán gave thanks to God and cursed the king,
wishing that he might wander naked through the world as he had
come naked into his presence.

Rónán went to Moira to make peace between Domnall and
Congal Claen, but without success. He and his clerics sprinkled holy
water on the armies, but when they sprinkled it on Suibhne he slew
one of the clerics with a spear and made a second cast at Rónán
himself. The second spear broke against the saint's bell, and the shaft
flew into the air. Rónán cursed Suibhne, wishing that he might fly

through the air like the shaft of his spear and that he might die of a
spear cast like the cleric whom he had slain.

Thereafter, when the battle was joined, the armies on both sides
raised three mighty shouts. Suibhne was terrified by the clamor. His
weapons fell from his hands. He was seized with trembling and fled in
a frenzy like a bird of the air. His feet rarely touched the ground in
his flight, and at last he settled upon a yew tree far from the battle-
field. There he was discovered by a kinsman, Aongus the Fat, who had
fled the field after the victory of Domnall. Aongus sought to persuade
Suibhne to join him, but Suibhne flew away like a bird and came to
Tír Conaill, where he perched on a tree near the church called Cill
Riagáin. It happened that the victorious army of Domnall had en-
camped there after the battle. Domnall recognized him and lamented
his misfortune.

[In a short poem Domnall reproaches Suibhne for his part in the
battle. Part of the poem however is a dialogue between Domnall and
Congal and is out of place here.]

Suibhne fled again and was for a long time traveling through
Ireland till he came to Glenn Bolcáin. It was there that the madmen
used to abide when their year of frenzy was over, for that valley is
always a place of great delight to madmen. Glenn Bolcáin has four
gaps to the wind and a lovely fragrant wood and clean-bordered wells
and cool springs, and a sandy stream of clear water with green cress
and long waving brooklime on its surface.

For seven years Suibhne wandered throughout Ireland, and
then he returned to Glenn Bolcáin. There Loingsechán came to seek
him. [Some say that Loingsechán was a son of Suibhne's mother, some
say that he was his foster-brother; but, however that may be, he was a
faithful friend, for he rescued Suibhne three times.] Loingsechán
found the footprints of Suibhne near the river where he came to eat
watercress, and the trace of his passage from tree to tree in the broken
branches, but he found not Suibhne. He slept one night in a hut and
Suibhne came near and heard him snore. And he uttered a lay:

> The man by the wall snores: I dare not sleep like that. For
> seven years since that Tuesday at Moira I have not slept for a
> moment.
> . . . .
>
> The cress of the well of Druim Cirb is my meal at terce. My
> face betrays it. Truly I am Suibhne the Madman.
> . . . .

Though I live from hill to hill on the mountain above the valley of yews, alas! that I was not left to lie with Congal Claen.

. . . .

Green cress and a drink of clear water is my fare. I do not smile. This is not the fate of the man by the wall.

. . . .

Eorann, Suibhne's wife, had gone to live with Guaire, one of the claimants to the kingdom. He visited her and spoke of their former happiness together, of her present comfort and his misery. (Their dialogue is in verse.) He reproaches her for enjoying the love of another man and the comfort of his house while her husband is an outcast; and she protests that she would rather live with Suibhne in the wilderness than with any man of Ireland or Scotland. Suibhne tells her that he does better to stay with Guaire than to share the life of a madman and that he bears her no grudge. As people approach he flies away.

Suibhne came to Ros Ercáin, where he had a house, and he settled in a yew tree there. Loingsechán came again to capture him. At first he pleaded with him to return home and resume the royal comforts that had been his. Suibhne bade Loingsechán leave him to his fate and asked for news of his country.

"Your father is dead." "That grieves me," said he. "Your mother is dead," said the lad. "Now all pity for me is at an end," said he. "Your brother is dead," said Loingsechán. "I am sorely wounded by that," said Suibhne. "Your daughter is dead," said Loingsechán. "And an only daughter is the needle of the heart," said Suibhne. "Dead is your son who used to call you 'Father,'" said Loingsechán. "Indeed," said he, "that is the drop that brings a man to the ground."

He fell down from the tree, and Loingsechán seized him and bound him and then told him that all his kindred were alive. Soon he recovered his reason and was king again, but he remained in the custody of Loingsechán. One day an old woman reminded him of his frenzy and so excited him that he flew away, and the hag followed him; and when at length he alighted on a tree she perched on a tree beside him. Then Suibhne heard the cry of hunters and the bellowing of the stag, and he made a poem in praise of the trees of Ireland and in memory of his hardships:

> O lowing stag, sweet clamorer, dear to me is the music thou makest in the valley.

Oak, elder, blackthorn, apple tree, briar, yew, holly, birch, and aspen are addressed in turn, and then he remembers his happy life as king and laments his fate. Then nature is praised in the spirit of some of the Fenian ballads:

> The starry frost will come, falling on every pool. I am wretched, wandering exposed to it on the mountain.
>
> The herons call in cold Glenn Aigle, swift flocks of birds coming and going.
>
> I love not the prattle that men and women make: sweeter to me is the song of the blackbird on his perch.
>
> I love not the trumpeting I hear in the morning: sweeter to me is the squeal of the badger in Benna Broc.
>
> I love not the loud horn I hear: sweeter to me is the belling of a twenty-pointed stag.
> . . . .
>
> The curse of fair-haired Rónán has made me thy companion, lowing stag, sweet clamorer.

After other adventures, Suibhne went again to visit his wife but refused to enter the house for fear that his people would confine him there. Eorann said that, since he would not stay with her, he had best be gone and not return, for she was ashamed that people should see him in his madness. [In a short poem Suibhne laments the frailty of women and recalls his feats of batttle when he was king. He flies away to Benn Boirche. Two short poems follow, the first somewhat in the spirit of Marbán's account of his life as a hermit, the second another lament for his misery.]

Then his reason returned to Suibhne, and he sought to go back to his people; but that was revealed to St. Rónán, and he prayed that

Suibhne might not be allowed to return to persecute the church as he had done before. When the madman was on his way, he was beset by a fearful apparition of headless bodies and trunkless heads, which pursued him through the air with frightful clamor until he escaped from them into the clouds.

At last Suibhne came to the monastery of St. Mo Ling. [In a poem of fifteen quatrains in dialogue between the saint and the madman, Suibhne foretells his death by the hand of a herdsman.] Mo Ling made him welcome and bade him return from his wanderings every evening so that his history might be written, for it was destined that his story should be written there and that he should receive a Christian burial. Mo Ling bade his cook give supper to Suibhne, and, wherever he traveled during the day, he would return at night. The cook would thrust her foot into some cowdung and fill the hole with milk, and Suibhne would lie down to drink. But the cook's husband, who was a herdsman, grew jealous of this attention by his wife, and he slew Suibhne with a spear as he lay drinking the milk one evening. [Others say that the herdsman placed the point of a deer's horn on the spot where Suibhne used to drink and that he fell upon it and so died.] Before his death he confessed his sin and received the body of Christ and was anointed. [The conversation of Suibhne, Mo Ling, and Mongán the herdsman is recorded in a poem of twenty-six quatrains, in which Suibhne says:

Sweeter to me once than the sound of a bell beside me was the song of a blackbird on the mountain and the belling of the stag in a storm.

Sweeter to me once than the voice of a lovely woman beside me was the voice of the mountain grouse at dawn.

Sweeter to me once was the cry of wolves than the voice of a cleric within bleating and whining.

Though you like to drink your ale in taverns with honor, I would rather drink water from my hand taken from the well by stealth.

Though sweet to you yonder in the church the smooth words of your students, sweeter to me the noble chant of the hounds of Glenn Bolcáin."

Then Suibhne swooned, and Mo Ling and his cleric brought each a stone for his monument, and Mo Ling said:

> Here is the tomb of Suibhne. His memory grieves my heart. Dear to me for love of him is every place the holy madman frequented.
> . . . .
> Dear to me each cool stream on which the green cress grew, dear each well of clear water, for Suibhne used to visit them.
>
> If the King of the stars allows it, arise and go with me. Give me, O heart, thy hand, and come from the tomb.
> Sweet to me was the conversation of Suibhne: long shall I remember it. I pray to the chaste King of heaven over his grave and tomb."

Suibhne arose out of his swoon, and Mo Ling took him by the hand, and they went together to the door of the church. And Suibhne leaned against the doorpost and gave a great sigh, and his spirit went to heaven, and he was buried with honor by Mo Ling.

summary by Myles Dillon

Further Readings for Early and Medieval Irish Literature

Translations

Carney, James. *Medieval Irish Lyrics*. Dublin: Dolmen Press, 1967.

Cross, Tom Peete, and Slover, Clark Harris, eds. *Ancient Irish Tales*. Revised bibliography by C. W. Dunn, New York: Barnes and Noble, 1969 (1936).

Doan, James. *The Romance of Cearbhall and Fearbhlaidh*. Mountrath, Republic of Ireland: Dolmen Press; Atlantic Highlands, N.J.: Humanities Press, 1985.

Flower, Robin. *Poems and Translations*. London: Constable and Co., 1931.

Gantz, Jeffrey. *Early Irish Myths and Sagas*. Harmondsworth: Penguin, 1981.

Gregory, Augusta. *Cuchulain of Muirthemne*. Introduction by Daniel Murphy, Gerrards Cross, England: Colin Smythe, 1984 (1902).

———. *Gods, Heroes and Fighting Men*. ed. T. R. Henn and Colin Smythe. Gerrards Cross, England: Colin Smythe, 1970 (1904).

Heaney, Seamus. *Sweeney Astray*. New York: Farrar, Straus and Giroux, 1984 (1983).

Jackson, Kenneth. *A Celtic Miscellany*. Rev. ed. Harmondsworth: Penguin, 1971 (1951).

Keefe, Joan. *Irish Poems: from Cromwell to the Famine*. Lewisburg, Pa.: Bucknell University Press, 1977.

Kelleher, John V. *Too Small for Stove Wood. Too Big for Kindling. Collected Verse and Translations*. Dublin: Dolmen Press, 1979.

Kinsella, Thomas. *The Tain*. Dublin: Dolmen; London and New York: Oxford University Press, 1970.

MacNeill, Eoin. *Duanaire Finn I: The Book of the Lays of Finn*. Irish Texts Society, 7. London: David Nutt, 1948 (1908).

Meyer, Kuno. *Selections from Ancient Irish Poetry*. London: Constable, 1959 (1911).

Murphy, Gerard. *Duanaire Finn* II, Irish Texts Society, 28. London: Simpkin and Marshall, 1933; III, Irish Texts Society, 43. Dublin: Educational Company of Ireland, 1953.

————. *Early Irish Lyrics*. Eighth to Twelfth Century. Oxford: Clarendon Press, 1956.

ní Shéaghdha, Nessa. *Tóruigheacht Dhiarmada agus Ghráinne* [The Pursuit of Diarmuid and Gráinne]. Irish Texts Society, 47. Dublin: Educational Company of Ireland, 1967.

O'Connor, Frank. *Kings, Lords and Commons*. New York: Alfred Knopf, 1959.

————, and Greene, David ed. *A Golden Treasury of Irish Poetry*, A.D. *600–1200*. London: Macmillan, 1967.

O'Faoláin, Seán. *The Silver Branch. A Collection of the Best Old Irish Lyrics Variously Translated*. London: Jonathan Cape, 1938.

O'Keeffe, J. G. *Buile Suibhne* [The Frenzy of Suibhne]. Irish Texts Society, 12. London: David Nutt, 1913.

Criticism

Bergin, Osborn. *Irish Bardic Poetry*. Dublin: Dublin Institute for Advanced Studies, 1970.

Carney, James, ed. *Early Irish Poetry*. Cork: Mercier, 1965.

————. *The Irish Bardic Poet*. Dublin: Dolmen Press, 1967.

Delargy, J. G. *The Gaelic Story-teller*. London: The Sir John Rhys Memorial Lecture, British Academy, 1945.

Dillon, Myles, ed. *Early Irish Literature*. Chicago: University of Chicago Press, 1948.

————, ed. *Early Irish Society*. Dublin: At the Sign of Three Candles, 1954.

————, ed. *Irish Sagas*. Dublin: Stationery Office, 1959.

Flower, Robin. *The Irish Tradition*. Oxford: Clarendon Press, 1963 (1947).

Knott, Eleanor. *Irish Classical Poetry*. Rev. ed. Cork: Mercier Press, 1973.

MacCana, Proinsias. *The Learned Tales of Medieval Ireland*. Dublin: Dublin Institute for Advanced Studies, 1980.

————. *Literature in Irish*. Dublin: Department of Foreign Affairs, 1980.

MacKillop, James. *Fionn mac Cumhaill. Celtic Myth in English Literature*. Syracuse, N.Y.: Syracuse University Press, 1986.

Murphy, Gerard. *Saga and Myth in Ancient Ireland*. Dublin: At the Sign of Three Candles, 1955.

———. *The Ossianic Lore and Romantic Tales of Medieval Ireland*. Dublin: At the Sign of Three Candles, 1955.

Nagy, Joseph Falaky. *The Wisdom of the Outlaw: The Boyhood Deeds of Finn in Gaelic Narrative Tradition*. Berkeley: University of California Press, 1985.

Rees, Alwyn, and Rees, Brinley. *Celtic Heritage: Ancient Tradition in Ireland and Wales*. New York: Grove Press, 1961.

EARLY MODERN IRISH POETRY

Loss is a major theme of early modern Irish poetry: political exile, lost or abandoned love, laments for the dead, nostalgia for a lost way of life. Much of the poetry reflects the times: the plantation of Ulster after the Flight of the Earls, the term for the migration of the great Earls of Tirconnell (O'Donnell) and Tyrone (O'Neill) and their followers, who left Ireland for the continent in 1607; and the further dispossession that resulted from the Cromwellian land confiscations of 1652–53.

One of the most poignant expressions of loss is the anonymous poem "Kilcash," which marks the passing of the house of one of the Butler family of County Tipperary.

ANONYMOUS

CILL CHAIS
[KILCASH]

Now what will we do for timber,
    with the last of the woods laid low?
There's no talk of Cill Chais or its household
    and its bell will be struck no more.
That dwelling where lived the good lady
    most honoured and joyous of women

—earls made their way over wave there
    and the sweet Mass once was said.

Ducks' voices nor geese do I hear there,
    nor the eagle's cry over the bay,
nor even the bees at their labour
    bringing honey and wax to us all.
No birdsong there, sweet and delightful,
    as we watch the sun go down,
nor cuckoo on top of the branches
    settling the world to rest.

A mist on the boughs is descending
    neither daylight nor sun can clear.
A stain from the sky is descending
    and the waters receding away.
No hazel nor holly nor berry
    but boulders and bare stone heaps,
not a branch in our neighbourly haggard,
    and the game all scattered and gone.

Then a climax to all of our misery:
    the prince of the Gael is abroad
oversea with that maiden of mildness
    who found honour in France and Spain.
Her company now must lament her,
    who would give yellow money and white
—she who'd never take land from the people
    but was friend to the truly poor.

I call upon Mary and Jesus
    to send her safe home again:
dances we'll have in long circles
    and bone-fires and violin music;
that Cill Chais, the townland of our fathers,
    will rise handsome on high once more
and till doom—or the Deluge returns—
    we'll see it no more laid low.

                        trans. Thomas Kinsella

SÉATHRÚN CÉITINN [GEOFFREY KEATING]
(1580–c. 1644)

This seventeenth-century priest-poet wrote one of the greatest of Irish love poems, a poem Seán Ó Tuama called "the most human and realistic renunciation of courtly love that I know."

O WOMAN FULL OF WILE

O woman full of wile,
Keep from me thy hand:
I am not a man of the flesh,
Tho' thou be sick for my love.

See how my hair is grey!
See how my body is powerless!
See how my blood hath ebbed!
For what is thy desire?

Do not think me besotted:
Bend not again thy head,
Let our love be without act
Forever, O slender witch.

Take thy mouth from my mouth,
Graver the matter so;
Let us not be skin to skin:
From heat cometh will.

'Tis thy curling ringleted hair,
Thy grey eye bright as dew,
Thy lovely round white breast,
That draw the desire of eyes.

Every deed but the deed of the flesh
And to lie in thy bed of sleep
Would I do for thy love,
O woman full of wile!

trans. Padraic Pearse

THOMAS FLAVELL (fl. late seventeenth century)

The historian James Hardiman published Thomas Flavell's "The County of Mayo" in *Irish Minstrelsy* (1831), characterizing the song as a favorite one in the west of Ireland. Flavell was a native of Inisbofin, the island off the Galway coast associated with the contemporary Irish poet Richard Murphy.

THE COUNTY OF MAYO

On the deck of Patrick Lynch's boat I sat in woeful
    plight,
Through my sighing all the weary day and weeping all
    the night.
Were it not that full of sorrow from my people forth I
    go,
By the blessed sun, 'tis royally I'd sing thy praise, Mayo.

When I dwelt at home in plenty, and my gold did much
    abound,
In the company of fair young maids the Spanish ale
    went round.
'Tis a bitter change from those gay days that now I'm
    forced to go,
And must leave my bones in Santa Cruz, far from my
    own Mayo.

They're altered girls in Irrul now; 'tis proud they're
    grown and high,
With their hair-bags and their top-knots—for I pass
    their buckles by.
But it's little now I heed their airs, for God will have it
    so,
That I must depart for foreign lands, and leave my
    sweet Mayo.

'Tis my grief that Patrick Loughlin is not Earl in Irrul
    still,
And that Brian Duff no longer rules as Lord upon the
    Hill;

And that Colonel Hugh MacGrady should be lying dead
and low,
And I sailing, sailing swiftly from the county of Mayo.

trans. George Fox

DONNCHADH RUA MAC CONMARA (1715–1810)

FAIR HILLS OF EIRE

Donnchadha Rua wrote "The Fair Hills of Eire" while in Hamburg.
His other well-known poem written in exile (in Newfoundland),
"Eachtra Ghiolla an Amaráin" [The adventures of a luckless fellow],
has been put into a lively modern translation by Arland Ussher. Born
in Cratloe, County Clare, Mac Conmara spent much of his life in
Waterford, where he was associated with the poets of the Sliabh
gCua district.

Take my heart's blessing over to dear Eire's strand—
    Fair Hills of Eire O!
To the Remnant that love her—Our Forefathers' Land!
    Fair Hills of Eire O!
How sweet sing the birds, o'er mount there and vale,
Like soft-sounding chords, that lament for the Gael,—
And I, o'er the surge, far, far away must wail
    The Fair Hills of Eire O.

How fair are the flowers on the dear daring peaks,
    Fair Hills of Eire O!
Far o'er foreign bowers I love her barest reeks,
    Fair Hills of Eire O!
Triumphant her trees, that rise on ev'ry height,
Bloom-kissed, the breeze comes odorous and bright,
The love of my heart!—O my very soul's delight!
    The Fair Hills of Eire O!

Still numerous and noble her sons who survive,
    Fair Hills of Eire O!

The true hearts in trouble,—the strong hands to strive—
    Fair Hills of Eire O!
Ah, 'tis this makes my grief, my wounding and my woe
To think that each chief is now a vassal low,
And my Country divided amongst the Foreign Foe—
    The Fair Hills of Eire O!

In purple they gleam, like our High Kings of yore,
    The Fair Hills of Eire O!
With honey and cream are her plains flowing o'er,
    Fair Hills of Eire O!
Once more I will come, or very life shall fail,
To the heart-haunted home of the ever-faithful Gael,
Than king's boon more welcome the swift swelling sail—
    For the Fair Hills of Eire O!

The dew-drops sparkle, like diamonds on the corn,
    Fair Hills of Eire O!
Where green boughs darkle the bright apples burn
    Fair Hills of Eire O!
Behold, in the valley, cress and berries bland,
Where streams love to dally, in that Wondrous Land,
While the great River-voices roll their music grand
    Round the Fair Hills of Eire O!

Oh, 'tis welcoming, wide-hearted, that dear land of love!
    Fair Hills of Eire O!
New life unto the martyred is the pure breeze above
    The Fair Hills of Eire O!
More sweet than tune flowing o'er the chords of gold
Comes the kine's soft lowing, from the mountain fold,—
    Oh, the Splendor of the Sunshine on them all,—
    Young and Old.
    'Mid the Fair Hills of Eire O!

trans. Dr. George Sigerson
(1836–1925)

AOGAN Ó RATHAILLE (c. 1675–1729)

Aogán Ó Rathaille's poetry reflects the turbulence of Ireland in the late seventeenth century: the dispossession, the lack of leadership, and—for poets who were part of the households of the great Gaelic families—the loss of their hereditary prerogatives. Ó Rathaille lived during the period of the penal laws, laws enacted after the Treaty of Limerick (1691) that maintained the transfer of Catholic lands to Protestant settlers and barred Catholics from parliament, government, and the professions.

The MacCarthys would have been the chiefs of the mountainous Sliabh Luachra region of Kerry where Ó Rathaille was born. They were succeeded by the Anglo-Irish Brownes, the first of whom—Sir Nicholas Browne—was a Catholic himself and sympathetic to the Irish. Ó Rathaille welcomes Sir Nicholas's son Sir Valentine with a poem celebrating the latter's marriage; however, Ó Rathaille later wrote the bitter "Valentine Browne." Bitterness had given way to despair—for himself, for Ireland—by his last poem, "No Help I'll Call."

Ó Rathaille's other poetic response to the broken world around him was the *aislingí*, or vision poems, a form he perfected in *aislingi* such as "Mac an Cheannaí" [The merchant's son] and "Gile na Gile" [Brightness of brightness]. An *aisling* is a political allegory, an interview between the poet and a *spéir-bhean* (literally, "sky woman") who is Ireland. The poet asks her why she mourns; she tells him her beloved is in exile, but that he will return and bring relief. The *aisling* is a virtuoso piece with elaborate descriptions of place and of the *spéir-bhean*, as well as with many allusions to Irish, classical, and Christian mythology.

BRIGHTNESS MOST BRIGHT

The Brightness of Brightness I saw in a lonely path,
Crystal of crystal, her blue eyes tinged with green,
Melody of melody, her speech not morose with age,
The ruddy and white appeared in her glowing cheeks.

Plaiting of plaiting in every hair of her yellow locks,
That robbed the earth of its brilliancy by their full
     sweeping,

An ornament brighter than glass on her swelling breast,
Which was fashioned at her creation in the world above.

A tale of knowledge she told me, all lonely as she was,
News of the return of HIM to the place which is his by
      kingly descent,
News of the destruction of the bands who expelled him,
And other tidings which, through sheer fear, I will not
      put in my lays.

Oh, folly of follies for me to go up close to her!
By the captive I was bound fast a captive;
As I implored the Son of Mary to aid me, she bounded
      from me,
And the maiden went off in a flash to the fairy
      mansion of Luachair.

I rush in mad race running with a bounding heart,
Through margins of a morass, through meads, through
      a barren moorland,
I reach the strong mansion—the way I came I know
      not—
That dwelling of dwellings, reared by wizard socery.

They burst into laughter, mockingly—a troop of wizards
And a band of maidens, trim, with plaited locks;
In the bondage of fetters they put me without much
      respite,
While to my maiden clung a clumsy, lubberly clown.

I told her then, in words the sincerest,
How it will became her to be united to an awkward,
      sorry churl,
While the fairest thrice over of all the Scotic race
Was waiting to receive her as his beauteous bride.

As she hears my voice she weeps through wounded
      pride,
The streams run down plenteously from her glowing
      cheeks,

She sends me with a guide for my safe conduct from
    the mansion,
She is the Brightness of Brightness I saw upon a lonely
    path.

THE BINDING.

O my sickness, my misfortune, my fall, my sorrow, my
    loss!
The bright, fond, kind, fair, soft-lipped, gentle maiden,
Held by a horned, malicious, croaking, yellow clown,
    with a black troop!
While no relief can reach her until the heroes come
    back across the main.

trans. Patrick S. Dinneen

VALENTINE BROWN

Darkness spreading over my age-crusted heart
As the foreign devils march through the green fields of
    Conn,
A cloud on the western sun whose right was Munster's
    throne,
—The reason I turn to you, Valentine Brown.

Cashel without company or horses, overgrown,
Brian's palace swamped with a black flood of otters,
No royal son of Munster ruling his own acres,
—The reason I turn to you, Valentine Brown.

The deer discarding the graceful shape by which she's
    known
Since the alien crow nested in the thick woods of Ross,
Fish leaving sunlit pools and hidden silent streams,
—The reason I turn to you, Valentine Brown.

Dar-Inish in the west mourning her earl of high
    renown,
In Hamburg, alas, our exiled noble lord,

An old gray eye weeping hard for all that is gone
—The reason I turn to you, Valentine Brown.

trans. Joan Keefe

THE GERALDINE'S DAUGHTER

A beauty all stainless, a pearl of a maiden,
    Has plunged me in trouble, and wounded my
        heart.
With sorrow and gloom are my soul overladen;
    An anguish is there that will never depart.
I could voyage to Egypt across the deep water,
    Nor care about bidding dear Eire farewell,
So I only might gaze on the Geraldine's daughter,
    And sit by her side in some green, pleasant dell!

Her curling locks wave round her figure of lightness,
    All dazzling and long, like the purest of gold;
Her blue eyes resemble twin stars in their brightness,
    And her brow is like marble or wax to behold!
The radiance of heaven illumines her features
    Where the snows and the rose have erected their
        throne;
It would seem that the sun had forgotten all creatures,
    To shine on the Geraldine's daughter alone!

Her bosom is swan-white, her waist smooth and slender;
    Her speech is like music, so sweet and so free;
The feelings that glow in her noble heart lend her
    A mien and a majesty lovely to see.
Her lips, red as berries, but riper than any,
    Would kiss away even a sorrow like mine.
No wonder such heroes and noblemen many
    Should cross the blue ocean to kneel at her shrine.

She is sprung from the Geraldine race, the great
    Grecians,
    Niece of Mileadh's sons of the Valorous Bands,
Those heroes, the seed of the olden Phenicians,

Though now trodden down, without fame, without
lands!
Of her ancestors flourished the Barrys and Powers,
To the Lords of Bunratty she too is allied;
And not a proud noble near Cashel's high towers
But is kin to this maiden—the Geraldine's Pride!

Of Saxon or Gael there are none to excel in
Her wisdom, her features, her figure, this fair;
In all she surpasses the far-famous Helen,
Whose beauty drove thousands to death and
despair.
Whoe'er could but gaze on her aspect so noble
Would feel from thenceforward all anguish depart,
Yet for me 'tis, alas! my worst woe and my trouble,
That her image must always abide in my heart!

trans. James Clarence Mangan

Further Readings on Aogan Ó Rathaille

Selected Works

Ua Duinnín, An tAthair Pádraig. *Dánta Aodhagáin Uí Rathaille*. Rev. ed. O'Donnchadha, Tadhg. Irish Texts Society, 3A. London: Simpkin, Marshall,
1909.

Biography and Criticism

Breatnach, R. "The Lady and the King." *Studies* 42: 321–36. A Study of the
aisling form.
Corkery, Daniel. *The Hidden Ireland. A Story of Gaelic Munster in the Eighteenth
Century*, pp. 160–92. Dublin: M. H. Gill, 1925.
Jordan, John. "Aogán Ó Rathaille." In *The Pleasures of Gaelic Poetry*, ed. Seán
MacReamoinn, pp. 81–91. Dublin: Allen Lane, 1982.
Ó Tuama, Seán. "Aogán O'Rathaille." In *File faoi Sceimhle*, pp. 87–124. Dublin:
Oifig an tSoláthair, 1978.

Eoghan Rua Ó Suilleabháin (1748–84)

Eoghan Rua ("Red Owen") or Eoghan an Bheóil Bhínn ("Owen of the Sweet Mouth") was born near Killarney, not far from where Aogán Ó Rathaille spent his life. Schooled in English, Irish, and probably a little Latin, he was by turns a schoolmaster and a *spalpín fánach* (wandering laborer) who left Kerry to work the harvest in neighboring counties and return in November or December.

Superficially, Eoghan Rua's poem to his friend the blacksmith Séamus Fitzgerald is a request for a new spade to take on the road, but it is in effect a statement about the migrant laborer's life: hard work by day, hard drinking by night. He is perhaps best remembered for his *aislingí* written in the classical manner. Eoghan Rua continues to be a popular and romantic figure in Irish-speaking Munster; the contemporary composer Seán Ó Riada wrote a play based on Eoghan Rua.

FRIEND OF MY HEART

Friend of my heart, Seamus, loving and witty,
Of Geraldine blood, Greek-tinged and poetic,
Make me a clean smooth handle to fit my spade
And add a nice crook as a crowning elegance.

Then I'll shoulder my tool and go on my way
Since my thirst for adventure has not been quenched
Without stop with my spade as far off as Galway
Where daily my pay will be breakfast and sixpence.

Before the day's end if my tired bones give out
And the steward says my grip of the spade is in doubt,
Then calmly I will tell him of the adventure of death
And of classical battles that left heroes weak.

Of Samson and high deeds I will talk for a while,
Of strong Alexander eager for enemies,
Of the Caesars' dictatorship, powerful and wise,
Or of Achilles who left many dead in the field,

Of the fall of the Fenians with terrible slaughter,
And the heartbreaking story of ravishing Deirdre.

And then with sweet coaxing I will sing songs,
An account of my day you have there now, Seamus.

After my labor I'll take my pay in a lump
And tie it with hemp in the breast of my shirt,
Still with a high heart I will head straight for home,
Not parting with sixpence till I come to your forge.

You are a man like me tormented with thirst,
So we will briskly set off for the inn down the road,
Ale and drams I will order to be arrayed on the table
And no ha'penny of hard-earned money will be spared.

trans. Joan Keefe

Further Readings on Eoghan Rua Ó Suilleabháin

Selected Works

Ua Duinnín, an tAthair Pádraig. *Amhráin Eoghain Ruaidh Uí Súilleabháin.* Dublin: Connradh na Gaeilge, 1923.

Biography and Criticism

Corkery, Daniel. *The Hidden Ireland. A Study of Gaelic Munster in the Eighteenth Century,* pp. 193–236. Dublin: M. H. Gill and Son, 1925.
Ua Duinnín, An tAthair Padraig. *Beatha Eoghan Ruaidh Uí Shuilleabháin.* Baile Átha Cliath: Connradh na Gaeilge, 1902.
O'Broin, Padraig. "The Wandering Spadesmen." *Éire-Ireland* 1:64–69.

EIBHLÍN DHUBH NÍ CHONAILL [EILEEN O'CONNELL] (c. 1770)

"Caoineadh Airt Uí Laoghaire" [The lament for Art O'Leary] is at once the best example of the *caoine* (keen), that unique expression of Irish grief, as well as one of the most passionate love poems in modern Irish. Daniel O'Connell's aunt Eibhlín Dhubh ní Chonaill made the song for her outlawed husband, a captain in the Hungarian Hussars, who returned from the Continent, quarrelled with the High Sheriff of Cork, and tried to kill him but was shot himself instead.

In his edition of the poem, Seán Ó Tuama identified a number of traditional elements: the address to the deceased, the use of formulaic language, the plea to rise up from the dead, the recital of praise, the description of the effect of the death on all nature, the singer's premonition of death, the curse laid on those responsible, and the dispute between the wife and her sister-in-law about whose is the greater loss. These elements suggest something of the community's values: family pedigrees, family relationships, physical grace, valor, and generosity—values reinforced by the *caoine* itself.

CAOINEADH AIRT UÍ LAOGHAIRE
[LAMENT FOR ART O'LEARY]

I

HIS WIFE:

My love forever!
The day I first saw you
At the end of the market-house,
My eye observed you,
My heart approved you,
I fled from my father with you,
Far from my home with you.

II

I never repented it:
You whitened a parlour for me,
Painted rooms for me,
Reddened ovens for me,
Baked fine bread for me,
Basted meat for me,
Slaughtered beasts for me;
I slept in ducks' feathers
Till midday milking-time
Or more if it pleased me.

III

My friend forever!
My mind remembers

That fine spring day
How well your hat suited you,
Bright gold-banded,
Sword silver-hilted—
Right hand steady—
Threatening aspect—
Trembling terror
On treacherous enemy—
You poised for a canter
On your slender bay horse.
The Saxons bowed to you,
Down to the ground to you,
Not for love of you
But for deadly fear of you,
Though you lost your life to them,
Oh my soul's darling.

IV

Oh white-handed rider!
How fine your brooch was
Fastened in cambric,
And your hat with laces
When you crossed the sea to us,
They would clear the street for you,
And not for love of you
But for deadly hatred.

V

My friend you were forever!
When they will come home to me,
Gentle little Conor
And Farr O'Leary, the baby,
They will question me so quickly,
Where did I leave their father.
I'll answer in my anguish
That I left him in Killnamartyr.
They will call out to their father:
And he won't be there to answer.

VI

My friend and my love!
Of the blood of Lord Antrim,
And of Barry of Allchoill,
How well your sword suited you,
Hat gold-banded,
Boots of fine leather,
Coat of broadcloth,
Spun overseas for you.

VII

My friend you were forever!
I knew nothing of your murder
Till your horse came to the stable
With the reins beneath her trailing,
And your heart's blood on her shoulders
Staining the tooled saddle
Where you used to sit and stand.
My first leap reached the threshold,
My second reached the gateway,
My third leap reached the saddle.

VIII

I struck my hands together
And I made the bay horse gallop
As fast as I was able,
Till I found you dead before me
Beside a little furze-bush.
Without Pope or bishop,
Without priest or cleric
To read the death-psalms for you,
But a spent old woman only
Who spread her cloak to shroud you—
Your heart's blood was still flowing;
I did not stay to wipe it
But filled my hands and drank it.

IX

My love you'll be forever!
Rise up from where you're lying

And we'll be going homewards.
We'll have a bullock slaughtered,
We'll call our friends together,
We'll get the music going.
I'll make a fine bed ready
With sheets of snow-white linen,
And fine embroidered covers
That will bring the sweat out through you
Instead of the cold that's on you!

X

ART'S SISTER: My friend and my treasure!
There's many a handsome woman
From Cork of the sails
To the bridge of Toames
With a great herd of cattle
And gold for her dowry,
That would not have slept soundly
On the night we were waking you.

XI

EIBHLÍN DHUBH: My friend and my lamb;
You must never believe it,
Nor the whisper that reached you,
Nor the venomous stories
That said I was sleeping.
It was not sleep was on me,
But your children were weeping,
And they needed me with them
To bring their sleep to them.

XII

Now judge, my people,
What woman in Ireland
That at every nightfall
Lay down beside him,
That bore his three children,
Would not lose her reason
After Art O'Leary

That's here with me vanquished
Since yesterday morning?

XIII

ART'S FATHER: Bad luck to you, Morris!—
May your heart's blood poison you!
With your squint eyes gaping!
And your knock-knees breaking!—
That murdered my darling,
And no man in Ireland
To fill you with bullets.

XIV

My friend and my heart!
Rise up again now, Art,
Leap up on your horse,
Make straight for Macroom town,
Then to Inchigeela back,
A bottle of wine in your fist,
The same as you drank with your dad.

XV

EIBHLÍN DHUBH: My bitter, long torment
That I was not with you
When the bullet came towards you,
My right side would have taken it
Or a fold of my tunic,
And I would have saved you
Oh smooth-handed rider.

XVI

ART'S SISTER: My sore sharp sorrow
That I was not behind you
When the gun-powder blazed at you,
My right side would have taken it,
Or a fold of my gown,
And you would have gone free then
Oh grey-eyed rider,
Since you were a match for them.

XVII

EIBHLÍN DHUBH: My friend and my treasure!
It's bad treatment for a hero
To lie hooded in a coffin,
The warm-hearted rider
That fished in bright rivers,
That drank in great houses
With white-breasted women,
My thousand sorrows
That I've lost my companion.

XVIII

Bad luck and misfortune
Come down on you, Morris!
That snatched my protector,
My unborn child's father:
Two of them walking
And the third still within me,
And not likely I'll bear it.

XIX

My friend and my pleasure!
When you went out through the gateway
You turned and came back quickly,
You kissed your two children,
You kissed me on the forehead,
You said: 'Eileen, rise up quickly,
Put your affairs in order
With speed and with decision.
I am leaving home now
And there's no telling if I'll return.'
I mocked this way of talking,
He had said it to me so often.

XX

My friend and my dear!
Oh bright-sworded rider,
Rise up this moment,
Put on your fine suit

Of clean, noble cloth,
Put on your black beaver,
Pull on your gauntlets.
Up with your whip;
Outside your mare is waiting.
Take the narrow road east,
Where the trees thin before you,
Where streams narrow before you,
Where men and women will bow before you,
If they keep their old manners—
But I fear they have lost them.

XXI

My love and my treasure!
Not my dead ancestors,
Nor the deaths of my three children,
Nor Domhnall Mór O'Connell,
Nor Connall that drowned at sea,
Nor the twenty-six years woman
Who went across the water
And held kings in conversation—
It's not on all of them I'm calling
But on Art who was slain last night
At the inch of Carriganima!—
The brown mare's rider
That's here with me only—
With no living soul near him
But the dark little women of the mill,
And my thousand sorrows worsened
That their eyes were dry of tears.

XXII

My friend and my lamb!
Arthur O'Leary,
Of Connor, of Keady,
Of Louis O'Leary,
From west in Geeragh
And from east in Caolchnoc,
Where berries grow freely
And gold nuts on branches

And great floods of apples
All in their seasons.
Would it be a wonder
If Ive Leary were blazing
Besides Ballingeary
And Guagán of the saint
For the firm-handed rider
That hunted the stag down,
All out from Grenagh
When slim hounds fell behind?
And Oh clear-sighted rider,
What happened last night?
For I thought to myself
That nothing could kill you
Though I bought your habit.

XXIII

ART'S SISTER: My friend and my love!
Of the country's best blood,
That kept eighteen wet-nurses at work,
And each received her pay—
A heifer and a mare,
A sow and her litter,
A mill at the ford,
Yellow gold and white silver,
Silks and fine velvets,
A holding of land—
To give her milk freely
To the flower of fair manhood.

XXIV

My love and my treasure
And my love, my white dove!
Though I did not come to you,
Nor bring my troops with me,
That was no shame to me
For they were all enclosed
In shut-up rooms,
In narrow coffins,
In sleep without waking.

XXV

Were it not for the small-pox
And the black death
And the spotted fever,
That powerful army
Would be shaking their harness
And making a clatter
On their way to your funeral,
Oh white-breasted Art.

XXVI

My love you were and my joy!
Of the blood of those rough horsemen
That hunted in the valley,
Till you turned them homewards
And brought them to your hall,
Where knives were being sharpened,
Pork laid out for carving
And countless ribs of mutton,
The red-brown oats were flowing
To make the horses gallop—
Slender, powerful horses
And stable-boys to care them
Who would not think of sleeping
Nor of deserting their horses
If their owners stayed a week,
Oh brother of many friends.

XXVII

My friend and my lamb!
A cloudy vision
Came last night to me
In Cork at midnight
Alone in my bed:
That our white court fell,
That the Geeragh withered,
That your slim hounds were still
And the birds without sweetness
When you were found vanquished
On the side of the mountain,

Without priest or cleric
But an old shrivelled woman
That spread her cloak over you,
Arthur O'Leary,
While your blood flowed freely
On the breast of your shirt.

XXVIII

My love and my treasure!
And well they suited you,
Five-ply stockings,
Boots to your knees,
A three-cornered Caroline,
A lively whip,
On a frisky horse—
Many a modest, mannerly maiden
Would turn to gaze after you.

XXIX

EIBHLÍN DHUBH: My love forever!
And when you went in cities,
Strong and powerful,
The wives of the merchants
All bowed down to you
For they knew in their hearts
What a fine man in bed you were,
And what a fine horseman
And father for children.

XXX

Jesus Christ knows
I'll have no cap on my head,
Nor a shift on my back,
Nor shoes on my feet,
Nor goods in my house,
Nor the brown mare's harness
That I won't spend on lawyers;
That I'll cross the seas
And talk to the king,
And if no one listens

That I'll come back
To the black-blooded clown
That took my treasure from me.

XXXI

My love and my darling!
If my cry were heard westwards
To great Derrynane
And to gold-appled Capling,
Many swift, hearty riders
And white-kerchiefed women
Would be coming here quickly
To weep at your waking,
Beloved Art O'Leary.

XXXII

My heart is warming
To the fine women of the mill
For their goodness in lamenting
The brown mare's rider.

XXXIII

May your black heart fail you,
Oh false John Cooney!
If you wanted a bribe,
You should have asked me.
I'd have given you plenty:
A powerful horse
That would carry you safely
Through the mob
When the hunt is out for you,
Or a fine herd of cattle,
Or ewes to bear lambs for you,
Or the suit of a gentleman
With spurs and top-boots—
Though it's sorry I'd be
To see you done up in them,
For I've always heard
You're a piddling lout.

XXXIV

Oh white-handed rider,
Since you are stuck down,
Rise and go after Baldwin,
The ugly wretch
With the spindle shanks,
And take your revenge
For the loss of your mare—
May he never enjoy her.
May his six children wither!
But no bad wish to Máire
Though I have no love for her,
But that my own mother
Gave space in her womb to her
For three long seasons.

XXXV

My love and my dear!
Your stooks are standing,
Your yellow cows milking;
On my heart is such sorrow
That all Munster could not cure it,
Nor the wisdom of the sages.
Till Art O'Leary returns
There will be no end to the grief
That presses down on my heart,
Closed up tight and firm
Like a trunk that is locked
And the key is mislaid.

XXXVI

All you women out there weeping,
Wait a little longer;
We'll drink to Art son of Connor
And the souls of all the dead,
Before he enters the school—
Not learning wisdom or music
But weighted down by earth and stones.

trans. Éilís Dillon

Further Readings on Caoineadh Airt Uí Laoghaire

Selected Works:

Dillon, Éilis. "Laoineadh Airt Uí. Lament for Art O'Leary." *Irish University Review* I, 198–210.

O'Connor, Frank. *A Lament for Art O'Leary: Translated from the Irish by Frank O'Connor.* Illustrated by Jack B. Yeats. Dublin: Cuala Press, 1940. Reprinted in *Kings, Lords and Commons,* pp. 110–19. New York: Alfred A. Knopf, 1959.

O'Tuama, Seán, ed. *Caoine Airt Uí Laoghaire.* Baile Átha Cliath: An Clóchomar, 1961.

Biography and Criticism

Bromwich, Rachel. "The Keen for Art O'Leary, Its Background and Its Place in the Tradition of Gaelic Keening." *Éigse* 5: 236–52.

Murphy, Gerard. "The Gaelic Background." In *Daniel O'Connell. Nine Centenary Essays,* pp. 1–24. Dublin: Browne and Nolan, 1948.

BRIAN MAC GIOLLA MEIDHRE [BRIAN MERRIMAN]
(1749?–1805)

The author of this ribald poem in the Irish language was born in Ennistymon, County Clare, about the year 1749. He farmed and taught in the village of Feakle in east Clare before settling in Limerick. The notice of his death in 1805 described him as a "teacher of mathematics, etc." "The Midnight Court," Merriman's long poem of some thousand lines, was not written in the classical literary language of eighteenth century Munster, but rather in vigorous Clare Irish. One of the most frequently translated Irish poems, there are versions by Arland Ussher, Frank O'Connor, Lord Longford, David Marcus, Patrick Power, and Cosslett O'Cuinn. In addition, Brendan Behan and Thomas Kinsella have made partial translations of the poem.

The Midnight Court of Eevell, queen of the Munster fairies, is convened to hear an assembly of unmarried women complain about their difficulties finding husbands. An old man charges that his wife presented him with a bastard on their wedding night; a young woman rebuts that the girl was forced into marrying him and that handsome young priests, who would make better mates, ought to be allowed to marry. Eevell leaves the priests to Rome, but rules that all other young men must marry or be tortured by women.

CÚIRT AN MHEADHON OIDHCHE
[THE MIDNIGHT COURT]

FROM PART ONE

'Twas my wont to wander beside the stream
On the soft greensward in the morning beam,
Where the woods stand thick on the mountain-side
Without trouble or care what might betide.
My heart would leap at the lake's near blue,
The horizon and the far-off view,
The hills that rear their heads on high
Over each other's backs to spy.
'Twould gladden the soul with dole oppressed,
With sorrows seared and with cares obsessed
Of the outcast Gael without gold or goods
To watch for a while o'er the tops of the woods
The ducks in their flocks on the tide, the swan
Gliding with stately gait along,
The fish that leap on the air with glee
And the speckled perch with gambols free,
The labouring waves laving the shore
With glistening spray and rumbling roar,
The sea-gulls shrieking and reeling wide,
And the red deer romping in woodland ride,
The bugle's blare and the huntsman's yell
And the hue and cry of the pack pell-mell.
Yesterday morn the sky was clear
In the dog-days' heat of the mad mid-year,
And the sun was scouring the slumb'rous air
With his burning beams and gleaming glare
And the leaves lay dense on the bending trees
And the lush grass waved in the scented breeze.
It's joyful hearing for Erin that
The Good Folk's Host have in Council sat
On the mountain's summit for three days' space

In Brean Moy Graney's meeting-place.
His Highness grieves and his noble throng
That Erin lingers in thraldom long,
Wasted by woe without respite,
To misery's hand abandoned quite,
Her land purloined, her laws decayed,
Her wealth destroyed and her trust betrayed,
Her fields and pastures with weeds o'ergrown,
Her ground untilled and her crops unsown,
Her chieftains banished and an upstart band
Of hirelings holding the upper hand,
Who'd skin the widow and orphan child
And grind the weak and the meek and mild.
Shame 'tis, sure, that the poor oppressed
By lawless might, in plight distressed,
Get nought for aught but extortion vile,
The judge's fraud and the lawyer's wile,
The tyrant's frown and the sycophant's sneer
Bribing with fee and with fawning leer.
'Twas among the plaints that there were pleaded—
For every wrong was heard and heeded—
A change in which you'll be implicated,
That the men and youths remain unmated,
And your maids in spinsterhood repining
And their bloom and beauty in age declining,
And the human race apace decreasing
With wars and famines and plagues unceasing,
The pride of kings and princes feeding,
Since your lads and lasses have left off breeding.
Your scanty brood 'tis sad to see
With women in bands on land and sea,
Buxom maids that fade obscure
And tender slips with lips that lure,
Damsels shy by shame retarded
And willing wenches unregarded.
'Tis sad no noble seed should rise
From lads of lusty thews and thighs,
'Twere well could all know what maids' woes are,
Prepared to fall on the first proposer.
To consider the case with due precision
The council came to a new decision,
To find the fittest among the throng

To learn the right and requite the wrong.
They appointed straight a maid serene,
Eevell of Craglee, Munster's queen,
To hold her court and preside there o'er it
And invite the plaintiffs to plead before it.
The gentle lady swore to elicit
Of falsehood purged the truth explicit,
To hear the plea of the unbefriended
And see the state of the hapless mended.
This court is seated in Feakle nov.,
Arise and trudge, for you thither must go,
Arise and trudge without more delay,
Arise at once for I'll take no nay!'
She clapped her claw on my cape behind
And whisked me away like a wisp on the wind
O'er mud and mire, mountain and valley,
To Moinmoy Hill at the churchyard alley.
'Tis sure I saw with torches flaring
A lofty hall with trumpets blaring,
With glare of light and brightly burnished,
With fleeces draped and great doors furnished,
And the portly queen with a courtly gesture
On the judge's bench in a splendid vesture,
And a troop of toughs with gruff demeanour
To clean the court and escort and screen her,
And people in throngs along the benches
Both women and men and boys and wenches,
And a weeping nymph in the witness-box
Of comely mould and golden locks,
With heaving breast and face aflame
And tears that gushed with grief and shame,
With flowing hair and staring eyes
And moans and groans and sobs and sighs.
Her passion's blast at last abated,
Weary of woe, with sorrow sated,
She dried her eyes, her sighs surmounted,
And in these words her woes recounted:—
'We give you greeting, Eevell fair,
Gracious queen, your people's care,
Who pity the poor and relieve their plight
And save the brave and retrieve the right.
'Tis the cause of my anguish and grief of heart,

The source of my sorrow and inward smart,
My wounding rending pain unending,
The way our women thro' life are wending,
Gray gloomy nuns with the grave pursuing,
Since our men and maidens have left off wooing;
Myself among them condemned to wait
Without hope and mope in the maiden state,
Without husband heaping the golden store
Or children creeping on hearth and floor,
In dread and fear—a drear subsistence—
Of finding nought to support existence,
By troubles pressed and by rest forsaken,
By cares consumed and by sorrows shaken.
Chaste Eevell, hasten to the relief
Of the women of Erin in their grief,
Wasting their pains in vain endeavour
To meet with mates who elude them ever,
Till in the ages is such disparity
We would not touch them except from charity,
With bleary eyes and wry grimaces
To scare a maiden from their embraces.
And if in manhood's warm pulsation
A youth is tempted to change his station,
He chooses a dour and sour-faced scold
Who's wasted her days in raising gold;
No lively lass of sweet seventeen
Of figure neat and features clean,
But blear-eyed hag or harridan brown
With toothless jaws and hairless crown
And snotty nose and dun complexion
And offering constant shrill correction.
My heart is torn and worn with grieving,
And my breast distressed with restless heaving,
With torture dull and with desperation
At the thought of my dismal situation,
When I see a bonny and bold young blade
With comely features and frame displayed,
A sturdy swearer or spanking buck,
A sprightly strapper with spunk and pluck,
A goodly wopper well made and planned,
A gamey walloper gay and grand,
Nimble and brave and bland and blithe,

Eager and active and brisk and lithe,
Of noted parts and of proved precocity,
Sold to a scold or old hidiosity,
Withered and worn and blear and brown,
A mumbling, grumbling, garrulous clown,
A surly, sluttish and graceless gawk
Knotted and gnarled like a cabbage's stalk,
A sleepy, sluggish decayed old stump,
A useless, juiceless and faded frump.
Ah, woe is me! there's a crumpled crone
Being buckled to-night while I'm left lone,
She's a surly scold and a bold-faced jade
And this moment she's merry—and me a maid!
Why wouldn't they have myself in marriage?
I'm comely and shapely, of stately carriage,
I've a mouth and a smile to make men dream
And a forehead that's fair with ne'er a seam,
My teeth are pearls in a peerless row,
Cherries to vie with my lips pray show,
I've a dancing, glancing, entrancing eye,
Roguish and rakish and takish and sly,
Gold lacks lustre beside my hair,
And every curl might a saint ensnare.

trans. Arland Ussher

Further Readings Brian Mac Giolla Meidhre

Standard Edition

Ó hUaithne, Dáithí, ed. *Cúirt an Mheán Oíche.* Foreword by Seán Ó Tuama. Dolmen Press, 1969.

Selected Translations

Marcus, David. *The Midnight Court.* Dublin: Dolmen Press, 1967.
O'Connor, Frank. *The Midnight Court. A Rhythmical Bacchanalia from the Irish of Bryan Merryman.* London: Maurice Fridberg, 1945.
Ussher, Percy Arland. *The Midnight Court and the Adventures of a Luckless Fellow.* Introduction by W. B. Yeats. New York: Boni and Liveright, 1900, 1985.

Selected Criticism

O'Cuinn, Cosslett. "Merriman's Court," in *The Pleasures of Gaelic Poetry,* ed. Seán Mac Réamoinn. London: Allen Lane, 1982, pp. 111–26.

IRISH FOLK SONGS

Like all folk songs, these Irish songs have been transmitted and perpetuated by oral tradition. While most are anonymous, some, like Padraic Colum's "She Moved Through the Fair" and Dion Boucicault's "The Wearin' o' the Green" have passed into folk tradition. "Shule Aroon" even emigrated to America, where "Johnny Has Gone for a Soldier" is often substituted for the Irish refrain.

Our selection offers some sense of the range of folk-song themes. Many of the best are love lyrics like "The Grief of a Girl's Heart," an example of the genre of laments of abandoned girls that Seán Ó Tuama has described as unique in European love literature. "Mary from Dungloe" is an emigration song, while "Sean O'Dwyer of the Glens" is a farewell to one of the O'Dwyers of Kilnamanagh, County Tipperary, who served with Colonel Edmund O'Dwyer and shared his fate after the defeat in the Cromwellian wars: exile to the Continent and service in the Spanish army.

"The Sorrowful Lamentation of Callaghan, Greally, and Mullen," a nineteenth century street ballad, describes the faction fight (or politicized fisticuffs) at the fair of Darrynaclougherg in 1843. The fight led to a confrontation with the police and the death of the lamented trio. The Mr. Brew who ordered the police to fire was the local magistrate; he died before he could stand trial.

These street ballads are an important source for social historians, and—with the patriotic ballads—are part of the Anglo-Irish ballad tradition rather than the Gaelic song tradition. "The Rising of the Moon" celebrates the 1798 Rising, especially in its promise of another rising. The song, often attributed to John Keegan Casey gives its title to Lady Gregory's famous play. Some readers consider

"Nell Flaherty's Drake" to be an allegorical song, promising ruin not only to "the monster that murdered" the unfortunate drake but to Ireland's oppressors as well.

The last three songs are of more literary interest. "The Star of Slane" is an *aisling* written in English, though preserving the Gaelic rhyme scheme based on assonance or vowel rhyme: "muses/refuses/infuses; favors/endeavours/labours." "The Night Before Larry was Stretched" is a pungent example of Irish gallows humor. "Finnegan's Wake," finally, possibly of American origin but widely known in Ireland, provided James Joyce with the title of his novel (although he misplaced the apostrophe). In both the song and the novel, a man thought dead comes back to life.

THE GRIEF OF A GIRL'S HEART

O Donall óg, if you go across the sea, bring myself with you and do not forget it; and you will have a sweetheart for fair days and market days, and the daughter of the King of Greece beside you at night.

It is late last night the dog was speaking of you; the snipe was speaking of you in her deep marsh. It is you are the lonely bird through the woods; and that you may be without a mate until you find me.

You promised me, and you said a lie to me, that you would be before me where the sheep are flocked; I gave a whistle and three hundred cries to you, and I found nothing there but a bleating lamb.

You promised me a thing that was hard for you, a ship of gold under a silver mast; twelve towns with a market in all of them, and a fine white court by the side of the sea.

You promised me a thing that is not possible, that you would give me gloves of the skin of a fish; that you would give me shoes of the skin of a bird; and a suit of the dearest silk in Ireland.

O Donnall óg, it is I would be better to you than a high, proud, spendthrift lady: I would milk the cow; I would bring help to you; and if you were hard pressed, I would strike a blow for you.

O, ochone, and it's not with hunger or with wanting food, or drink, or sleep, that I am growing thin, and my life is shortened; but it is the love of a young man has withered me away.

It is early in the morning that I saw him coming, going along the road on the back of a horse; he did not come to me; he made nothing of me; and it is on my way home that I cried my fill.

When I go by myself to the Well of Loneliness, I sit down and I go through my trouble; when I see the world and do not see my boy, he that has an amber shade in his hair.

It was on that Sunday I gave my love to you; the Sunday that is last before Easter Sunday. And myself on my knees reading the Passion; and my two eyes giving love to you for ever.

O, aya! my mother, give myself to him; and give him all that you have in the world; get out yourself to ask for alms, and do not come back and forward looking for me.

My mother said to me not to be talking with you to-day, or tomorrow, or on the Sunday; it was a bad time she took for telling me that; it was shutting the door after the house was robbed.

My heart is as black as the blackness of the sloe, or as the black coal that is on the smith's forge; or as the sole of a shoe left in white halls; it was you put that darkness over my life.

You have taken the east from me; you have taken the west from me; you have taken what is before me and what is behind me; you have taken the moon, you have taken the sun from me, and my fear is great that you have taken God from me!

trans. Lady Gregory

BRÍGHIDÍN BÁN MO STÓRE [BRIDGET, MY TREASURE]

I am a wand'ring minstrel man,
And Love my only theme:

I've strayed beside the pleasant Bann,
    And eke the Shannon's stream;
I've piped and played to wife and maid
    By Barrow, Suir, and Nore,
But never met a maiden yet
    Like *Bríghidín bán mo stóre.*

My girl hath ringlets rich and rare,
    By Nature's fingers wove—
Loch-Carra's swan is not so fair
    As is her breast of love;
And when she moves, in Sunday sheen,
    Beyond our cottage door,
I'd scorn the high-born Saxon queen
    For *Bríghidín bán mo stóre.*

It is not that thy smile is sweet,
    And soft thy voice of song—
It is not that thou fleest to meet
    My comings lone and long:
But that doth rest beneath thy breast
    A heart of purest core,
Whose pulse is known to me alone,
    My *Bríghidín bán mo stóre.*

trans. Edward Walsh

HAVE YOU BEEN AT CARRICK?

Have you been at Carrick, and saw you my true-love there,
And saw you her features, all beautiful, bright and fair?
Saw you the most fragrant, flowery, sweet apple-tree?
Oh! saw you my loved one, and pines she in grief like
    me?

"I have been at Carrick, and saw thy own true-love
    there;
And saw, too, her features, all beautiful, bright and fair;
And saw the most fragrant, flowering, sweet apple-
    tree—

I saw thy loved one—she pines *not* in grief like thee."

Five guineas would price every tress of her golden
    hair—
Then think what a treasure her pillow at night to share!
These tresses thick-clust'ring and curling around her
    brow—
O Ringlet of Fairness! I'll drink to thy beauty now.

When, seeking to slumber, my bosom is rent with
    sighs—
I toss on my pillow till morning's blest beams arise;
No aid, bright beloved! can reach me save God above.
For a blood-lake is formed of the light of my eyes with
    love.

Until yellow autumn shall usher the Paschal day,
And Patrick's gay festival come in its train alway—
Until through my coffin the blossoming boughs shall
    grow,
My love on another I'll never in life bestow!

Lo! yonder the maiden illustrious, queen-like, high.
With long-flowing tresses adown to her sandal-tie—
Swan, fair as the lily, descended of high degree,
A myriad of welcomes, dear mind of my heart, to thee:

trans. Edward Walsh

SHULE AROON
A BRIGADE BALLAD

I would I were on yonder hill,
'T is there I'd sit and cry my fill,
And every tear would turn a mill,
Is go d-teidh tú, a mhúrnín, slán!

Siubhail, siubhail, siubhail, a rúin!
Siubhail go socair, agus siubhail go ciúin,

Siubhail go dtí an doras agus eulaigh liom,
Is go d-teidh tú, a mhúrnín, slán!

I'll sell my rock, I'll sell my reel,
I'll sell my only spinning-wheel,
To buy for my love a sword of steel,
Is go d-teidh tú, a mhúrnín, slán!
                Siubhail etc.

I'll dye my petticoats, I'll dye them red,
And round the world I'll beg my bread,
Until my parents shall wish me dead,
Is go d-teidh tú, a mhúrnín, slán!
                Siubhail etc.

I wish, I wish, I wish in vain,
I wish I had my heart again,
And vainly think I'd not complain,
Is go d-teidh tú, a mhúrnín, slán!
                Siubhail etc.

But now my love has gone to France,
To try his fortune to advance;
If he e'er come back, 't is but a chance,
Is go d-teidh tú, a mhúrnín, slán!
                Siubhail etc.

MARY FROM DUNGLOE

Oh, then, fare ye well, sweet Donegal, the Rosses and
    Gweedore
I'm crossing the main ocean, where the foaming billows
    roar.
It breaks my heart from you to part, where I spent
    many happy days
Farewell to kind relations, I'm bound for Amerikay.

Oh, my love is tall and handsome and her age is scarce
    eighteen

She far exceeds all other fair maids when she trips over
 the green
Her lovely neck and shoulders are fairer than the snow
Till the day I die I'll ne'er deny my Mary from
 Dungloe.

If I was at home in sweet Dungloe a letter I would
 write
Kind thoughts would fill my bosom for Mary my
 delight
'Tis in her father's garden, the fairest violets grow
And 'twas there I came to court the maid, my Mary
 from Dungloe.

Ah then, Mary you're my heart's delight my pride and
 only care
It was your cruel father, would not let me stray there.
But absence makes the heart grow fond and when I'm
 o'er the main
May the Lord protect my darling girl till I return again.

And I wished I was in sweet Dungloe and seated on the
 grass
And by my side a bottle of wine and and on my knee a
 lass.
I'd call for liquor of the best and I'd pay before I
 would go
And I'd roll my Mary in my arms in the town of sweet
 Dungloe.

SEAN O'DWYER OF THE GLEN

Rising in the morning
The summer sun shining,
I have heard the chant weaving
And the sweet songs of birds,
Badgers and small creatures,
The woodcock with his long beak,
The sounding of echoes,

The firing of strong guns,
The red fox on the crag.
Thousand yells of huntsmen
And a woman glumly in the pathway
Counting her flock of geese,
But now the woods are being cut
We will cross over the sea
And, Sean O'Dwyer of the Glen,
You are left weak.

This is my long loneliness,
the shelter for my head being cut,
The North wind lashing me
And death in the sky;
My happy dog being tied up
With no right to move or gambol
Who would take bad temper from a child
In the bright noon day;
The hearts of nobles on the rock
Capering, proud, prancing,
Who would climb up beyond the furze
Until their final day.
So if I get a little peace soon
From the gentry of the town
I will make my way to Galway
And leave the rout behind.

Meadows in stream-cut valleys
Have no vigor, no strength of men,
No glass or cup is raised
To health or happy life;
My bare hills! loss of hedges
From low field to mountain stacks
Leaves the hare on thickets' edges,
A vagrant on the plain.
What is this raid of strangers
But long-drawn cutting and clearing?
Sweet-whistled thrush and blackbird
Without branches for their singing,
An omen of coming troubles
Burdened priest and people

Adrift in empty harbors
Of deep mountain glens.

This is my daily bitterness,
To have lived to the age of sin,
To see this heavy scandal fall
On my people, my own kind.
How often on those long fine days
There were apples on the trees,
Green leaves on the oak,
Fresh dew on the grass;
Now I am driven from my acres,
In lonely cold without friends,
Hiding sadly in holes
And hollows of the mountain.
If I don't get some peace soon
And the right to stay at home
I must give up my own ground,
My country and my life.

trans. Joan Keefe

THE SORROWFUL LAMENTATION OF CALLAGHAN, GREALLY, AND MULLEN

"Come, tell me, dearest mother, what makes my father
    stay,
Or what can be the reason that he's so long away?"
"Oh! hold your tongue, my darling son, your tears do
    grieve me sore;
I fear he has been murdered in the fair of
    Turloughmore."

Come, all you tender Christians, I hope you will draw
    near;
It's of this dreadful murder I mean to let you hear,
Concerning those poor people whose loss we do deplore
The Lord have mercy on their souls they died at
    Turloughmore.

It is on the First of August, the truth I will declare,
Those people they assembled that day all at the fair;
But little was their notion what evil was in store,
All by the bloody Peelers at the fair of Turloughmore.

Were you to see that dreadful sight 'twould grieve your
    heart, I know,
To see the comely women and the men all lying low;
God help their tender parents, they will never see them
    more,
For cruel was their murder at the fair of Turloughmore.

It's for that base bloodthirsty crew, remark the word I
    say,
The Lord He will reward them against the judgment
    day;
The blood they have taken innocent, for it they'll suffer
    sore,
And the treatment that they gave to us that day at
    Turloughmore.

The morning of their trial as they stood up in the dock,
The words they spoke were feeling, the people round
    them flock;
"I tell you, Judge and Jury, the truth I will declare,
It was Brew that ordered us to fire that evening at the
    fair."

Now to conclude and finish this sad and doleful fray,
I hope their souls are happy against the judgment day;
It was little time they got, we know, when they fell like
    new-mowed hay,
May the Lord have mercy on their souls against the
    judgment day.

THE RISING OF THE MOON

"Tell me, tell me, Seán O'Farrell, tell me why you hurry
    so."

"Hush, a bhuachaill, hush and listen," and his cheeks
    were all aglow.
"I bear orders from the Captain, get you ready quick
    and soon,
For the pikes must be together at the rising of the
    moon."

"Oh! then, tell me, Seán O'Farrell, where the gatherin'
    is to be?"
"In the old spot by the river, right well-known to you
    and me.
One word more, for signal token whistle up the
    marchin' tune,
With your pike upon your shoulder at the rising of the
    moon."

Out from many a mud-wall cabin eyes were watching
    thro' the night.
Many a manly heart was throbbing for that blessed
    warning light;
Murmurs passed along the valley, like the banshee's
    lonesome croon,
And a thousand blades were flashing at the rising of the
    moon.

There beside the singing river that dark mass of men
    was seen,
High above their shining weapons flew their own
    beloved green,
"Death to every foe and traitor! forward! strike the
    marchin' tune!
And hurra! my boys, for freedom; 'tis the rising of the
    moon!"

Well they fought for poor old Ireland, and full bitter
    was their fate;
Oh! what glorious pride and sorrow fill the name of
    'Ninety-eight.
But, thank God, there still are beating strong young
    hearts in manhood's bloom,

Who will follow in their footsteps at the rising of the
    moon.

THE WEARIN' O' THE GREEN

Oh, Paddy dear! an' did ye hear the news that's goin'
    round?
The shamrock is by law forbid to grow on Irish
    ground.
No more St. Patrick's Day we'll keep, his color can't be
    seen,
For there's a cruel law agin the wearin' o' the green!

I met wid Napper Tandy, and he took me by the hand.
And he said, "How's poor Ould Ireland, and how does
    she stand?"
She's the most disthressful country that iver yet was
    seen,
For they're hangin' men and women there for wearin' o'
    the green.

An' if the color we must wear is England's cruel red,
Let it remind us of the blood that Ireland has shed;
Then pull the shamrock from your hat, and throw it on
    the sod,—
And never fear, 'twill take root there, tho' under foot
    'tis trod!

When law can stop the blades of grass from growin' as
    they grow,
And when the leaves in summer-time their color dare
    not show,
Then I will change the color, too, I wear in my
    caubeen,
But till that day, plaze God, I'll stick to wearin' o' the
    green.

trans. Dion Boucicault

NELL FLAHERTY'S DRAKE

My name it is Nell, quite candid I tell,
    That I live near Coote hill, I will never deny;
I had a fine drake, the truth for to spake,
    That my grandmother left me and she going to
        die;
He was wholesome and sound, he would weigh twenty
    pound,
    The universe round I would rove for his sake—
Bad wind to the robber—be he drunk or sober—
    That murdered Nell Flaherty's beautiful drake.

His neck it was green—most rare to be seen,
    He was fit for a queen of the highest degree;
His body was white—and would you delight—
    He was plump, fat and heavy, and brisk as a bee.
The dear little fellow, his legs they were yellow,
    He would fly like a swallow and dive like a hake,
But some wicked savage, to grease his white cabbage,
    He murdered Nell Flaherty's beautiful drake.

May his pig never grunt, may his cat never hunt,
    May a ghost ever haunt him at dead of the night;
May his hen never lay, may his ass never bray,
    May his goat fly away like an old paper kite.
That the flies and the fleas may the wretch ever tease,
    And the piercing north breeze make him shiver
        and shake,
May a lump of a stick raise bumps fast and thick
    On the monster that murdered Nell Flaherty's
        drake.

May his cradle ne'er rock, may his box have no lock,
    May his wife have no frock for to cover her back;
May his cock never crow, may his bellows ne'er blow,
    And his pipe and his pot may be evermore lack.
May his duck never quack, may his goose turn black,
    And pull down his turf with her long yellow beak;
May the plague grip the scamp, and his villainy stamp

On the monster that murdered Nell Flaherty's
      drake.

May his pipe never smoke, may his teapot be broke,
      And to add to the joke, may his kettle ne'er boil;
May he keep to the bed till the hour that he's dead,
      May he always be fed on hogwash and boiled oil.
May he swell with the gout, may his grinders fall out,
      May he roll, howl and shout with the horrid
            toothache;
May the temples wear horns, and the toes many corns,
      Of the Monster that murdered Nell Flaherty's
            drake.

May his spade never dig, may his sow never pig,
      May each hair in his wig be well thrashed with a
            flail;
May his door have no latch, may his house have no
      thatch,
      May his turkey not hatch, may the rats eat his meal.
May every old fairy, from Cork to Dunleary,
      Dip him snug and airy in river or lake,
Where the eel and the trout may feed on the snout
      Of the monster that murdered Nell Flaherty's
            drake.

May his dog yelp and howl with the hunger and cold,
      May his wife always scold till his brains go astray;
May the curse of each hag that e'er carried a bag
      Alight on the vag, till his hair turns gray.
May monkeys affright him, and mad dogs still bite him,
      And every one slight him, asleep or awake;
May weasels still gnaw him, and jackdaws still claw
      him—
      The monster that murdered Nell Flaherty's drake.

The only good news that I have to infuse
      Is that old Peter Hughes and blind Peter McCrake,
And big-nosed Bob Manson, and buck-toothed Ned
      Hanson,

Each man had a grandson of my lovely drake.
My treasure had dozens of nephews and cousins,
    And one I must get or my heart it will break;
To keep my mind easy, or else I'll run crazy—
    This ends the whole song of my beautiful drake.

THE STAR OF SLANE

Ye brilliant muses, who ne'er refuses,
    But still infuses in the poet's mind,
Your kind sweet favors to his endeavors.
    That his ardent labors should appear sublime;
Preserve my study from getting muddy,
    My idea's ready, so inspire my brain;
My quill refine, as I write each line,
    On a nymph divine called the Star of Slane.

In beauteous Spring, when the warblers sing,
    And their carols ring through each fragrant grove;
Bright Sol did shine, which made me incline
    By the river Boyne for to go to rove,
I was ruminating and meditating
    And contemplating as I paced the plain,
When a charming fair, beyond compare,
Did my heart ensnare near the town of Slane.

Had Paris seen this young maid serene,
    The Grecian queen he would soon disdain,
And straight embrace this virgin chaste,
    And peace would grace the whole Trojan plain.
If Ancient Caesar could on her gaze. sir,
    He'd stand amazed for to view this dame;
Sweet Cleopatra he would freely part her.
    And his crown he'd barter for the Star of Slane.

There's Alexander, that famed commander,
    Whose triumphant standard it did conquer all,
Who proved a victor over crowns and scepters,
    And great warlike structures did before him fall;

Should he behold her, I will uphold, sir,
    From pole to pole he would then proclaim,
For the human race in all that wide space,
    To respect the chaste blooming Star of Slane.

To praise her beauty then is my duty,
    But alas! I'm footy in this noble part,
And to my sorrow, sly Cupid's arrow
    Full deep did burrow in my tender heart;
In pain and trouble yet I will struggle,
    Though sadly hobbled by my stupid brain,
Yet backed by Nature I can tell each feature
    Of this lovely creature called the Star of Slane.

Her eyes it's true are an azure blue,
    And her cheeks the hue of the crimson rose;
Her hair behold it does shine like gold,
    And is finely rolled and so nicely grows;
Her skin is white as the snow by night,
    Straight and upright is her supple frame;
The chaste Diana, or fair Susanna,
    Are eclipsed in grandeur by the Star of Slane.

Her name to mention it might cause contention,
    And it's my intention for to breed no strife;
For me to woo her I am but poor,
    I'm deadly sure she won't be my wife;
In silent anguish I here must languish
    Till time does banish all my love-sick pain,
And my humble station I must bear with patience,
    Since great exaltation suits the Star of Slane.

THE NIGHT BEFORE LARRY WAS STRETCHED

The night before Larry was stretched,
    The boys they all paid him a visit;
A bait in their sacks, too, they fetched;
    They sweated their duds till they riz it:
For Larry was ever the lad,

When a boy was condemned to the squeezer,
Would fence all the duds that he had
    To help a poor friend to a sneezer,
        And warm his gob 'fore he died.

The boys they came crowding in fast,
    They drew all their stools round about him,
Six glims round his trap-case were placed,
    He couldn't be well waked without 'em.
When one of us asked could he die
    Without having duly repented,
Says Larry, "That's all in my eye;
    And first by the clargy invented,
        To get a fat bit for themselves."

"I'm sorry, dear Larry," says I,
    "To see you in this situation;
And, blister my limbs if I lie,
    I'd as lieve it had been my own station."
"Ochone! it's all over," says he,
    "For the neckcloth I'll be forced to put on
And by this time to-morrow you'll see
    Your poor Larry as dead as a mutton,"
        Because, why, his courage was good.

"And I'll be cut up like a pie,
    And my nob from my body be parted."
"You're in the wrong box, then," says I,
    "For blast me if they're so hard-hearted:
A chalk on the back of your neck
    Is all that Jack Ketch dares to give you;
Then mind not such trifles a feck,
For why should the likes of them grieve you?
        And now, boys, come tip us the deck."

The cards being called for, they played,
Till Larry found one of them cheated;
A dart at his napper he made
    (The boy being easily heated):
"Oh, by the hokey, you thief,
    I'll scuttle your nob with my daddle!

You cheat me because I'm in grief,
  But soon I'll demolish your noddle,
   And leave you your claret to drink."

Then the clergy came in with his book,
  He spoke him so smooth and so civil;
Larry tipped him a Kilmainham look,
  And pitched his big wig to the devil;
Then sighing, he threw back his head
  To get a sweet drop of the bottle,
And pitiful sighing, he said:
"Oh, the hemp will be soon round my throttle
   And choke my poor windpipe to death.

"Though sure it's the best way to die,
  Oh, the devil a betther a-livin'!
For, sure, when the gallows is high
  Your journey is shorter to Heaven:
But what harasses Larry the most,
  And makes his poor soul melancholy,
Is to think of the time when his ghost
  Will come in a sheet to sweet Molly—
   Oh, sure it will kill her alive!"

So moving these last words he spoke,
  We all vented our tears in a shower;
For my part, I thought my heart broke,
  To see him cut down like a flower,
On his travels we watched him next day;
  Oh, the throttler! I thought I could kill him;
But Larry not one word did say,
  Nor changed till he come to "King William"—
   Then, *musha!* his color grew white.

When he came to the nubbling chit,
  He was tucked up so neat and so pretty,
The rumbler jogged off from his feet,
  And he died with his face to the city;
He kicked, too—but that was all pride,
  For soon you might see 't was all over;
Soon after the noose was untied,

And at darky we waked him in clover,
And sent him to take a ground sweat.

FINNEGAN'S WAKE

Tim Finnegan liv'd in Walkin Street
    a gentleman Irish mighty odd.
He had a tongue both rich and sweet,
    an' to rise in the world he carried a hod.
Now Tim had a sort of a tipplin' way,
    with the love of the liquor he was born,
An' to help him on with his work each day
    he'd a drop of the craythur ev'ry morn.

Chorus: Whack fol the dah,
        dance to your partner
        Welt the flure yer trotters shake
        Wasn't it the truth I told you,
        Lot's of fun at Finnegan's wake.

One morning Tim was rather full,
    His head felt heavy which made him shake,
He fell from the ladder and broke his skull,
    So they carried him home his corpse to
wake,
They rolled him up in a nice clean sheet
And laid him out upon the bed,
With a gallon of whiskey at his feet,
    And a barrel of porter at his head.

His friends assembled at the wake,
    And Mrs. Finnegan called for lunch,
First they brought in tay and cake,
    The pipes, tobacco, and whiskey punch.
Miss Biddy O'Brien began to cry,
    "Such a neat clean corpse, did you ever see,
Arrah, Tim avourneen, why did you die?"
    "Ah, hould your gab," said Paddy McGee.

Then Biddy O'Connor took up the job,
  "Biddy," says she, "you're wrong, I'm sure,"
But Biddy gave her a belt in the gob,
  And left her sprawling on the floor;
Oh, then the war did soon enrage;
  'Twas woman to woman and man to man,
Shillelagh law did all engage,
  And a row and a ruction soon began.

Then Micky Maloney raised his head,
  When a noggin of whiskey flew at him,
It missed and falling on the bed,
  The liquor scattered over Tim;
Bedad he revives, see how he rises,
  And Timothy rising from the bed,
Says, "Whirl your liquor round like blazes,
  Thanam o'n dhoul, do ye think I'm dead?"

Further Readings on Irish Folk Songs

Collections

O'Lochlainn, Colm, ed. *The Bunting Collection of Irish Folk Music and Songs: I-VI.* Journal of the Irish Folk Song Society, XXII–XXIX, 1927–1939.
———, ed. *Irish Street Ballads.* Appreciation by Frank O'Connor. Dublin: The Sign of the Three Candles, 1939; New York; Corinth Books, 1960.
———, ed. *More Irish Street Ballads.* Dublin: The Three Candles, 1965.
O'Sullivan, Donal. *Songs of the Irish.* Dublin: Browne and Nolan; New York: Crown Publishers, 1960.

Studies

Golden, Sean V. "Traditional Irish Music in Contemporary Irish Literature." *MOSAIC* 12: 1–23.
Ó Canainn, Tomás. *Traditional Music in Ireland.* London and Boston: Routledge and Kegan Paul, 1978.
Ó Riada, Seán. *Our Musical Heritage.* Edited by Tomas Kinsella. Music edited by Tomás OCanainn. Dublin: Dolmen Press, 1982.
O'Sullivan, Donal. *Irish Folk Music and Song.* Rev. ed. Dublin: The Cultural Relations Committee, 1961.
Ó Tuama, Seán. *An Grá in Amhráin na nDaoine.* Dublin: An Clóchomhar, 1960.
Zimmerman, George-Denis. *Songs of the Irish Rebellion.* Reprint. Detroit: Gale, 1967.

NINETEENTH-CENTURY PROSE

Maria Edgeworth (1767–1849)

There are those who date the beginning of Anglo-Irish literature with the publication of Maria Edgeworth's *Castle Rackrent* (1800). Certainly, it was she who first cultivated the untilled field of the regional novel, and in so doing inspired Sir Walter Scott, William Makepeace Thackeray, James Fenimore Cooper—perhaps even Ivan Turgenev.

The eldest daughter and favorite child among Richard Lovell Edgeworth's twenty children, Maria Edgeworth helped run her father's estate at Edgeworthtown (Mostrim), County Longford, and collaborated with her father on a series of educational and moral tales. It was while her father was taken up with the Act of Union that she published anonymously at first, her novel *Castle Rackrent*.

Using their steward John Langan as a model, she created the narrator Thady Quirk, the first of a line of family retainers that would become a standard feature of nineteenth century Irish fiction. Thady's ironic account of three generations of Rackrents opens with with a description of Sir Patrick Rackrent, whom Thady's grandfather served and from whom Thady learned the facts of life in the Big House: lavish entertainment, hard drinking, and debt. The litigious Sir Kit follows, and then Thady's favorite, Sir Condy, who finally loses the estate to Thady's shrewd son Jason. *Castle Rackrent* is a cautionary tale, as strong a statement of the failure of responsibility of the landlord class as exists in Irish literature.

Edgeworth's own notes follow the narrative.

88

From *CASTLE RACKRENT*

Monday Morning.[1]

Having, out of friendship for the family, upon whose estate, praised
be Heaven! I and mine have lived rent-free, time out of mind, voluntarily undertaken to publish the Memoirs of the Rackrent Family, I
think it my duty to say a few words, in the first place, concerning
myself. My real name is Thady Quirk, though in the family I have
always been known by no other than *"honest Thady,"*—afterward, in the
time of Sir Murtagh, deceased, I remember to hear them calling me
"old Thady," and now I'm come to "poor Thady"; for I wear a long
great coat winter and summer, which is very handy, as I never put my
arms into the sleeves; they are as good as new, though come Holantide
next I've had it these seven years; it holds on by a single button round
my neck, cloak fashion. To look at me, you would hardly think "poor
Thady" was the father of attorney Quirk; he is a high gentleman, and
never minds what poor Thady says, and having better than fifteen
hundred a year, landed estate, looks down upon honest Thady; but I
wash my hands of his doings, and as I have lived so will I die, true and
loyal to the family. The family of the Rackrents is, I am proud to say,
one of the most ancient in the kingdom. Every body knows this is not
the old family name, which was O'Shaughlin, related to the kings of
Ireland—but that was before my time. My grandfather was driver to
the great Sir Patrick O'Shaughlin, and I heard him, when I was a boy,
telling how the Castle Rackrent estate came to Sir Patrick; Sir Tallyhoo
Rackrent was cousin-german to him, and had a fine estate of his own,
only never a gate upon it, it being his maxim that a car was the best
gate. Poor gentleman! he lost a fine hunter and his life, at last, by it, all
in one day's hunt. But I ought to bless that day, for the estate came
straight into *the* family, upon one condition, which Sir Patrick
O'Shaughlin at the time took sadly to heart, they say, but thought
better of it afterwards, seeing how large a stake depended upon it,
that he should, by act of parliament, take and bear the surname and
arms of Rackrent.

Now it was that the world was to see what was *in* Sir Patrick. On
coming into the estate, he gave the finest entertainment ever was
heard of in the country; not a man could stand after supper but Sir
Patrick himself, who could sit out the best man in Ireland, let alone
the three kingdoms itself.[2] He had his house, from one year's end to
another, as full of company as ever it could hold, and fuller; for rather
than be left out of the parties at Castle Rackrent, many gentlemen,

and those men of the first consequence and landed estates in the country, such as the O'Neills of Ballynagrotty, and the Moneygawls of Mount Juliet's Town, and O'Shannons of New Town Tullyhog, made it their choice, often and often, when there was no room to be had for love nor money, in long winter nights, to sleep in the chickenhouse, which Sir Patrick had fitted up for the purpose of accommodating his friends and the public in general, who honoured him with their company unexpectedly at Castle Rackrent; and this went on, I can't tell you how long. The whole country rang with his praises!—Long life to him! I'm sure I love to look upon his picture, now opposite to me; though I never saw him, he must have been a portly gentleman—his neck something short, and remarkable for the largest pimple on his nose, which, by his particular desire, is still extant in his picture, said to be a striking likeness, though taken when young. He is said also to be the inventor of raspberry whiskey, which is very likely, as nobody has ever appeared to dispute it with him, and as there still exists a broken punch-bowl at Castle Rackrent, in the garret, with an inscription to that effect—a great curiosity. A few days before his death he was very merry; it being his honour's birth-day, he called my grandfather in, God bless him! to drink the company's health, and filled a bumper himself, but could not carry it to his head, on account of the great shake in his hand; on this he cast his joke, saying, "What would my poor father say to me if he was to pop out of the grave, and see me now? I remember when I was a little boy, the first bumper of claret he gave me after dinner, how he praised me for carrying it so steady to my mouth. Here's my thanks to him—a bumper toast." Then he fell to singing the favourite song he learned from his father—for the last time, poor gentleman—he sung it that night as loud and as hearty as ever with a chorus:

> He that goes to bed, and goes to bed sober,
> Falls as the leaves do, falls as the leaves do, and dies in October;
> But he that goes to bed, and goes to bed mellow,
> Lives as he ought to do, lives as he ought to do, and dies an
>   honest fellow.

Sir Patrick died that night: just as the company rose to drink his health with three cheers, he fell down in a sort of fit, and was carried off; they sat it out, and were surprised, on inquiry, in the morning, to find that it was all over with poor Sir Patrick. Never did any gentleman

live and die more beloved in the country by rich and poor. His funeral
was such a one as was never known before or since in the country! All
the gentlemen in the three counties were at it; far and near, how they
flocked! my great grandfather said, that to see all the women even in
their red cloaks, you would have taken them for the army drawn out.
Then such a fine whillaluh![3] you might have heard it to the farthest
end of the county, and happy the man who could get but a sight of the
hearse! But who'd have thought it? Just as all was going on right,
through his own town they were passing, when the body was seized
for debt—a rescue was apprehended from the mob; but the heir who
attended the funeral was against that, for fear of consequences, seeing
that those villains who came to serve acted under the disguise of the
law: so, to be sure, the law must take its course, and little gain had the
creditors for their pains. First and foremost, they had the curses of
the country: and Sir Murtagh Rackrent, the new heir, in the next
place, on account of this affront to the body, refused to pay a shilling
of the debts, in which he was countenanced by all the best gentlemen
of property, and others of his acquaintance; Sir Murtagh alleging in
all companies, that he all along meant to pay his father's debts of
honour, but the moment the law was taken of him, there was an end
of honour to be sure. It was whispered (but none but the enemies of
the family believe it), that this was all a sham seizure to get quit of the
debts, which he had bound himself to pay in honour.

NOTES

1. *Monday morning.*—Thady begins his memoirs of the Rackrent Family by dating *Monday morning*, because no great undertaking can be auspiciously commenced in
Ireland on any morning but *Monday morning.* "Oh, please God we live till Monday
morning, we'll set the slater to mend the roof of the house. On Monday morning we'll
fall to, and cut the turf. On Monday morning we'll see and begin mowing. On Monday
morning, please your honour, we'll begin and dig the potatoes," &c.

All the intermediate days, between the making of such speeches and the ensuing
Monday, are wasted: and when Monday morning comes, it is ten to one that the
business is deferred to *the next* Monday morning. The Editor knew a gentleman, who, to
counteract this prejudice, made his workmen and labourers begin all new pieces of
work upon a Saturday.

2. *Let alone the three kingdoms itself.*—*Let alone, in this sentence, means put out of
consideration.* The phrase, *let alone,* which is now used as the imperative of a verb, may in
time become a conjunction, and may exercise the ingenuity of some future etymologist.
The celebrated Horne Tooke has proved most satisfactorily, that the conjunction *but*
comes from the imperative of the Anglo-Saxon verb *(beoutan) to be out;* also, that *if*
comes from *gif,* the imperative of the Anglo-Saxon verb which signifies to *give,* &c.

3. *Whillaluh.*—Ullaloo, Gol, or lamentation over the dead

"Magnoque ululante tumultu."—Virgil.
"Ululatibus omne
Implevere nemus."—Ovid.

A full account of the Irish Gol, or Ullaloo, and of the Caoinan or Irish funeral song, with its first semichorus, second semichorus, full chorus of sighs and groans, together with the Irish words and music, may be found in the fourth volume of the transactions of the Royal Irish Academy. For the advantage of *lazy* readers, who would rather read a page than walk a yard, and from compassion, not to say sympathy, with their infirmity, the Editor transcribes the following passages:

The Irish have been always remarkable for their funeral lamentations; and this peculiarity has been noticed by almost every traveller who visited them; and it seems derived from their Celtic ancestors, the primæval inhabitants of this isle. . . .

It has been affirmed of the Irish, that to cry was more natural to them than to any other nation, and at length the Irish cry became proverbial. . . .

Cambrensis in the twelfth century says, the Irish then musically expressed their griefs; that is, they applied the musical art, in which they excelled all others, to the orderly celebration of funeral obsequies, by dividing the mourners into two bodies, each alternately singing their part, and the whole at times joining in full chorus. . . . The body of the deceased, dressed in grave clothes, and ornamented with flowers, was placed on a bier, or some elevated spot. The relations and keepers *(singing mourners)* ranged themselves in two divisions, one at the head, and the other at the feet of the corpse. The bards and croteries had before prepared the funeral Caoinan. The chief bard of the head chorus began by singing the first stanza, in a low, doleful tone, which was softly accompanied by the harp: at the conclusion, the foot semichorus began the lamantation, or Ullaloo, from the final note of the preceding stanza, in which they were answered by the head semichorus; then both united in one general chorus. The chorus of the first stanza being ended, the chief bard of the foot semichorus began the second Gol or lamentation, in which he was answered by that of the head; and then, as before, both united in the general full chorus. Thus alternately were the song and choruses performed during the night. The genealogy, rank, possessions, the virtues and vices of the dead were rehearsed, and a number of interrogations were addressed to the deceased; as, Why did he die? If married, whether his wife was faithful to him, his sons dutiful, or good hunters or warriors? If a woman, whether her daughters were fair or chaste? If a young man, whether he had been crossed in love; or if the blue-eyed maids of Erin treated him with scorn?

We are told, that formerly the feet (the metrical feet) of the Caoinan were much attended to; but on the decline of the Irish bards these feet were gradually neglected, and the Caoinan fell into a sort of slipshod metre amongst women. Each province had different Caoinans, or at least different imitations of the original. There was the

Munster cry, the Ulster cry, &c. It became an extempore performance, and every set of keepers varied the melody according to their own fancy.

It is curious to observe how customs and ceremonies degenerate. The present Irish cry, or howl, cannot boast of such melody, nor is the funeral procession conducted with much dignity. The crowd of people who assemble at these funerals sometimes amounts to a thousand, often to four or five hundred. They gather as the bearers of the hearse proceed on their way, and when they pass through any village, or when they come near any houses, they begin to cry—Oh! Oh! Oh! Oh! Oh! Agh! Agh! raising their notes from the first *Oh!* to the last *Ah!* in a kind of mournful howl. This gives notice to the inhabitants of the village that a *funeral is passing,* and immediately they flock out to follow it. In the province of Munster it is a common thing for the women to follow a funeral, to join in the universal cry with all their might and main for some time, and then to turn and ask—"Arrah! who is it that's dead?—who is it we're crying for?" Even the poorest people have their own burying-places, that is, spots of ground in the church-yards where they say that their ancestors have been buried ever since the wars of Ireland; and if these burial-places are ten miles from the place where a man dies, his friends and neighbours take care to carry his corpse thither. Always one priest, often five or six priests, attend these funerals; each priest repeats a mass, for which he is paid, sometimes a shilling, sometimes half-a-crown, sometimes half-a-guinea, or a guinea, according to their circumstances, or, as they say, according to the *ability* of the deceased. After the burial of any very poor man, who has left a widow or children, the priest makes what is called *a collection* for the widow; he goes round to every person present, and each contributes sixpence or a shilling, or what they please.

Certain old women, who cry particularly loud and well, are in great request, and, as a man said to the Editor, "Every one would wish and be proud to have such at his funeral, or at that of his friends." The lower Irish are wonderfully eager to attend the funerals of their friends and relations, and they make their relationships branch out to a great extent. The proof that a poor man has been well beloved during his life is his having a crowded funeral. To attend a neighbour's funeral is a cheap proof of human-ity, but it does not, as some imagine, cost nothing. The time spent in attending funerals may be safely valued at half a million to the Irish nation; the Editor thinks that double that sum would not be too high an estimate. The habits of profligacy and drunkenness which are acquired at *wakes,* are here put out of the question. When a labourer, a carpenter, or a smith, is not at his work, which frequently happens, ask where he is gone, and ten to one the answer is—"Oh, faith, please your honour, he couldn't do a stroke to-day, for he's gone to *the* funeral."

Even beggars, when they grow old, go about begging *for their own funerals*; that is, begging for money to buy a coffin, candles, pipes, and tobacco.

Those who value customs in proportion to their antiquity, and nations in propor-tion to their adherence to ancient customs, will doubtless, admire the Irish *Ullaloo,* and the Irish nation, for persevering in this usage from time immemorial. The Editor, however, has observed some alarming symptoms, which seem to prognosticate the declining taste for the Ullaloo in Ireland. In a comic theatrical entertainment, repre-sented not long since on the Dublin stage, a chorus of old women was introduced, who set up the Irish howl round the relics of a physician, who is supposed to have fallen under the wooden sword of Harlequin. After the old women have continued their Ullaloo for a decent time, with all the necessary accompaniments of wringing their hands, wiping or rubbing their eyes with the corners of their gowns or aprons, &c. one of the mourners suddenly suspends her lamentable cries, and, turning to her neighbour, asks, "Arrah now, honey, who is it we're crying for?"

Further Readings on Maria Edgeworth

Bibliography

Butler, Marilyn. *Maria Edgeworth: A Literary Biography*, pp. 501–9. Oxford: Clarendon Press, 1972.
Newcomber, James. *Maria Edgeworth*, pp. 88–94. Lewisburg, Pa: Bucknell University Press, 1973.
Slade, Bertha Coolidge. *Maria Edgeworth: A Bibliographical Tribute*. London: Constable, 1937.

Selected Works

Castle Rackrent. Edited by George Watson. London: Oxford University Press, 1964 (1800).
Castle Rackrent and The Absentee. Everyman's Library. Introduction by Brander Matthews. London: Dent and Sons, 1934 (1800, 1812).
Ormond. Introduction by A. Norman Jeffares, Shannon: Irish University Press, 1972 (1817).
Memoirs of Richard Lovell Edgeworth, Esq., Begun by Himself and Concluded by his Daughter, Maria Edgeworth. 2 vols. Introduction by Desmond Clarke. Shannon: Irish University Press, 1970 (1820).
Tales and Novels of Maria Edgeworth. New York: AMS, 1967 (1893).
Tour in Connemara and the Martins of Ballinahinch. Edited by Harold Edgeworth Butler. London: Constable and Co., 1950.

Biography and Criticism

Butler, Marilyn. *Maria Edgeworth: A Literary Biography*. Oxford: Clarendon Press, 1972.
Clarke, Desmond. *The Ingenious Mr. Edgeworth*. London: Oldbourne, 1965.
Clarke, Isabel C. *Maria Edgeworth: Her Family and Friends*. London: Hutchinson and Co., 1950.
Flanagan, Thomas J. *The Irish Novelists, 1800–1850*, pp. 53–106. New York: Columbia University Press, 1959.
Harden, O. Elizabeth. *Maria Edgeworth*. Boston: Twayne Publishers, 1984.
———*Maria Edgeworth's Art of Prose Fiction*. The Hague: Mouton, 1971.
Hare, Augustus J. C. *The Life and Letters of Maria Edgeworth*. 2 vols. Freeport, N.Y.: Books for Libraries Press, 1971 (1894).
Hawthorne, Mark D. *Doubt and Dogma in Maria Edgeworth*. Gainesville: University of Florida Press, 1967.

Inglis-Jones, Elisabeth. *The Great Maria*. London: Faber and Faber, 1959.

McHugh, Roger. "Maria Edgeworth's Irish Novels." *Studies* 27:556–70.

Newcomber, James. *Maria Edgeworth*. Lewisburg, Pa: Bucknell University Press, 1973.

———. *Maria Edgeworth the Novelist. 1767–1849. A Bicentennial Study*. Fort Worth: Texas Christian University Press, 1967.

Tracy, Robert. "Maria Edgeworth and Lady Morgan: Legality versus Legitimacy." *Nineteenth Century Fiction* 40:1–22.

Woolf, Virginia. "The Taylors and the Edgeworths." In *The Common Reader*. New York: Harcourt, Brace and World, 1953.

WILLIAM CARLETON (1794–1869)

William Carleton's fiction is unique for its description of Irish rural life in the early nineteenth century—especially the world of the tenant farmer and landless laborer, a world destroyed by the famine of 1845–48. W. B. Yeats judged him a great Irish historian: "The history of a nation is not parliaments and battle-fields, but in what the people say to each other on fair-days and high days, and in how they farm, and quarrel, and go on pilgrimage. These things has Carleton recorded." Carleton himself realized the value of this work. He introduced *Tales of Ireland* (1834) as follows:

> I found them a class unknown in literature, unknown by their landlords, and unknown by those in whose hands much of their destiny was placed. If I became the historian of their habits and manners, their feelings, their prejudices, their superstitions and their crimes, if I have attempted to delineate their moral, religious and physical state, it was because I saw no person willing to undertake a task which surely must be looked on as an important one. . . .

He was one of their own, too. Son of a tenant farmer and a mother celebrated locally as a singer, Carleton was born in Prillisk, Clogher parish, County Tyrone, was steeped in oral tradition in both Irish and English. Like Jemmy M'Evoy, the hero of "The Poor Scholar," Carleton set off to Munster; however, he quickly returned home. Later, he went to Dublin where his struggle with poverty was responsible for his uneven career—much of his output consisted of potboilers and propaganda—and for his broken health.

Jemmy was more fortunate. His first bit of luck was meeting the hospitable farmer who took him home for the night. The passage illustrates Carleton's adroit use of language—a combination of authentic dialect and rich dialogue that anticipates Synge and O'Casey.

From "THE POOR SCHOLAR"

There is no country on the earth in which either education, or the desire to procure it, is so much reverenced as in Ireland. Next to the claims of the priest and schoolmaster come those of the poor scholar for the respect of the people. It matters not how poor or how miserable he may be; so long as they see him struggling with poverty in the prosecution of a purpose so laudable, they will treat him with attention and kindness. Here there is no danger of his being sent to the workhouse, committed as a vagrant—or passed from parish to parish until he reaches his own settlement. Here the humble lad is not met by the sneer of purse-proud insolence, or his simple tale answered only by the frown of heartless contempt. No—no—no. The best bit and sup are placed before him; and whilst his poor, but warm-hearted entertainer can afford only potatoes and salt to his own half-starved family, he will make a struggle to procure something better for the poor scholar; *"Bekase he's far from his own, the crathur!* An' sure the intintion in him is good, any how; the Lord prosper him, an' every one that has the heart set upon the larnin'!"

As Jemmy proceeded, he found that his satchel of books and apparel gave as clear an intimation of his purpose, as if he had carried a label to that effect upon his back.

"God save you, a bouchal!" said a warm, honest-looking countryman, whom he met driving home his cows in the evening, within a few miles of the town in which he purposed to sleep.

"God save you kindly!"

"Why, thin, 'tis a long journey you have before you, alanna, for I know well it's for Munster you're bound."

"Thrue for you, 'tis there wid the help of God I'm goin'. A great scarcity of larnin' was in my own place, or I wouldn't have to go at all," said the boy, whilst his eyes filled with tears.

"'Tis no discredit in life," replied the countryman, with untaught natural delicacy, for he perceived that a sense of pride lingered about the boy which made the character of poor scholar sit painfully upon him; "'tis no discredit, dear, nor don't be cast down. I'll warrant you that God will prosper you; an' that He may, avick, I pray this day!" and as he spoke, he raised his hat in reverence to the Being whom he invoked. "An' tell me, dear—where do you intend to sleep to-night?"

"In the town forrid here," replied Jemmy. "I'm in hopes I'll be able to reach it before dark."

"Pooh! asy you will. Have you any friends or acquaintances there that'ud welcome you, *a bouchal dhas* [my handsome boy]?"

"No, indeed," said Jemmy, "they're all strangers to me; but I can stop in 'dhry lodgin',' for it's chaper."

"Well, alanna, I believe you; but *I'm no stranger to you*—so come home wid me to-night; where you'll get a good bed, and betther thratement nor in any of their dhry lodgins. Give me your books, and I'll carry them for you. Ethen, but you have a great batch o' them entirely. Can you make any hand o' the Latin at all yet?"

"No, indeed," replied Jemmy, somewhat sorrowfully; "I didn't ever open a Latin book, at all at all."

"Well, acushla, everything has a beginnin';—you won't be so. An' I know by your face that you'll be bright at it, an' a credit to them that owes you. There's my house in the fields beyant, where you'll be well kept for one night, any way, or for twinty, or for ten times twinty, if you wanted them."

The honest farmer then commenced the song of *Colleen dhas Crotha na Mho,* which he sang in a clear mellow voice, until they reached the house.

"Alley," said the man to his wife, on entering, "here's a stranger I've brought you."

"Well," replied Alley, "he's welcome sure, any way; *Kead millia failta ghud,* alanna! sit over to the fire. Brian, get up, dear," said she to one of the children, "an' let the stranger to the hob."

"He's goin' on a good errand, the Lord bless him!" said the husband, "up the country for the larnin'. Put thim books over on the settle; an' whin the *girshas* are done milkin,' give him a brave dhrink of the sweet milk; it's the stuff to thravel on."

"Troth, an' I will, wid a heart an' a half, wishin' it was better I had to give him. Here, Nelly, put down a pot o' wather, an' lave soap an' a *praskeen,* afore you go to milk, till I bathe the dacent boy's feet. Sore an' tired they are afther his journey, poor young crathur."

When Jemmy placed himself upon the hob, he saw that some

peculiarly good fortune had conducted him to so comfortable a rest-ing-place. He considered this as a good omen, and felt, in fact, much relieved, for the sense of loneliness among strangers was removed.

The house evidently belonged to a wealthy farmer, well to do in the world; the chimney was studded with sides upon sides of yellow smoke-dried bacon, hams, and hung beef in abundance. The kitchen tables were large, and white as milk; and the dresser rich in its shining array of delf and pewter. Everything, in fact, was upon a large scale. Huge meal chests were ranged on one side, and two or three settle beds on the other, conspicuous, as I have said, for their uncommon cleanliness; whilst hung from the ceiling were the *glaiks*, a machine for churning; and beside the dresser stood an immense churn, certainly too unwieldy to be managed except by machinery. The farmer was a ruddy-faced Milesian, who wore a drab frieze coat, with a velvet collar, buff waistcoat, corduroy small-clothes, and top-boots well greased from the tops down. He was not only an agriculturist, but a grazier— remarkable for shrewdness and good sense, generally attended fairs and markets, and brought three or four large droves of fat cattle to England every year. From his fob hung the brass chain and almost rusty key of a watch, which he kept certainly more for use than ornament.

"A little sup o' this," said he, "won't take your life," approaching Jemmy with a bottle of as good poteen as ever escaped the eye of an exciseman; "it'll refresh you—for you're tired, or I wouldn't offer it, by rason that one bint on what you're bint on, oughtn't to be makin' freedoms wid the same dhrink. But there's a time for everything, an' there's a time for this.—Thank you, agra," he added, in reply to Jemmy, who had drunk his health. "Now, don't be frettin'—but make yourself as aisy as if you were at your own father's hearth. You'll have everything to your heart's contint for this night; the carts are goin' in to the market to-morrow airly—you can sit upon them, an' maybe you'll get somethin' more nor you expect: sure the Lord has given it to me, an' why wouldn't I share it wid them that wants it more nor I do?"

[Jemmy is given his dinner and later the local schoolmaster arrives.]

As she spoke, a short thickset man, with black twinkling eyes and ruddy cheeks entered. This personage was no other than the school-master of that district, who circulated, like a newspaper, from one farmer's house to another, in order to expound for his kind entertainers the news of the day, his own learning, and the very evident extent of their ignorance.

The moment he came in, the farmer and his wife rose with an air of much deference, and placed, a chair for him exactly opposite the fire, leaving a respectful distance on each side, within which no illiterate mortal durst presume to sit.

"Misther Corcoran," said the farmer, presenting Jemmy's satchel, through which the shapes of the books were quite plain, *"thig in thu shinn?"* and as he spoke he looked significantly at its owner.

"Ah;" replied the man of letters, *"thigum, thigum.* God be wid the day when I carried the likes of it. 'Tis a badge of polite genius, that no boy need be ashamed of. So my young suckling of litherature, you're bound for Munster?—for that counthry where the swallows fly in conic sections—where the magpies and the turkeys confab in Latin, and the cows and bullocks will roar you Doric Greek—bo-a-o—clamo. What's your pathronymic? *quo nomine gowdes, Domine doctissime?"*

The lad was silent; but the farmer's wife turned up the whites of her eyes with an expression of wonder and surprise at the erudition of the "masther."

"I persave you are as yet uninitiated into the elementary *principia* of the languages; well—the honour is still before you. What's your name?'

"James M'Evoy, Sir."

Just now the farmer's family began to assemble round the spacious hearth; the yound lads, whose instruction the worthy teacher claimed as his own peculiar task, came timidly forward, together with two or three pretty bashful girls with sweet flashing eyes, and countenances full of feeling and intelligence. Behind on the settles, half-a-dozen servants of both sexes sat in pairs—each boy placing himself beside his favourite girl. These *appeared* to be as strongly interested in the learned conversation which the master held, as if they were masters and mistresses of Munster Latin and Doric Greek themselves; but an occasional thump cautiously bestowed by no slender female hand upon the sturdy shoulder of her companion, or a dry cough from one of the young men, fabricated to drown the coming blow, gave slight indications that they contrived to have a little amusement among themselves, altogether independent of Mr. Corcoran's erudition.

When the latter came in, Jemmy was taking the tumbler of punch which the farmer's wife had mixed for him; on this he fixed an expressive glance, which instantly reverted to the *vanithee,* and from her to the large bottle which stood in a window to the right of the fire. It is a quick eye, however, that can anticipate Irish hospitality.

"Sure, I am," she replied, "an' will have it for you in less than no time."

She accordingly addressed herself to the bottle, and in a few minutes handed a reeking jug of punch to the *Farithee,* or good man.

"Come, Masther, by the hand o' my body, I don't like dhry talk so long as I can get anything to moisten the discoorse. Here's your health, Masther," continued the farmer, winking at the rest, "and a speedy conclusion to what you know! In throth, she's the pick of a good girl—not to mintion what she has for her portion. I'm a friend to the same family, an' will put a spoke in your wheel, Masther, that'll sarve you."

"Oh, Mr. Lanigan, very well, Sir—very well—you're becoming quite facetious upon me," said the little man, rather confused; "but upon my credit and reputation, except the amorous inclination in regard to me is on *her* side," and he looked sheepishly at his hands, "I can't say that the arrows of Cupid have as yet pinethrated the sintimintal side of *my* heart. It is not with me as it was wid Dido—hem—

Non 'hæret lateri lethalis arundo,'

as Virgil says. Yet I can't say, but if a friend were to become spokesman for me, and insinuate in my behalf a small taste of amorous sintimintality, why—hem, hem, hem! The company's health! Lad, James M'Evoy, *your* health, and success to you, my good boy!— hem, hem!"

"Here's wishin' him the same!" said the farmer.

"James," said the schoolmaster, "you are goin' to Munsther, an' I can say that I have travelled it from end to end, not to a bad purpose, I hope—hem! Well, a bouchal, there are hard days and nights before you, so keep a firm heart. If you have money, as 'tis likely you have, don't let a single rap of it into the hands of the schoolmaster, although the first thing he'll do will be to bring you home to his own house, an' palaver you night an' day, till he succeeds in persuading you to leave it in his hands for security. You might, if not duly pre-adominished, surrender it to his solicitations, for—

'Nemo mortalium omnibus horis sapit.'

Michael, what case is *mortalium?*" added he, suddenly addressing one of the farmer's sons: "come now, Michael, where's your brightness? What case is *mortalium?*"

The boy was taken by surprise, and for a few minutes could not reply.

"Come man," said the father, "be sharp, spake out bravely, an' don't be afeard; nor don't be in a hurry aither, we'll wait for you."

"Let him alone—let him alone," said Corcoran; "I'll face the same boy agin the county for *cuteness*. If he doesn't expound that, I'll never consthre a line of Latin, or Greek, or Masoretic, while I'm livin'."

His cunning master knew right well that the boy, who was only confused at the suddenness of the question, would feel no difficulty in answering it to his satisfaction. Indeed, it was impossible for him to miss it, as he was then reading the seventh book of Virgil, and the fourth of Homer. It is, however, a trick with such masters to put simple questions of that nature to their pupils, when at the houses of their parents, as knotty and difficult, and when they are answered, to assume an air of astonishment at the profound reach of thought displayed by the pupil.

When Michael recovered himself, he instantly replied, "*Mortalium* is the genitive case of *nemo*, by '*Nomina Partitiva*.'"

Corcoran laid down the tumbler, which he was in the act of raising to his lips, and looked at the lad with an air of surprise and delight, then at the farmer and his wife, alternately, and shook his head with much mystery. "Michael," said he to the lad, "will you go out, and tell us what the night's doin'."

The boy accordingly went out—"Why," said Corcoran, in his absence, "if ever there was a phanix, and that boy will be an the bird— an Irish phanix he will be, a

Rara avis in terris, nigorque simillima cygno!

There is no batin' him at anything he undhertakes. Why, there's thim that are makin' good bread by their larnin', that couldn't resolve that; and you all saw how he did it widout the book! Why, if he goes on at this rate, I'm afraid he'll soon be too many for myself—hem!"

"Too many for yourself! Fill the masther's tumbler, Alley. Too many for yourself! No, no! I doubt he'll never see that day, bright as he is, an' cute. That's it—put a hape upon it. Give me your hand, masther. I thank you for your attintion to him, an' the boy *is* a credit to us. Come over, Michael, avourneen. Here, take what's in this tumbler, an' finish it. Be a good boy, an' mind your lessons, an' do everything the masther here—the Lord bless him!—bids you; an' you'll never want a frind, masther, nor a dinner, nor a bed, nor a guinea, while the Lord spares me aither the one or the other."

"I know it, Mr. Lanigan, I know it; and I will make that boy the pride of Ireland, if I'm spared. I'll show him *cramboes* that would puzzle the great Scaliger himself; and many other difficulties I'll let him into, that I have never let out yet, except to Tim Kearney, that bate them all at Thrinity College in Dublin up, last June."

"Arrah, how was that, Masther?"

"Tim, you see, went in to his Entrance Examinayshuns, and one of the Fellows came to examine him, but divil a long it was till Tim sacked him.

" 'Go back agin,' says Tim, 'and sind some one that's *able* to tache me, for you're *not*.'

"So another greater scholar agin came to thry Tim, and *did* thry him, and Tim made a hare of *him*, before all that was in the place—five or six thousand ladies and gintlemen, at laste!

"The great learned Fellows thin began to look odd enough; so they picked out the best scholar among them but one, and slipped him at Tim: but well becomes Tim, the never a long it was still he had *him*, too, as dumb as a post. The fellow went back—

" 'Gintlemen,' says he to the rest, 'we'll be disgraced all out,' says he, 'for except the Prowost sacks that Munsther spalpeen, he'll bate us all, an' we'll never be able to hould up our heads afther.'

"Accordingly, the Prowost attacks Tim; and such a meetin' as they had, never was seen in Thrinity College since its establishment. At last when they had been nine hours and a half at it, the Prowost put one word to him that Tim couldn't expound, so he lost it by *one* word only. For the last two hours the Prowost carried an the examinashun in Hebrew, thinking, you see, he *had* Tim there; but he was mistaken for Tim answered him in good Munsther Irish, and it so happened that they understood each other, for the two languages are first cousins, or, at all evints, close blood relations. Tim was then pronounced to be the best scholar in Ireland except the Prowost; though among ourselves they might have thought of the man that *taught* him. That, however, wasn't all. A young lady fell in love wid Tim, and is to make him a present of herself and her great fortune (three estates) the moment he becomes a counsellor; and in the meantime she allows him thirty pounds a year to bear his expenses, and live like a gintleman.

"Now to return to the youth in the corner: *Nemo mortalium omnibus horis sapit,* Jemmy keep your money, or give it to the priest to keep, and it will be safest; but by no means let the Hyblean honey of the schoolmaster's blarney deprive you of it, otherwise it will be a *vale, vale, longum vale* between you."

Further Readings on William Carleton

Bibliography

Hayley, Barbara. *The William Carleton Bibliography.* Gerrards Cross, England: Colin Smythe, 1985.

Selected Works

The Black Prophet. New York: Garland Press, 1979 (1847).
Denis O'Shaughnessy Going to Maynooth. Introduction by Maurice Harmon. Cork: Mercier Press, 1973.
The Emigrants of Ahadarra. New York: Garland Publishing, 1979 (1848).
The Life of William Carleton. 2 vols. Edited by David J. O'Donoghue. Introduction by Mrs. Cashel Hoey. New York: Garland Publishing, 1979 (1896).
Stories from Carleton. Edited and with an introduction by W. B. Yeats. New York: Lemma, 1973 (1889).
Traits and Stories of the Irish Peasantry. New York: Garland Publishing, 1979 (1830, 1833).
Valentine M'Clutchy, The Irish Agent. New York: Garland Publishing, 1979 (1847).
The Works of Carleton. Freeport, N.Y.: Books for Libraries Press, 1970 (1880).

Biography and Criticism

Bell, Sam Hanna. "William Carleton and his Neighbors." *Ulster Folk Life* 7: 37–40.
Boué, André. *William Carleton, romancier irlandais (1794–1869).* Lille: Université de Lille, III, 1973. Reprinted, Paris: Publications de la Sorbonne, 1978.
Flanagan, Thomas. *The Irish Novelists, 1800–1850,* pp. 255–330. New York: Columbia University Press, 1958.
Hayley, Barbara. *Carleton's "Traits and Stories" and the 19th Century Anglo-Irish Tradition.* Gerrards Cross: Colin Smythe; New York: Barnes and Noble, 1983.

Kiely, Benedict. *Poor Scholar. A Study of the Works and Days of William Carleton (1794–1869)*. New York: Sheed and Ward, 1948.

Ó hAinle, Cathal G. "The Gaelic Background of Carleton's *Traits and Stories*." *Eire-Ireland* 18: 6–19.

Shaw, Rose. *Carleton Country*. Introduction by Shane Leslie. Dublin: Talbot Press, 1930.

Sullivan, Eileen. *William Carleton*. Boston: Twayne Publishers, 1983.

NINETEENTH-CENTURY POETRY

Thomas Moore (1779–1852)

Lionized in his own day, popular still in 1879, the year of his centenary, Thomas Moore's bicentenary passed with scant attention; yet, some would argue he is Ireland's national poet. People have sung Moore's *Irish Melodies* with great feeling for more than one hundred and fifty years, and while it may be true that other, less sentimental music better embodies Irish identity today, generations of Irish at home and abroad have found an expression of national aspiration in Moore's imagery.

Born to a middle-class Dublin family, Moore attended Trinity College, Dublin, where Robert Emmet became a good friend. Here, too, he discovered Edward Bunting's *Irish Airs,* and first conceived the idea to provide lyrics for that music. He left Ireland to spend the required terms at the Middle Temple to become a barrister; however, he abandoned law after he published his translation of the Greek poet Anacreon. Moore's patron, the Earl of Moira, arranged for him to be the Registrar of the court of Admiralty at Bermuda in 1803. Leaving a deputy in charge there, Moore traveled in the United States. He was taken with the country's natural beauty but disapproved of American democracy, prophesying that it would not succeed.

Eventually, Moore returned to London, to the drawing-room society where his vivacious personality, his wit, and his ability to entertain made him, in Byron's words, "the poet of all circles and the idol of his own." Byron himself made Moore the custodian of his memoirs, which Moore published in 1830 as *Letters and Journals of*

Lord Byron: with Notes of His Life. Despite his popularity and his commercial successes—his Oriental romance *Lalla Rookh* (1816) brought him a 3,000-guinea advance—his last years were darkened by the death of his children and his own mental deterioration.

Moore found the story of the children of Lir among the Irish manuscripts belonging to the Countess of Moira. Noting that the entire narrative would require more verses "than anyone is authorized to inflict upon an audience at once," Moore offered the two-stanza "Song of Fionnuala," which suggests that the Lir's children were a metaphor for Ireland, since both were enchanted and both waited for heaven to deliver them.

THE MINSTREL BOY

The minstrel boy to the war is gone,
        In the ranks of death you'll find him,
His father's sword he has girded on,
        And his wild harp slung behind him.
"Land of song!" said the warrior bard,
        "Though all the world betrays thee,
One sword, at least, thy rights shall guard,
        One faithful harp shall praise thee!"

The minstrel fell!—but the foeman's chain
        Could not bring his proud soul under;
The harp he loved ne'er spoke again,
        For he tore its chords asunder;
And said, "No chains shall sully thee,
        Thou soul of love and bravery!
Thy songs were made for the pure and free,
        They shall never sound in slavery!"

THE SONG OF FIONNUALA

Silent, O Moyle! be the roar of thy water,
        Break not, ye breezes, your chain of repose,
While, murmuring mournfully, Lir's lonely daughter
        Tells to the night-star her tale of woes.

EIGHTH CENTURY—IRISH RENAISSANCE

When shall the swan, her death-note singing,
    Sleep, with wings in darkness furled?
When will heaven, its sweet bell ringing,
    Call my spirit from this stormy world?

Sadly, O Moyle! to thy winter wave weeping,
    Fate bids me languish long ages away!
Yet still in her darkness doth Erin lie sleeping,
    Still doth the pure light its dawning delay!
When will that day-star, mildly springing,
    Warm our isle with peace and love?
When will heaven, its sweet bell ringing,
    Call my spirit to the fields above?

Further Readings on Thomas Moore

Bibliography

MacManus, M. J. *A Bibliographical Hand-List of the First Editions of Thomas Moore.* Dublin, 1934.

Selected Works

A Centenary Selection of Moore's Melodies. Edited by David Hammond. Introduction by Seamus Heaney. Dublin: Gilbert Dalton, 1979.

Letters and Journals of Lord Byron: with Notes of His Life. London: John Murray, 1830.

The Letters of Thomas Moore. 2 vols. Edited by Wilfred S. Dowden. Oxford: Clarendon Press, 1964.

The Memoirs, Journal and Correspondence of Thomas Moore. Edited by Lord John Russell. London: Longmans, 1853–1856.

The Poetical Works of Thomas Moore. Edited A. D. Godley. London: Henry Frowde, 1910.

Biography and Criticism

de Ford, Miriam Allen. *Thomas Moore.* New York: Twayne, 1967.

Jordan, Hoover. *Bolt Upright: The Life of Thomas Moore.* 2 vols. Salzburg, 1975.

Tessier, Therese. *The Bard of Erin. A Study of Thomas Moore's "Irish Melodies," 1808–1834.* Atlantic Highlands, N.J.: Humanities Press, 1981.

White, Terence de Vere. *Tom Moore. The Irish Poet.* London: Hamish Hamilton, 1977.

ANTHONY RAFTERY (1784–1835)

One still hears Raftery's songs sung in the west of Ireland—love songs like "An Pósae Glégeal" [The bright flower], written to celebrate Mary Hynes, a local beauty, or "Anach-Cuain" (Annaghdown), which commemorates a local tragedy: the drowning in Lough Corrib of nineteen young people on their way to a fair in Galway. One can not compare Raftery with such sophisticated and accomplished Munster poets as Aogán Ó Rathaille and Eoghan Rua Ó Suilleabháin; nevertheless, Raftery's songs share the simplicity and passion of the best of Irish folk songs and ballads.

Raftery was born in Lios Ard, County Mayo, near Killedan, the house of his landlord Frank Taafe. He received some education at a local hedge school, but left when he was blinded by smallpox at the age of nine. He was encouraged to take up music by Mrs. Taafe, but—though he was said to have been "taught by the fairies"—he was only a poor fiddler. After Taafe banished him in connection with the accidental death of a favorite horse, Raftery went to South Galway, where he remained a wandering minstrel until his death on Christmas Eve, 1835. Raftery was something of a cult figure for Hyde, Yeats, and Lady Gregory. Indeed, the latter arranged for a stone to mark his grave in Killeenin, near Craughwell; it was dedicated at a *feis* in August, 1900.

Douglas Hyde published two collections of Raftery's poems, the first with help from Lady Gregory. Hyde's play "An Posadh" [The marriage] is based on an account of Raftery at the wedding of a poor pair near Cappaghtagle. Yeats cited Raftery's "Antoine Ó Dalaigh" and "An Pósae Glégeal" in his essays "The Literary Movement in Ireland" and "Dust Hath Closed Helen's Eye," and alludes to Raftery in both section 2 of "The Tower" and "Coole Park and Ballylee, 1931." A number of writers have made their own translations or adaptations of Raftery's work, including Padraic Fallon, Lady Gregory, Thomas Kinsella, Donagh MacDonagh, and Desmond O'Grady. Finally, he is a figure in three of Austin Clarke's poems: "A Centenary Tribute," "F. R. Higgins," and "Paupers."

Scholars have concluded that the language, rhyme, and thought in "Mise Raifterí" strongly suggest it was written by someone else (perhaps Hyde himself), although based on a genuine tradition that owes much of its flavor, at the very least, to the poet. James Stephens made another translation of it, while Derek Mahon's "I Am Raftery" is a modern parody.

I AM RAFTERY

Said to have been Raftery's response to someone who asked who he was.

> I am Raftery the poet,
> Full of hope and love,
> With eyes that have no light,
> With gentleness that has no misery.
>
> Going west upon my pilgrimage
> By the light of my heart,
> Feeble and tired
> To the end of my road.
>
> Behold me now,
> And my face to a wall,
> A-playing music
> Unto empty pockets.

trans. Douglas Hyde

RAFTERY'S PRAISE OF MARY HYNES

Going to Mass by the will of God, the day came wet and the wind rose; I met Mary Hynes at the cross of Kiltartan, and I fell in love with her there and then.

I spoke to her kind and mannerly, as by report was her own way; and she said "Raftery, my mind is easy; you may come to-day to Ballylee."

When I heard her offer I did not linger; when only talk went to my heart my heart rose. We have only to go across the three fields; we had daylight with us to Ballylee.

The table was laid with glasses and a quart measure; she had fair hair and she sitting beside me; and she said "drink, Raftery, and a hundred welcomes; there is a strong cellar in Ballylee,"

O star of light and O sun in harvest; O amber hair, O my share of the world! Will you come with me on the Sunday, till we agree together before all the people?

I would not begrudge you a song every Sunday evening; punch on the table or wine if you would drink it. But O King of Glory, dry the roads before me till I find the way to Ballylee.

There is sweet air on the side of the hill, when you are looking down upon Ballylee; When you are walking in the valley picking nuts and blackberries, there is music of the birds in it and music of the Sidhe.

What is the worth of greatness till you have the light of the flower of the branch that is by your side? There is no good to deny it or to try and hide it; she is the sun in the heavens who wounded my heart.

There was no part in Ireland I did not travel, from the rivers to the tops of the mountains; to the edge of Lough Greine whose mouth is hidden, and I saw no beauty but was behind hers.

Her hair was shining and her brows were shining too; her face was like herself, her mouth pleasant and sweet; She is the pride and I give her the branch; she is the shining flower of Ballylee.

It is Mary Hynes, the calm and easy woman, has beauty in her mind and in her face. If a hundred clerks were gathered together, they could not write down a half of her ways.

trans. Lady Gregory

ANACH-CUAIN
[THE DROWNING OF ANNACH DOON]

If I get health, it is long there shall be talk,
    Of all who were drowned at Annach Down,
And my grief: on the morrow each father and mother,
    Wife and child a-shedding eyes;
O, King of the Graces, who hast shaped Heaven and
      Paradise
    Were it not small the grief to us two or three,
But a day so fine as it was, without wind, without rain,
    To sweep away the full of a boat of them!

Was it not great the wonder, forenent the people,
    To see them stretched on the backs of their heads,

Screaming and crying that would terrify people,
    Hair a-dishevelling, and the spoil being divided?
There were young boys there on the coming of harvest,
    Being stretched on the bier and being taken to the
        churchyard,
And sure it was the materials for their wedding that
    served for their wake,
    And, O God of Glory, is it not great the pity!

It was on Friday you would hear the keening
    Coming on every side, and the clapping of hands
        together,
And numbers of people, after the night, heavy, weary,
    overthrown,
    With nothing for them to do but to lay-out corpses.
O God, and O Christ, who suffered as an offering (?),
    Who hast purchased truly the poor and the naked,
To holy Paradise, mayest Thou bring free with Thee
    Each creature of them who has fallen beneath the
        lot,

A bitter blame to be on the same place [where they
    died],
    That star may never shine on it and that sun may
        never rise on it!
Which has drowned all those who journeyed together
    To Galway, to the fair, early a-Thursday.
The men who used to get-ready harrow and plough,
    Who used to turn-up fallows and scatter seed,
And the women according, who would make everything
    Who would spin freize and then linen.

Ballyclare was nigh hand,
    But the luck did not suffer them to go up to it;
Death was so strong that he gave no respite
    To a single mother's son of all that were ever born.
Unless it be a thing that was decreed for them, on this
    day of their drowning,
    O King of Graces! was it not a poor thing!
But to lose them all, without (their being on) lake or
    brine,

Through a vile old boat, and they close to land!

O King of Graces, who hast created Heaven and
      Paradise,
      And O God! what were the grief to us, two or
            three,
But on a day so fine, without wind, without rain,
      And the full of the boat of them to go to the
            bottom.
The boat broke and the people were drowned,
      The sheep scattered over in the water;
And O God, is it not there the great slaughter was
      made
      Of eleven men and of eight women.

There were fathers and mothers there, women and
      children,
      Crying and calling and shedding tears,
Women accordingly, who would make anything,
      Who would spin freize and then linen.
O Thomas O'Cahill, you were the great pity;
      You would plough the fallow-land and you would
            scatter seed,
And the numbers of boys who used to shake hands
      with you!
      My grief, and you drowned in Annaghdown!

O John O Cosgair [Cosgrave] you were the great pity
      That you ever stood in ship or boat,
And all the vigorous steps you travelled
      From London over to Beltra.
When you thought to make a swimming
      The young women caught hold of you on this side
            and that,
And sure your little-mother thought though a hundred
      men might be drowned
      That yourself [at least] would come home to her
            safe.

There was Mary Ruane there, a bright young-shoot,
      The sky-like girl that we had in the place;

She dressed herself up, early a Wednesday,
 To go to the fair from Knock Delain.
She had a coat upon her of choice cloth,
 A lace cap, and white ribbons,
And she has left her little-mother sorrowful, ruined,
 Shedding the tears again for ever.

A mountain-burning and a scalding breast
 Be on the place where they expired, and a hard
  reproach,
For it is many is the creature it has left bitterly-weeping,
 Shedding tears, and lamenting each Monday
  morning.
It was no lack of knowledge that sent them out of their
 right-direction.
 But great misfortune that was in Caislean-Nuadh,
And the finishing of the song is—that many were
 drowned,
 Which has left cause of grief to Annach Doon.

trans. Douglas Hyde

Further Readings on Anthony Raftery

Selected Works

Hyde, Douglas. *Abhráin atá Leagtha ar an Reachtúire* [Songs of Raftery]. Shannon: Irish University Press, 1979 (1903).

Biography and Criticism

Gregory, Augusta. "Raftery", "The Poet Raftery", "Raftery's Repentance"; "A Red-Letter Day in Killeenan." In *Poets and Dreamers*. Foreword by T. R. Henn. Gerrards Cross, England: Colin Smythe, 1974 (1903).

ní Cheannain, Áine. *Raifteirí an File*. Dublin: Foilseacháin Náisiúnta, 1984.

O'Rourke, Brian. "County Mayo in Gaelic Folksong." In *Mayo. Aspects of its Heritage,* ed. Bernard O'Hara, pp. 153–56, 291–96. Galway: Corrib, 1982.

JAMES CLARENCE MANGAN (1803–49)

Mangan is often cited as the most significant poetic precursor of the Irish Renaissance: no less than Yeats and Joyce became his champions in later generations. Born to an impoverished Dublin Catholic grocer, Mangan led a life of unrelieved misery and died, perhaps of starvation or malnutrition, during a cholera epidemic. He was a lonely, sickly, eccentric character, addicted either to alcohol or to opium. Much in his life and work invite comparisons with Poe: both were fascinated by extreme states of psychic distress and both experimented in verse techniques. Despite his isolation, Mangan was published in the leading Dublin journals, including the first edition of *The Nation* (1842), the organ of Young Ireland, and *The Dublin University Review*. Many of Mangan's best works are "translations" from languages he had not studied. His translations from the Irish, for example, rely on the prose paraphrases of intermediaries.

"Dark Rosaleen" is Mangan's version of *Róisín Dubh*, a 17th century poem ascribed to Owen Roe MacWard. Mangan produced three versions, the best-known of which, from *The Nation* of May 30, 1846, appears here; a later version, though less favored by critics, is arguably closer to the original text. The phrases *Róisín Dubh* and "Dark Rosaleen" both indicate a personification of Ireland.

DARK ROSALEEN

O my Dark Rosaleen,
    Do not sigh, do not weep!
The priests are on the ocean green,
    They march along the Deep.
There's wine . . . from the royal Pope
    Upon the ocean green;
And Spanish ale shall give you hope,
    My Dark Rosaleen!
    My own Rosaleen!
Shall glad your heart, shall give you hope,
Shall give you health, and help, and hope,
    My Dark Rosaleen.

Over hills and through dales
    Have I roamed for your sake;

All yesterday I sailed with sails
    On river and on lake.
The Erne . . . at its highest flood
    I dashed across unseen,
For there was lightning in my blood,
    My Dark Rosaleen!
    My own Rosaleen!
Oh! there was lightning in my blood,
Red lightning lightened through my blood,
    My Dark Rosaleen!

All day long in unrest
    To and fro do I move
The very soul within my breast
    Is wasted for you, love!
The heart . . . in my bosom faints
    To think of you, my Queen,
My life of life, my saint of saints,
    My Dark Rosaleen!
    My own Rosaleen!
To hear your sweet and sad complaints,
My life, my love, my saint of saints,
    My Dark Rosaleen!

Woe and pain, pain and woe,
    Are my lot night and noon,
To see your bright face clouded so,
    Like to the mournful moon.
But yet . . . will I rear your throne
    Again in golden sheen;
'Tis you shall reign, shall reign alone,
    My Dark Rosaleen!
    My own Rosaleen!
'Tis you shall have the golden throne,
'Tis you shall reign, and reign alone,
    My Dark Rosaleen!

Over dews, over sands
    Will I fly for your weal;
Your holy delicate white hands
    Shall girdle me with steel.

At home . . . in your emerald bowers,
    From morning's dawn till e'en,
You'll pray for me, my flower of flowers,
    My Dark Rosaleen!
    My fond Rosaleen!
You'll think of me through daylight's hours,
My virgin flower, my flower of flowers,
    My Dark Rosaleen!

I could scale the blue air,
    I could plough the high hills,
Oh, I could kneel all night in prayer,
    To heal your many ills!
And one . . . beamy smile from you
    Would float like light between
My toils and me, my own, my true,
    My Dark Rosaleen!
    My fond Rosaleen!
Would give me life and soul anew,
A second life, a soul anew,
    My Dark Rosaleen!

O! the Erne shall run red
    With redundance of blood,
The earth shall rock beneath our tread,
    And flames wrap hill and wood,
And gun-peal, and slogan cry,
    Wake many a glen serene,
Ere you shall fade, ere you shall die,
    My Dark Rosaleen!
    My own Rosaleen!
The Judgement Hour must first be nigh,
Ere you can fade, ere you can die,
    My Dark Rosaleen!

THE NAMELESS ONE

Roll forth, my song, like the rushing river,
    That sweeps along to the mighty sea;

God will inspire me while I deliver
    My soul of thee!

Tell thou the world, when my bones lie whitening
    Amid the last homes of youth and eld,
That there was once one whose veins ran lightning
    No eye beheld.

Tell how his boyhood was one drear night-hour,
    How shone for *him,* through is griefs and gloom,
No star of all heaven sends to light our
    Path to the tomb.

Roll on, my song, and to after ages
    Tell how, disdaining all earth can give,
He would have taught men, from wisdom's pages,
    The way to live.

And tell how trampled, derided, hated,
    And worn by weakness, disease, and wrong,
He fled for shelter to God, who mated
    His soul with song—

With song which alway, sublime or vapid,
    Flowed like a rill in the morning beam,
Perchance not deep, but intense and rapid—
    A mountain stream.

Tell how this Nameless, condemned for years long
    To herd with demons from hell beneath,
Saw things that made him, with groans and tears, long
    For even death.

Go on to tell how, with genius wasted,
    Betrayed in friendship, befooled in love,
With spirit shipwrecked, and young hopes blasted,
    He still, still strove.

Till, spent with toil, dreeing death for others,
    And some whose hands should have wrought for *him*
(If children live not for sires and mothers),
    His mind grew dim.

And he fell far through that pit abysmal
    The gulf and grave of Maginn and Burns,
And pawned his soul for the devil's dismal
    Stock of returns

But yet redeemed it in days of darkness
    And shapes and signs of the final wrath,
When death, in hideous and ghastly starkness,
    Stood on his path.

And tell how now, amid wreck and sorrow,
    And want, and sickness, and houseless nights,
He bides in calmness the silent morrow,
    That no ray lights.

And lives he still, then? Yes! Old and hoary
    At thirty-nine, from despair and woe,
He lives enduring what future story
    Will never know.

Him grant a grave to, ye pitying noble,
    Deep in your bosoms! There let him dwell!
He, too, had tears for all souls in trouble,
    Here and in hell.

SHAPES AND SIGNS

I see black dragons mount the sky,
    I see earth yawn beneath my feet—
    I feel within the asp, the worm
That will not sleep and cannot die,
    Fair though may show the winding-sheet!
    I hear all night as through a storm
    Hoarse voices calling, calling
    My name upon the wind—
    All omens monstrous and appalling
    Affright my guilty mind.

I exult alone in one wild hour—
    That hour in which the red cup drowns

The memories it anon renews
In ghastlier guise, in fiercer power—
Then Fancy brings me golden crowns,
And visions of all brilliant hues
Lap my lost soul in gladness,
Until I wake again,
And the dark lava-fires of madness
Once more sweep through my brain.

Further Readings on James Clarence Mangan

Bibliography

Chutto, Jacques. *The James Clarence Mangan Bibliography*. Dublin: Wolfhound Press, 1981.
Holzapfel, Rudi P. *James Clarence Mangan: A Checklist of Printed and Other Sources*. Dublin: Scepter, 1969.
———. "Mangan's Poetry in the *Dublin University Magazine:* A Bibliography." *Hermathena* 105: 40–54.

Selected Works

Autobiography. Edited by James Kilroy. Dublin: Dolmen, 1968.
James Clarence Mangan: His Selected Poems. Edited and with a study by L. I. Guiney. Boston: Lamson-Wolfe, 1897.
Poems. Edited and with preface and notes by D. J. O'Donoghue. Dublin: O'Donoghue & Co., 1903.
The Prose Writings. Edited by D. J. O'Donoghue. Essay by Lionel Johnson. Dublin: O'Donoghue, 1904.

Biography and Criticism

D'Alton, Louis. *The Man in the Cloak: A Play About James Clarence Mangan.* In *Two Plays*. London: Macmillan, 1938. Reprinted, Dublin: Bourke, 1971.
Donaghy, Henry J. *James Clarence Mangan*. New York: Twayne, 1974.
Joyce, James. "James Clarence Mangan." Reprinted in: 1–16. *James Joyce: The Critical Writings*, pp. 73–83. New York: Viking, 1959.
Kilroy, James. *James Clarence Mangan*. Lewisburg, Pa.: Bucknell University Press, 1970.
Lloyd, David. *Nationalism and Minor Literature: James Clarence Mangan and the Emergence of Irish Cultural Nationalism*. Berkeley: University of California Press, 1987.
O'Donoghue, D. J. *The Life and Writings of J. C. Mangan*. Edinburgh: P. Geddes, 1897.

Sheridan, Desmond. *James Clarence Mangan*. Dublin: Talbot, 1936.
Yeats, William Butler. "Clarence Mangan." *Irish Fireside* Reprinted in *Uncollected Prose*. vol. 1, pp. 114–19. Edited by John Frayne. New York: Columbia University Press, 1970.

SAMUEL FERGUSON (1810–86)

Samuel Ferguson was one of the first writers to realize the possibilities of a national literature based on Irish myth and legend. Born in Belfast and educated at the Belfast Academical Institute and at Trinity College, Dublin, Ferguson was trained as a lawyer and called to the Irish bar in 1838. However, he gave up his practice to become the first Deputy Keeper of Records in 1869, and was knighted for his service to the state in 1878.

Ferguson's poetry was informed by his knowledge of Irish antiquarianism. More than a keen amateur, though, he was elected President of the Royal Irish Academy in 1881. The Ordnance Survey project (1828) which brought together such brilliant scholars as John O'Donovan, Eugene O'Curry, and Sir Charles Petrie to collect place-names and topograhical lore stimulated Ferguson's interest in antiquuities. O'Donovan's translation of the Battle of Magh Rath inspired Ferguson's *Congal* (written 1861, published 1872), an epic describing the conflict between Congal and Donald which is to say between paganism and Christianity. Yeats later drew upon Congal as a source for *On Baile's Strand* (1904) and *The Herne's Egg* (1938).

Ferguson turned to translating when he reviewed James Hardiman's *Irish Minstrelsy or Bardic Remains of Ireland* (1831) in a series of essays for the *Dublin University Review* in 1834. He judged Hardiman's translations to be too artificial, and offered instead his own, which were more faithful to the original and which retained their Irish rhythms. Indeed, poems like "Cashel of Munster" and "Dear Dark Head" demonstrated the potential for Irish metrics in Anglo-Irish poetry to such distinguished successors as Yeats and Austin Clarke.

CASHEL OF MUNSTER

I'd wed you without herds, without money, or rich
    array,

And I'd wed you on a dewy morning at day-dawn gray;
My bitter woe it is, love, that we are not far away
In Cashel town, though the bare deal board were our
    marriage bed this day!

Oh, fair maid, remember the green hill side,
Remember how I hunted about the valleys wide;
Time now has worn me; my locks are turned to gray,
The year is scarce and I am poor, but send me not,
    love, away!

Oh, deem not my blood is of base strain, my girl,
Oh, deem not my birth was as the birth of the churl;
Marry me, and prove me, and say soon you will,
That noble blood is written on my right side still!

My purse holds no red gold, no coin of the silver white,
No herds are mine to drive through the long twilight!
But the pretty girl that would take me, all bare though
    I be and lone,
Oh, I'd take her with me kindly to the county Tyrone.

Oh, my girl, I can see 'tis in trouble you are,
And, oh, my girl, I see 'tis your people's reproach you
    bear;
"I am a girl in trouble for his sake with whom I fly,
And, oh, may no other maiden know such reproach as
    I!"

DEAR DARK HEAD

Put your head, darling, darling, darling,
    Your darling black head my heart above;
Oh, mouth of honey, with the thyme for fragrance,
    Who, with heart in breast, could deny you love?
Oh, many and many a young girl for me is pining,
    Letting her locks of gold to the cold wind free,
For me, the foremost of our gay young fellows;
    But I'd leave a hundred, pure love, for thee!

Then put your head, darling, darling, darling,
Your darling black head my heart above;
Oh, mouth of honey, with the thyme for fragrance,
Who, with heart in breast, could deny you love?

Further Readings on Samuel Ferguson

Bibliography

Ferguson, Lady Mary Catherine. *Sir Samuel Ferguson in the Ireland of His Day.* Vol. 2, pp. 369–74. Edinburgh: William Blackwood and Sons, 1896.

Selected Works

Congal. London: G. Bell and Sons, 1872.
Lays of the Western Gael. London: Bell, 1862.
Poems. Edited by Padraic Colum. Dublin: Hodges, Figges, 1963.
The Poetry of Sir Samuel Ferguson. Edited by John O'Hagan. Dublin: Gill, 1887.

Biography and Criticism

Brown, Malcolm. *Sir Samuel Ferguson.* Lewisburg, Pa.: Bucknell University Press, 1973.
Ferguson, Lady Mary Catherine. *Sir Samuel Ferguson in the Ireland of His Day.* 2 vols. Edinburgh: William Blackwood and Sons, 1896.
O'Driscoll, Robert. "Sir Samuel Ferguson and the Idea of an Irish National Literature." *Eire-Ireland* 6: 82–95.
Yeats, W. B. "The Poetry of Sir Samuel Ferguson—I," "The Poetry of Sir Samuel Ferguson—II," ed. John P. Frayne, *Uncollected Prose by W. B. Yeats.* Vol. I: First Reviews and Articles, 1886–1896. New York: Columbia University Press, 1970. pp. 81–87; 87–104 (1886).

THOMAS DAVIS (1814–45)

Thomas Davis was to nineteenth century Irish cultural unity what Daniel O'Connell was to nineteenth century Irish political unity. His 1840 valedictory speech to the Historical Society of Trinity College, Dublin, can be compared with Ralph Waldo Emerson's 1837 Phi Beta Kappa address, "The American Scholar," in its call for cultural autonomy.

In September 1842, Davis founded *The Nation* with John Blake

Dillon and Charles Gavan Duffy. The paper's nationalist ideals informed Irish politics for the rest of the century, and on into our own time. When *The Nation* proposed compiling a ballad history of Ireland, Davis wrote that such a project would ". . . make Irish history familiar to the minds, pleasant to the ears, dear to the passions and powerful over the taste and conduct of Irish people in times to come." His own contributions, especially ballads like the "Lament for the Death of Eoghan Ruadh O'Neill," awaken in the Irish people a sense of the nobility of the Irish past. (The death of O'Neill, who had been responsible for a brilliant victory at Benburb in 1649, removed the only Irish leader who could have challenged Cromwell.) "The West's Asleep" alludes to the familiar Barbarossa legend of the sleeping hero who will awaken to help his people in their hour of need.

"Our National Language" (1843), one of a series of essays about the relationships between Irish cultural and national identity, anticipates the work of the Gaelic League fifty years later. His admonition, "Educate that you may be free," has been commemorated in the Thomas Davis Lectures, long a feature of Radio Eireann.

David died suddenly on September 16, 1845—just one week after the first reports of a potato blight in Ireland.

LAMENT FOR THE DEATH OF EOGHAN RUADH O'NEILL

TIME—*10th November, 1649.* SCENE—*Ormond's Camp, County Waterford.* SPEAKERS—*A veteran of Eoghan O'Neill's clan, and one of the horsemen, just arrived with an account of his death.*

I.

"Did they dare, did they dare, to slay Eoghan Ruadh
    O'Neill?"
"Yes, they slew with poison him, they feared to meet
    with steel."
"May God wither up their hearts! May their blood cease
    to flow!
"May they walk in living death, who poisoned Eoghan
    Ruadh!

II.

"Though it break my heart to hear, say again the bitter
    words."

"From Derry, against Cromwell, he marched to measure
     swords:
But the weapon of the Sassanach met him on his way,
And he died at Cloch Uachtar, upon St. Leonard's day.

II.

"Wail, wail ye for the Mighty One! Wail, wail, ye for the
     Dead!
Quench the hearth, and hold the breath—with ashes
     strew the head.
How tenderly we loved him! How deeply we deplore!
Holy Saviour! but to think we shall never see him more.

IV.

"Sagest in the council was he, kindest in the hall!
Sure we never won a battle—'twas Eoghan won them
     all.
Had he lived—had he lived—our dear country had
     been free;
But he's dead, but he's dead, and 'tis slaves we'll ever
     be.

V.

"O'Farrell and Clanrickarde, Preston and Red Hugh,
Audley, and MacMahon, ye are valiant, wise, and true;
But—what, what are ye all to our darling who is gone?
The Rudder of our Ship was he, our Castle's corner
     stone!

VI.

"Wail, wail him through the Island! Weep, weep, for our
     pride!
Would that on the battle-field our gallant chief had
     died!
Weep the Victor of Beann-bhorb—weep him, young
     men and old;
Weep for him, ye women—your Beautiful lies cold!

VII.

"We thought you would not die—we were sure you
    would not go,
And leave us in our utmost need to Cromwell's cruel
    blow—
Sheep without a shepherd, when the snow shuts out the
    sky—
Oh! why did you leave us, Eoghan? Why did you die?

VIII.

"Soft as woman's was your voice, O'Neill! bright was
    your eye,
Oh! why did you leave us, Eoghan? Why did you die?
Your troubles are all over, you're at rest with God on
    high,
But we're slaves, and we're orphans, Eoghan!—why
    didst thou die?"

THE WEST'S ASLEEP

AIR—*The Brink of the White Rocks.*

I.

When all beside a vigil keep,
The West's asleep, the West's asleep—
Alas! and well may Erin weep,
When Connacht lies in slumber deep.
There lake and plain smile fair and free,
'Mid rocks—their guardian chivalry—
Sing oh! let man learn liberty
From crashing wind and lashing sea.

II.

That chainless wave and lovely land
Freedom and Nationhood demand—
Be sure, the great God never planned,
For slumbering slaves, a home so grand.

And, long, a brave and haughty race
Honoured and sentinelled the place—
Sing oh! not even their sons' disgrace
Can quite destroy their glory's trace.

III.

For often, in O'Connor's van,
To triumph dashed each Connacht clan—
And fleet as deer the Normans ran
Through Corlieu's Pass and Ardrahan.
And later times saw deeds as brave;
And glory guards Clanrickarde's grave—
Sing oh! they died their land to save,
At Aughrim's slopes and Shannon's wave.

IV.

And if, when all a vigil keep,
The West's asleep, the West's asleep—
Alas! and well may Erin weep,
That Connacht lies in slumber deep.
But, hark! some voice like thunder spake:
"The West's awake! the West's awake!"—
"Sing oh! hurra! let England quake,
We'll watch till death for Erin's sake!"

From "OUR NATIONAL LANGUAGE," PART I
[THE NATION, APRIL 1, 1843]

Men are ever valued most for peculiar and original qualities.

A man who can only talk common-place, and act according to routine, has little weight. To speak, look, and do what your own soul from its depths orders you, are credentials of greatness which all men understand and acknowledge. Such a man's dictum has more influence than the reasoning of an imitative or common-place man. He fills his circle with confidence. He is self-possessed, firm, accurate, and daring. Such men are the pioneers of civilization, and the rulers of the human heart.

Why should not nations be judged thus? Is not a full indulgence of its natural tendencies essential to a people's greatness? Force the manners, dress, language, and constitution of Russia, on Italy, or Norway, or America, and you instantly stunt and distort the whole mind of either people.

The language, which grows up with a people, is conformed to their organs, descriptive of their climate, constitution, and manners, mingled inseparably with their history, and their soil, fitted beyond any other language to express their prevalent thoughts in the most natural efficient way.

To impose another language on such a people is to send their history adrift among the accidents of translation—'tis to tear their identity from all places—'tis to substitute arbitrary signs for picturesque and suggestive names—'tis to cut off the entail of feeling, and separate the people from their forefathers by deep gulf—'tis to corrupt their very organs, and abridge their power of expression.

The language of a nation's youth is the only easy and full speech for its manhood and for its age. And when the language of its cradle goes, itself craves a tomb.

What business has a Russian for the rippling language of Italy or India? How could a Greek distort his organs and his soul to speak Dutch upon the sides of the Hymettus, or the beach of Salamis, or on the waste where once was Sparta? And is it befitting the fiery, delicate-organed Celt to abandon his beautiful tongue, docile and spirited as an Arab, "sweet as music, strong as the wave"—is it befitting in him to abandon this wild liquid speech for the mongrel of a hundred breeds called English, which, powerful though it be, creaks, and bangs about the Celt who tries to use it?

We lately met a glorious thought in the *Triads of Mochmed,* printed in one of the Welsh codes by the Record Commission.. "There are three things without which there is no country—common language, common judicature, and co-tillage land—for without these a country cannot support itself in peace and social union."

A people without a language of its own is only half a nation. A nation should guard its language more that its territories—'tis a surer barrier, and more important frontier, than fortress or river.

And in good times it has ever been thought so. Who had dared to propose the adoption of Persian or Egyptian in Greece?—how had Pericles thundered at the barbarian! How had Cato scourged from the forum him who would have given the Attic or Gallic speech to men of Rome! How proudly and how nobly Germany stopped "the incipient creeping" progress of French! And no sooner had she succeeded than her genius, which had tossed in a hot trance, sprung up fresh and triumphant.

Had Pyrrhus quelled Italy, or Xerxes subdued Greece for a time long enough to impose new languages, where had been the literature which gives a pedigree to human genius? Even liberty recovered had been sickly and insecure without the language with which it had hunted in the woods, worshipped at the fruit-strewn altar, debated on the council-hill, and shouted in the battle-charge.

There is a fine song of the Frisians which describes *"language linked to liberty."* To lose your native tongue, and learn that of an alien, is the worst badge of conquest—it is the chain on the soul. To have lost entirely the national language is death; the fetter has worn through. So long as the Saxon held to his German speech he could hope to resume his land from the Norman; now, if he is to be free and locally governed, he must build himself a new home. There is hope for Scotland—strong hope for Wales—sure hope for Hungary. The speech of the alien is not universal in the one; is gallantly held at bay in the other; is nearly expelled from the third.

How unnatural—how corrupting—'tis for us, three-fourths of whom are of Celtic blood, to speak a medley of Teutonic dialects. If we add the Celtic Scots, who came back here from the thirteenth to the seventeenth centuries, and the Celtic Welsh, who colonised many parts of the Wexford and other Leinster counties, to the Celts who never left Ireland, probably five-sixths, or more of us are Celts. What business have we with the Norman-Sasanach?

Nor let any doubt these proportions because of the number of English names in Ireland. With a politic cruelty, the English of the Pale passed an Act compelling every Irishman within English jurisdiction, "to go like to one Englishman in apparel, and shaving off his beard above the mouth," "and shall take to him an English sirname of one town, as Sutton, Chester, Trym, Skyrne, Corke, Kinsale; or colour, as White, Blacke, Browne; or art of science, as Smith, or Carpenter; or office, as Cook, Butler; and that he and his issue shall use this name under pain of forfeiting his goods yearly."

And just as this parliament before the Reformation, so did another after the Reformation. By the 28th Henry VII, the dress and language of the Irish were insolently described as barbarous by the minions of that ruffian king, and were utterly forbidden and abolished under many penalties and incapacities. These laws are still in force; but whether the Archaeological Society, including Peel and O'Connell, will be prosecuted, seems doubtful.

There was also, 'tis to be feared, an adoption of English names, during some periods, from fashion, fear, or meanness. Some of our best Irish names, too, have been so mangled as to require some scholarship to identify them. For these and many other reasons, the members of the Celtic race here are immensely greater than at first appears.

But this is not all; for even the Saxon and Norman colonist, notwithstanding these laws, melted down into the Irish, and adopted all their ways and language. For centuries upon centuries Irish was spoken by men of all bloods in Ireland, and English was unknown, save to a few citizens and nobles of the Pale. 'Tis only within a very later period that the majority of the people learned English.

But, it will be asked, how can the language be restored now?

We shall answer this partly by saying that, through the labours of the Archaeological and many lesser societies, it is being revived rapidly.

Nothing can make us believe that it is natural or honourable for the Irish to speak the speech of the alien, the invader, the Sasanach tyrant, and to abandon the language of our kings and heroes. What! give up the tongue of Ollamh Fodhla and Brian Boru, the tongue of M'Carthy, and the O'Neills, the tongue of Sarsfield's, Curran's, Mathew's, and O'Connell's boyhood, for that of Strafford and Poynings, Sussex, Kirk, and Cromwell!

No! oh, no! the "brighter days shall surely come," and the green flag shall wave on our towers, and the sweet old language be heard once more in college, mart, and senate.

But, even should the effort to save it as the national language fail, by the attempt we will rescue its old literature, and hand down to our descendants proofs that we had a language as fit for love, and war, and business, and pleasure, as the world ever knew, and that we had not the spirit and nationality to preserve it!

Had Swift known Irish he would have sowed its seed by the side of that nationality which he planted, and the close of the last century would have seen the one as flourishing as the other. Had Ireland used Irish in 1782, would it not have impeded England's re-conquest of us? But 'tis not yet too late.

Further Readings on Thomas Davis

Bibliography

Moody, T. W. "Thomas Davis and the Irish Nation." *Hermathena,* 102: 5–31.

Selected Works

Essays and Poems with a Centenary Memoir. 1845–1945. Introduction by Eamon de Valera. Dublin: M. H. Gill and Sons, 1945.

Biography and Criticism

Duffy, Charles Gavan. *Thomas Davis: The Memoirs of an Irish Patriot, 1840–1846.* London: T. Fisher Unwin, 1890.
———. *Young Ireland: A Fragment of Irish History, 1840–1845.* 2 vols. London: T. Fisher Unwin, 1896.
Moody, T. W. *Thomas Davis, 1814–1815.* Dublin: The Stationery Office, 1945.
O'Sullivan, T. F. *The Young Irelanders.* Tralee: The Kerryman, 1944.
Yeats, W. B., and Kinsella, Thomas. *Davis, Mangan, Ferguson?*, pp. 15–20. Dublin: The Dolmen Press, 1970.

PART II
THE IRISH LITERARY RENAISSANCE

DOUGLAS HYDE
(1860–1949)

D ouglas Hyde wrote prolifically in both English and Irish, sometimes using the pseudonym "An Craoibhín Aoibhinn" [The
pleasant (or delightful) little branch]. At turns, he was a poet,
scholar, translator, folklorist, playwright, academic, and Ireland's
president. His *Leabhar Sgéulaigheachta* (1889), a collection of
folklore, was the first of its kind in the Irish language. He helped to
found and became the first president of the Gaelic League (1893),
which was dedicated to the revival of the Irish language. In response
to the criticism that there was little to read in the native language, he
produced *A Literary History of Ireland* (1899). His contribution to the
revived theater movement that began under Yeats and Lady Gregory
was *Casadh an tSúgáin* [the twisting of the rope] (1901), the first
drama in the Irish language to be performed in modern times. He
served as a professor of the Irish language at University College,
Dublin and was elected unopposed as president of Ireland in 1938.

The Love Songs of Connacht, begun serially in 1890, showed a
generation of younger poets the means of finding a new tone and
idiom in English. Using materials he had collected from unlettered
peasants, Hyde gave side-by-side translations that attempted to carry
the Irish vowel sounds and meters into English. The *Love Songs*
served as a handbook for poetic diction as well as a dual-language
learning text.

"The Necessity for De-Anglicising Ireland" (1892), Hyde's decla-
ration of cultural and linguistic independence, predates the Easter
Rising by more than twenty-three years. Writing at a time when the
Irish language was disparaged and fast disappearing, Hyde saw
seeds of renewal in what others saw as a language of poverty.

Selections from THE LOVE SONGS OF CONNACHT

MY GRIEF ON THE SEA

My grief on the sea,
    How the waves of it roll!
For they heave between me
    And the love of my soul!

Abandoned, forsaken,
    To grief and to care,
Will the sea ever waken
    Relief from despair?

My grief, and my trouble!
    Would he and I were
In the province of Leinster,
    Or county of Clare.

Were I and my darling—
    Oh, heart-bitter wound!—
On board of the ship
    For America bound.

On a green bed of rushes
    All last night I lay,
And I flung it abroad
    With the heat of the day.

And my love came behind me—
    He came from the South;
His breast to my bosom,
    His mouth to my mouth.

RINGLETED YOUTH OF MY LOVE

Ringleted youth of my love,
    With thy locks bound loosely behind thee,

You passed by the road above,
        But you never came in to find me;
Where were the harm for you
        If you came for a little to see me,
Your kiss is a wakening dew
        Were I ever so ill or so dreamy.

If I had golden store
        I would make a nice little boreen
To lead straight up to his door,
        The door of the house of my storeen;
Hoping to God not to miss
        The sound of his footfall in it,
I have waited so long for his kiss
        That for days I have slept not a minute.

I thought, O my love! you were so—
        As the moon is, or sun on a fountain,
And I thought after that you were snow,
        The cold snow on top of the mountain;
And I thought after that, you were more
        Like God's lamp shining to find me,
Or the bright star of knowledge before,
        And the star of knowledge behind me.

You promised me high-heeled shoes,
        And satin and silk, my storeen,
And to follow me, never to lose,
        Though the ocean were round us roaring;
Like a bush in a gap in a wall
        I am now left lonely without thee,
And this house I grow dead of, is all
        That I see around or about me.

MY LOVE, OH, SHE IS MY LOVE

She casts a spell, oh, casts a spell,
        Which haunts me more than I can tell.

Dearer, because she makes me ill,
Than who would will to make me well.

She is my store, oh, she my store,
Whose grey eye wounded me so sore,
Who will not place in mine her palm,
Who will not calm me any more.

She is my pet, oh, she my pet,
Whom I can never more forget;
Who would not lose by me one moan,
Nor stone upon my cairn set.

She is my roon, oh, she my roon,
Who tells me nothing, leaves me soon;
Who would not lose by me one sigh,
Were death and I within one room.

She is my dear, oh, she my dear,
Who cares not whether I be here.
Who would not weep when I am dead,
Who makes me shed the silent tear.

Hard my case, oh, hard my case,
How have I lived so long a space,
She does not trust me any more,
But I adore her silent face.

She is my choice, oh, she my choice,
Who never made me to rejoice;
Who caused my heart to ache so oft,
Who put no softness in her voice.

Great my grief, oh, great my grief,
Neglected, scorned beyond belief,
By her who looks at me askance,
By her who grants me no relief.

She's my desire, oh, my desire,
More glorious than the bright sun's fire;

Who were than wind-blown ice more cold,
Had I the boldness to sit by her.

She it is who stole my heart,
But left a void and aching smart,
And if she soften not her eye
Then life and I shall shortly part.

THE NECESSITY FOR DE-ANGLICISING IRELAND

When we speak of "The Necessity for De-Anglicising the Irish Nation," we mean it, not as a protest against imitating what is *best* in the English people, for that would be absurd, but rather to show the folly of neglecting what is Irish, and hastening to adopt, pell-mell, and indiscriminately, everything that is English, simply because it *is* English.

This is a question which most Irishmen will naturally look at from a National point of view, but it is one which ought also to claim the sympathies of every intelligent Unionist, and which, as I know, does claim the sympathy of many.

If we take a bird's-eye view of our island to-day, and compare it with what it used to be, we must be struck by the extraordinary fact that the nation which was once, as every one admits, one of the most classically learned and cultured nations in Europe, is now one of the least so; how one of the most reading and literary peoples has become one of the *least* studious and most *un*-literary, and how the present art products of one of the quickest, most sensitive, and most artistic races on earth are now only distinguished for their hideousness.

I shall endeavour to show that this failure of the Irish people in recent times has been largely brought about by the race diverging during this century from the right path, and ceasing to be Irish without becoming English. I shall attempt to show that with the bulk of the people this change took place quite recently, much more recently than most people imagine, and is, in fact, still going on. I should also like to call attention to the illogical position of men who drop their own language to speak English, of men who translate their euphonious Irish names into English monosyllables, of men who read English books, and know nothing about Gaelic literature, nevertheless protesting as a matter of sentiment that they hate the country which at every hand's turn they rush to imitate.

I wish to show you that in Anglicising ourselves wholesale we have thrown away with a light heart the best claim which we have upon the world's recognition of us as a separate nationality. What did Mazzini say? What is Goldwin Smith never tired of declaiming? What do the *Spectator* and *Saturday Review* harp on? That we ought to be content as an integral part of the United Kingdom because we have lost the notes of nationality, our language and customs.

It has always been very curious to me how Irish sentiment sticks in this half-way house—how it continues to apparently hate the English, and at the same time continues to imitate them; how it continues to clamour for recognition as a distinct nationality, and at the same time throws away with both hands what would make it so. If Irishmen only went a little farther they would become good Englishmen in sentiment also. But—illogical as it appears—there seems not the slightest sign or probability of their taking that step. It is the curious certainty that come what may Irishmen will continue to resist English rule, even though it should be for their good, which prevents many of our nation from becoming Unionists upon the spot. It is a fact, and we must face it as a fact, that although they adopt English habits and copy the English in every way, the great bulk of Irishmen and Irishwomen over the whole world are known to be filled with a dull, ever-abiding animosity against her, and—right or wrong—to grieve when she prospers, and to joy when she is hurt. Such movements as Young Irelandism, Fenianism, Land Leagueism, and Parliamentary obstruction seem always to gain their sympathy and support. It is just because there appears no earthly chance of their becoming good members of the Empire that I urge that they should not remain in the anomalous position they are in, but since they absolutely refuse to become the one thing, that they become the other; cultivate what they have rejected, and build up an Irish nation on Irish lines.

But you ask, why should we wish to make Ireland more Celtic than it is—why should we de-Anglicise it at all?

I answer because the Irish race is at present in a most anomalous position, imitating England and yet apparently hating it. How can it produce anything good in literature, art, or institutions as long as it is actuated by motives so contradictory? Besides I believe it is our Gaelic past which, though the Irish race does not recognise it just at present, is really at the bottom of the Irish heart, and prevents us becoming citizens of the Empire, as, I think, can be easily proved.

To say that Ireland has not prospered under English rule is simply a truism; all the world admits it, England does not deny it. But the English retort is ready. You have not prospered, they say, because you would not settle down contentedly, like the Scotch, and form part of the Empire. "Twenty years of good, resolute, grandfatherly government," said a well-known Englishman, will solve the Irish question. He possibly made the period too short, but let us suppose this. Let us suppose for a moment—which is impossible—that there were to arise a series of Cromwells in England for the space of one hundred years, able administrators of the Empire, careful rulers of Ireland, developing to the utmost our national resources, whilst they unremittingly stamped out every spark of national feeling, making Ireland a land of wealth and factories, whilst they extinguished every thought and every idea that was Irish, and left us, at last, after a hundred years of good government, fat, wealthy, and populous, but with all our characteristics gone, with every external that at present differentiates us from the English lost or dropped; all our Irish names of places and people turned into English names; the Irish language completely extinct; the O's and the Macs dropped; our Irish intonation changed, as far as possible, by English schoolmasters into something English; our history no longer remembered or taught; the names of our rebels and martyrs blotted out; our battlefields and traditions forgotten; the fact that we were not of Saxon origin dropped out of sight and memory, and let me now put the question—How many Irishmen are there who would purchase material prosperity at such a price? It is exactly such a question as this and the answer to it that shows the difference between the English and Irish race. Nine Englishmen out of ten would jump to make the exchange, and I as firmly believe that nine Irishmen out of ten would indignantly refuse it.

And yet this awful idea of complete Anglicisation, which I have here put before you in all its crudity, is, and has been, making silent inroads upon us for nearly a century.

Its inroads have been silent, because, had the Gaelic race perceived what was being done, or had they been once warned of what was taking place in their own midst, they would, I think, never have allowed it. When the picture of complete Anglicisation is drawn for them in all its nakedness Irish sentimentality becomes suddenly a power and refuses to surrender its birthright.

What lies at the back of the sentiments of nationality with which the Irish millions seem so strongly leavened, what can prompt them to applaud such sentiments as:

They say the British Empire owes much to Irish hands,
That Irish valour fixed her flag o'er many conquered lands;
And ask if Erin takes no pride in these her gallant sons,
Her Wolseleys and her Lawrences, her Wolfes and Wellingtons.

Ah! these were of the Empire—we yield them to her fame,
And ne'er in Erin's orisons are heard their alien name;
But those for whom her heart beats high and benedictions swell,
They died upon the scaffold and they pined within the cell.

Of course it is a very composite feeling which prompts them; but I believe that what is largely behind it is the half unconscious feeling that the race which at one time held possession of more than half Europe, which established itself in Greece, and burned infant Rome, is now—almost extirpated and absorbed elsewhere—making its last stand for independence in this island of Ireland; and do what they may the race of to-day cannot wholly divest itself from the mantle of its own past. Through early Irish literature, for instance, can we best form some conception of what that race really was, which, after overthrowing and trampling on the primitive peoples of half of Europe, was itself forced in turn to yield its speech, manners, and independence to the victorious eagles of Rome. We alone of the nations of Western Europe escaped the claws of those birds of prey; we alone developed ourselves naturally upon our own lines outside of and free from all Roman influence; we alone were thus able to produce an early art and literature, *our* antiquities can best throw light upon the pre-Romanised inhabitants of half Europe, and—we are our father's sons.

There is really no exaggeration in all this, although Irishmen are sometimes prone to overstating as well as to forgetting. Westwood himself declares that, were it not for Irishmen these islands would possess no primitive works of art worth the mentioning; Jubainville asserts that early Irish literature is that which best throws light upon the manners and customs of his own ancestors the Gauls; and Zimmer, who has done so much for Celtic philology, has declared that only a spurious criticism can make an attempt to doubt about the historical character of the chief persons of our two epic cycles, that of Cuchullain and that of Finn. It is useless elaborating this point; and Dr. Sigerson has already shown in his opening lecture the debt of gratitude which in many respects Europe owes to ancient Ireland. The dim consciousness of this is one of those things which are at the back of Irish national sentiment, and our business, whether we be Unionists or Nationalists, should be to make this dim consciousness an active and potent feeling, and thus increase our sense of self-respect and of honour.

What we must endeavour to never forget is this, that the Ireland of to-day is the descendant of the Ireland of the seventh century, then the school of Europe and the torch of learning. It is true that Northmen made some minor settlements in it in the ninth and tenth centuries, it is true that the Normans made extensive settlements during the succeeding centuries, but none of those broke the continuity of the social life of the island. Dane and Norman drawn to the kindly Irish breast issued forth in a generation or two fully Irishised, and more Hibernian than the Hibernians themselves, and even after the Cromwellian plantation the children of numbers of the English soldiers who settled in the south and midlands, were, after forty years' residence, and after marrying Irish wives, turned into good Irishmen, and unable to speak a word of English, while several Gaelic poets of the last century have, like Father English, the most unmistakably English names. In two points only was the continuity of the Irishism of Ireland damaged. First, in the north-east of Ulster, where the Gaelic race was expelled and the land planted with aliens, whom our dear mother Erin, assimilative as she is, has hitherto found it difficult to absorb, and in the ownership of the land, eight-ninths of which belongs to people many of whom always lived, or live, abroad, and not half of whom Ireland can be said to have assimilated.

During all this time the continuation of Erin's national life centred, according to our way of looking at it, not so much in the Cromwellian or Williamite landholders who sat in College Green, and governed the country, as in the mass of the people whom Dean Swift considered might be entirely neglected, and looked upon as hewers of wood and drawers of water; the men who, nevertheless, constituted the real working population, and who were living on in the hopes of better days; the men who have since made America, and have within the last ten years proved what an important factor they may be in wrecking or in building the British Empire. These are the men of whom our merchants, artisans, and farmers mostly consist, and in whose hands is to-day the making or marring of an Irish nation. But, alas, *quantum mutatus ab illo!* What the battleaxe of the Dane, the sword of the Norman, the wile of the Saxon were unable to perform, we have accomplished ourselves. We have at last broken the continuity of Irish life, and just at the moment when the Celtic race is presumably about to largely recover possession of its own country, it finds itself deprived and stript of its Celtic characteristics, cut off from the past, yet scarcely in touch with the present. It has lost since the beginning of this century almost all that connected it with the era of Cuchullain and of Ossian, that connected it with the Christianisers of Europe, that connected it with Brian Boru and the heroes of Clontarf, with the O'Neills and O'Donnells, with Roy O'More, with the Wild Geese, and even to some extent with the men of '98. It has lost all that they had— language, traditions, music, genius, and ideas. Just when we should be starting to build up anew the Irish race and the Gaelic nation—as within our own recollection Greece has been built up anew—we find ourselves despoiled of the bricks of nationality. The old bricks that lasted eighteen hundred years are destroyed; we must now set to, to bake new ones, if we can, on other ground and of other clay. Imagine for a moment the restoration of a German-speaking Greece.

The bulk of the Irish race really lived in the closest contact with the traditions of the past and the national life of nearly eighteen hundred years, until after the beginning of this century. Not only so, but during the whole of the dark Penal times they produced amongst themselves a most vigorous literary development. Their school-masters and wealthy farmers, unwearied scribes, produced innumera-ble manuscripts in beautiful writing, each letter separated from another as in Greek, transcripts both of the ancient literature of their sires and of the more modern literature produced by themselves. Until the beginning of the present century there was no county, no barony, and, I may almost say, no townland which did not boast of an Irish poet, the people's representative of those ancient bards who died out with the extirpation of the great Milesian families. The literary activity of even the eighteenth century among the Gaels was very great, not in the South alone, but also in Ulster—the number of poets it produced was something astonishing. It did not, however, produce many works in Gaelic prose, but it propagated translations of many pieces from the French, Latin, Spanish, and English. Every well-to-do farmer could read and write Irish, and many of them could under-stand even archaic Irish. I have myself heard persons reciting the poems of Donogha More O'Daly, Abbot of Boyle, in Roscommon, who died sixty years before Chaucer was born. To this very day the people have a word for archaic Irish, which is much the same as though Chaucer's poems were handed down amongst the English peasantry, but required a special training to understand. This training, however, nearly every one of fair education during the Penal times possessed, nor did they begin to lose their Irish training and knowledge until the establishment of Maynooth and the rise of O'Connell. These two events made an end of the Gaelicism of the Gaelic race, although a great number of poets and scribes existed even down to the forties and fifties of the present century, and a few may linger on yet in remote localities. But it may be said, roughly speaking, that the ancient Gaelic civilisation died with O'Connell, largely, I am afraid, owing to his example and his neglect of inculcating the necessity of keeping alive racial customs, language, and traditions, in which with the one notable exception of our scholarly idealist, Smith O'Brien, he has been followed until a year ago by almost every leader of the Irish race.

Thomas Davis and his brilliant band of Young Irelanders came just at the dividing of the line, and tried to give to Ireland a new literature in English to replace the literature which was just being discarded. It succeeded and it did not succeed. It was a most brilliant effort, but the old bark had been too recently stripped off the Irish tree, and the trunk could not take as it might have done to a fresh one. It was a new departure, and at first produced a violent effect. Yet in the long run it failed to properly leaven our peasantry who might, perhaps, have been reached upon other lines. I say they *might* have been reached upon other lines because it is quite certain that even well on into the beginning of this century, Irish poor scholars and schoolmasters used to gain the greatest favour and applause by reading out manuscripts in the people's houses at night, some of which manuscripts had an antiquity of a couple of hundred years or more behind them, and which, when they got illegible from age, were always recopied. The Irish peasantry at that time were all to some extent cultured men, and many of the better off ones were scholars and poets. What have we now left of all that? Scarcely a trace. Many of them read newspapers indeed, but who reads, much less recites, an epic poem or chants an elegiac or even a hymn?

Wherever Irish throughout Ireland continued to be spoken, there the ancient MSS. continued to be read, there the epics of Cuchullain, Conor MacNessa, Deirdre, Finn, Oscar, and Ossian continued to be told, and there poetry and music held sway. Some people may think I am exaggerating in asserting that such a state of things existed down to the present century, but it is no exaggeration. I have myself spoken with men from Cavan and Tyrone who spoke excellent Irish. Carleton's stories bear witness to the prevalence of the Irish language and traditions in Ulster when he began to write. My friend

Mr. Lloyd has found numbers in Antrim who spoke good Irish. And, as for Leinster, my friend Mr. Cleaver informed me that when he lived in Wicklow a man came by from the County Carlow in search of work who could not speak a word of English. Old labourers from Connacht, who used to go to reap the harvest in England and take shipping at Drogheda, told me that at that time, fifty years ago, Irish was spoken by every one round that town. I have met an old man in Wicklow, not twenty miles from Dublin, whose parents always repeated the Rosary in Irish. My friend Father O'Growney, who has done and is doing so much for the Irish language and literature at Maynooth, tells me that there, within twenty miles of Dublin, are three old people who still speak Irish. O'Curry found people within seven miles of Dublin city who had never heard English in their youth at all, except from the car-drivers of the great town. I gave an old man in the street who begged from me, a penny, only a few days ago, saying, 'Sin pighin agad' [Here's a penny for you], and when he answered in Irish I asked him where he was from, and he said from *Newna (n' Eamhain)*, i.e., Navan. Last year I was in Canada and out hunting with some Red Indians, and we spent a night in the last white man's house in the last settlement on the brink of the primeval forest; and judging from a peculiarly Hibernian physiognomy that the man was Irish, I addressed him in Gaelic, and to the intense astonishment both of whites and Indians we entered into a conversation which none of them understood; and it turned out that he was from within three miles of Kilkenny, and he had been forty years in that country without forgetting the language he had spoken as a child, and I, although from the centre of Connacht, understood him perfectly. When my father was a young boy in the county Leitrim, not far from Longford, he seldom heard the farm labourers and tenants speak anything but Irish amongst themselves. So much for Ulster and Leinster, but Connacht and Munster were until quite recently completely Gaelic. In fact, I may venture to say, that, up to the beginning of the present century, neither man, woman, nor child of the Gaelic race, either of high blood or low blood, existed in Ireland who did not either speak Irish or understand it. But within the last ninety years we have, with an unparalleled frivolity, deliberately thrown away our birthright and Anglicised ourselves. None of the children of those people of whom I have spoken know Irish, and the race will from henceforth be changed; for as Monsieur Jubainville says of the influence of Rome upon Gaul, England "has definitely conquered us, she has even imposed upon us her language, that is to say, the form of our thoughts

during every instant of our existence." It is curious that those who
most fear West Britonism have so eagerly consented to imposing upon
the Irish race what, according to Jubainville, who in common with all
the great scholars of the continent, seems to regret it very much, is
"the form of our thoughts during every instant of our existence."

So much for the greatest stroke of all in our Anglicisation, the
loss of our language. I have often heard people thank God that if the
English gave us nothing else they gave us at least their language. In
this way they put a bold face upon the matter, and pretend that the
Irish language is not worth knowing, and has no literature. But the
Irish language *is* worth knowing, or why would the greatest phi-
lologists of Germany, France, and Italy be emulously studying it, and
it *does* possess a literature, or why would a German savant have made
the calculation that the books written in Irish between the eleventh
and seventeenth centuries, and still extant, would fill a thousand
octavo volumes.

I have no hesitation at all in saying that every Irish-feeling
Irishman, who hates the reproach of West-Britonism, should set himself to encourage the efforts which are being made to keep alive our
once great national tongue. The losing of it is our greatest blow, and
the sorest stroke that the rapid Anglicisation of Ireland has inflicted
upon us. In order to de-Anglicise ourselves we must at once arrest the
decay of the language. We must bring pressure upon our politicians
not to snuff it out by their tacit discouragement merely because they
do not happen themselves to understand it. We must arouse some
spark of patriotic inspiration among the peasantry who still use the
language, and put an end to the shameful state of feeling—a thou-
sand-tongued reproach to our leaders and statesmen—which makes
young men and women blush and hang their heads when overheard
speaking their own language.* Maynooth has at last come splendidly

* As an instance of this, I mention the case of a young man I met on the road coming
from the fair of Tuam, some ten miles away. I saluted him in Irish, and he answered me
in English. "Don't you speak Irish," said I. "Well, I declare to God, sir," he said, "My
father and mother hasn't a word of English, but still, I don't speak Irish." This was
absolutely true for him. There are thousands upon thousands of houses all over
Ireland to-day where the old people invariably use Irish in addressing the children, and
the children as invariably answer in English, the children understanding Irish but not
speaking it, the parents understanding their children's English but unable to use it
themselves. In a great many cases, I should almost say most, the children are not
conscious of the existence of two langauges. I remember asking a gossoon a couple of
miles west of Ballaghaderreen in the Co. Mayo, some questions in Irish and he
answered them in English. At last I said to him, *"Nach labhrann tú Gaedheilg?"* (*i.e.*,

to the front, and it is now incumbent upon every clerical student to attend lectures in the Irish language and history during the first three years of his course. But in order to keep the Irish language alive where it is still spoken—which is the utmost we can at present aspire to—nothing less than a house-to-house visitation and exhortation of the people themselves will do, something—though with a very different purpose—analogous to the procedure that James Stephens adopted throughout Ireland when he found her like a corpse on the dissecting table. This and some system of giving medals or badges of honour to every family who will guarantee that they have always spoken Irish amongst themselves during the year. But, unfortunately, distracted as we are and torn by contending factions, it is impossible to find either men or money to carry out this simple remedy, although to a dispassionate foreigner—to a Zeuss, Jubainville, Zimmer, Kuno Meyer, Windisch, or Ascoli, and the rest—this is of greater importance than whether Mr. Redmond or Mr. MacCarthy lead the largest wing of the Irish party for the moment, or Mr. So-and-So succeed with his election petition. To a person taking a birds-eye view of the situation a hundred or five hundred years hence, believe me, it will also appear of greater importance than any mere temporary wrangle, but, unhappily, our countrymen cannot be brought to see this.

We can, however, insist, and we *shall* insist if Home Rule be carried, that the Irish language, which so many foreign scholars of the first calibre find so worthy of study, shall be placed on a par with—or even above—Greek, Latin, and modern languages, in all examinations held under the Irish Government. We can also insist, and we *shall* insist, that in those baronies where the children speak Irish, Irish shall be taught, and that Irish-speaking schoolmasters, petty sessions clerks, and even magistrates be appointed in Irish-speaking districts. If all this were done, it should not be very difficult, with the aid of the

---

"Don't you speak Irish?") and his answer was, "And isn't it Irish I'm spaking?" "No *a-chuisle*," said I, "it's not Irish you're speaking, but English." "Well then," said he, "that's how I spoke it ever!" He was quite unconscious that I was addressing him in one language and he answering in another. On a different occasion I spoke Irish to a little girl in a house near Kilfree Junction, Co. Sligo, into which I went while waiting for a train. The girl answered me in Irish until her brother came in. "Arrah now, Mary," said he, with what was intended to be a most bitter sneer; "and isn't that a credit to you!" And poor Mary—whom I had with difficulty persuaded to begin—immediately hung her head and changed to English. This is going on from Malin Head to Galway, and from Galway to Waterford, with the exception possibly of a few spots in Donegal and Kerry, where the people are wiser and more national.

foremost foreign scholars, to bring about a tone of thought which would make it disgraceful for an educated Irishman—especially of the old Celtic race, MacDermotts, O'Conors, O'Sullivans, MacCarthys, O'Neills—to be ignorant of his own language—would make it at least as disgraceful as for an educated Jew to be quite ignorant of Hebrew.

Further Readings on Douglas Hyde

Bibliography

de Bhaldraithe, Tomás. "Aguiín le clár saothair An Craoibhín." *Galvia* 4: 18–24.

Kersnowski, Frank L., *et al. A Bibliography of Modern Irish and Anglo-Irish Literature*, pp. 54–60. San Antonio, Tex.: Trinity University Press, 1976.

O'Hegarty, P. S. *A Bibliography of Dr. Douglas Hyde*. Dublin: Alex Thorn, 1939.

Selected Works

Leabhar Sgéulaighteachta. Dublin: M. H. Gill, 1889. Reprinted, with additions, Dublin: Oifig Díolta Foillseacháin Rialtais, 1931.

Beside the Fire. London: Nutt, 1890. Reprinted, New York: Lemma, 1973.

"The Necessity for De-Anglicising Ireland." Address, 25 November 1892. In *The Revival of Irish Literature*, ed. Lady Gregory. London: Unwin, 1894, 1901.

The Love Songs of Connacht. Dublin: M. H. Gill, 1893. Reprinted, Shannon: Irish University Press, 1969.

The Story of Early Gaelic Literature. Dublin: Sealy, Bryers; London: Unwin; New York: Kenedy, 1895. Rev. ed., London: Unwin, 1920.

The Literary History of Ireland from the Earliest Times to the Present. London: Unwin; New York: Scribner's, 1899. Reprinted with revisions by Brian Ó Cuiv, London: Ernest Benn; New York: Barnes & Noble, 1967.

Casadh an tSugáin. Drama, first performed 21 October 1901. Translated by Lady Gregory as *The Twisting of the Rope*. In Gregory's *Poets and Dreamers*. Dublin: Figgis; London: Murray, 1903. Reprinted, Gerrards Cross,: Colin Smythe; New York: Oxford, 1974.

Biography and Criticism

Coffey, Diarmid. *Douglas Hyde: President of Ireland*. Dublin: Talbot, 1938.

Daly, Dominic. *The Young Douglas Hyde: The Dawn of the Irish Revolution and Renaissance 1874–1893*. Totowa, N.J.: Rowman & Littlefield, 1974.

Dunleavy, Gareth W. *Douglas Hyde*. Lewisburg, Pa.: Bucknell University Press, 1974.

ISABELLA AUGUSTA, LADY GREGORY
(1852–1932)

The godmother of the Irish Literary Renaissance was born of a landed, Protestant, Unionist, and nonliterary family. Lady Gregory did not begin an active career in literature, however, until she was widowed and past forty. But once awakened, she gave of herself tirelessly, usually as a champion of the traditions and culture of the Catholic peasant underclass. She worked as a folklorist, recording narratives and beliefs in her own poetic version of folk language called "Kiltartanese," after the region around her estate, Coole Park, in County Galway. With William Butler Yeats she founded the Irish Literary Theatre in 1899, and then the Abbey Theatre five years later. When the works of others failed to draw crowds, she wrote her own plays, many in Kiltartanese, and these were often highly popular with audiences. Her two retellings (in Kiltartanese) of Old Irish heroic literature, *Cuchulain of Muirthemne* (1902) and *Gods and Fighting Men* (1904), fusing disparate narratives into a continuous whole, have been compared to the work of Thomas Malory with the Arthurian legends. Lady Gregory was a prudent manager of the Abbey Theatre, where she promoted the careers of many younger playwrights, notably Sean O'Casey.

"The Only Son of Aoife," from her *Cuchulain*, adapts an Irish variant of an international tale sometimes known by its Persian title, "Sohrub and Rustum." (The title of the Irish text is *Aided Oenfir Aífe*.) Yeats used versions of the narrative in his poem "Cuchulain's Fight with the Sea" (1892), and in his play *On Baile's Strand* (1904). In other texts, the name of the main characters may be spelled differently: Aoife/Aífe, Conlaoch/Connla, and Cuchulain/Cúchulainn.

The Rising of the Moon, one of her best-known short plays, was published in 1904 but not performed until 1907. Alluding to the 1798 revolution, the title of the play is taken from the patriotic ballad of the same name, attributed to John Keegan Casey (1846–70). An adaptation of Lady Gregory's play appears in John Ford's film (1958), again of the same title.

THE ONLY SON OF AOIFE

The time Cuchulain came back from Alban, after he had learned the use of arms under Scathach, he left Aoife, the queen he had overcome in battle, with child.

And when he was leaving her, he told her what name to give the child, and he gave her a gold ring, and bade her keep it safe till the child grew to be a lad, and till his thumb would fill it; and he bade her to give it to him then, and to send him to Ireland, and he would know he was his son by that token. She promised to do so, and with that Cuchulain went back to Ireland.

It was not long after the child was born, word came to Aoife that Cuchulain had taken Emer to be his wife in Ireland. When she heard that, great jealousy came on her, and great anger, and her love for Cuchulain was turned to hatred; and she remembered her three champions that he had killed, and how he had overcome herself, and she determined in her mind that when her son would come to have the strength of a man, she would get her revenge through him. She told Conlaoch her son nothing of this, but brought him up like any king's son; and when he was come to sensible years, she put him under the teaching of Scathach, to be taught the use of arms and the art of war. He turned out as apt a scholar as his father, and it was not long before he had learnt all Scathach had to teach.

Then Aoife gave him the arms of a champion, and bade him go to Ireland, but first she laid three commands on him: the first, never to give way to any living person, but to die sooner than be made turn back; the second, not to refuse a challenge from the greatest champion alive, but to fight him at all risks, even if he was sure to lose his life; the third, not to tell his name on any account, though he might be threatened with death for hiding it. She put him under *geasa*, that is, under bonds, not to do these things.

Then the young man, Conlaoch, set out, and it was not long before his ship brought him to Ireland, and the place he landed at was Baile's Strand, near Dundealgan.

It chanced that at that time Conchubar, the High King, was holding court there, for it was a convenient gathering-place for his chief men, and they were settling some business that belonged to the government of that district.

When word was brought to Conchubar that there was a ship come to the strand, and a young lad in it armed as if for fighting, and armed men with him, he sent one of the chief men of his household to ask his name, and on what business he was come.

The messenger's name was Cuinaire, and he went down to the strand, and when he saw the young man he said: "A welcome to you, young hero from the east, with the merry face. It is likely, seeing you come armed as if for fighting, you are gone astray on your journey; but as you are come to Ireland, tell me your name and what your deeds have been, and your victories in the eastern bounds of the world."

"As to my name," said Conlaoch, "it is of no great account; but whatever it is, I am under bonds not to tell it to the stoutest man living."

"It is best for you to tell it at the king's desire," said Cuinaire, "before you get your death through refusing it, as many a champion from Alban and from Britain has done before now." "If that is the order you put on us when we land here, it is I will break it," said Conlaoch, "and no one will obey it any longer from this out."

So Cuinaire went back and told the king what the young lad had said. Then Conchubar said to his people: "Who will go out into the field, and drag the name and the story out of this young man?" "I will go," said Conall, for his hand was never slow in fighting. And he went out, and found the lad angry and destroying, handling his arms, and they attacked one another with a great noise of swords and shouts, and they were gripped together, and fought for a while, and then Conall was overcome, and the great name and the praise that was on Conall, it was on the head of Conlaoch it was now.

Word was sent then to where Cuchulain was, in pleasant, bright-faced Dundealgan. And the messenger told him the whole story, and he said: "Conall is lying humbled, and it is slow the help is in coming; it is a welcome there would be before the Hound."

Cuchulain rose up then and went to where Conlaoch was, and he still handling his arms. And Cuchulain asked him his name and said: "It would be well for you, young hero of unknown name, to loosen yourself from this knot, and not to bring down my hand upon you, for it will be hard for you to escape death." But Conlaoch said: "If I put you down in the fight, the way I put down your comrade, there will be a great name on me; but if I draw back now, there will be mockery on me, and it will be said I was afraid of the fight. I will never give in to any man to tell the name, or to give an account of myself. But if I was not held with a command," he said, "there is no man in the world I would sooner give it to than to yourself, since I saw your face. But do not think, brave champion of Ireland, that I will let you take away the fame I have won, for nothing."

With that they fought together, and it is seldom such a battle was seen, and all wondered that the young lad could stand so well against Cuchulain.

So they fought a long while, neither getting the better of the other, but at last Cuchulain was charged so hotly by the lad that he was forced to give way, and although he had fought so many good fights, and killed so many great champions, and understood the use of arms better than any man living, he was pressed very hard.

And he called for the Gae Bulg, and his anger came on him, and the flames of the hero-light began to shine about his head, and by that sign Conlaoch knew him to be Cuchulain, his father. And just at that time he was aiming his spear at him, and when he knew it was Cuchulain, he threw his spear crooked that it might pass beside him. But Cuchulain threw his spear, the Gae Bulg, at him with all his might, and it struck the lad in the side and went into his body, so that he fell to the ground.

And Cuchulain said: "Now, boy, tell your name and what you are, for it is short your life will be, for you will not live after that wound."

And Conlaoch showed the ring that was on his hand, and he said: "Come here where I am lying on the field, let my men from the east come round me. I am suffering for revenge. I am Conlaoch, son of the Hound, heir of dear Dundealgan; I was bound to this secret in Dun Scathach, the secret in which I have found my grief."

And Cuchulain said: "It is a pity your mother not to be here to see you brought down. She might have stretched out her hand to stop the spear that wounded you." And Conlaoch said: "My curse be on my mother, for it was she put me under bonds; it was she sent me here to try my strength against yours." And Cuchulain said: "My curse be on your mother, the woman that is full of treachery; it is through her harmful thoughts these tears have been brought on us." And Conlaoch said: "My name was never forced from my mouth till now; I never gave an account of myself to any man under the sun. But, O

Cuchulain of the sharp sword, it was a pity you not to know me the time I threw the slanting spear behind you in the fight."

And then the sorrow of death came upon Conlaoch, and Cuchulain took his sword and put it through him, sooner than leave him in the pain and the punishment he was in.

And then great trouble and anguish came on Cuchulain, and he made this complaint:

"It is a pity it is, O son of Aoife, that ever you came into the province of Ulster, that you ever met with the Hound of Cuailgne.

"If I and my fair Conlaoch were doing feats of war on the one side, the men of Ireland from sea to sea would not be equal to us together. It is no wonder I to be under grief when I see the shield and the arms of Conlaoch. A pity it is there is no one at all, a pity there are not hundreds of men on whom I could get satisfaction for his death.

"If it was the king himself had hurt your fair body, it is I would have shortened his days.

"It is well for the House of the Red Branch, and for the heads of its fair army of heroes, it was not they that killed my only son.

"It is well for Laegaire of Victories it is not from him you got your heavy pain.

"It is well for the heroes of Conall they did not join in the killing of you; it is well that travelling across the plain of Macha they did not fall in with me after such a fight.

"It is well for the tall, well-shaped Forbuide; well for Dubthach, your Black Beetle of Ulster.

"It is well for you, Cormac Conloingeas, your share of arms gave no help, that it is not from your weapons he got his wound, the hard-skinned shield or the blade.

"It is a pity it was not one on the plains of Munster, or in Leinster of the sharp blades, or at Cruachan of the rough fighters, that struck down my comely Conlaoch.

"It is a pity it was not in the country of the Cruithne, of the fierce Fians, you fell in a heavy quarrel, or in the country of the Greeks, or in some other place of the world, you died, and I could avenge you.

"Or in Spain, or in Sorcha, or in the country of the Saxons of the free armies; there would not then be this death in my heart.

"It is very well for the men of Alban it was not they that destroyed your fame; and it is well for the men of the Gall.

"Och! It is bad that it happened; my grief! it is on me is the misfortune, O Conlaoch of the Red Spear, I myself to have spilled your blood.

"I to be under defeat, without strength. It is a pity Aoife never taught you to know the power of my strength in the fight.

"It is no wonder I to be blinded after such a fight and such a defeat.

"It is no wonder I to be tired out, and without the sons of Usnach beside me.

"Without a son, without a brother, with none to come after me; without Conlaoch, without a name to keep my strength.

"To be without Naoise, without Ainnle, without Ardan; is it not with me is my fill of trouble?

"I am the father that killed his son, the fine green branch; there is no hand or shelter to help me.

"I am a raven that has no home; I am a boat going from wave to wave; I am a ship that has lost its rudder; I am the apple left on the tree; it is little I thought of falling from it; grief and sorrow will be with me from this time."

Then Cuchulain stood up and faced all the men of Ulster. "There is trouble on Cuchulain," said Conchubar; "he is after killing his own son, and if I and all my men were to go against him, by the end of the day he would destroy every man of us. Go now," he said to Cathbad, the Druid, "and bind him to go down to Baile's Strand, and to give three days fighting against the waves of the sea, rather than to kill us all."

So Cathbad put an enchantment on him, and bound him to go down. And when he came to the strand, there was a great white stone before him, and he took his sword in his right hand, and he said: "If I had the head of the woman that sent her son to his death, I would split it as I split this stone." And he made four quarters of the stone.

Then he fought with the waves three days and three nights, till he fell from hunger and weakness, so that some men said he got his death there. But it was not there he got his death, but on the plain of Muirthemne.

THE RISING OF THE MOON

Persons

SERGEANT.
POLICEMAN X.
POLICEMAN B.
A RAGGED MAN.

SCENE. *Side of a quay in a seaport town. Some posts and chains. A large barrel. Enter three policemen. Moonlight.*

(SERGEANT, *who is older than the others, crosses the stage to right and looks down steps. The others put down a pastepot and unroll a bundle of placards.*)

POLICEMAN B. I think this would be a good place to put up a notice. (*He points to barrel.*)

POLICEMAN X. Better ask him. (*Calls to* SERGEANT) Will this be a good place for a placard?

(*No answer.*)

POLICEMAN B. Will we put up a notice here on the barrel?

(*No answer.*)

SERGEANT. There's a flight of steps here that leads to the water. This is a place that should be minded well. If he got down here, his friends might have a boat to meet him; they might send it in here from outside.

POLICEMAN B. Would the barrel be a good place to put a notice up?

SERGEANT. It might; you can put it there.

(*They paste the notice up.*)

SERGEANT (*reading it*). Dark hair—dark eyes, smooth face, height five feet five—there's not much to take hold of in that—It's a pity I had no chance of seeing him before he broke out of gaol. They say he's a wonder, that it's he makes all the plans for the whole organization. There isn't another man in Ireland would have broken gaol the way he did. He must have some friends among the gaolers.

POLICEMAN B. A hundred pounds is little enough for the Government to offer for him. You may be sure any man in the force that takes him will get promotion.

SERGEANT. I'll mind this place myself. I wouldn't wonder at all if he came this way. He might come slipping along there (*points to side of quay*), and his friends might be waiting for him there (*points down steps*), and once he got away it's little chance we'd have of finding him; it's maybe under a load of kelp he'd be in a fishing boat, and not one to help a married man that wants it to the reward.

POLICEMAN X. And if we get him itself, nothing but abuse on our heads for it from the people, and maybe from our own relations.

SERGEANT. Well, we have to do our duty in the force. Haven't we the whole country depending on us to keep law and order? It's those that are down would be up and those that are up would be down, if it wasn't for us. Well, hurry on, you have plenty of other places to placard yet, and come back here then to me. You can take the lantern. Don't be too long now. It's a very lonesome here with nothing but the moon.

POLICEMAN B. It's a pity we can't stop with you. The Government should have brought more police into the town, with *him* in gaol, and at assize time too. Well, good luck to your watch.

(They go out.)

SERGEANT *(walks up and down once or twice and looks at placard)*. A hundred pounds and promotion sure. There must be a great deal of spending in a hundred pounds. It's a pity some honest man not to be better of that.

(A RAGGED MAN appears at left and tries to slip past. SERGEANT suddenly turns.)

SERGEANT. Where are you going?

MAN. I'm a poor ballad-singer, your honour. I thought to sell some of these *(holds out bundle of ballads)* to the sailors.

(He goes on.)

SERGEANT. Stop! Didn't I tell you to stop? You can't go on there.

MAN. Oh, very well. It's a hard thing to be poor. All the world's against the poor!

SERGEANT. Who are you?

MAN. You'd be as wise as myself if I told you, but I don't mind. I'm one Jimmy Walsh, a ballad-singer.

SERGEANT. Jimmy Walsh? I don't know that name.

MAN. Ah, sure, they know it well enough in Ennis. Were you ever in Ennis, sergeant?

SERGEANT. What brought you here?

MAN. Sure, it's to the assizes I came, thinking I might make a few shillings here or there. It's in the one train with the judges I came.

SERGEANT. Well, if you came so far, you may as well go farther, for you'll walk out of this.

MAN. I will, I will; I'll just go on where I was going.

(Goes towards steps.)

SERGEANT. Come back from those steps; no one has leave to pass down them to-night.

MAN. I'll just sit on the top of the steps till I see will some sailor buy a ballad off me that would give me my supper. They do be late going back to the ship. It's often I saw them in Cork carried down the quay in a hand-cart.

SERGEANT. Move on, I tell you. I won't have any one lingering about the quay to-night.

MAN. Well, I'll go. It's the poor have the hard life! Maybe yourself might like one, sergeant. Here's a good sheet now. (*Turns one over.*) "Content and a pipe"—that's not much. "The Peeler and the goat"— you wouldn't like that. "Johnny Hart"—that's a lovely song.

SERGEANT. Move on.

MAN. Ah, wait till you hear it. (*Sings:*)

There was a rich farmer's daughter lived near the town
    of Ross;
She courted a Highland soldier, his name was Johnny
    Hart;
Says the mother to her daughter, "I'll go distracted mad
If you marry that Highland soldier dressed up in
    Highland plaid."

SERGEANT. Stop that noise.

(MAN *wraps up his ballads and shuffles towards the steps.*)

SERGEANT. Where are you going?

MAN. Sure you told me to be going, and I am going.

SERGEANT. Don't be a fool. I didn't tell you to go that way; I told you to go back to the town.

MAN. Back to the town, is it?

SERGEANT (*taking him by the shoulder and shoving him before him*). Here, I'll show you the way. Be off with you. What are you stopping for?

MAN (*who has been keeping his eye on the notice, points to it*). I think I know what you're waiting for, sergeant.

SERGEANT. What's that to you?

MAN. And I know well the man you're waiting for—I know him well—I'll be going.

(*He shuffles on.*)

SERGEANT. You know him? Come back here. What sort is he?

MAN. Come back is it, sergeant? Do you want to have me killed?

SERGEANT. Why do you say that?

MAN. Never mind. I'm going. I wouldn't be in your shoes if the reward was ten times as much. (*Goes on off stage to left.*) Not if it was ten times as much.

SERGEANT (*rushing after him*). Come back here, come back. (*Drags him back.*) What sort is he? Where did you see him?

MAN. I saw him in my own place, in the County Clare. I tell you you wouldn't like to be looking at him. You'd be afraid to be in the one place with him. There isn't a weapon he doesn't know the use of, and as to strength, his muscles are as hard as that board (*slaps barrel*).

SERGEANT. Is he as bad as that?

MAN. He is then.

SERGEANT. Do you tell me so?

MAN. There was a poor man in our place, a sergeant from Ballyvaughan.—It was with a lump of stone he did it.

SERGEANT. I never heard of that.

MAN. And you wouldn't, sergeant. It's not everything that happens gets into the papers. And there was a policeman in plain clothes, too . . . It is in Limerick he was. . . . It was after the time of the attack on the police barrack at Kilmallock. . . . Moonlight . . . just like this . . . waterside. . . . Nothing was known for certain.

SERGEANT. Do you say so? It's a terrible county to belong to.

MAN. That's so, indeed! You might be standing there, looking out that way, thinking you saw him coming up this side of the quay *(points)*, and might be coming up this other side *(points)*, and he'd be on you before you knew where you were.

SERGEANT. It's a whole troop of police they ought to put here to stop a man like that.

MAN. But if you'd like me to stop with you, I could be looking down this side. I could be sitting up here on this barrel.

SERGEANT. And you know him well, too?

MAN. I'd know him a mile off, sergeant.

SERGEANT. But you wouldn't want to share the reward?

MAN. Is it a poor man like me, that has to be going the roads and singing in fairs, to have the name on him that he took a reward? But you don't want me. I'll be safer in the town.

SERGEANT. Well, you can stop.

MAN *(getting up on barrel)*. All right, sergeant. I wonder, now, you're not tired out, sergeant, walking up and down the way you are.

SERGEANT. If I'm tired I'm used to it.

MAN. You might have hard work before you to-night yet. Take it easy while you can. There's plenty of room up here on the barrel, and you see farther when you're higher up.

SERGEANT. Maybe so. *(Gets up beside him on barrel, facing right. They sit back to back, looking different ways.)* You made me feel a bit queer with the way you talked.

MAN. Give me a match, sergeant *(he gives it and man lights pipe)*; take a draw yourself? It'll quiet you. Wait now till I give you a light, but you needn't turn round. Don't take your eye off the quay for the life of you.

SERGEANT. Never fear, I won't. *(Lights pipe. They both smoke.)*

Indeed it's a hard thing to be in the force, out at night and no thanks for it, for all the danger we're in. And it's little we get but abuse from the people, and no choice but to obey our orders, and never asked when a man is sent into danger, if you are a married man with a family.

MAN (*sings*)—

As through the hills I walked to view the hills and
     shamrock plain,
I stood awhile where nature smiles to view the rocks
     and streams,
On a matron fair I fixed my eyes beneath a fertile vale,
And she sang her song it was on the wrong of poor old
     Granuaile.

SERGEANT. Stop that; that's no song to be singing in these times.

MAN. Ah, sergeant, I was only singing to keep my heart up. It sinks when I think of him. To think of us two sitting here, and he creeping up the quay, maybe, to get to us.

SERGEANT. Are you keeping a good lookout?

MAN. I am; and for no reward too. Amn't I the foolish man? But when I saw a man in trouble, I never could help trying to get him out of it. What's that? Did something hit me?

(*Rubs his heart.*)

SERGEANT (*patting him on the shoulder*). You will get your reward in heaven.

MAN. I know that, I know that, sergeant, but life is precious.

SERGEANT. Well, you can sing if it gives you more courage.

MAN (*sings*)—

Her head was bare, her hands and feet with iron bands
     were bound,
Her pensive strain and plaintive wail mingles with the
     evening gale,
And the song she sang with mournful air, I am old
     Granuaile.
Her lips so sweet that monarchs kissed . . .

SERGEANT. That's not it. . . . "Her gown she wore was stained with gore." . . . That's it—you missed that.

MAN. You're right, sergeant, so it is; I missed it. (*Repeats line.*) But to think of a man like you knowing a song like that.

SERGEANT. There's many a thing a man might know and might not have any wish for.

MAN. Now, I daresay, sergeant, in your youth, you used to be sitting up on a wall, the way you are sitting up on this barrel now, and the other lads beside you, and you singing "Granuaile"? . . .

SERGEANT. I did then.

MAN. And the "Shan Van Vocht"? . . .

SERGEANT. I did then.

MAN. And the "Green on the Cape"?

SERGEANT. That was one of them.

MAN. And maybe the man you are watching, for to-night used to be sitting on the wall, when he was young, and singing those same songs. . . . It's a queer world. . . .

SERGEANT. Whisht! . . . I think I see something coming. . . . It's only a dog.

MAN. And isn't it a queer world? . . . Maybe it's one of the boys you used to be singing with that time you will be arresting to-day or to-morrow, and sending into the dock. . . .

SERGEANT. That's true indeed.

MAN. And maybe one night, after you had been singing, if the other boys had told you some plan they had, some plan to free the country, you might have joined with them . . . and maybe it is you might be in trouble now.

SERGEANT. Well, who knows but I might? I had a great spirit in those days.

MAN. It's a queer world, sergeant, and it's little any mother knows when she sees her child creeping on the floor what might happen to it before it has gone through its life, or who will be who in the end.

SERGEANT. That's a queer thought now, and a true thought. Wait now till I think it out. . . . If it wasn't for the sense I have, and for my wife and family, and for me joining the force the time I did, it might be myself now would be after breaking gaol and hiding in the dark, and it might be him that's hiding in the dark and that got out of gaol would be sitting up here where I am on this barrel. . . . And it might be myself would be creeping up trying to make my escape from himself, and it might be himself would be keeping the law, and myself would be breaking it, and myself would be trying to put a bullet in his head, or to take up a lump of stone the way you said he did . . . no, that myself did. . . . Oh! *(Gasps. After a pause)* What's that? *(Grasps man's arm.)*

MAN (*jumps off barrel and listens, looking over the water*). It's nothing, sergeant.

SERGEANT. I thought it might be a boat. I had a notion there might be friends of his coming about the quays with a boat.

MAN. Sergeant, I am thinking it was with the people you were, and not with the law you were, when you were a young man.

SERGEANT. Well, if I was foolish then, that time's gone.

MAN. Maybe, sergeant, it comes into your head sometimes, in spite of your belt and your tunic, that it might have been as well for you to have followed Granuaile.

SERGEANT. It's no business of yours what I think.

MAN. Maybe, sergeant, you'll be on the side of the country yet.

SERGEANT (*gets off barrel*). Don't talk to me like that. I have my duties and I know them. (*Looks round.*) That was a boat; I hear the oars.

(*Goes to the steps and looks down.*)

MAN (*sings*)—

> O, then, tell me, Shawn O'Farrell,
>   Where the gathering is to be.
> In the old spot by the river
>   Right well known to you and me!

SERGEANT. Stop that! Stop that, I tell you!

MAN (*sings louder*)—

> One word more, for signal token,
>   Whistle up the marching tune,
> With your pike upon your shoulder,
>   At the Rising of the Moon.

SERGEANT. If you don't stop that, I'll arrest you.

(*A whistle from below answers, repeating the air.*)

SERGEANT. That's a signal. (*Stands between him and steps.*) You must not pass this way. . . . Step farther back. . . . Who are you? You are no ballad-singer.

MAN. You needn't ask who I am; that placard will tell you. (*Points to placard.*)

SERGEANT. You are the man I am looking for.

MAN (*takes off hat and wig.* SERGEANT *seizes them*). I am. There's a hundred pound on my head. There is a friend of mine below in a boat. He knows a safe place to bring me to.

SERGEANT *(looking still at hat and wig.).* It's a pity! It's a pity. You deceived me. You deceived me well.

MAN. I am a friend of Granuaile. There is a hundred pounds on my head.

SERGEANT. It's a pity, it's a pity!

MAN. Will you let me pass, or must I make you let me?

SERGEANT. I am in the force. I will not let you pass.

MAN. I thought to do it with my tongue. *(Puts hand in breast.)* What is that?

(VOICE OF POLICEMAN X *outside*). Here, this is where we left him.

SERGEANT. It's my comrades coming.

MAN. You won't betray me . . . the friend of Granuaile. *(Slips behind barrel.)*

(Voice of POLICEMAN B.). That was the last of the placards.

POLICEMAN X. *(as they come in).* If he makes his escape it won't be unknown he'll make it.

(SERGEANT *puts hat and wig behind his back.)*

POLICEMAN B. Did any one come this way?

SERGEANT. *(after a pause).* No one.

POLICEMAN B. No one at all?

SERGEANT. No one at all.

POLICEMAN B. We had no orders to go back to the station; we can stop along with you.

SERGEANT. I don't want you. There is nothing for you to do here.

POLICEMAN B. You bade us to come back here and keep watch with you.

SERGEANT. I'd sooner be alone. Would any man come this way and you making all that talk? It is better the place to be quiet.

POLICEMAN B. Well, we'll leave you the lantern anyhow.

(Hands it to him.)

SERGEANT. I don't want it. Bring it with you.

POLICEMAN B. You might want it. There are clouds coming up and you have the darkness of the night before you yet. I'll leave it over here on the barrel. *(Goes to barrel.)*

SERGEANT. Bring it with you I tell you. No more talk.

POLICEMAN B. Well, I thought it might be a comfort to you. I often think when I have it in my hand and can be flashing it about into every dark corner *(doing so)* that it's the same as being beside the fire at home, and the bits of bogwood blazing up now and again.

(Flashes it about, now on the barrel, now on SERGEANT.)

SERGEANT *(furious).* Be off the two of you, yourselves and your lantern!

(They go out. MAN *comes from behind barrel. He and* SERGEANT *stand looking at one another.)*

SERGEANT. What are you waiting for?

MAN. For my hat, of course, and my wig. You wouldn't wish me to get my death of cold?

(SERGEANT *gives them.)*

MAN *(going towards steps.)* Well, good-night, comrade, and thank you. You did me a good turn to-night, and I'm obliged to you. Maybe I'll be able to do as much for you when the small rise up and the big fall down . . . when we all change places at the Rising *(waves his hand and disappears)* of the Moon.

SERGEANT *(turning his back to audience and reading placard).* A hundred pounds reward! A hundred pounds! *(Turns towards audience.)* I wonder, now, am I as great a fool as I think I am?

Further Readings on Isabella Augusta, Lady Gregory

Bibliography

Carens, James F. "Lady Gregory." In *Anglo-Irish Literature: A Review of Research,* edited by R. J. Finneran, pp. 437–46. New York: Modern Language Association, 1976.

Selected Works

Collected Works of Lady Gregory. The Coole Edition. Edited by T. R. Henn and Colin Smythe. 21 vols. Gerrards Cross, England: Colin Smythe; New York: Oxford University Press, 1969–1976.

Cuchulain of Muirthemne: The Story of the Men of the Red Branch of Ulster. London: Murray, 1902 Reprinted, Gerrards Cross, England: Colin Smythe; New York: Oxford University Press, 1970.

Gods and Fighting Men: The Story of the Tuatha de Danaan and of the Fianna of Ireland. London: Murray; New York: Scribner's, 1904. Reprinted, Gerrards Cross, England: Colin Smythe; New York: Oxford University Press, 1970.

The Rising of the Moon. First published in *Samhain* (December 1904). Also in *Seven Short Plays.* Dublin: Maunsel, 1909; and in *Collected Plays.* vol. 1. Gerrards Cross, England: Colin Smythe; New York: Oxford University Press, 1971.

Selected Plays of Lady Gregory. Edited by Mary FitzGerald. Gerrards Cross, England: Colin Smythe; Washington: Catholic University Press, 1983.

Biography and Criticism

Adams, Hazard. *Lady Gregory.* Irish Writers Series. Lewisburg, Pa.: Bucknell University Press, 1973.

Coxhead, Elizabeth. *Lady Gregory: A Literary Portrait.* London and Toronto: Macmillan; New York: Harcourt, 1961.

Kohfeldt, Mary Lou. *Lady Gregory, The Woman Behind the Irish Literary Renaissance.* London: Andre Deutsch, 1985.

Kopper, Richard A., Jr. *Lady Isabella Persse Gregory.* Boston: Twayne, 1976.

Saddlemyer, Ann. *In Defence of Lady Gregory, Playwright.* Dublin: Dolmen, 1966.

LYRIC VOICES OF THE
IRISH RENAISSANCE

Although William Butler Yeats was the dominant Irish poet to emerge in the Irish Literary Renaissance (1895–1916), the movement allowed many distinctive talents to speak. Many, though not all, defined themselves in terms of their relation to Yeats, accepting or rejecting his visions of the Irish tradition, of nature, and of a world beyond the senses.

T[homas] W[illiam] Rolleston (1857–1920) was better known in his lifetime as scholar and translator than as poet. He championed Walt Whitman, wrote commentaries on ancient philosophers, translated the works of Richard Wagner, and popularized Old Irish heroic narratives. His "Clonmacnoise" contemplates the Irish past at the monastic ruin on east bank of the Shannon in County Offaly, a seat of learning in the golden age of the Celtic church, c. A.D. 700–1100.

Katharine Tynan, or Tynan Hinkson (1861–1931), was a close friend of Yeats from her youth. At first a poet of nationalist sympathies, she became an astoundingly prolific prose writer with pro-British views. She published 105 novels, 18 collections of poetry, and 38 other volumes, including a valuable memoir of the beginnings of the Irish Renaissance, *Twenty-Five Years* (1913). Her poem, "The Children of Lir," draws on an Old Irish story, much invested with mythological symbolism, in which the children of the sea god Lir are transformed by a cruel stepmother into swans, and remain so for nine hundred years until they return to human form.

George W. Russell, or "AE" (1867–1935), was an early friend and rival of Yeats, as well as a fellow-mystic who was later eclipsed by him. Like Yeats, he was a man of action as well of words. He edited several publications, fostered the careers of many younger writers, and became an authority on agricultural economy. A career of more than forty years produced many volumes of poetry, drama, and journalistic gleanings, as well as a number of distinguished paintings. "The Winds of Angus" alludes to the Old Irish god of poetry and love. Terence MacSwiney, Lord Mayor of Cork from 1879 to 1920, died as a result of a hunger strike protesting his imprisonment by the British. (Russell's familiar pseudonym, "AE," comes from a printer's misunderstanding of an earlier pen-name, Aeon.)

Francis Ledwidge (1887–1917) was a self-educated farm laborer who wrote nature poetry in evocation of Thomas Gray and Keats. Befriended by the fantasy-fiction writer Lord Dunsany (1878–1957), Ledwidge was introduced to Yeats's literary circle. Although a nationalist and a labor activist, he volunteered for the British Army and survived the disastrous invasion at Gallipoli only to be killed in action in Belgium.

T. W. ROLLESTON (1857–1920)

CLONMACNOISE

In a quiet water'd land, a land of roses,
    Stands Saint Kieran's city fair;
And the warriors of Erin in their famous generations
    Slumber there.

There beneath the dewy hillside sleep the noblest
    Of the clan of Conn,
Each below his stone with name in branching Ogham
    And the sacred knot thereon.

There they laid to rest the seven Kings of Tara,
    There the sons of Cairbrè sleep—
Battle-banners of the Gael that in Kieran's plain of crosses
    Now their final hosting keep.

And in Clonmacnoise they laid the men of Teffia,
    And right many a lord of Breagh;

Deep the sod above Clan Creidè and Clan Conaill,
   Kind in hall and fierce in fray

Many and many a son of Conn the Hundred-fighter
   In the red earth lies at rest;
Many a blue eye of Clan Colman the turf covers,
   Many a swan-white breast.

KATHARINE TYNAN HINKSON (1861–1931)

THE CHILDREN OF LIR

Out upon the sand-dunes thrive the coarse
      long grasses,
   Herons standing knee-deep in the
         brackish pool,
Overhead the sunset fire and flame amasses,
   And the moon to eastward rises pale and
         cool:
Rose and green about her, silver-grey and
      pearly,
   Chequered with the black rooks flying
         home to bed;
For, to wake at daybreak, birds must couch
      them early,
   And the day's a long one since the dawn
         was red.

On the chilly lakelet, in that pleasant
      gloaming,
   See the sad swans sailing: they shall have
         no rest:
Never a voice to greet them save the bittern's
      booming
   Where the ghostly sallows sway against
         the West.
"Sister," saith the grey swan, "Sister, I am
      weary,"

Turning to the white swan wet,
　　despairing eyes;
"Oh," she saith, "my young one, oh," she
　　saith, "my dearie,"
　　Casts her wings about him with a storm
　　　　of cries.

Woe for Lir's sweet children whom their vile
　　stepmother
　　Glamoured with her witch-spells for a
　　　　thousand years;
Died their father raving, on his throne
　　another,
　　Blind before the end came from the
　　　　burning tears.
Long the swans have wandered over lake and
　　river.
　　Gone is all the glory of the race of Lir,
Gone and long forgotten like a dream of
　　fever:
　　But the swans remember the sweet days
　　　　that were.

Dews are in the clear air, and the roselight
　　paling,
　　Over sands and sedges shines the evening
　　　　star,
And the moon's disc lonely high in heaven is
　　sailing,
　　Silvered all the spear-heads of the rushes
　　　　are,—
Housed warm are all things as the night
　　grows colder,
　　Water-fowl and sky-fowl dreamless in the
　　　　nest;
But the swans go drifting, drooping wing and
　　shoulder
　　Cleaving the still water where the fishes
　　　　rest.

GEORGE W. RUSSELL ["AE"] (1867–1935)

THE GREAT BREATH

Its edges foamed with amethyst and rose,
Withers once more the old blue flower of day:
There where the ether like a diamond glows
    Its petals fade away.

A shadowy tumult stirs the dusky air;
Sparkle the delicate dews, the distant snows;
The great deep thrills, for through it everywhere
    the breath of Beauty blows.

I saw how all the trembling ages past,
Moulded to her by deep and deeper breath,
Neared to the hour when Beauty breathes her last
    And knows herself in death.

PARTING

As from our dream we died away
Far off I felt the outer things;
Your wind-blown tresses round me play,
Your bosom's gentle murmurings.

And far away our faces met
As on the verge of the vast spheres;
And in the night our cheeks were wet,
I could not say with dew or tears.

As one within the Mother's heart
In that hushed dream upon the height
We lived, and then we rose to part,
Because her ways are infinite.

THE WINDS OF ANGUS

The grey road whereupon we trod became as holy
      ground:
The eve was all one voice that breathed its message with
      no sound:
And burning multitudes pour through my heart, too
      bright, too blind,
Too swift and hurried in their flight to leave their tale
      behind.
Twin gates unto that living world, dark honey-coloured
      eyes,
The lifting of whose lashes flushed the face with
      Paradise,
Beloved, there I saw within their ardent rays unfold
The likeness of enraptured birds that flew from deeps
      of gold
To deeps of gold within my breast to rest, or there to
      be
Transfigured in the light, or find a death to life in me.
So love, a burning multitude, a seraph wind that blows
From out the deep of being to the deep of being goes.
And sun and moon and starry fires and earth and air
      and sea.
Are creatures from the deep let loose, who pause in
      ecstasy,
Or wing their wild and heavenly way until again they
      find
The ancient deep, and fade therein, enraptured, bright,
      and blind.

IMMORTALITY

We must pass like smoke or live within the spirit's fire;
For we can no more than smoke unto the flame return
If our thought has changed to dream, our will unto
      desire,
      As smoke we vanish though the fire may burn.

Lights of infinite pity star the grey dusk of our days:
Surely here is soul: with it we have eternal breath:
In the fire of love we live, or pass by many ways,
    By unnumbered ways of dream to death.

TERENCE MacSWINEY

See, though the oil be low more purely still and higher
The flame burns in the body's lamp! The watchers still
Gaze with unseeing eyes while the Promethean Will,
The Uncreated Light, the Everlasting Fire
Sustains itself against the torturer's desire
Even as the fabled Titan chained upon the hill.
Burn on, shine on, thou immortality, until
We, too, have lit our lamps at the funereal pyre;
Till we, too, can be noble, unshakable, undismayed:
Till we, too, can burn with the holy flame, and know
There is that within us can triumph over pain,
And go to death, alone, slowly, and unafraid.
The candles of God are already burning row on row:
Farewell, lightbringer, fly to thy heaven again!

FRANCIS LEDWIDGE (1887–1917)

JUNE

Broom out the floor now, lay the fender by,
And plant this bee-sucked bough of woodbine there,
And let the window down. The butterfly
Floats in upon the sunbeam, and the fair
Tanned face of June, the nomad gipsy, laughs
Above her widespread wares, the while she tells
The farmer's fortunes in the fields, and quaffs
The water from the spider-peopled wells.

The hedges are all drowned in green grass seas,
And bobbing poppies flare like Elmo's light,

While siren-like the pollen-stainèd bees
Drone in the clover depths. And up the height
The cuckoo's voice is hoarse and broke with joy.
And on the lowland crops the crows make raid,
Nor fear the clappers of the farmer's boy,
Who sleeps, like drunken Noah, in the shade.

And loop this red rose in that hazel ring
That snares your little ear, for June is short
And we must joy in it and dance and sing,
And from her bounty draw her rosy worth.
Ay! soon the swallows will be flying south,
The wind wheel north to gather in the snow,
Even the roses split on youth's red mouth
Will soon blow down the road all roses go.

THOMAS MacDONAGH

He shall not hear the bittern cry
In the wild sky, where he is lain,
Nor voices of the sweeter birds
Above the wailing of the rain.

Nor shall he know when loud March blows
Thro' slanting snows her fanfare shrill,
Blowing to flame the golden cup
Of many an upset daffodil.

But when the Dark Cow leaves the moor,
And pastures poor with greedy weeds,
Perhaps he'll hear her low at morn
Lifting her horn in pleasant meads.

Further Reading on Lyric Voices of the Irish Renaissance

Bibliography

Carens, James F. "AE (George W. Russell)." In *Anglo-Irish Literature: A Review of Research,* ed. R. J. Finneran, p. 446–52. New York: Modern Language Association, 1976.

Denson, Alan. *Printed Writings by George W. Russell (AE): A Bibliography.* Evanston, Ill.: Northwestern University Press, 1961. Reprinted, Gerrards Cross, England: Colin Smythe, 1975.

Kersnowski, Frank, *et al.* "Katharine Tynan Hinkson." In *A Bibliography of Modern Irish and Anglo-Irish Literature,* p. 135–44. San Antonio, Tex.: Trinity University Press, 1976.

Selected Works

Ledwidge, Francis. *Complete Poems.* Edited by A. Curtayne. London: Martin Brian & O'Keefe, 1974.

Rolleston, T. W. *Sea Spray: Verses and Translations.* Dublin: Maunsel, 1909.

———. *The High Deeds of Finn MacCool.* London: Harrap, 1910.

———. *Myths and Legends of the Celtic Race.* London: Harrap, 1911.

Russell, George W. *Collected Poems.* London: Macmillan, 1913. Reprinted, St. Clair Shores, Mi.: Scholarly Press, 1970.

Tynan Hinkson, Katharine. *Collected Poems.* London: Macmillan, 1930.

———. *Twenty-Five Years.* London: Smith Elder, 1913.

Biography and Criticism

Boyd, Ernest A. *Ireland's Literary Renaissance.* Rev. ed. New York: Knopf, 1922. Reprinted, New York: Barnes & Noble, 1968.

Curtayne, Alice. *Francis Ledwidge: A Life of the Poet.* London: Martin Brian & O'Keefe, 1972.

Davis, Robert B. *George William Russell* ("AE"). Boston: Twayne, 1977.

Fallis, Richard. *The Irish Renaissance.* Syracuse, N.Y.: Syracuse University Press, 1977.

Hall, Wayne E. *Shadowy Heroes: Irish Literature of the 1890s.* Syracuse, N.Y.: Syracuse University Press, 1980.

Howarth, Herbert. *Irish Writers 1880–1940.* New York: Hill & Wang, 1958.

Kain, Richard M., and O'Brien, J. H. *George Russell ("AE").* Lewisburg, Pa.: Bucknell University Press, 1976.

Kuch, Peter. *Yeats and AE.* Gerrards Cross: Colin Smyth; Totowa, N.J.: Barnes and Noble, 1986.

Marcus, Phillip L. *Yeats and the Beginning of the Irish Renaissance.* Ithaca, N.Y.: Cornell University Press, 1970.

Rolleston, Charles H. *Portrait of an Irishman* [T. W. Rolleston]. London: Methuen, 1939.

Rose, Marilyn Gaddis. *Katharine Tynan.* Lewisburg, Pa.: Bucknell University Press, 1973.

Sommerfield, Henry. *That Myriad-Minded Man. A Biography of George William Russell.* Gerrards Cross, England: Colin Smythe, 1975.

JOHN MILLINGTON SYNGE
(1871–1909)

John Millington Synge (pronounced "sing") is the author of *The Playboy of the Western World* (1907), the most admired of all Irish dramas. The child of a Protestant family of the professional classes, Synge had a diverse cultural education in addition to his degree from Trinity College. He studied the violin in Germany and literature in Paris, and he knew Hebrew, German, French, and Irish. An oft-repeated, but inaccurate, story has it that Synge was struggling as a translator in Paris when Yeats suggested he find his theme for writing in the Aran Islands on Ireland's remote west coast. In fact, Synge had visited the Islands before this time, and in the four years after Yeats is supposed to have advised him he spent only four and a half months on the Islands but 43 months in Paris! Nevertheless, the inaccurate story is instructive, since Synge indeed took his most important themes from the Irish peasantry—of the Aran Islands, the western counties of Mayo, Galway, Clare, and Kerry, as well as in Wicklow, whose glens he had walked in his youth.

Synge described his travelogue-memoir *The Aran Islands*, which he completed in 1901 but which was not published until 1907, as his "first serious piece of work." He continued to produce essays, translations, and poetry, but he would make his greatest contribution in his literature for the stage. His first tentative effort was *When the Moon Has Set* (1900), but more successful works followed: *In the Shadow of the Glen* (1903), *Riders to the Sea* (1904), *The Well of the Saints* (1905), *The Playboy of the Western World* and *The Tinker's Wedding* (both 1907), and *Deirdre of the Sorrows* (posthumously published in 1910). Although Synge was the most significant playwright to emerge from Yeats and Lady Gregory's efforts to found a

173

national theater, controversy often followed his work. The riots that greeted the opening of *Playboy* in January, 1907, for example, marked one of the most infamous (and most widely reported) episodes in Irish literary history. Similarly, his outrageous farce, *The Tinker's Wedding*, was thought to be "too dangerous to be performed in Dublin" for almost fifty years.

As early as 1897, when he was only 26, Synge had the first indications of the Hodgkins disease that would eventually kill him, but mercifully he was not in pain until 1907, two years before he died. Many of the poems included here date from those later years, when he knew that his own death was as imminent as that of the fishermen in *Riders to the Sea*.

Based on a story he had heard in the Aran Islands, *Riders to the Sea* embodies an important theme in Synge's writing: that people living at the edge of life and death know life more fully. Often described as the "only one-act tragedy in the English language," *Riders to the Sea* has an international reputation among non-Irish readers and theater-goers. The English composer Ralph Vaughan Williams turned it into an opera in 1936.

RIDERS TO THE SEA

MAURYA *(an old woman)*
BARTLEY *(her son)*
CATHLEEN *(her daughter)*
NORA *(a younger daughter)*
MEN and WOMEN

SCENE. *An Island off the West of Ireland. (Cottage kitchen, with nets, oil-skins, spinning wheel, some new boards standing by the wall, etc. Cathleeen, a girl of about twenty, finishes kneading cake, and puts it down in the pot-oven by the fire; then wipes her hands, and begins to spin at the wheel. Nora, a young girl, puts her head in at the door.)*

NORA *(in a low voice)*. Where is she?

CATHLEEN. She's lying down, God help her, and may be sleeping, if she's able.

[NORA *comes in softly, and takes a bundle from under her shawl.*]

CATHLEEN *(spinning the wheel rapidly)*. What is it you have?

NORA. The young priest is after bringing them. It's a shirt and a plain stocking were got off a drowned man in Donegal.

[CATHLEEN *stops her wheel with a sudden movement, and leans out to listen.*]

NORA. We're to find out if it's Michael's they are, some time herself will be down looking by the sea.

CATHLEEN. How would they be Michael's, Nora. How would he go the length of that way to the far north?

NORA. The young priest says he's known the like of it. "If it's Michael's they are," says he, "you can tell herself he's got a clean burial by the grace of God, and if they're not his, let no one say a word about them, for she'll be getting her death," says he, "with crying and lamenting."

[*The door which* NORA *half closed is blown open by a gust of wind.*]

CATHLEEN (*looking out anxiously*). Did you ask him would he stop Bartley going this day with the horses to the Galway fair?

NORA. "I won't stop him," says he, "but let you not be afraid. Herself does be saying prayers half through the night, and the Almighty God won't leave her destitute," says he, "with no son living."

CATHLEEN. Is the sea bad by the white rocks, Nora?

NORA. Middling bad, God help us. There's a great roaring in the west, and it's worse it'll be getting when the tide's turned to the wind.

[*She goes over to the table with the bundle.*]

Shall I open it now?

CATHLEEN. Maybe she'd wake up on us, and come in before we'd done. (*Coming to the table.*) It's a long time we'll be, and the two of us crying.

NORA (*goes to the inner door and listens*). She's moving about on the bed. She'll be coming in a minute.

CATHLEEN. Give me the ladder, and I'll put them up in the turf-loft, the way she won't know of them at all, and maybe when the tide turns she'll be going down to see would he be floating from the east.

[*They put the ladder against the gable of the chimney;* CATHLEEN *goes up a few steps and hides the bundle in the turf-loft.* MAURYA *comes from the inner room.*]

MAURYA (*looking up at* CATHLEEN *and speaking querulously*). Isn't it turf enough you have for this day and evening?

CATHLEEN. There's a cake baking at the fire for a short space (*throwing down the turf*) and Bartley will want it when the tide turns if he goes to Connemara.

[NORA *picks up the turf and puts it round the pot-oven.*]

MAURYA (*sitting down on a stool at the fire*). He won't go this day with the wind rising from the south and west. He won't this day, for the young priest will stop him surely.

NORA. He'll not stop him, mother, and I heard Eamon Simon and Stephen Pheety and Colum Shawn saying he would go.

MAURYA. Where is he itself?

NORA. He went down to see would there be another boat sailing in the week, and I'm thinking it won't be long till he's here now, for the tide's turning at the green head, and the hooker's tacking from the east.

CATHLEEN. I hear some one passing the big stones.

NORA (looking out). He's coming now, and he in a hurry.

BARTLEY (comes in and looks round the room. Speaking sadly and quietly). Where is the bit of new rope, Cathleen, was bought in Connemara?

CATHLEEN (coming down). Give it to him, Nora; it's on a nail by the white boards. I hung it up this morning, for the pig with the black feet was eating it.

NORA (giving him a rope). Is that it, Bartley?

MAURYA. You'd do right to leave that rope, Bartley, hanging by the boards. (BARTLEY takes the rope.) It will be wanting in this place, I'm telling you, if Michael is washed up to-morrow morning, or the next morning, or any morning in the week, for it's a deep grave we'll make him by the grace of God.

BARTLEY (beginning to work with the rope). I've not halter the way I can ride down on the mare, and I must go now quickly. This is the one boat going for two weeks or beyond it, and the fair will be a good fair for horses I heard them saying below.

MAURYA. It's a hard thing they'll be saying below if the body is washed up and there's no man in it to make the coffin, and I after giving a big price for the finest white boards you'd find in Connemara.

[She looks round at the boards.]

BARTLEY. How would it be washed up, and we after looking each day for nine days, and a strong wind blowing a while back from the west and south?

MAURYA. If it wasn't found itself, that wind is raising the sea, and there was a star up against the moon, and it rising in the night. If it was a hundred horses, or a thousand horses you had itself, what is the price of a thousand horses against a son where there is one son only?

BARTLEY (working at the halter, to CATHLEEN). Let you go down each day, and see the sheep aren't jumping in on the rye, and if the jobber comes you can sell the pig with the black feet if there is a good price going.

MAURYA. How would the like of her get a good price for a pig?

BARTLEY (*to* CATHLEEN). If the west wind holds with the last bit of the moon let you and Nora get up weed enough for another cock for the kelp. It's hard set we'll be from this day with no one in it but one man to work.

MAURYA. It's hard set we'll be surely the day you're drownd'd with the rest. What way will I live and the girls with me, and I an old woman looking for the grave?

[BARTLEY *lays down the halter, takes off his old coat, and puts on a newer one of the same flannel.*]

BARTLEY (*to* NORA). Is she coming to the pier?

NORA (*looking out*). She's passing the green head and letting fall her sails.

BARTLEY (*getting his purse and tobacco*). I'll have half an hour to go down, and you'll see me coming again in two days, or in three days, or maybe in four days if the wind is bad.

MAURYA (*turning round to the fire, and putting her shawl over her head*). Isn't it a hard and cruel man won't hear a word from an old woman, and she holding him from the sea?

CATHLEEN. It's the life of a young man to be going on the sea, and who would listen to an old woman with one thing and she saying it over?

BARTLEY (*taking the halter*). I must go now quickly. I'll ride down on the red mare, and the gray pony 'll run behind me. . . . The blessing of God on you.

[*He goes out.*]

MAURYA (*crying out as he is in the door*). He's gone now, God spare us, and we'll not see him again. He's gone now, and when the black night is falling I'll have no son left me in the world.

CATHLEEN. Why wouldn't you give him your blessing and he looking round in the door? Isn't it sorrow enough is on every one in this house without your sending him out with an unlucky word behind him, and a hard word in his ear?

[MAURYA *takes up the tongs and begins raking the fire aimlessly without looking around.*]

NORA (*turning towards her*). You're taking away the turf from the cake.

CATHLEEN (*crying out*). The Son of God forgive us, Nora, we're after forgetting his bit of bread.

[*She comes over to the fire.*]

NORA. And it's destroyed he'll be going till dark night, and he after eating nothing since the sun went up.

CATHLEEN (*turning the cake out of the oven*). It's destroyed he'll be, surely. There's no sense left on any person in a house where an old woman will be talking for ever.

[MAURYA *sways herself on her stool.*]

CATHLEEN (*cutting off some of the bread and rolling it in a cloth; to* MAURYA). Let you go down now to the spring well and give him this and he passing. You'll see him then and the dark word will be broken, and you can say, "God speed you," the way he'll be easy in his mind.

MAURYA (*taking the bread*). Will I be in it as soon as himself?

CATHLEEN. If you go now quickly.

MAURYA (*standing up unsteadily*). It's hard set I am to walk.

CATHLEEN *Looking at her anxiously*). Give her the stick, Nora, or maybe she'll slip on the big stones.

NORA. What stick?

CATHLEEN. The stick Michael brought from Connemara.

MAURYA (*taking a stick* NORA *gives her*). In the big world the old people do be leaving things after them for their sons and children, but in this place it is the young men do be leaving things behind for them that do be old.

[*She goes out slowly.* NORA *goes over to the ladder.*]

CATHLEEN. Wait, Nora, maybe she'd turn back quickly. She's that sorry, God help her, you wouldn't know the thing she'd do.

NORA. Is she gone round by the bush?

CATHLEEN (*looking out*). She's gone now. Throw it down quickly, for the Lord knows when she'll be out of it again.

NORA (*getting the bundle from the loft*). The young priest said he'd be passing to-morrow, and we might go down and speak to him below if it's Michael's they are surely.

CATHLEEN (*taking the bundle*). Did he say what way they were found?

NORA (*coming down*). "There were two men," says he, "and they rowing round with poteen before the cocks crowed, and the oar of one of them caught the body, and they passing the black cliffs of the north."

CATHLEEN (*trying to open the bundle*). Give me a knife, Nora, the string's perished with the salt water, and there's a black knot on it you wouldn't loosen in a week.

NORA (*giving her a knife*). I've heard tell it was a long way to Donegal.

CATHLEEN (*cutting the string*). It is surely. There was a man in here a while ago—the man sold us that knife—and he said if you set off walking from the rocks beyond, it would be seven days you'd be in Donegal.

NORA. And what time would a man take, and he floating?

[*Cathleen opens the bundle and takes out a bit of a stocking. They look at them eagerly.*]

CATHLEEN *(in a low voice)*. The Lord spare us, Nora! isn't it a queer hard thing to say if it's his they are surely?

NORA. I'll get his shirt off the hook the way we can put the one flannel on the other. *(She looks through some clothes hanging in the corner.)* It's not with them, Cathleen, and where will it be?

CATHLEEN. I'm thinking Bartley put it on him in the morning, for his own shirt was heavy with the salt in it *(pointing to the corner)*. There's a bit of a sleeve was of the same stuff. Give me that and it will do.

[NORA *brings it to her and they compare the flannel.*]

CATHLEEN. It's the same stuff, Nora; but if it is itself aren't there great rolls of it in the shops of Galway, and isn't it many another man may have a shirt of it as well as Michael himself?

NORA *(who has taken up the stocking and counted the stitches, crying out)*. It's Michael, Cathleen, it's Michael; God spare his soul, and what will herself say when she hears this story, and Bartley on the sea?

CATHLEEN *(taking the stocking)*. It's a plain stocking.

NORA. It's the second one of the third pair I knitted, and I put up three score stitches, and I dropped four of them.

CATHLEEN *(counts the stitches)*. It's that number is in it *(crying out)*. Ah, Nora, isn't it a bitter thing to think of him floating that way to the far north, and no one to keen him but the black hags that do be flying on the sea?

NORA *(swinging herself round, and throwing out her arms on the clothes)*. And isn't it a pitiful thing when there is nothing left of a man who was a great rower and fisher, but a bit of an old shirt and a plain stocking?

CATHLEEN *(after an instant)*. Tell me is herself coming, Nora? I hear a little sound on the path.

NORA *(looking out)*. She is, Cathleen. she's coming up to the door.

CATHLEEN. Put these things away before she'll come in. Maybe it's easier she'll be after giving her blessing to Bartley, and we won't let on we've heard anything the time he's on the sea.

NORA *(helping CATHLEEN to close the bundle)*. We'll put them here in the corner.

[*They put them into a hole in the chimney corner.* CATHLEEN *goes back to the spinning-wheel.*]

NORA. Will she see it was crying I was?

CATHLEEN. Keep your back to the door the way the light'll not be on you.

[NORA *sits down at the chimney corner, with her back to the door.* MAURYA *comes in very slowly, without looking at the girls, and goes over to her stool at the other side of the fire. The cloth with the bread is still in her hand. The girls look at each other, and* NORA *points to the bundle of bread.*]

CATHLEEN (*after spinning for a moment*). You didn't give him his bit of bread?

[MAURYA *begins to keen softly, without turning round.*]

CATHLEEN. Did you see him riding down?

[MAURYA *goes on keening.*]

CATHLEEN (*a little impatiently*). God forgive you; isn't it a better thing to raise your voice and tell what you seen, than to be making lamentation for a thing that's done? Did you see Bartley, I'm saying to you.

MAURYA (*with a weak voice*). My heart's broken from this day.

CATHLEEN (*as before*). Did you see Bartley?

MAURYA. I seen the fearfulest thing.

CATHLEEN (*leaves her wheel and looks out*). God forgive you; he's riding the mare now over the green head, and the gray pony behind him.

MAURYA (*starts, so that her shawl falls back from her head and shows her white tossed hair. With a frightened voice*). The gray pony behind him.

CATHLEEN (*coming to the fire*). What is it ails you, at all?

MAURYA (*speaking very slowly*). I've seen the fearfulest thing any person has seen, since the day Bride Dara seen the dead man with the child in his arms.

CATHLEEN and NORA. Uah.

[*They crouch down in front of the old woman at the fire.*]

NORA. Tell us what it is you seen.

MAURYA. I went down to the spring well, and I stood there saying a prayer to myself. Then Bartley came along, and he riding on the red mare with the gray pony behind him. (*She puts up her hands, as if to hide something from her eyes.*) The Son of God spare us, Nora!

CATHLEEN. What is it you seen.

MAURYA. I seen Michael himself.

CATHLEEN (*speaking softly*). You did not, mother; It wasn't Michael you seen, for his body is after being found in the far north, and he's got a clean burial by the grace of God.

MAURYA (*a little defiantly*). I'm after seeing him this day, and he riding and galloping. Bartley came first on the red mare; and I tried to say "God speed you," but something choked the words in my throat. He went by quickly; and "the blessing of God on you," says he, and I could say nothing. I looked up then, and I crying, at the gray pony, and there was Michael upon it—with fine clothes on him, and new shoes on his feet.

CATHLEEN *(begins to keen)*. It's destroyed we are from this day. It's destroyed, surely.

NORA. Didn't the young priest say the Almighty God wouldn't leave her destitute with no son living?

MAURYA *(in a low voice, but clearly)*. It's little the like of him knows of the sea. . . . Bartley will be lost now, and let you call in Eamon and make me a good coffin out of the white boards, for I won't live after them. I've had a husband, and a husband's father, and six sons in this house—six fine men, though it was a hard birth I had with every one of them and they coming to the world—and some of them were found and some of them were not found, but they're gone now the lot of them. . . . There were Stephen, and Shawn, were lost in the great wind, and found after in the Bay of Gregory of the Golden Mouth, and carried up the two of them on the one plank, and in by that door.

[*She pauses for a moment, the girls start as if they heard something through the door that is half open behind them.*]

NORA *(in a whisper)*. Did you hear that, Cathleen? Did you hear a noise in the north-east?

CATHLEEN *(in a whisper)*. There's some one after crying out by the seashore.

MAURYA *(continues without hearing anything)*. There was Sheamus and his father, and his own father again, were lost in a dark night, and not a stick or sign was seen of them when the sun went up. There was Patch after was drowned out of a curagh that turned over. I was sitting here with Bartley, and he a baby, lying on my two knees, and I seen two women, and three women, and four women coming in, and they crossing themselves, and not saying a word. I looked out then, and there were men coming after them, and they holding a thing in the half of a red sail, and water dripping out of it—it was a dry day, Nora—and leaving a track to the door.

[*She pauses again with her hand stretched out towards the door. It opens softly and old women begin to come in, crossing themselves on the threshold, and kneeling down in front of the stage with red petticoats over their heads.*]

MAURYA *(half in a dream, to* CATHLEEN*)*. Is it Patch, or Michael, or what is it at all?

CATHLEEN. Michael is after being found in the far north, and when he is found there how could he be here in this place?

MAURYA. There does be a power of young men floating round in the sea, and what way would they know if it was Michael they had, or another man like him, for when a man is nine days in the sea, and the wind blowing, it's hard set his own mother would be to say what man was it.

CATHLEEN. It's Michael, God spare him, for they're after sending us a bit of his clothes from the far north.

[*She reaches out and hands Maurya the clothes that belonged to Michael. Maurya stands up slowly and takes them in her hands.* NORA *looks out.*]

NORA. They're carrying a thing among them and there's water dripping out of it and leaving a track by the big stones.

CATHLEEN (*in a whisper to the women who have come in*). Is it Bartley it is?

ONE OF THE WOMEN. It is surely, God rest his soul.

[*Two younger* WOMEN *come in and pull out the table. Then men carry in the body of* BARTLEY, *laid on a plank, with a bit of a sail over it, and lay it on the table.*]

CATHLEEN (*to the women, as they are doing so*). What way was he drowned?

ONE OF THE WOMEN. The gray pony knocked him into the sea, and he was washed out where there is a great surf on the white rocks.

[MAURYA *has gone over and knelt down at the head of the table. The women are keening softly and swaying themselves with a slow movement.* CATHLEEN *and* NORA *kneel at the other end of the table. The* MEN *kneel near the door.*]

MAURYA (*raising her head and speaking as if she did not see the people around her*). They're all gone now, and there isn't anything more the sea can do to me. . . . I'll have no call now to be up crying and praying when the wind breaks from the south, and you can hear the surf is in the east, and the surf is in the west, making a great stir with the two noises, and they hitting one on the other. I'll have no call now to be going down and getting Holy Water in the dark nights after Samhain, and I won't care what way the sea is when the other women will be keening. (*To* NORA.) Give me the Holy Water, Nora, there's a small sup still on the dresser.

[NORA *gives it to her.*]

MAURYA (*drops Michael's clothes across* BARTLEY'S *feet, and sprinkles the Holy Water over him*). It isn't that I haven't prayed for you, Bartley, to the Almighty God. It isn't that I haven't said prayers in the dark night till you wouldn't know what I'ld be saying; but it's a great rest I'll have now, and great sleeping in the long nights after Samhain, if it's only a bit of wet flour we do have to eat, and maybe a fish that would be stinking.

[*She kneels down again, crossing herself, and saying prayers under her breath.*]

CATHLEEN (*to an old man*). Maybe yourself and Eamon would make a coffin when the sun rises. We have fine white boards herself bought, God help her, thinking Michael would be found, and I have a new cake you can eat while you'll be working.

THE OLD MAN (*looking at the boards*). Are there nails with them?

CATHLEEN. There are not, Colum; we didn't think of the nails.

ANOTHER MAN. It's a great wonder she wouldn't think of the nails, and all the coffins she's seen made already.

CATHLEEN. It's getting old she is, and broken.

[MAURYA *stands up again very slowly and spreads out the pieces of Michael's clothes beside the body, sprinkling them with the last of the Holy Water.*]

NORA (*in a whisper to* CATHLEEN). She's quiet now and easy; but the day Michael was drowned you could hear her crying out from this to the spring well. It's fonder she was of Michael, and would any one have thought that?

CATHLEEN (*slowly and clearly*). An old woman will be soon tired with anything she will do, and isn't it nine days herself is after crying and keening, and making great sorrow in the house?

MAURYA (*puts the empty cup mouth downwards on the table, and lays her hands together on* BARTLEY's *feet*). They're all together this time, and the end is come. May the Almighty God have mercy on Bartley's soul, and on Michael's soul, and on the souls of Sheamus and Patch, and Stephen and Shawn (*bending her head*); and may He have mercy on my soul, Nora, and on the soul of every one is left living in the world.

[*She pauses, and the keen rises a little more loudly from the women, then sinks away.*]

MAURYA (*continuing*). Michael has a clean burial in the far north, by the grace of the Almighty God. Bartley will have a fine coffin out of the white boards, and a deep grave surely. What more can we want than that? No man at all can be living for ever, and we must be satisfied.

[*She kneels down again and the curtain falls slowly.*]

PRELUDE

Still south I went and west and south again,
Through Wicklow from the morning till the night,
And far from cities, and the sites of men,
Lived with the sunshine and the moon's delight.

I knew the stars, the flowers, and the birds,
The grey and wintry sides of many glens,
And did but half remember human words,
In converse with the mountains, moors, and fens.

ON AN ANNIVERSARY
AFTER READING THE DATES IN A BOOK OF LYRICS

With Fifteen-ninety or Sixteen-sixteen
We end Cervantes, Marot, Nashe or Green:
Then Sixteen-thirteen till two score and nine,
Is Crashaw's niche, that honey-lipped divine.
And so when all my little work is done
They'll say I came in Eighteen-seventy-one,
And died in Dublin. . . . What year will they write
For my poor passage to the stall of Night?

QUEENS

Seven dog-days we let pass
Naming Queens in Glenmacnass,
All the rare and royal names
Wormy sheepskin yet retains,
Etain, Helen, Maeve, and Fand,
Golden Deirdre's tender hand,
Bert, the big-foot, sung by Villon,
Cassandra, Ronsard found in Lyon.
Queens of Sheba, Meath and Connaught,
Coifed with crown, or gaudy bonnet,
Queens whose finger once did stir men,

Queens were eaten of fleas and vermin,
Queens men drew like Monna Lisa,
Or slew with drugs in Rome and Pisa,
We named Lucrezia Crivelli,
And Titian's lady with amber belly,
Queens acquainted in learned sin,
Jane of Jewry's slender shin:
Queens who cut the bogs of Glanna,
Judith of Scripture, and Gloriana,
Queens who wasted the East by proxy,
Or drove the ass-cart, a tinker's doxy,
Yet these are rotten—I ask their pardon—
And we've the sun on rock and garden,
These are rotten, so you're the Queen
Of all are living, or have been.

THE PASSING OF THE SHEE
AFTER LOOKING AT ONE OF A.E.'S PICTURES

Adieu, sweet Angus, Maeve and Fand,
Ye plumed yet skinny Shee,
That poets played with hand in hand
To learn their ecstasy.

We'll search in Red Dan Sally's ditch,
And drink in Tubber fair,
Or poach with Red Dan Philly's bitch
The badger and the hare.

ON AN ISLAND

You've plucked a curlew, drawn a hen,
Washed the shirts of seven men,
You've stuffed my pillow, stretched the sheet,
And filled the pan to wash your feet,
You've cooped the pullets, wound the clock,
And rinsed the young men's drinking crock;

And now we'll dance to jigs and reels,
Nailed boots chasing girls' naked heels,
Until your father'll start to snore,
And Jude, now you're married, will stretch on the floor.

IS IT A MONTH

Is it a month since I and you
In the starlight of Glen Dubh
Stretched beneath a hazel bough
Kissed from ear and throat to brow,
Since your fingers, neck, and chin
Made the bars that fenced me in,
Till Paradise seemed but a wreck
Near your bosom, brow, and neck
And stars grew wilder, growing wise,
In the splendour of your eyes!
Since the weasel wandered near
Whilst we kissed from ear to ear
And the wet and withered leaves
Blew about your cap and sleeves,
Till the moon sank tired through the ledge
Of the wet and windy hedge?
And we took the starry lane
Back to Dublin town again.

BEG-INNISH

Bring Kateen-beug and Maurya Jude
To dance in Beg-Innish,
And when the lads (they're in Dunquin)
Have sold their crabs and fish,
Wave fawny shawls and call them in,
And call the little girls who spin,
And seven weavers from Dunquin,
To dance in Beg-Innish.

I'll play you jigs, and Maurice Kean,
Where nets are laid to dry,
I've silken strings would draw a dance
From girls are lame or shy;
Four strings I've brought from Spain and France
To make your long men skip and prance,
Till stars look out to see the dance
Where nets are laid to dry.

We'll have no priest or peeler in
To dance in Beg-Innish;
But we'll have drink from M'riarty Jim
Rowed round while gannets fish,
A keg with porter to the brim,
That every lad may have his whim,
Till we up sails with M'riarty Jim
And sail from Beg-Innish.

TO THE OAKS OF GLENCREE

My arms are round you, and I lean
Against you, while the lark
Sings over us, and golden lights, and green
Shadows are on your bark.

There'll come a season when you'll stretch
Black boards to cover me:
Then in Mount Jerome I will lie, poor wretch,
With worms eternally.

THE CURSE
TO A SISTER OF AN ENEMY OF THE AUTHOR'S
WHO DISAPPROVED OF "THE PLAYBOY"

Lord, confound this surly sister,
Blight her brow with blotch and blister,

Cramp her larynx, lung, and liver,
In her guts a galling give her.
Let her live to earn her dinners
In Mountjoy with seedy sinners:
Lord, this judgment quickly bring,
And I'm your servant, J. M. Synge.

IN KERRY

We heard the thrushes by the shore and sea,
And saw the golden stars' nativity,
Then round we went the lane by Thomas Flynn,
Across the church where bones lie out and in;
And there I asked beneath a lonely cloud
Of strange delight, with one bird singing loud,
What change you'd wrought in graveyard, rock and sea,
This new wild paradise to wake for me . . .
Yet knew no more than knew these merry sins
Had built this stack of thigh-bones, jaws and shins.

ON A BIRTHDAY

Friend of Ronsard, Nashe, and Beaumont,
Lark of Ulster, Meath and Thomond,
Heard from Smyrna and Sahara
To the surf of Connemara,
Lark of April, June, and May,
Sing loudly this my Lady-day.

A QUESTION

I asked if I got sick and died, would you
With my black funeral go walking too,
If you'd stand close to hear them talk or pray
While I'm let down in that steep bank of clay.

And, No, you said, for if you saw a crew
Of living idiots, pressing round that new
Oak coffin—they alive, I dead beneath
That board,—you'd rave and rend them with your teeth.

Further Readings on John Millington Synge

Bibliography

Levitt, Paul. *John Millington Synge: A Bibliography of Published Criticism.* New York: Barnes & Noble, 1973.
Mikhail, E. H. *John Millington Synge: A Bibliography of Criticism.* Totowa, N.J.: Rowman and Littlefield, 1975.
Thornton, Weldon. "J. M. Synge." In *Anglo-Irish Literature: A Review of Research,* ed. R. J. Finneran, pp. 315–65. New York: Modern Language Association, 1976.

Selected Works

Collected Works. Edited by Robin Skelton and Ann Saddlemyer. 4 vols. London: Oxford University Press, 1962–1968. Reprinted, Washington, D.C.: Catholic University Press, 1983.
Letters to Molly: John Millington Synge to Máire O'Neill, 1906–1909. Edited by Ann Saddlemyer. Cambridge: Harvard University Press, 1971.

Biography and Criticism

Benson, Eugene. *J. M. Synge.* London: Macmillan, 1983.
Bushrui, Suheil B., ed. *Sunshine and the Moon's Delight: A Centenary Tribute to John Millington Synge, 1871–1909.* Gerrards Cross, England: Colin Smythe; New York: Barnes & Noble, 1972.
Corkery, Daniel. *Synge and Anglo-Irish Literature: A Study.* Cork: Cork University Press; New York: Longmans Green, 1931. Reprinted, Cork: Mercier Books. 1966.
Coxhead, Elizabeth. *J. M. Synge and Lady Gregory.* London and New York: Longmans, 1962.
Gerstenberger, Donna. *John Millington Synge.* New York: Twayne, 1964.
Greene, David Herbert, and Stephens, Edward M. *J. M. Synge, 1871–1909.* New York: Macmillan, 1959.
Grene, Nicholas. *Synge: A Critical Interpretation of the Plays.* London: Macmillan, 1975.
Harmon, Maurice, ed. *J. M. Synge Centenary Papers, 1971.* Dublin: Dolmen, 1972.

Johnson, Toni O'Brien. *Synge: The Medieval and the Grotesque.* Gerrards Cross, England: Colin Smythe: New York: Barnes & Noble, 1982.

Johnston, Denis. *John Millington Synge.* New York: Columbia University Press, 1965.

Kiberd, Declan. *Synge and the Irish Language.* Totowa, N.J.: Rowman and Littlefield, 1979.

Kilroy, James. *The "Playboy" Riots.* Dublin: Dolmen, 1971.

King, Mary C. *The Drama of J. M. Synge.* Syracuse, N.Y.: Syracuse University Press, 1986.

Price, Alan Frederick. *Synge and Anglo-Irish Drama.* London: Methuen, 1961.

Saddlemyer, Ann. *J. M. Synge and Modern Comedy.* Dublin: Dolmen Press, 1968.

Skelton, Robin. *J. M. Synge.* Lewisburg, Pa.: Bucknell University Press, 1972.

———. *J. M. Synge and His World.* New York: Viking, 1971.

———. *The Writings of J. M. Synge.* London: Thames & Hudson; Indianapolis: Bobbs Merrill, 1971.

Thornton, Weldon. *J. M. Synge and the Western Mind.* New York: Harper and Row, 1979.

Whitaker, Thomas R., ed. *Twentieth Century Interpretations of "The Playboy of the Western World."* Englewood Cliffs, N.J.: Prentice-Hall. 1969.

GEORGE MOORE
(1852–1933)

George Moore was one of the most cosmopolitan Irish authors of any generation. Born in County Mayo to landed gentry, he was equally at home in Paris, where he studied art from 1873 to 1880, and in London, where he was something of a literary lion. From 1901 to 1911 he resided in Dublin, where he was active in the Irish literary revival, and where he served as an advisor and sometime collaborator of Yeats. His memoir of the years in Dublin, the three-volumed *Hail and Farewell* (*Ave* [1911]; *Salve* [1912]; and *Vale* [1914]), is one of the most personal (if mordant) retellings of those glory years. Moore achieved distinction as novelist, short-story writer, dramatist, essayist, art critic, and poet. His best-known (if not best) work, *Esther Waters* (1894), is set in England. A symbolic novel set in rural Ireland, *The Lake*, has been praised by critic John V. Kelleher as the finest of all Irish novels excepting *Ulysses*. As a dramatist, he was a disciple of Ibsen in his *Strike at Arlingford* (1893). Yet he also co-wrote *Diarmuid and Grania* with Yeats in 1901.

"Julia Cahill's Curse" comes from Moore's collection *Untilled Field* (1903), based on perceptions of a homeland revisited in middle age. In his own words, the stories were written. . . "out of no desire of self-expression, but in the hope of furnishing the young Irish of the future with models." The collection was translated into the Irish language and published in 1902, with the thought that the English originals would be burned. But when sales for the Irish language volume were disappointing, *The Untilled Field* was issued in its present form. In the collection, Moore draws from such Continental writers as Dostoevski, Zola, and Turgenev, and anticipates an Irish one: James Joyce.

191

JULIA CAHILL'S CURSE

"And what has become of Margaret?"

"Ah, didn't her mother send her to America as soon as the baby was born? Once a woman is waked here she has to go. Hadn't Julia to go in the end, and she the only one that ever said she didn't mind the priest?"

"Julia who?" said I.

"Julia Cahill."

The name struck my fancy, and I asked the driver to tell me her story.

"Wasn't it Father Madden who had her put out of the parish, but she put her curse on it, and it's on it to this day."

"Do you believe in curses?"

"Bedad I do, sir. It's a terrible thing to put a curse on a man, and the curse that Julia put on Father Madden's parish was a bad one, the divil a worse. The sun was up at the time, and she on the hilltop raising both her hands. And the curse she put on the parish was that every year a roof must fall in and a family go to America. That was the curse, your honour, and every word of it has come true. You'll see for yourself as soon as we cross the mearing."

"And what became of Julia's baby?"

"I never heard she had one, sir."

He flicked his horse pensively with his whip, and it seemed to me that the disbelief I had expressed in the power of the curse disinclined him for further conversation.

"But," I said, "who is Julia Cahill, and how did she get the power to put a curse upon the village?"

"Didn't she go into the mountains every night to meet the fairies, and who else could've given her the power to put a curse on the village?"

"But she couldn't walk so far in one evening."

"Them that's in league with the fairies can walk that far and as much farther in an evening, your honour. A shepherd saw her; and you'll see the ruins of the cabins for yourself as soon as we cross the mearing, and I'll show you the cabin of the blind woman that Julia lived with before she went away."

"And how long is it since she went?"

"About twenty year, and there hasn't been a girl the like of her in these parts since. I was only a gossoon at the time, but I've heard tell she was as tall as I'm myself, and as straight as a poplar. She walked with a little swing in her walk, so that all the boys used to be looking after her, and she had fine black eyes, sir, and she was nearly always laughing. Father Madden had just come to the parish; and there was courting in these parts then, for aren't we the same as other people— we'd like to go out with a girl well enough if it was the custom of the country. Father Madden put down the ball alley because he said the boys stayed there instead of going into Mass, and he put down the cross-road dances because he said dancing was the cause of many a bastard, and he wanted none in his parish. Now there was no dancer like Julia; the boys used to gather about to see her dance, and who ever walked with her under the hedges in the summer could never think about another woman. The village was cracked about her. There was fighting, so I suppose the priest was right: he had to get rid of her. But I think he mightn't have been as hard on her as he was.

"One evening he went down to the house. Julia's people were well-to-do people, they kept a grocery-store in the village; and when he came into the shop who should be there but the richest farmer in the country, Michael Moran by name, trying to get Julia for his wife. He didn't go straight to Julia, and that's what swept him. There are two counters in that shop, and Julia was at the one on the left hand as you go in. And many's the pound she had made for her parents at that counter. Michael Moran says to the father, 'Now, what fortune are you going to give with Julia?' And the father says there was many a man who would take her without any; and that's how they spoke, and Julia listening quitely all the while at the opposite counter. For Michael didn't know what a spirited girl she was, but went on arguing till he got the father to say fifty pounds, and thinking he had got him so far he said, 'I'll never drop a flap to her unless you give the two heifers.' Julia never said a word, she just sat listening. It was then that the priest came in. And over he goes to Julia; 'And now,' says he, 'aren't you proud to hear that you'll have such a fine fortune, and it's I that'll be glad to see you married, for I can't have any more of your goings-on in my parish. You're the encouragement of the dancing and courting here; but I'm going to put an end to it.' Julia didn't answer a word, and he went over to them that were arguing about the sixty pounds. 'Now why not make it fifty-five?' says he. So the father agreed to that since the priest had said it. And all three of them thought the marriage was settled. 'Now what will you be taking, Father Tom?' says Cahill, 'and you, Michael?' Sorra one of them thought of asking her if she was pleased with Michael; but little did they know what was passing in her mind, and when they came over to the counter to tell her what they had settled, she said, 'Well, I've just been listening to you, and 'tis well for you to be wasting your time talking about me,' and she tossed her head, saying she would just pick the boy out of the parish that pleased her best. And what angered the priest most of all was her way of saying it—that the boy that would marry her would be marrying herself and not the money that would be paid when the book was signed or when the first baby was born. Now it was agin girls marrying according to their fancy that Father Madden had set himself. He had said in his sermon the Sunday before that young people shouldn't be allowed out by themselves at all, but that the parents should make up the marriages for them. And he went fairly wild when Julia told him the example she was going to set. He tried to keep his temper, sir, but it was getting the better of him all the while, and Julia said, 'My boy isn't in the parish now, but maybe he is on his way here, and he may be here to-morrow or the next day.' And when Julia's father heard her speak like that he knew that no one would turn her from what she was saying, and he said, 'Michael Moran, my good man, you may go your way: you'll never get her.' Then he went back to hear what Julia was saying to the priest, but it was the priest that was talking. 'Do you think,' says he, 'I am going to let you go on turning the head of every boy in the parish? Do you think, says he, I'm going to see you gallavanting with one and then with the other? Do you think I'm going to see fighting and quarrelling for your like? Do you think I'm going to hear stories like I heard last week about poor Patsy Carey, who has gone out of his mind, they say, on account of your treatment? No,' says he, 'I'll have no more of that. I'll have you out of my parish, or I'll have you married.' Julia didn't answer the priest, she tossed her head, and went on making up parcels of tea and sugar and getting the steps and taking down candles, though she didn't want them, just to show the priest that she didn't mind what he was saying. And all the while her father trembling, not knowing what would happen, for the priest had a big stick, and there was no saying that he wouldn't strike her. Cahill tried to quiet the priest, he promising him that Julia shouldn't go out any more in the evenings, and bedad, sir, she was out the same evening with a young man and the priest saw them, and the next evening she was out with another and the priest saw them, nor was she minded at the end of the month to marry any of them. Then the priest went down to the shop to speak to her a second time, and he went down again a third time, though what he said the third time no one knows, no one being there at the time. And next Sunday he spoke out, saying that a disobedient daughter would have the worst devil in hell to attend on her. I've heard tell that he called her the evil spirit that set men mad. But most of the people that were there are dead or gone to America, and no one rightly knows what he did say, only that the words came pouring out of his mouth, and the people when they saw Julia crossed themselves, and even the boys who were most mad after Julia were afraid to speak to her. Cahill had to put her out."

"Do you mean to say that the father put his daughter out?"

"Sure, didn't the priest threaten to turn him into a rabbit if he didn't, and no one in the parish would speak to Julia, they were so afraid of Father Madden, and if it hadn't been for the blind woman that I was speaking about a while ago, sir it is to the Poor House she'd have to go. The blind woman has a little cabin at the edge of the bog— I'll point it out to you, sir; we do be passing it by—and she was with the blind woman for nearly two years disowned by her own father. Her clothes wore out, but she was as beautiful without them as with them. The boys were told not to look back, but sure they couldn't help it.

"Ah, it was a long while before Father Madden could get shut of her. The blind woman said she wouldn't see Julia thrown out on the road-side, and she was as good as her word for wellnigh two years, till Julia went to America, so some do be saying, sir, whilst others do be saying she joined the fairies. But 'tis for sure, sir, that the day she left the parish Pat Quinn heard a knocking at his window and somebody asking if he would lend his cart to go to the railway station. Pat was a heavy sleeper and he didn't get up, and it is thought that it was Julia who wanted Pat's cart to take her to the station; it's a good ten mile; but she got there all the same!"

"You said something about a curse?"

"Yes, sir. You'll see the hill presently. A man who was taking some sheep to the fair saw her there. The sun was just getting up and he saw her cursing the village, raising both her hands, sir, up to the sun, and since that curse was spoken every year a roof has fallen in, sometimes two or three."

I could see he believed the story, and for the moment I, too, believed in an outcast Venus becoming the evil spirit of a village that would not accept her as divine.

"Look, sir, the woman coming down the road is Bridget Coyne. And that's her house," he said, and we passed a house built of loose stones without mortar, but a little better than the mud cabins I had seen in Father MacTurnan's parish.

"And now, sir, you will see the loneliest parish in Ireland."

And I noticed that though the land was good, there seemed to be few people on it, and what was more significant than the untilled fields were the ruins for they were not the cold ruins of twenty, or thirty, or forty years ago when the people were evicted and their tillage turned into pasture—the ruins I saw were the ruins of cabins that had been lately abandoned, and I said:

"It wasn't the landlord who evicted these people."

"Ah, it's the landlord who would be glad to have them back, but there's no getting them back. Everyone here will have to go, and 'tis said that the priest will say Mass in an empty chapel, sorra a one will be there but Bridget, and she'll be the last he'll give communion to. It's said, your honour, that Julia has been seen in America, and I'm going there this autumn. You may be sure I'll keep a lookout for her."

"But all this is twenty years ago. You won't know her. A woman changes a good deal in twenty years."

"There will be no change in her, your honour. Sure hasn't she been with the fairies?"

Further Readings on George Moore

Bibliography

English Literature [Formerly, *Fiction*] *in Transition.* Annual bibliography, 1959–.

Gerber, Helmut E. "George Moore." In *Anglo-Irish Literature: A Review of Research,* ed. R. J. Finneran, pp. 138–66. New York: Modern Language Association, 1976.

Gilcher, Edwin. *A Bibliography of the Writings of George Moore.* DeKalb, Ill.: Northern Illinois University Press, 1970.

Selected Works

Collected Works. Carra Edition. 22 vols. New York: Boni and Liveright, 1922–1926.

Diarmuid and Grania. With W. B. Yeats. Edited by A. Farrow. Chicago: DePaul University Press, 1974.

Esther Waters. London: W. Scott, 1894. Reprinted, London and New York: Everyman's Library, 1983.

Hale and Farewell (Ave [1911]; *Salve* [1912]; *Valve* [1914]). London: Heinemann, 1914; reprint. Atlantic Highlands: Humanities Press, 1980.

In Minor Keys: The Uncollected Short Stories. Edited by D. Eakin and H. Gerber. Syracuse, N.Y.: Syracuse University Press, 1985.

The Lake. London: Heinemann, 1905. Reprinted, Gerrards Cross, England: Colin Smythe; Atlantic Highlands, N.J.: Humanities Press, 1981.
The Untilled Field. London: T. F. Unwin, 1903. Reprinted, Freeport, N.Y.: Books for Libraries, 1970.
The Works of George Moore. Uniform Edition. 20 vols. London: Heinemann, 1924–1933.

Biography and Criticism

Brown, Malcolm. *George Moore: A Reconsideration.* Seattle: University of Washington Press, 1955.
Dunleavy, Janet Egleson. *George Moore: The Artist's Vision, The Storyteller's Art.* Lewisburg, Pa.: Bucknell, 1973.
———, ed. *George Moore in Perspective.* Naas, Ireland: Malton Books; Totowa, N.J.: Barnes and Noble Books, 1984.
Farrow, Anthony. *George Moore.* Boston: Twayne, 1978.
Hone, Joseph. *The Life of George Moore.* New York: Macmillan, 1936.
Hughes, Douglas A., ed. *The Man of Wax: Critical Essays on George Moore.* New York: New York University Press, 1971.
Jeffares, A. Norman. *George Moore.* London: Longmans, 1965.

OLIVER ST. JOHN GOGARTY
(1878–1957)

Like Socrates, Oliver St. John Gogarty is better remembered today for what others wrote of him than for what he wrote himself. He was the model for the character of Buck Mulligan in James Joyce's *Ulysses,* and his name was borrowed for the protagonist of George Moore's *The Lake* (1905). In life Gogarty was a colorful conversationalist and wit whose words survive in a half-dozen memoirs. Gogarty was also a man of action and athletic prowess, with great skills as a swimmer and cyclist; when his life was threatened in the Civil War, he made a daring escape by swimming the Liffey. After the signing of the Anglo-Irish Treaty in 1922, Gogarty was appointed to the Free State Senate, later becoming a bitter opponent of the Republican leadership, especially of Eamon de Valera. By profession Gogarty was a medical doctor, but his writing output was large, diverse, and distinguished. He wrote dramas in youth, novels in maturity, and poetry all his life, as well as lively volumes of memoirs and autobiography. Gogarty's poetry has little in common with the Eliot/Pound-inspired metaphysical taste of many of his contemporaries but harks back instead to Elizabethan and classical models. After losing a libel suit over his memoir, *As I was Going Down Sackville Street,* Gogarty emigrated to the United States in 1939, where he publishing much more prose in the last two decades of his life.

His best-known poem, "Ringsend," is an ironic response to reading Leo Tolstoy (or Tolstoi), the Russian novelist who recommended spiritual renewal through a peasant-like rejection of middle-class values and comforts. (Ringsend is a neighborhood south and east of Dublin, adjacent to the harbor.)

198

The title of Gogarty's memoir *As I Was Going Down Sackville Street* is taken from a traditional ballad. Sackville Street, now called O'Connell Street, is Dublin's principal commercial thoroughfare. A revised version published after Gogarty's loss of the libel suit was retitled *As I Was Walking Down Sackville Street*.

RINGSEND
AFTER READING TOLSTOI

I will live in Ringsend
With a red-headed whore,
And the fan-light gone in
Where it lights the hall-door;
And listen each night
For her querulous shout,
As at last she streels in
And the pubs empty out.
To soothe that wild breast
With my old-fangled songs,
Till she feels it redressed
From inordinate wrongs,
Imagined, outrageous,
Preposterous wrongs,
Till peace at last comes,
Shall be all I will do,
Where the little lamp blooms
Like a rose in the stew;
And up the back-garden
The sound comes to me
Of the lapsing, unsoilable,
Whispering sea.

THE CRAB TREE

Here is the crab tree,
Firm and erect,
In spite of the thin soil,
In spite of neglect.

The twisted root grapples
For sap with the rock,
And draws the hard juice
To the succulent top:
Here are wild apples,
Here's a tart crop!

No outlandish grafting
That ever grew soft
In a sweet air of Persia,
Or safe Roman croft;
Unsheltered by steading,
Rock-rooted and grown,
A great tree of Erin,
It stands up alone,
A forest tree spreading
Where forests are gone.

Of all who pass by it
How few in it see
A westering remnant
Of days when Lough Neagh
Flowed up the long dingles
Its blossom had lit,
Old days of glory
Time cannot repeat;
And therefore it mingles
The bitter and sweet.

It takes from the West Wind
The thrust of the main;
It makes from the tension
Of sky and of plain,
Of what clay enacted,
Of living alarm,
A vitalised symbol
Of earth and of storm,
Of Chaos contracted
To intricate form.

Unbreakable wrestler!
What sapling or herb

Has core of such sweetness
And fruit so acerb?
So grim a transmitter
Of life through mishap,
That one wonders whether
If that in the sap,
Is sweet or is bitter
Which makes it stand up.

From *AS I WAS GOING DOWN SACKVILLE STREET*
ON SYNGE, GREGORY, AND JOYCE

Then, farther up the town in Camden Street, Synge would be sitting watching his rehearsals. He sat silent, holding his stick between his knees, his chin resting on his hands. He spoke seldom. When he did, the voice came in a short rush, as if he wished to get the talk over as soon as possible. A dour, but not a forbidding man. Had he been less competent it might have been said of him on account of his self-absorption that he "stood aloof from other minds. In impotence of fancied power." He never relaxed his mind from its burden.

I asked him if he did not intend his *Playboy* for a satire to show up, for one thing, how lifeless and inert was the country where a man could be hailed as a hero for doing something kinetic even though it were a murder, and how ineffectual, for, as the event showed, even that had not been committed. He gave me a short glance and looked straight in front of himself, weighing me up and thinking how hard it would be to get the public to appreciate his play as a work of art, when one who should know better was reading analogies and satire into it already. He shook my question off with a shake of his head.

We were nearer to poetic drama than we shall ever be again. Intellectual life was astir. Joyce and I used to go to see how the actors were getting on with John Elwood, a medical student, who enjoyed the licence allowed to medical students by the tolerant goodwill of a people to whom Medicine with its traffic in Life and Death had something of the mysterious and magical about it. To be a medical student's pal by virtue of the glamour that surrounded a student of medicine was almost a profession in itself. Joyce was the best example of a medical student's pal Dublin produced, or rather the best example of the type, extinct since the Middle Ages, of a Goliard, a wandering scholar. The theatre off Camden Street was approached through a narrow passage. John Elwood got so drunk one night that he lamented that he could not even see the ladies stepping over him as they came out.

"Synge looks like a fellow who would sip a pint."

"John," I said, "if you had done more sipping and less swallowing you would not have got us all kicked out."

Joyce knew far better than I what was in the air, and what was likely to be the future of the theatre in Ireland.

Who can measure how great was its loss when Lady Gregory gave him the cold shoulder? Maybe her much-announced search for talent did not contemplate the talent latent in medical students' pals or wandering minstrels. After an unsuccessful interview he met us in a "snug," where, very solemnly, with his high, well-stocked forehead bulging over his nose, he recited, waving his finger slowly:

> There was a kind Lady called Gregory,
> Said, "Come to me poets in beggery."
> But found her imprudence
> When thousands of students
> Cried, "All we are in that catégory"!

The elision of "who" before the "Said" in the second line is a parody on the synthetic folk speech in Synge's *Playboy*. And the strained "catégory" the beginning of his own experiment with words. She had no room for playboys except on the stage. . . . So Ulysses had to strike out for himself. Dublin's Dante had to find a way out of his own Inferno. But he had lost the key. James Augustine Joyce slipped politely from the snug with an "Excuse me!"

"Whist! He's gone to put it all down!"

"Put what down?"

"Put *us* down. A chiel's among us takin' notes. And, faith, he'll print it."

Now, that was a new aspect of James Augustine. I was too unsophisticated to know that even outside Lady Gregory's presence, notes made of those contemporary with the growing "Movement" would have a sale later on, and even an historical interest.

Further Readings on Oliver St. John Gogarty

Bibliography

Carens, James F. "Oliver St. John Gogarty." In *Anglo-Irish Literature: A Review of Research,* ed. R. J. Finneran, pp. 452–59. New York: Modern Language Association, 1976.

Selected Works

As I Was Going Down Sackville Street. London: Rich & Cowan; New York: Reynal & Hitchcock, 1937; New York: Harvest Books of Harcourt Brace, 1965. Rev. ed., *As I Was Walking Down Sackville Street.* London: Rich & Cowan, 1939.
Blight, the Tragedy of Dublin. With Joseph O'Connor (under the pseudonyms Alpha and Omega). Dublin: Talbot, 1971. Reprinted in *The Plays of Oliver St. John Gogarty,* ed. J. F. Carens. Newark, Del.: Proscenium, 1972.
Collected Poems. Prefaces by W. B. Yeats, "AE," and Horace Reynolds. London: Constable, 1951; New York & Toronto: Longmans, 1952; New York: Devin-Adair, 1954.
I Follow St. Patrick. London: Rich & Cowan; New York: Reynal & Hitchcock, 1938. Rev. ed. London: Constable; New York: Longmans, 1939.
Tumbling in the Hay: A Novel. London: Constable; New York: Reynal & Hitchcock, 1939.
William Butler Yeats: A Memoir. Dublin: Dolmen, 1963.

Biography and Criticism

Carens, James F. *Surpassing Wit: Oliver St. John Gogarty, His Poetry and His Prose.* Dublin: Gill and Macmillan, 1979.
Jeffares, A. Norman. "Oliver St. John Gogarty." *Proceedings of the British Academy,* 46: 73–98.
Lyons, J. B. *Oliver St. John Gogarty.* Lewisburg, Pa.: Bucknell University Press, 1976.
O'Connor, Ulick. *The Times I've Seen: Oliver St. John Gogarty. A Biography.* New York: Obolensky, 1963; London: Cape, 1964.

PADRAIC COLUM
(1881–1972)

Padraic Colum had such a long and diverse career that he might easily be mistaken for three or four different writers instead of only one. In the course of more than sixty years he published sixty-one books, in addition to hundreds of essays and articles. Although he is best remembered today as a poet, he achieved distinction in all genres. Much of his poetry celebrates the pastoralism of his home in the Irish midlands, but his later work, especially in his last volume, *Images of Departure* (1969), has an affecting spareness more characteristic of late-century poets. As a young man, he appeared to be among the most promising playwrights at the Abbey Theatre, especially with *The Land* (1905), *The Fiddler's House* (1907), and *Thomas Muskerry* (1910). After emigrating to the United States in 1914, he made his living largely as a writer of children's books. In many of these books he reinterpreted classical literature without ever being condescending to his youthful readers.

Colum was so highly regarded as a folklorist that he was invited by the legislature of the Territory of Hawaii to collect a volume of folklore of those islands. His two volumes of biography show Colum's great range; his *Ourselves Alone* (1959), is a thoroughly researched study of Arthur Griffith and the beginnings of the Irish Free State, while *Our Friend, James Joyce* (1958), done with wife Mary Colum, is light and anecdotal. With all this, there was still time for prose fiction, including two historical novels, *Castle Conquer* (1923) and *The Flying Swans* (1957), and a volume of short stories. In the last decade of his life he returned to the dramatic form, writing a series of Noh plays in the style of the poetic theater of Japan. During much of his later career, Colum became a familiar figure on the

American literary scene, attending conferences, contributing to journals, and the like. As he lived until the time of the Vietnam War, he was by all odds the longest surviving writer of the Irish Renaissance—a one-time intimate of Yeats, Lady Gregory, and Joyce who yet outlived Brendan Behan!

"The Plougher" is probably Colum's single best-known poem, representative of much of his earlier output. His "Book of Kells" shows his understanding of the continuity of Irish artistry. The actual Book of Kells is the greatest example of the art of Irish illuminated manuscripts from the early Christian period, A.D. 700–1100. It is named for Kells, County Meath, site of the monastery where the book was compiled. "In Saint Stephen's Green" and "Expecting No One" were published when the poet was eighty-eight years old.

Colum reportedly pronounced his first name "PAW-derig," but the name is also pronounced "PORR-ek" and "PARR-ek" in rural Ireland.

THE PLOUGHER

Sunset and silence! A man; around him earth savage,
    earth broken;
Beside him two horses, a plough!

Earth savage, earth broken, the brutes, the dawn-man
    there in the sunset,
And the plough that is twin to the sword, that is
    founder of cities!

"Brute-tamer, plough-maker, earth-breaker! Canst hear?
    There are ages between us—
Is it praying you are as you stand there alone in the
    sunset?

Surely our sky-born gods can be nought to you, earth
    child and earth-master—
Surely your thoughts are of Pan, or of Wotan, or Dana?

Yet why give thought to the gods? Has Pan led your
    brutes where they stumble?

Has Dana numbed pain of the child-bed, or Wotan put
  hands to your plough?

What matter your foolish reply! O man standing lone
  and bowed earthward,
Your task is a day near its close. Give thanks to the
  night-giving god."

Slowly the darkness falls, the broken lands blend with
  the savage;
The brute-tamer stands by the brutes, a head's breadth
  only above them.

A head's breadth? Aye, but therein is hell's depth and
  the height up to heaven,
And the thrones of the gods and their halls, their
  chariots, purples, and splendours.

THE BOOK OF KELLS

First, make a letter like a monument—
An upright like the fast-held hewn stone
Immovable, and half-rimming it
The strength of Behemoth his neck-bone,
And underneath that yoke, a staff, a rood
Of no less hardness than the cedar wood.

Then, on a page made golden as the crown
Of sainted man, a scripture you enscroll
Blackly, firmly, with the quickened skill
Lessoned by famous masters in our school,
And with an ink whose lustre will keep fresh
For fifty generations of our flesh.

And limn below it the Evangelist
In raddled coat, on bench abidingly,
Simple and bland: Matthew his name or Mark,
Or Luke or John; the book is by his knee,
And thereby its similitudes: Lion,
Or Calf, or Eagle, or Exalted Man.

The winds that blow around the world—the four
Winds in their colours on your pages join—
The Northern Wind—its blackness interpose;
The Southern Wind—its blueness gather in;
In redness and in greenness manifest
The splendours of the Winds of East and West.

And with these colours on a ground of gold
Compose a circuit will be seen by men
As endless patience, but is nether web
Of endless effort—a strict pattern:
Illumination lighting interlace
Of cirque and scroll, of panel and lattice.

A single line describes them and enfolds,
One line, one course where term there is none,
Which in its termlessness is envoying
The going forth and the return one.
With man and beast and bird and fish therein
Transformed to species that have never been.

With mouth a-gape or beak a-gape each stands
Initial to a verse of miracle,
Of mystery and of marvel (Depth of God!)
That Alpha or Omega may not spell,
Then finished with these wonders and these signs,
Turn to the figures of your first outlines.

Axal, our angel, has sustained you so
In hand, in brain; now to him seal that thing
With figures many as the days of man,
And colours, like the fire's enamelling—
That baulk, that letter you have greatly reared
To stay the violence of the entering Word!

IN SAINT STEPHEN'S GREEN

Bare branches: on the tree above
A nest from seasons gone

That keeps in spite of all that blew
A lone, wild homeliness.

And they that have the lease of it,
Two magpies, flit around;
Their magpie-minds are bent upon
The matter of repair.

Renewal! Like some other beings,
They're claimant of a day
Whose grant is lodging, prospect, store,
Companionship renewed.

The magpies fly with tuft and twig
Up to the nest regained:
Elated by their enterprise
They patch, and probe, and pull.

And in the shadow, not a pair,
A triad: one lets fall
To one below the thread she's spun
Who measures, passes down

To one who's seated: on her lap
The shears, the cutting shears—
Three bronzen women at a task
That is from ancientry.

Like nuns of order so severe
None have remained but they:
They look out on a world where we
A homeliness repair.

EXPECTING NO ONE

The bridge we often crossed, one to the other—
I lean upon its ledge, expecting no one
From north or south, a pilgrim who is mindful
Of all he left behind, and mindful, too,
Of disrepair in all he has come back to.

The seagulls fly up from the darkened river—
Their flight disordered—there is emblem here.

I lean upon the ledge this stilly night—
The word that Thomas Moore has in his song
That's of departures—his statue is within
The watch I keep—the town's worst monument.
No more than he of "banquet hall deserted"
Am I in hope of one to re-appear.

Expecting no one—
Regretting this—that you had come so often
To where I crossed, and that so seldom I,
Moved from set purposes, made a festival
Of your approach, you who were attuned
To all the harps that sounded in the air.
And here I stand with all those purposes
Signed, sealed, delivered as a book in vault,
Between the statue in his metal cloak
And seagulls making their disordered flight,
Expecting no one from the south or north.

Further Readings on Padraic Colum

Bibliography

Denson, Alan. "Padraic Colum: An Appreciation with a Checklist of His
     Publications," *Dublin Magazine* 6: 50–65, 83–85.
Kersnowski, Frank, *et al. A Bibliography of Modern Irish and Anglo-Irish Literature*
     pp. 15–21 San Antonio, Tex.: Trinity University Press, 1976.

Selected Works

A Boy in Eirinn. New York: E. P. Dutton, 1913.
Castle Conquer. New York and London: Macmillan, 1923.
The Collected Poems of Padraic Colum. New York: Devin-Adair, 1953.
The Flying Swans. New York: Crown, 1957.
The Frenzied Prince, Being Heroic Stories of Ancient Ireland. Philadelphia: McKay,
     1943.
Images of Departure. Dublin: Dolmen, 1969.
Our Friend James Joyce. With Mary Colum. Garden City: Doubleday, 1958.
Ourselves Alone: The Story of Arthur Griffith and the Origins of the Irish Free State.

New York: Crown, 1959 Published under the title *Arthur Griffith*. Dublin: Brown and Nolan, 1959.

The Poet's Circuits. Collected Poems of Ireland. London: Oxford University Press, 1960. Reprinted, Dublin: Doleman, 1986.

Selected Plays of Padraic Colum. Edited by Sanford Sternlicht. Syracuse, N.Y.: Syracuse University Press, 1986.

Selected Short Stories of Padraic Colum. Edited by Sanford Sternlicht. Syracuse, N.Y.: Syracuse University Press, 1984.

Three Plays: The Fiddler's House, The Land, Thomas Muskerry. Boston: Little Brown, 1916; Dublin: Maunsel, 1917. Rev. ed., New York: Macmillan, 1925; Dublin: Figgis, 1963.

Biography and Criticism

Bowen, Zack. *Padraic Colum. A Biographical-Critical Introduction.* Carbondale, Ill.: Southern Illinois University Press, 1970.

Journal of Irish Literature. Padraic Colum number, ed. Zack Bowen and Gordon Henderson. 2: (January 1973).

Sternlicht, Sanford. *Padraic Colum.* Boston: Twayne, 1985.

PÁDRAIC O'CONAIRE
(1882–1928)

A Galway landmark is Albert Power's statue of a small man sitting on a wall with his hand holding his lapel and his hat on the back of his head. The figure is that of Pádraic O'Conaire, who traveled the roads of the west of Ireland with a donkey and cart and who is remembered in F. R. Higgins's poem as well as in Power's stone:

> Dear Pádraic of the wide and sea-cold eyes—
> So lovable, so courteous and noble,
> The very West was in his soft replies.

O'Conaire was the first significant writer in Modern Irish. Stephen McKenna described him in 1925 as "absolutely the only writer you can imagine a European reading." Later, the best Irish language prose writer of his generation, Máirtín O'Cadháin, judged him the "most successful exponent in Irish," and went on to point out that "this is no mean praise in a country which is world famous for its short-story writers."

O'Conaire was not a native speaker of Irish; he went to his uncle's house in Rosmuc in the Connemara Gaeltacht as a schoolboy of eleven. He spent fifteen years as a minor clerk in London before he became involved with the Gaelic League. Most of his best stories as well as his novel *Deoraídheacht* (In Exile) were written before he returned to Ireland in 1914.

"An Bhean a Ciapadh" [The woman who was made to suffer], entitled "Put to the Rack" in this translation, criticizes the old *cleam-*

211

hnas or matchmaking system with its sympathetic portrait of a young woman married off to a prosperous middle-aged farmer who has returned to Ireland from America. George Moore's "Julia Cahill's Curse" treats the same theme, as does Liam O'Flaherty's "The Touch," William Carleton's *The Immigrants of Ahadarra* and many folk songs that encourage young people to marry for love rather than for money. O'Conaire's story not only discloses a heartbroken young girl facing a "made" marriage, but digs deep into the reality of that loveless arrangement: the isolation, the lack of communication, and the inutterable loneliness.

PUT TO THE RACK

Next month in the City of Galway a judge and jury will try an action for slander. Burke of Knockmore and Andrew Finnerty are the parties to the dispute and as judgment will have been given before these words are in print, it is no harm to tell the whole story fully.

One day, after his return from America, when Burke was sitting on the ditch where the idlers foregather in the City of Galway, he saw coming up the road towards him a girl who walked with the lightest tread and who had the finest bearing he had ever seen. She appeared to be not more than eighteen, but so dainty were her feet that the marks of her footsteps on the muddy street seemed to be those of a child of twelve.

Burke fell in love with the girl of the tiny feet as she passed him by humming an air to herself. He had a piece of chewing gum in his mouth, but he ejected it through a gap in his upper teeth and it fell circling into the water.

"Who is that young woman?" said he to a hulk of a fellow who sat on the ditch.

"What woman?"

"The little light-footed woman."

"She is a daughter of Andrew Finnerty's, who keeps the shop near the dock."

"Andrew Finnerty?" repeated Burke with deliberation.

"Is he a tall dark man?" he inquired, suddenly.

"He is."

"And has he a mole under his left ear?"

"He has, indeed, and a big one too."

"And has he lost the top of his right thumb?"

"You know all about him, it seems."

Burke jumped off the ditch, seized his umbrella, and made off at top speed. He crossed the bridge in a great hurry and never cried halt until he reached the dock.

Finnerty's shop was stocked mostly with boating gear, and the stranger paused a bit outside looking at the shop and trying to think what he had best buy in such a place.

He walked in.

"Sixpence worth of mackerel hooks," he said.

The proprietor himself was present and he handed them to him.

"Isn't it queer that you don't know your old friend? What a bad memory you have!" said Burke.

The shopkeeper scrutinised him closely.

"It can't be that you are James Burke—you are very like him."

"I'm the same man."

Finnerty gave him a hearty welcome. They had not met for twenty-seven years, since both were working together in the States.

The stranger was invited into the room behind the shop. The two old comrades sat down, glasses were filled, and they began to chat.

"How long is it since we were in Panama?" asked the shopkeeper.

"Twenty-seven years this Christmas."

"And I suppose you got married?"

"I didn't. I never had time."

"I suppose you have made a tidy bit of money, James?"

"I have some."

They heard a sailor in the shop asking for a couple of fathoms of cord. The shopkeeper went to the door, told him to sit down and said he would not keep him long. He filled the glasses again.

"As for you," said Burke, "I needn't ask you."

"No. I'm a widower with a houseful of children. All daughters, except one son."

"Do you say so?"

The sailor in the shop was getting impatient and the shopkeeper had to go out and serve him. When he had gone, Burke began to think. Why should he go away again? Hadn't he made enough money? Wasn't a rest good after such strenuous work? And where could he find a nicer place to spend the rest of his life in than the place where he was born? When leaving the States he had intended to pay only a short visit to Ireland, but as the days and the months slipped by his desire to return became less and less. The old enchantment! The old call of the blood!

When Finnerty came back from the shop his friend said to him—

"I came home to get married, Andrew! I am tired of the life over there."

"One of the Blakes has a fine farm for sale over at Knockmore, if you know the place. You'd get it for a thousand pounds. He wants twelve hundred, and there is as fine a house on it as you ever saw."

"Have you a car?"

"I have."

"Yoke the horse at once, and let us go and look at it."

While the horse was being harnessed, they spoke as follows:

"You have a very bad memory, Andrew!" said Burke. "Don't you remember the Christmas night long ago when we gave our word that one of us wouldn't want for a wife so long as the other had a daughter?"

"I do remember it, and I'll keep my promise if what you tell me about the money is true."

"If she herself is willing."

"Why shouldn't she be?"

"Women nowadays are astonishing. Look at them in England. There's no limit to what they'll do."

Before the car reached the door the match was agreed upon.

A few nights afterwards Mary Finnerty and her father were together. He told her about the match. She was not satisfied with her proposed husband and said she would never marry him. Her father insisted that she should. Mary swore that she would not.

All the same they were married.

It is true that they had a fine house in Knockmore and everything in keeping with it. The house had been built for a gentleman, but in the course of time he became impoverished, and he had to sell out and go away. No wonder the people thought it a fine match for Miss Finnerty. What had the Finnertys ever had even at their best? And even if her husband was getting on in years, who would realise that he was nearing fifty? Was there a young man in the Parish of Knockmore who could work like him? Where was there anyone with the same "go" in him? Wouldn't it delight your heart to see him working? And he was so fond of her! The insignificant little thing without energy, or health, or anything!

The neighbors were right. He was a vigorous man. He was fond of work, and he was very fond of the little woman he married.

But she was not content, and her dissatisfaction was due to the

queer way in which he showed his affection. He was a bit rough.
Perhaps this was due to his life in America, to the grinding work there
and to all he had seen. Anyway, she trembled a little when he came
near her for fear he would prove too loving. A little shudder of goose-
flesh passed over her as he touched her.

She would not confess to this feeling for anything in the world.
She thought it would be a great sin to do so, but nevertheless, she was
pleased in spite of herself when he told her that he was going to such
and such a fair and would be away for a few days. She could not help
her feelings. She could not possibly love him in the way a woman loves
a man, and as soon as he had departed she tried to find out whether
many women of her acquaintance were in a similar plight.

He did not understand how matters were with her. He was
clever, intelligent and vigorous-minded. In a bargain he would certainly not come off second best. He was well-informed in business
matters and on political questions, but he failed to understand people
who had not his own rough outlook. What was the cause of this? His
life in the States, his incessant labour, his strenuous existence, and the
scramble for money? Or was it a natural warp in his temperament?

Often when his wife was discontented and out of sorts, and when
an appropriate word would have made her all right, he would say
something rough that would make her worse. He often noticed her in
this way, but he did not understand the cause of it. He had never met
a woman like that before. The women whom he had come across in
the big cities of America liked nothing better than flattery and pre-
sents.

He resolved to give his wife a beautiful present in the hope that it
would dispel her queer moods. He went to Galway for the sole
purpose of buying this present. He visited all the shops and he finally
decided on a fine dress of glacé silk made in the latest fashion. In
addition he bought her a large gold brooch. He was always most
generous to her, but in the purchase of these articles he went somewhat beyond measure. It was of no consequence, however. Wouldn't
she be delighted when she saw them?

And she was delighted. She had never seen such a lovely dress
and its style was perfect. When her husband held it up to show it to
her it seemed so dainty that it would not fit even the most slender
woman.

His wife took it to put it on.

"I am most grateful to you, James! Most grateful indeed," said
she.

She put on the dress and it was too small for her. He told her so.
"I'd prefer it that way, James! I'll be in the fashion."

"But in a month or two you won't be able to put it on at all." He said a great deal more to her that I will not mention. It displeased her and when he would not stop she burst into tears and fled to her own room.

He was sorry for having spoken to her in that way. He knew that she did not like such language and he knocked at the door to go in and apologise to her. She would not let him, however.

"Open the door," he said.

"I won't," she answered.

He was getting angry.

"The longer you stay outside the better I'll be pleased," said she.

She opened the door slightly, and flung out the dress.

"And if you want to give a present in future," she said, "give it to somebody else."

He was very angry. He stood for a few minutes at the door between two minds. He would have liked to put his shoulder to the door, to break it in and to thrash her soundly. He did not do it, however, but he took up the fine dress from the floor and threw it into the fire.

"The devil take her!" he said, "but I'll teach her manners," and with that he flung out of the house, rode off on a white horse of his, and never stopped till he reached the town.

He was seen that night on the road swearing terribly and beating his poor horse unmercifully.

When her baby boy was born it never saw the light. Two doctors from Galway were called in, but the child was born dead, and the doctors expressed the opinion that if she had another child she would not survive.

When she got better her husband took practically no notice of her. About this time he commenced going from fair to fair buying cattle to fatten on Knockmore, and often she did not see him or hear from him for a week. She did not mind this in the least. Even when he was at home they spoke but seldom. He got up, ate his breakfast, went out to look after the stock and she would not see him till dinner time. Almost every night he had company in the kitchen and spent a good part of the night playing cards and carousing. He had always drunk a fair share, but he was as strong as a bull and was well able to stand it. But his bad habits were gradually getting the upper hand of him, and it was often daylight before he went to bed. Oftener still he did not speak to his wife for a whole day or two days on end unless to ask whether she had done this or that, or whether she wanted money for household expenses.

She was of opinion that he had no longer any respect for her, and where there is no respect there is no love. She was pleased that this was so. She would have been content, or half-content, if he had left her alone except for the necessary few words. She would have a wretched life tied to a man whom she hated, but how could she escape it?

He had bought out his land completely and one night that he came home drunk from the fair of Galway his wife learned something of what was troubling him.

"He won't get it whoever gets it," said he to himself as he sat by the fire while she got ready the supper.

"He won't get it, the fool, the cursed knave, the rogue!" said he not noticing the presence of his wife.

It was not long until she knew what was in his mind.

"He knows that none of my people are living, but neither he, nor his people will get it. I'd rather sell the land and throw the money into the sea."

He raised his head and saw his wife. It was very late and she had got up to let him in for fear he might be killed on the flags outside. If he had met his end far from home and unknown to her she would not have cared. When he raised his head and when she looked at him she thought that she had never seen, and hoped that she would never see again, a human face so ugly. She tried to get away from him and get to her own room, but with a coarse remark he caught her by the shoulder.

She succeeded in shaking him off he had so much drink taken, and he fell on to the floor and remained on the cold flags till morning.

He rode the white horse from fair to fair and from town to town, and man and horse were frequently seen travelling the road at midnight—the rider in a drunken sleep and the horse guiding him itself. His wife was at home and any night she expected him she could not sleep till he arrived. She remained up not because of any remnant of affection for him, but she sat at the window listening for the horse's hoofs on the road, hoping she might never hear them and that the rider would drink that last drop that would precipitate him from the saddle on his head on the road.

And visions came before her eyes. She saw her husband being brought home some morning dead. The neighbours would condole with her on the loss of a good husband, and she thought of what she would say to them, or whether she could mourn his loss.

She was, however, a good pious woman, and such thoughts came to her in spite of herself. She never willingly harboured them.

Then she would hear the horse, far away, trotting on the hard road, and she would strain her ears to catch the sound of her husband's voice and to learn from it in what state he was, for she knew how drunk he was by his voice and her terror varied with its sound. When he came home in a maudlin state and showed her affection in his rough way she tried to elude him, but seldom succeeded. How she hated him! How she loathed him as she felt his heavy drunken breath on her cheek! She was a timid little thing by nature and she would never have taken any steps if it were not for something he said to her one morning at breakfast. He made it clear to her that he had no respect for her and that he could not think much of such a woman— who had not given him an heir.

Before he left the house he said a lot more that troubled her greatly. She saw him go down the road on the white horse, and she prayed that he might never return.

But the same night she was at her post at the window listening for the horse. It did not come. Midnight passed, and one, two and three o'clock and no sign. She had time to think of the wretched life she was leading, but what pained her most was what he had said to her that morning and the manner in which he had said it. It was a bright moonlit night, and a sudden desire seized her to go out.

She left the house, and no sooner was she outside than she resolved never to return. She drew her cloak round her, and, setting out to walk to Galway, she did not halt until, before dawn, she stood on her father's hearth.

After three days Burke went to Galway to her. He found Finnerty at home, and he was taken into the room behind the shop.

His glass was filled, as was always done.

"This is a very bad business," said Finnerty.

"She herself is to blame," replied Burke.

Her father had heard only part of her story. The young woman had been ashamed to tell him the worst, and even if she had done so he would not have understood aright. He thought that it was nothing but a young woman's whim, and that it could be easily remedied. He had advised her to go back to her husband, but she refused. This was, in his opinion, only youthful nonsense, but he thought it well to teach her husband a lesson and to give him a fright. He had been too long indulging in drink and late hours.

"I suppose you have come for her," said Finnerty.

"And so she is here?"

He had suspected that she was not.

"Where else would she be? And she says that here she will stay."

"Not here. I am her husband."

Burke assumed a bold attitude. Right was on his side, he thought.

"You've been drinking and carousing too much for the past year," said Finnerty. "I wouldn't blame a man for taking a drink now and again, but every night in the year! Wherever I go I hear nothing but 'did you hear what Burke of Knockmore did lately?' or 'isn't he a terrible drinker?' It's a shame, man! It's a shame!"

"I don't care a straw what they say. I know my own business best—but where is Mary?"

"You know your own business all right, but my daughter is married to you!"

"If they haven't the truth they will tell lies."

"And the truth is bad enough."

"Yes," said Burke in a hesitating tone, as he tried to guess how much of the truth had been told to his old friend.

"Make it up in God's name," said Finnerty, "and don't let the world be laughing at us. I'll call her."

He called her and she came in hurriedly. She bowed to the two men.

"If you have come for me, James!" she said to her husband, "your journey has been in vain."

"You will have to come with me. I am your husband."

"Oughtn't you take advice?" interposed her father. "However wise you are you cannot understand everything."

"I was terribly foolish when I gave in to you both at first, but I have bought sense since then, and I have bought it dearly, and you both know that I have had a hard teacher."

She went on to speak, and the two men were surprised at the vigour and boldness of her remarks.

"Is it go back to that fine house in Knockmore and live there with that man who has insulted me every day—that man who is so coarse that he doesn't even know when he is insulting! The man who never wanted anything but to satisfy his unbridled appetite!"

Her father tried to stop her. He had not thought that things were so bad. If he had known perhaps he would not have advised her to go back.

But now she had put aside all shyness and timidity. She would speak her mind out whatever would be the consequence. The two men were at either side of the table and she stood at the head, but she was so excited that she had, at times, to take hold of a chair to steady herself.

"I would far rather spend my life and my health begging from door to door than spend a single night in the same house with you, James Burke!"

Her father made a quiet remark. He was rather afraid of her.

"And I am far from being grateful to you," she said to him. "You only wanted to get me a husband and you didn't care a jot what sort of a man he was so long as he had a little money. To sell me—that is all you wanted. There are some men and God shouldn't give them daughters. There are others and it is a great crime for them to get wives—"

"Stop, woman! Be silent, I say," shouted Burke in a threatening tone. "I have only one word to say," he continued. "You are my wife, and where I am you are, and unless you come home willingly with me, I'll find other means."

He attempted to take hold of her, but Finnerty went between them, and for a moment it looked as if there was going to be a struggle.

"You had better go home to-night, Burke!" said her father. "The matter is not going to be settled in that way."

Burke went away.

That night two men—one in Galway and one in Knockmore—thought long and deeply on the surprises of woman's soul.

A week afterwards Burke was astonished to get a letter from his wife saying that she was willing to return if he would come for her.

He came and on their return home on the car it occurred to Burke to ask her why she had given in. He was proud that he had brought her to reason.

"There was no use in your tormenting yourself," he said. "Didn't you know that you would have to come back? I suppose your father told you that he couldn't keep you at home with his big family."

"That isn't the reason why I am here with you now," she answered. "If he had only a second bit in the house he'd give me one."

"Why, then, have you given in?"

"Whisper," she said, and she spoke a word in his ear known only to him and her.

It was nightfall. The old white horse was ambling along in his own way. There was not a breath of air. The birds had ceased their song. The couple on the car heard no sound except that made by the horse and car. One thought was troubling them both. Burke looked at his wife. She was sad and deep in thought, and her hand lay wearily on the well of the car. He put his hand on her hand and stroked it gently, fearing in his heart that she might draw it away. She did not withdraw it.

"Mary! Mary!" he exclaimed, but could say nothing else.

She bore a son, but died at its birth.

. . . .

Some time after this a young man was walking the road near Knockmore when he heard a car behind him. Burke was on the car, and as the young man knew his late wife and her father he gave him a lift. Burke was on for talking, and the young man contented himself with listening.

"He'll pay dearly for it," said Burke. "The idea of saying that I killed her, considering how fond of her I was! But there is law in the land still, and I'll show him that he cannot call me a murderer."

They were passing Knockmore Cemetery.

"She is buried there," said Burke. "There is her grave."

He stopped the horse.

"We may as well go in and say a prayer for her soul."

The two men knelt over her grave, and when they had prayed for her soul, Burke said:

"I thank you, God! that you did not lay too heavy a hand on me, and even if you have taken away the woman I loved since first I saw her, she has left me an heir."

A feeling of disgust seized the young man at the thought that the other man did not care what had happened to his wife so long as he had a son, and he let him continue his journey alone.

Further Readings on Pádraic O'Conaire

Bibliography

ní Cnionnaith, An tSr. Eibhlín. "Pádraic O'Conaire: Liosta Saothair" *Pádraic O'Conaire. Léachtaí Cuimhneacháin*, pp. 65–83. Indreabháin: Cló Chonamara, 1983.

Selected Works

Aistí Phádraic Uí Chonaire. Edited by Gearóid Denvir. RosMuc: Cló Chois Fharraige, 1978.

Deoraíocht. Cló Talbot, 1974.

Field and Fair. Translated by Cormac Breathnach. Dublin: Cló Talbot, 1974. Dublin and Cork: Talbot Press, 1929.

Pádraic O'Conaire. Dublin: Poolbeg Press, 1982. (Fifteen stories by fifteen different translators.)

Scothscéalta le Pádraic O'Conaire. Edited by Tomás de Bhaldraithe. Dublin: Sáirséal agus Dill, 1962 (1956).

Seacht mBua Éirí Amach. Baile Átha Cliath: Maunsel, 1918.

The Woman at the Window. Translated by Eamonn O'Neill. Illustrated by Mícheál MacLiammóir. Dublin and Cork: Talbot Press, n.d.

Biography and Criticism

Denvir, Gearóid. *Pádraic Ó Conaire. Léachtaí Cuimhneacháin.* Indreabháin: Clò Chonamara, 1983.

Higgins, F. R. "An Appreciation." In *Field and Fair,* pp. 11–15. Dublin and Cork: Talbot Press, 1929.

Jordan, John. "On *Deoraíocht,*" *The Pleasures of Gaelic Literature.* Edited by John Jordan. Cork: Mercier Press, 1972.

MacGrianna, Seosamh. "Pádraic O'Conaire," *Pádraic O'Conaire agus Aistí Eile.* Baile Átha Cliath: Oifig an tSolathair, 1969 (1936).

Murphy, Maureen. "The Short Story in Irish." *Mosaic* 12:81–89.

Ó Cadháin, Máirtin. "Irish Prose in the Twentieth Century." *Literature in Celtic Countries,* ed. J. E. Caerwyn Williams. Cardiff: University of Wales Press, 1971.

Ó Maille, Pádraic. "Pádraic O'Conaire—Prince of Storytellers." *The Ireland-American Review* 1:379–88.

Ó Néill, Séamus. "Gaelic Writing." *Irish Writing* 33: 7–10.

JAMES STEPHENS
(1880[82?]–1950)

J ames Stephens was often called a leprechaun of literature during
his lifetime. Not only was he short, standing only four feet ten
inches, but his writing, both in poetry and prose, displays a charged
mixture of fantasy and athletic verve. He did not, however, look away
from the sometimes sordid reality of everyday Irish life. One of his
earliest works, *The Charwoman's Daughter* (1912), is a fantasy set
amid the poverty of a Dublin Stephens had known well in his childhood. Stephens is probably best-remembered today for his imaginative retellings of Old Irish stories that reveal his personal vision of
youth and of a world beyond the senses. These include *The Crock of
Gold* (1912), *The Demi-Gods* (1914), *Irish Fairy Tales* (1920), *Deirdre*
(1923), and *In the Land of Youth* (1924). The American musical *Finian's
Rainbow* (1947) might also be cited as a work by Stephens, as it is an
adaptation of *The Crock of Gold*.

Stephens was not so much interested in making old stories
accessible to the modern reader as in recreating distinctively Irish
stories in his own way. His own way included borrowings from
Eastern philosophies as well as from the writings of the English
mystical poet William Blake, with whom he is often compared.
While not a nationalist in the conventional sense, Stephens was
greatly moved by the Easter Rising of 1916 and wrote an eye-witness
account of it. Later, he was unhappy with the changes wrought by
revolution and so emigrated to England in 1924. Late in life, with his
best works behind him, Stephens achieved some of his widest popularity as a commentator and storyteller for the British Broadcasting
Corporation. Although Stephens appealed to a popular readership,
his writing enjoyed the esteem of some of his most demanding

contemporaries. James Joyce, for example, found Stephens to be a kindred spirit, and asked that he be ready to complete the incomparably abstruse work, *Finnegans Wake*, should the author be unable to. Joyce believed that he and Stephens were born on the same day, February 2, 1882—an assertion not supported, however, by birth records.

Stephens wrote poetry throughout his career, and it became his dominant concern in the years following the disappointing reception of *In the Land of Youth*. In *Irish Fairy Tales*, the youthful Fionn speaks for Stephens's aesthetic.

From THE INSURRECTION IN DUBLIN

MONDAY

On the way home I noticed that many silent people were standing in their doorways—an unusual thing in Dublin outside the back streets. The glance of a Dublin man or woman conveys generally a criticism of one's personal appearance, and is a little hostile to the passer. The look of each person as I passed was steadfast, and contained an enquiry instead of a criticism. I felt faintly uneasy, but withdrew my mind to a meditation which I had covenanted with myself to perform daily, and passed to my house.

There I was told that there had been a great deal of rifle firing all the morning, and we concluded that the military recruits or Volunteer [i.e., rebel] detachments were practising that arm. My return to business was by the way I had already come. At the corner of Merrion Row I found the same silent groups, who were still looking in the direction of the Green, and addressing each other occasionally with the detached confidence of strangers. Suddenly, and on the spur of the moment, I addressed one of these silent gazers.

"Has there been an accident?" said I.

I indicated the people standing about.

"What's all this for?"

He was a sleepy, rough-looking man about forty years of age, with a blunt red moustache, and the distant eyes which one sees in sailors. He looked at me, stared at me as at a person from a different country. He grew wakeful and vivid.

"Don't you know?" said he.

And then he saw that I did not know.

"The Sinn Feiners have seized the city this morning."

"Oh!" said I.

He continued with the savage earnestness of one who has amazement in his mouth:

"They seized the city at eleven o'clock this morning. The Green there is full of them. They have captured the Castle. They have taken the Post Office."

"My God!" said I, staring at him, and instantly I turned and went running towards the Green.

TUESDAY

There had been looting in the night about Sackville Street, and it was current that the Volunteers had shot twenty of the looters.

The shops attacked were mainly haberdashers, shoe shops, and sweet shops. Very many sweet shops were raided, and until the end of the rising, sweet shops were the favourite mark of the looters. There is something comical in this looting of sweet shops—something almost innocent and child-like. Possibly most of the looters are children who are having the sole gorge of their lives. They have tasted sweetstuffs they had never toothed before, and will never taste again in this life, and until they die the insurrection of 1916 will have a sweet savour for them.

WEDNESDAY

Today the *Irish Times* was published. It contained a new military proclamation, and a statement that the country was peaceful, and told that in Sackville Street some houses were burned to the ground.

On the outside railings a bill proclaiming martial law was posted.

Into the newspaper statement that peace reigned in the country one was inclined to read more of disquietude than truth, and one said: Is the country so extraordinarily peaceful that it can be dismissed in three lines? There is too much peace or too much reticence, but it will be some time before we hear from outside of Dublin.

Meanwhile the sun was shining. It was a delightful day, and the streets outside and around the areas of fire were animated and even gay. In the streets of Dublin there were no morose faces to be seen. Almost everyone was smiling and attentive, and a democratic feeling was abroad, to which our city is very much a stranger; for while in private we are a social and talkative people, we have no street manners or public ease whatever. Every person spoke to every other person, and men and women mixed and talked without constraint.

FRIDAY

Many English troops have been landed each night, and it is believed that there are more than sixty thousand soldiers in Dublin alone, and that they are supplied with every offensive contrivance which military art has invented.

Merrion Square is strongly held by the soldiers. They are posted along both sides of the road at intervals of about twenty paces, and their guns are continually barking up at the roofs which surround them in the great square. It is said that these roofs are held by the Volunteers from Mount Street Bridge to the Square, and that they hold in like manner wide stretches of the city.

They appear to have mapped out the roofs with all the thoroughness that had hitherto been expended on the roads, and upon these roofs they are so mobile and crafty and so much at home that the work of the soldiers will be exceedingly difficult as well as dangerous.

Still, and notwithstanding, men can only take to the roofs for a short time. Up there, there can be no means of transport, and their ammunition, as well as their food, will very soon be used up. It is the beginning of the end, and the fact that they have to take to the roofs, even though that be in their programme, means that they are finished.

From the roof there comes the sound of machine guns. Looking towards Sackville Street one picks out easily Nelson's Pillar, which towers slenderly over all the buildings of the neighbourhood. It is wreathed in smoke. Another towering building was the D.B.C. Café. Its Chinese-like pagoda was a landmark easily to be found, but today I could not find it. It was not there, and I knew that, even if all Sackville Street was not burned down, as rumour insisted, this great Café had certainly been curtailed by its roof and might, perhaps, have been completely burned.

On the gravel paths I found pieces of charred and burnt paper. These scraps must have been blown remarkably high to have crossed all the roofs that lie between Sackville Street and Merrion Square.

At eleven o'clock there is continuous firing, and snipers firing from the direction of Mount Street, and in every direction of the city these sounds are being duplicated.

In Camden Street the sniping and casualties are said to have been very heavy. One man saw two Volunteers taken from a house by the soldiers. They were placed kneeling in the centre of the road, and within one minute of their capture they were dead. Simultaneously there fell several of the firing party.

An officer in this part had his brains blown into the roadway. A young girl ran into the road, picked up his cap and scraped the brains into it. She covered this poor debris with a little straw, and carried the lot piously to the nearest hospital in order that the brains might be buried with their owner.

From IRISH FAIRY TALES

FIONN'S FAVORITE MUSIC

Once, as they rested on a chase, a debate arose among the Fianna-Finn as to what was the finest music in the world.

"Tell us that," said Fionn, turning to Oisín.

"The cuckoo calling from the tree that is highest in the hedge," cried his merry son.

"A good sound," said Fionn. "And you, Oscar," he said, "what is to your mind the finest of music?"

"The top of music is the ring of a spear on a shield," cried the stout lad.

"It is a good sound," said Fionn.

And the other champions told their delight: the belling of a stag across water, the baying of a tuneful pack heard in the distance, the song of a lark, the laugh of a gleeful girl, or the whisper of a moved one.

"They are good sounds all," said Fionn.

"Tell us, chief," one ventured, "what you think?"

"The music of what happens," said great Fionn, "that is the finest music in the world."

Further Readings on James Stephens

Bibliography

Bramsbäck, Birgit. *James Stephens: A Literary and Bibliographical Study.* Uppsala: Lundequist; Cambridge: Harvard University Press, 1959, 1973.

Carens, James F. "James Stephens." In *Anglo-Irish Literature: a Review of Research,* ed. R. J. Finneran, pp. 459–69. New York: Modern Language Association, 1976.

Selected Works

The Charwoman's Daughter. London: Macmillan, 1912. Reprinted, Dublin: Gill
    and Macmillan, 1972.
Collected Poems. 2nd ed. London and New York: Macmillan, 1954.
Deirdre. London and New York: Macmillan, 1923.
The Demi-Gods. London and New York: Macmillan, 1914.
The Insurrection in Dublin. Dublin and London: Maunsel, 1916.
In the Land of Youth. London and New York: Macmillan, 1924.
Irish Fairy Tales. London and New York: Macmillan, 1920. Reprinted, New
    York: Abaris, 1978.
James, Seumas and Jacques: Unpublished Writings by James Stephens. Edited by
    Lloyd Frankenberg. London and New York: Macmillan, 1964.
James Stephens: A Selection. Edited by Lloyd Frankenberg. London: Macmillan,
    1962. Under the title *A James Stephens Reader.* New York: Macmillan,
    1962.
Letters of James Stephens. Edited by Richard J. Finneran. London and New
    York: Macmillan, 1974.
Uncollected Prose. Edited by Patricia A. McFate, New York: St. Martin's, 1983.

Biography and Criticism

Journal of Irish Literature. James Stephens number 4. 1975.
McFate. Patricia A. *The Writings of James Stephens: Variations on a Theme of Love.*
    London: Macmillan, 1979.
Martin, Augustine. *James Stephens: A Critical Study.* Dublin: Gill and Mac-
    millan, 1977.
Pyle, Hilary. *James Stephens: His Works and an Account of His Life.* London:
    Routledge and Kegan Paul; New York: Barnes and Noble, 1965.

THE POETS OF 1916

The single most electrifying moment in twentieth-century Irish history was the armed seizure of the General Post Office, the "G.P.O.," during Easter Week, April 24–29, 1916. The building itself was of small consequence, but it represented British imperial power on Dublin's main commercial thoroughfare, then called Sackville Street. Sentiment for independence had been diffused before Easter Week, especially since so many Irishmen were off fighting for Britain in World War I. But after the Rising, and especially after the executions of most of its leaders in the first weeks of May, the popular will for freedom solidified, never to be broken.

Among the seven signers of the Proclamation of the Irish Republic were three poets: Padraic Pearse, Thomas MacDonagh, and Joseph Plunkett. Men of action as well as of letters, the three played leading roles in the Rising. Viewed from a global perspective, the Easter Rising in Ireland is distinct for having been led by poets, rather than by soldiers, lawyers, or political ideologues.

P[atrick] H[enry] (or Padraic) Pearse (1879–1916) committed his life to the cause of Ireland from the time he joined the Gaelic League when he was sixteen. Although born of an English father, his knowledge of the Irish language was so proficient that he edited a journal in the language, *An Claidheamh Soluis* [The sword of light], and published collections of Irish-language short stories as well (*Íosagán* [1907]). The most important crucible for revolutionary activity as far as Pearse was concerned was the bi-lingual school, St. Enda's (*Scoil Énna*), which had attracted a wide range of partisan support after its foundation in 1908. A play written for students of

229

the school, *The Singer*, was a literary analogue for the Easter Rising. Some of Pearse's most famous sentiments are to be found in his August 1, 1915, oration at the burial of Jeremiah O'Donovan Rossa (1831–1915), a Fenian leader who advocated armed action for independence. Pearse was executed May 4, 1916.

Thomas MacDonagh (1878–1916) was closely associated with Pearse on many projects, but retained his own distinctive poetic voice. Steeped in both Irish and non-Irish tradition, MacDonagh's poetry shows the influence of such diverse writers as Walt Whitman and A. E. Housman. In an early play, *When the Dawn Is Come* (1908), he envisioned an Ireland free of Britain. Like Pearse, he became proficient in the Irish language and worked at St. Enda's School. With Padraic Colum and Mary Maguire later, Colum's wife, he founded the influential journal, *The Irish Review* (1911–15), which published some of the most significant writers of his generation. Even as the revolutionary fires were rising, MacDonagh was working on his critical history, *Literature in Ireland*, which would be published posthumously. A son, Donagh MacDonagh (1912–68), was also a poet and playwright of distinction. Thomas MacDonagh was executed May 3, 1916.

Joseph Mary Plunkett (1887–1916) died before his poetic style fully matured. Always in ill health, Plunkett spent much of his short life abroad in the warmer, drier climates of Italy, Algeria, and Egypt. He assisted Thomas MacDonagh with *The Irish Review*. In the months before the Rising, he helped Sir Roger Casement (1864–1916) in the thwarted attempt to smuggle German arms into Ireland. On the Good Friday before Easter, Plunkett was hospitalized for throat surgery, and so had to rise from a sickbed in order to enter the fray. He was executed May 4, 1916.

PROCLAMATION OF THE IRISH REPUBLIC

Irishmen and Irishwomen: In the name of God and of the dead generations from which she receives her old tradition of nationhood, Ireland, through us, summons her children to her flag and strikes for her freedom.

Having organised and trained her manhood through her secret

revolutionary organisation, the Irish Republican Brotherhood, and through her open military organisations, the Irish Volunteers and the Irish Citizen Army, having patiently perfected her discipline, having resolutely waited for the right moment to reveal itself, she now seizes that moment, and, supported by her exiled children in America and by gallant allies in Europe, but relying in the first on her own strength, she strikes in full confidence of victory.

We declare the right of the people of Ireland to the ownership of Ireland, and to the unfettered control of Irish destinies, to be sovereign and indefeasible. The long usurpation of that right by a foreign people and government has not extinguished the right, nor can it ever be extinguished except by the destruction of the Irish people. In every generation the Irish people have asserted their right to national freedom and sovereignty; six times during the past three hundred years they have asserted it in arms. Standing on that fundamental right and again asserting it in arms in the face of the world, we hereby proclaim the Irish Republic as a Sovereign Independent State, and we pledge our lives and the lives of our comrades-in-arms to the cause of its freedom, of its welfare, and of its exaltation among the nations.

The Irish Republic is entitled to, and hereby claims, the allegiance of every Irishman and Irishwoman. The Republic guarantees religious and civil liberty, equal rights and equal opportunities to all its citizens, and declares its resolve to pursue the happiness and prosperity of the whole nation and of all its parts, cherishing all the children of the nation equally, and oblivious of the differences carefully fostered by an alien government, which have divided a minority from the majority in the past.

Until our arms have brought the opportune moment for the establishment of a permanent National Government, representative of the whole people of Ireland and elected by the suffrages of all her men and women, the Provisional Government, hereby constituted, will administer the civil and military affairs of the Republic in trust for the people.

We place the cause of the Irish Republic under the protection of the Most High God, Whose blessing we invoke upon our arms, and we pray that no one who serves that cause will dishonour it by cowardice, inhumanity, or rapine. In this supreme hour the Irish nation must, by its valour and discipline and by the readiness of its children to sacrifice themselves for the common good, prove itself worthy of the august destiny to which it is called.

Signed on Behalf of the Provisional Government,
THOMAS J. CLARKE,

SEAN MACDIARMADA,   THOMAS MACDONAGH,
P. H. PEARSE,   EAMONN CEANNT,
JAMES CONNOLLY.   JOSEPH PLUNKETT.

P. H. PEARSE (1879–1916)

I AM IRELAND

I am Ireland:
I am older than the Old Woman of Beare.

Great my glory:
I that bore Cuchulainn the valiant.

Great my shame:
My own children that sold their mother.

I am Ireland:
I am lonelier than the Old Woman of Beare.

IDEAL, OR RENUNCIATION

Naked I saw thee,
O beauty of beauty!
And I blinded my eyes
For fear I should flinch.

I heard thy music,
O sweetness of sweetness!
And I shut my ears
For fear I should fail.

I kissed thy lips
O sweetness of sweetness!

And I hardened my heart
For fear of my ruin.

I blinded my eyes
And my ears I shut,
I hardened my heart
And my love I quenched.

I turned my back
On the dream I had shaped,
And to this road before me
My face I turned.

I set my face
To the road here before me,
To the work that I see,
To the death that I shall meet.

THE REBEL

I am come of the seed of the people, the people that
    sorrow,
That have no treasure but hope,
No riches laid up but a memory
Of an Ancient glory.
My mother bore me in bondage, in bondage my mother
    was born,
I am of the blood of serfs;
The children with whom I have played, the men and
    women with whom I have eaten,
Have had masters over them, have been under the lash
    of masters,
And, though gentle, have served churls;
The hands that have touched mine, the dear hands
    whose touch is familiar to me,
Have worn shameful manacles, have been bitten at the
    wrist by manacles,

Have grown hard with the manacles and the task-work
of strangers,
I am flesh of the flesh of these lowly, I am bone of
their bone,
I that have never submitted;
I that have a soul greater than the souls of my people's
masters,
I that have vision and prophecy and the gift of fiery
speech,
I that have spoken with God on the top of His holy hill.

And because I am of the people, I understand the
people,
I am sorrowful with their sorrow, I am hungry with
their desire:
My heart has been heavy with the grief of mothers,
My eyes have been wet with the tears of children,
I have yearned with old wistful men,
And laughed or cursed with young men;
Their shame is my shame, and I have reddened for it,
Reddened for that they have served, they who should be
free,
Reddened for that they have gone in want, while others
have been full,
Reddened for that they have walked in fear of lawyers
and of their jailors
With their writs of summons and their handcuffs,
Men mean and cruel!
I could have borne stripes on my body rather than this
shame of my people.

And now I speak, being full of vision;
I speak to my people, and I speak in my people's name
to the masters of my people.
I say to my people that they are holy, that they are
august, despite their chains,
That they are greater than those that hold them, and
stronger and purer,
That they have but need of courage, and to call on the
name of their God,

God the unforgetting, the dear God that loves the
     peoples
For whom He died naked, suffering shame.
And I say to my people's masters: Beware,
Beware of the thing that is coming, beware of the risen
     people,
Who shall take what ye would not give. Did ye think to
     conquer the people,
Or that Law is stronger than life and than men's desire
     to be free?
We will try it out with you, ye that have harried and
     held,
Ye that have bullied and bribed, tyrants, hypocrites,
     liars!

TO DEATH

I have not gathered gold;
     The fame that I won perished;
In love I found but sorrow,
     That withered my life.

Of wealth or of glory
I shall leave nothing behind me
(I think it, O God, enough!)
     But my name in the heart of a child.

AT THE GRAVE OF O'DONOVAN ROSSA

It has seemed right, before we turn away from this place in which we
have laid the mortal remains of O'Donovan Rossa, that one among us
should, in the name of all, speak the praise of that valiant man, and
endeavour to formulate the thought and the hope that are in us as we
stand around his grave. And if there is anything that makes it fitting
that I, rather than some other, I rather than one of the grey-haired

men who were young with him and shared in his labour and in his suffering, should speak here, it is perhaps that I may be taken as speaking on behalf of a new generation that has been re-baptised in the Fenian faith, and that has accepted the responsibility of carrying out the Fenian programme. I propose to you then that, here by the grave of this unrepentant Fenian, we renew our baptismal vows; that, here by the grave of this unconquered and unconquerable man, we ask of God, each one for himself, such unshakable purpose, such high and gallant courage, such unbreakable strength of soul as belonged to O'Donovan Rossa.

Deliberately here we avow ourselves, as he avowed himself in the dock, Irishmen of one allegiance only. We of the Irish Volunteers, and you others who are associated with us in today's task and duty, are bound together and must stand together henceforth in brotherly union for the achievement of the freedom of Ireland. And we know only one definition of freedom: it is Tone's definition, it is Mitchel's definition, it is Rossa's definition. Let no man blaspheme the cause that the dead generations of Ireland served by giving it any other name and definition than their definition.

We stand at Rossa's grave not in sadness but rather in exaltation of spirit that it has been given to us to come thus into so close a communion with that brave and splendid Gael. Splendid and holy causes are served by men who are themselves splendid and holy. O'Donovan Rossa was splendid in the proud manhood of him, splendid in the heroic grace of him, splendid in the Gaelic strength and clarity and truth of him. And all that splendour and pride and strength was compatible with a humility and a simplicity of devotion to Ireland, to all that was olden and beautiful and Gaelic in Ireland, the holiness and simplicity of patriotism of a Michael O'Clery or of an Eoghan O'Growney. The clear true eyes of this man almost alone in his day visioned Ireland as we of today would surely have her: not free merely, but Gaelic as well; not Gaelic merely, but free as well.

In a closer spiritual communion with him now than ever before or perhaps ever again, in a spiritual communion with those of his day, living and dead, who suffered with him in English prisons, in communion of spirit too with our own dear comrades who suffer in English prisons today, and speaking on their behalf as well as our own, we pledge to Ireland our love, and we pledge to English rule in Ireland our hate. This is a place of peace, sacred to the dead, where men should speak with all charity and with all restraint; but I hold it a Christian thing, as O'Donovan Rossa held it, to hate evil, to hate untruth, to hate oppression, and, hating them, to strive to overthrow them. Our foes are strong and wise and wary; but, strong and wise and wary as they are, they cannot undo the miracles of God who ripens in the hearts of young men the seeds sown by the young men of a former generation. And the seeds sown by the young men of '65 and '67 are coming to their miraculous ripening today. Rulers and Defenders of Realms had need to be wary if they would guard against such processes. Life springs from death; and from the graves of patriot men and women spring living nations. The Defenders of this Realm have worked well in secret and in the open. They think that they have pacified Ireland. They think that they have purchased half of us and intimidated the other half. They think that they have foreseen everything, think that they have provided against everything; but the fools the fools, the fools!—they have left us our Fenian dead, and while Ireland holds these graves, Ireland unfree shall never be at peace.

THOMAS MACDONAGH (1878–1916)

THE MAN UPRIGHT

I once spent an evening in a village
Where the people are all taken up with tillage,
Or do some business in a small way
Among themselves, and all the day
Go crooked, doubled to half their size,
Both working and loafing, with their eyes
Stuck in the ground or in a board,—
For some of them tailor, and some of them hoard
Pence in a till in their little shops,
And some of them shoe-soles—they get the tops
Ready-made from England, and they die cobblers—
All bent up double, a village of hobblers
And slouchers and squatters, whether they straggle
Up and down, or bend to haggle
Over a counter, or bend at a plough,
Or to dig with a spade, or to milk a cow,

Or to shove the goose-iron stiffly along
The stuff on the sleeve-board, or lace the thong
In the boot on the last, or to draw the wax-end
Tight cross-ways—and so to make or to mend
What will soon be worn out by the crooked people.
The only thing straight in the place was the steeple,
I thought at first. I was wrong in that;
For there past the window at which I sat
Watching the crooked little men
Go slouching, and with the gait of a hen
An odd little woman go pattering past,
And the cobbler crouching over his last
In his window opposite, and next door
The tailor squatting inside on the floor—
While I watched them, as I have said before,
And thought that only the steeple was straight,
There came a man of a different gait—
A man who neither slouched nor pattered,
But planted his steps as if each step mattered;
Yet walked down the middle of the street
Not like a policeman on his beat,
But like a man with nothing to do
Except walk straight upright like me and you.

THE YELLOW BITTERN

The yellow bittern that never broke out
    In a drinking bout, might as well have drunk;
His bones are thrown on a naked stone
    Where he lived alone like a hermit monk.
O yellow bittern! I pity your lot,
    Though they say that a sot like myself is curst—
I was sober a while, but I'll drink and be wise
    For I fear I should die in the end of thirst.

It's not for the common birds that I'd mourn,
    The black-bird, the corn-crake, or the crane,
But for the bittern that's shy and apart
    And drinks in the marsh from the long bog-drain.

Oh! if I had known you were near your death,
    While my breath held out I'd have run to you,
Till a splash from the Lake of the Son of the Bird
    Your soul would have stirred and waked anew.

My darling told me to drink no more
    Or my life would o'er in a little short while;
But I told her 'tis drink gives me health and strength
    And will lengthen my road by many a mile.
You see how the bird of the long smooth neck
    Could get his death from the thirst at last—
Come, son of my soul, and drain your cup,
    You'll get no sup when your life is past.

In a wintering island by Constantine's halls
    A bittern calls from a wineless place,
And tells me that hither he cannot come
    Till the summer is here and the sunny days.
When he crosses the stream there and wings o'er the sea
    Then a fear comes to me he may fail in his flight—
Well, the milk and the ale are drunk every drop,
    And a dram won't stop our thirst this night.

    from the Irish of Cathal Buidhe Mac Giolla Ghunna

OF A POET PATRIOT

His songs were a little phrase
    Of eternal song,
Drowned in the harping of lays
    More loud and long.

His deed was a single word,
    Called out alone
In a night when no echo stirred
    To laughter or moan.

But his songs new souls shall thrill,
    The loud harps dumb,

And his deed the echoes fill
When the dawn is come.

JOSEPH MARY PLUNKETT (1887–1916)

THE LITTLE BLACK ROSE SHALL BE RED AT LAST

Because we share our sorrows and our joys
And all your dear and intimate thoughts are mine
We shall not fear the trumpets and the noise
Of battle, for we know our dreams divine,
And when my heart is pillowed on your heart
And ebb and flowing of their passionate flood
Shall beat in concord love through every part
Of brain and body—when at last the blood
O'erleaps the final barrier to find
Only one source wherein to spend its strength.
And we two lovers, long but one in mind
And soul, are made only flesh at length;
Praise God if this my blood fulfils the doom
When you, dark rose, shall redden into bloom.

THIS HERITAGE TO THE RACE OF KINGS

This heritage to the race of kings
Their children and their children's seed
Have wrought their prophecies in deed
Of terrible and splendid things.

The hands that fought, the hearts that broke
In old immortal tragedies,
These have not failed beneath the skies,
Their children's heads refuse the yoke.

And still their hands shall guard the sod
That holds their father's funeral urn,

Still shall their hearts volcanic burn
With anger of the sons of God.

No alien sword shall earn as wage
The entail of their blood and tears,
No shameful price for peaceful years
Shall ever part this heritage.

Further Readings on the Poets of 1916

Bibliography

O'Hegarty, P. S. "P. H. Pearse." *Dublin Magazine* 6:3, 44–49. Reprinted, Dublin: Thom, 1931.

Selected Works

MacDonagh, Thomas. *When the Dawn is Come*. Dublin: Maunsel, 1908. Reprinted, Chicago: DePaul University. 1973.
———. *Literature in Ireland: Studies in Irish and Anglo-Irish*. Dublin: Talbot Press, 1916.
———. *Poetical Works*. Dublin: Talbot Press; London: Unwin, 1916.
Pearse, P. H. *Collected Works*. 3 vols. Dublin: Maunsel; New York: Stokes, 1917–1922.
———. *Scríbhinní. Collected Works in Gaelic*. Dublin and London: Maunsel, 1919.
———. *Collected Works*. 5 vols. Dublin, Cork, and Belfast: Phoenix, 1924.
———. *Short Stories*. Cork: Mercier Press, 1968.
———. *Literary Writings*. Edited by Séamas Ó Buachalla. Dublin: Mercier Press, 1979.
Plunkett, Joseph Mary. *Sword* [poems]. Dublin: Maunsel, 1911.
———. *Poems*. Dublin: Talbot; London: Unwin, 1916.
Ryan, Desmond, ed. *The 1916 Poets*. Dublin: Allen Figgis, 1963. Reprinted Westport, Conn.: Greenwood Press, 1979; Dublin: Carraig, 1980.

Biography and Criticism

Coffey, Thomas M. *Agony at Easter*. New York: Macmillan, 1969. Reprinted, Baltimore: Penguin, 1971.
Greaves, C. Desmond. *The Easter Rising in Song and Ballad*. London: Kahn and Averill (for the Workers' Music Association), 1980.
Loftus, Richard J. *Nationalism in Moderen Anglo-Irish Poetry*. Madison and Milwaukee: University of Wisconsin Press, 1964.

Martin, F. X., ed. *Leaders and Men of the Easter Rising: Dublin 1916.* London: Methuen, 1967.

Ryan, Desmond. *The Rising,* 4th ed. Dublin: Golden Eagle Books, 1966.

Thompson, William Irwin. *The Imagination of an Insurrection: Dublin, Easter 1916.* New York: Oxford University Press, 1967. Reprinted, New York: Harper Colophon Books, 1972.

Edwards, Ruth Dudley. *Patrick Pearse: The Truimph of Failure.* London: Gollancz, 1977.

McCay, Hedley. *Padraic Pearse: A New Biography.* Cork: Mercier Press, 1966.

Porter, Raymond. *P. H. Pearse.* New York: Twayne, 1973.

Norstedt, Johann. *Thomas MacDonagh: A Critical Biography.* Charlottesville: University Press of Virginia, 1980.

Parks, Edd Winfield, and Parks, Aileen Wells. *Thomas MacDonagh: The Man, The Patriot, The Writer.* Athens: University of Georgia Press, 1967.

PART III
IRELAND SINCE INDEPENDENCE

❧

DANIEL CORKERY
(1878–1964)

R eaders of Frank O'Connor's autobiography *An Only Child* will remember the young teacher whose passion for the Irish language as an expression of Irish national identity inspired his young students. A versatile artist-playwright as well as novelist, watercolorist as well as writer—Daniel Corkery was mentor to a generation that included Seán O'Faoláin as well as O'Connor. Describing his influence, O'Faoláin wrote: "In the boredom of Cork I do not know what I would have done without his friendly door."

A National Teacher who was Professor of English at University College, Cork from 1931 to 1947, and a member of the Seanad Éireann (1951–54), Corkery is best known for *The Hidden Ireland: A Story of Gaelic Munster in the Eighteenth Century,* a study of the poets of West Cork. A controversial and somewhat simplistic view of Irish history, it nevertheless introduces the reader to the work of such major Munster poets as Aogán Ó Rathaille and Eoghan Rua Ó Suilleabháin. These figures were models for the character of Eoghan Mor O'Donovan in "Solace," Corkery's fictional portrayal of a dispossessed poet. Indeed, Eoghan Mor's song reminds one of Aogán Ó Rathaille's "Cabhair ní ghairfead" [Help I'll not call].

SOLACE

TIME: THE EIGHTEENTH CENTURY

When Eoghan Mor O'Donovan, poet, stooped down and came in over his threshold he saw in spite of the gloom that his son Diarmuid, who all day long had been with him leading the cow at the ploughing, had

245

eaten his evening meal of potatoes and milk, and in his exhaustion had leant his head down on the deal table and fallen asleep. The boy's unkempt head was almost buried in the potato refuse. No one else the poet found before him in the cabin; and the only light was the glow of the broad fire of turf sods. Looking on the weary figure of the boy, in a flash of thought the poet beheld more plainly than when he had stood in it, the stone-strewn patch of mountainside they had been trying to soften up beneath the plough that bitter February day, and he, with the pride of the Gael in his soul, felt more deeply than ever before the hopelessness of his position, the slavery and indignity. Yes, there it was before his eyes: the dark-coloured patch of turfy hillside, with the weather-bleached rocks sticking up through its surface and piled upon them the stones and shale his bleeding hands had gathered from it winter after winter. But the vision made his voice gentle, whereas the living sight of it would have filled him with anger.

"Where's your mother, lad?" he said, laying his earthy, toil-thickened fingers on the boy's shoulder, not without gentleness and warm love in the touch. Diarmuid struggled with his sleepiness.

"Father?" he said, having failed to catch the question.

"Your mother, lad, where has she gone?"

"As I came in she was crying out angrily at a stranger, and he was laughing, mocking her, as he went away."

At the words the weariness fell from the poet's limbs. He was again a strong, gaunt peasant, his voice harsh:

"It it of Tadhg Smith the Bailiff you are speaking?" he asked, his eyes on fire.

"It is."

The poet wheeled and made passionately for the door. He stared a moment into the gathering night. Then he returned. And weariness was again in his limbs, making them heavy and awkward. Without a word he seated himself listlessly on the settle, and, a hand on either knee, stared helplessly before him. The sound of waters falling among the rocks outside, the roaring of a far-off bull on a mountain ledge, and, occasionally, the stir of the turf sods as they fell on the flagstone were the only sounds until he spoke:

"We might have left our ploughing till to-morrow—or the day after," he said.

The boy was blinking at him. The sleep had brought back some fulness to his eyes; but they were still jaded-looking.

"Yes!" he answered, not having caught all the meaning in his father's words, and "'Tis yes! indeed," replied the poet, with a return of the gentleness the first glance at the spent figure had inspired.

The boy's head went slowly down among the refuse again.

"And I might have left my new song till to-morrow or the next day," the poet added, half to himself.

But though he said the words as if he saw and felt what a foolish thing it was that he should have slipped unknowingly into the making of one more vision-song while this storm was gathering above his weed-tattered roof of scraps, the power of song was already surging up within him; and a riot of words, golden and flashing with fire and sound and colour, was already taking his brain captive, making it reel for very bliss. But it was not the words of his half-made vision-song were rioting within him now; that song was definitely done with; in the deeper inspiration the bursting of the storm had unloosed, the half-made song seemed but an idle, cold-hearted thing indeed. A new song had leaped within him, leaped with such a strength as made him reckless of the smaller things of life.

His wife entering found him as still as a tree in the evening. She too had had time to shed the first madness of despair: she spoke calmly:

"We will be saying farewell to Gortinfliuch," she said; "you have ploughed the ground for a stranger."

He was sensitive; but his song was struggling within him, growing from moment to moment, its promise vast and great: his spirit was on the heights:

"Gortinfliuch!" he said, with earnest scorn—"'tis a poor place for such as you to dwell in."

She was in the act of shaking Diarmuid from his sleep, fearing some fever was overcoming him; but she paused and looked at Eoghan; though always a wildly-earnest man, it was not often he had spoken in such a strain.

"One would think you were one of those poets who teach school, like Eoghan Ruadh," she replied, "wanderers, with whom one place is as good as another."

"One would think," he answered, in the same tone of sad earnestness, "your name had never been put into a song."

Whatever look was in his face it made her recollect the many songs he and other poets had sung to her name; she guessed that the same phrases of these old songs as were in her brain now, were singing also in his. And so she drew quietly away from the sleeping boy and, her hood still hiding her face and head, seated herself on a sugawn chair before the flameless glow; she turned to speak, but speech failed her, she could see that her husband's thoughts were gone far away. Through the one dim little pane of glass the poet saw the white stars sparkling in the sky, the night-blue of which appeared deepened and enriched by reason of the red turf-glow with which the cabin was filled. He thought of the clods in the new-ploughed field as crumbling under the touch of the keen frost—a thing that had happened ever since the beginning of the world, that would continue until the end, whatever woe befell the world of the Gael.

"God's will be done!" he said aloud out of his thoughts, and bent his head.

"Amen, O Lord," his wife answered.

They both sank again into themselves; and the silence was again deep, except when the boy would stir or snort in his sleep, but at last the woman began to rock herself, and wail in a low and constrained and unnatural tone that had but little resemblance to human speech. Uch! Uch! Ochone! she would cry at the opening of each phrase of her keening; and the name Gortinfliuch was sure to come into every sentence of it: about that homely word she was gathering up the most intimate memories in traditional phrases of woe. One would think that Gortinfliuch was a pleasant, sunny place, and a soil of good heart, instead of being what it was. And she keened old chieftains of the O'Donovans and old dynasties of the MacCarthys, the MacCarthys who once were overlords of all those bleak uplands, their sunken rivers and hidden woodlands.

To that long-continued wail of sorrow, the poet gave no heed. An odd phrase would strike on his ear and stir memories or flash landscapes on his eye. But just then the keening was of no more moment to him than all the other sorrows of men's life; the keen was a part of that life which his spirit was shaping anew, at its own imperious will. He gave no sign when her voice died away into a long litany of the saints of the Gael, and finished with the name of the Mother of God. There was then a deeper silence than before: the poet was conscious of its breadth, its grandeur. The wheeling of the night's great shield of stars had carried that heart-broken keen away with it, as it had done with a hundred others from the same stricken land; and that great shield of blue and gold had dipped its eastern rim in the western sea before any other sound except the regular breathing of the boy disturbed the fire-lit gloom.

Silent but not asleep as yet, the woman's mind was dulled and tired; her grief had spent itself; her spirit had reached that tranquil shore which lies beyond a flood of tears. Her eyes were wide, cold-lidded, piteous; and the fire of anger was entirely quenched in them. The poet's eyes were different: in them was an ever-increasing glow, but it was the heat of great energy of creation, not of anger. Except for the eyes and the tense brows, the man's tall and haggard frame might have been asleep. All day long his body had lurched and swung to the timber plough, as it skirted the rocks; now his body was having its waking rest, while his mind had taken up the ploughing—ploughing of another sort. And the fierce labour held him until at last the grey dawn touched the beams of the hut with its wan light; at which moment it seemed his song came finally to perfection. The tri-umphant "ceangal", or envoi, his first enraptured line had aspired to was reached just as the last star drew back into the spreading light of the sky. He rose silently up and stretched himself and appeared to notice for the first time the uneasy attitude of his only child, his head resting on the table, the uneasy attitude of his wife, her head fallen low on her breast. Looking at their pathetic figures, for the first time he became conscious of how the night had passed; and conscious too that a new day was come upon the uplands. There was indignity in either thought, a sense of uncomeliness, of fear; and his hut looked miserable in the cold light of morning; the golden song within his brain, however, he soon recollected, was lavish recompense not alone for this night of stormy wailing, this unhappy dawn, but for all the abiding sorrows he and his had ever wrestled with, only to be at last overthrown. It was more than recompense. It was they themselves— these sorrows of his years—crystallised, transfigured, recreated—the same in elements, the self-same, yet a solace instead of a despair, rest instead of worry, triumph instead of defeat! He had often wondered at the miracle of song; the immediate needs of his spirit bade him now not to wonder but to accept. Because he had accepted his face was calm. ‑

Fearing to awaken his little clan, it was on tip-toe he stepped from the room into the haggard. From a brad he took down a huge, clumsy-handled mall. As if still pursued with the fear of waking the sleepers, he stepped gently towards the tumble-down cow-house where their one beast—their whole wealth—had passed the night. He undid the wood bolt, stooped his head, and entered the close-smell-ing, brown-hued darkness in a gush of lovely sunbeams. The cow was lying lazily on her belly, staring up at him with mild eyes that blinked in the sudden glare. This the poet saw. Without a moment's delay, he raised the mall, swung it and struck one swift, smashing blow at the animal's skull above the eyes. The mall sank in a little way. It was withdrawn, swung again, and there was again the sound of crunching bone, less sudden, less loud. A quiver that began at the hind feet travelled through the animal's frame like a wave, another, yet another; then the life went out, and there on the floor was a high mass of bones and flesh. The poet went for his butcher's knife to let the blood run from the veins.

After a short time he re-entered his hut: his wife, his boy still slept. He wondered a moment at the silence. Then in a voice of authority, and speaking the Irish of the Bardic Schools, most classical of tongues, he cried out: "Maire, the daughter of Kearney, and Diarmuid, the son of Eoghan Mor of the Aislings, awaken! Awaken and order the house for feasting and revelling—the house of Eoghan Mor of the vision songs. Before the coming of night some of them will have gathered at our threshold—the poets of Muskerry and Carbery, Iveleary, and Iveragh and Uibhrathach, of Slieve Luchra and Corkaguiney, of Imokilly and Deise; and it will not be long until they will all have come. After the feasting I will silence them and recite, so that they may know it for ever, the song I have made in the night that has passed over us."

The glow of triumph in his appearance was more radiant than his wife had ever seen there before; yet she made bold to answer, speaking with reverence however, and as one who would urge a necessary consideration, and in the common language of the people:

"The feasting will not last for long; the poets will leave us in the end as desolate as we are now in this dawning: when at last it comes to the nailing up of the door there will be few except ourselves to behold it. Have you thought of the days that will follow on the feasting?"

"Woman," he answered her, "the sorrow that has made us desolate has this night given birth to a song that will live for ever; because of it my name and your name and our son's name, which are woven into its *amhrán* metre, will not pass: were I given my choice this moment to choose between Gortinfliuch and my song, to which would I reach my hand? This trouble that has come to our doors is as nothing to the rapture in this song of mine!"

That day the poet went east and around by the north; and his son went north and around by the west; and other messengers went in other directions announcing the Bardic Sessions that were to be held at the house of Eoghan Mor O'Donovan, and as they sped, the messengers could not refrain from hinting at a new song that had just been made which was thought to excel even Egan O'Rahilly's "Gile na Gile."

*   *   *   *   *

In the eighteenth century a certain traveller, an Englishman, wrote a book of his experiences in the south of Ireland. In one chapter he deals both with Carbery and Iveragh—in neither of which he found much to dwell on. He tells how as he left Carbery and made northwards he came to a curious scene:

> As my servant—the droll-spoken Hibernian I have previously made mention of—and myself rode through the mountain pass we became aware that some gathering must be about to take place farther on towards the west. We overtook and passed several knots of those tatterdemalion figures without which no Irish landscape seems complete; and these little groups—some of the wayfarers curiously excited in appearance, wildly gesticulating, which seems to be a national characteristic—were all making, we observed, in the one direction. Over the mountains we would notice other groups coming to swell the gathering: it was not wonderful therefore that one in whom curiosity is ever alive, as it seems to be in all those who travel much, more especially if their wanderings take them into foreign lands—should set his horse's head in the same path as these turbulent-looking figures. As daylight failed we came on a miserable hut on the fringe of a bleak upland. Several peat-fires, which had been used apparently for the cooking of huge meals, had begun to die: but their relics still encircled the house and set it apart from the one or two others in the same district. The house itself, a miserable cabin, was crowded to the door with wild and picturesque figures. We heard no language but the Gaelic. In the midst of the assembly, as I took trouble to note, a huge gaunt man was reciting what was apparently a very violent poem—to judge by the excitement under which he laboured. I can recall but two lines which run (by the way my guide offered to translate the whole poem into Latin, as he did not seem satisfied that he could appositely render it in such English as he knew):

> Till through my coffin-wood white blossoms start to grow
> No grace I'll beg from one of Cromwell's crew.

It was a strange scene to come on in the midst of lonely mountains at the close of the day; but I could not help reflecting that these strong-bodied, though ill-clad peasants, might have found better employment on an evening admirably suited for ploughing. I noticed in a patch of bogland not far from the hut some ploughing gear lying haphazardly in a half-length of furrow, as if some peasant had flung it down on hearing a call to join the curious throng. But such reflections come into the mind of the observant traveller at every hand's turn in this strange land.

Further Readings on Daniel Corkery

Bibliography

Saul, George Brandon. *Daniel Corkery*. Lewisburg, Pa.: Bucknell University Press, 1973.

Selected Works

The Hounds of Banba. New York: Viking Press, 1922.
A Munster Twilight. Cork: Mercier Press, 1963.
The Stormy Hills, London: Jonathan Cape, 1929.
The Threshold of Quiet. New York: Stokes, 1918.
The Wager and Other Stories, New York: The Devin-Adair Co., 1950.
The Yellow Bittern and Other Plays. Dublin: Talbot Press, 1920.

Studies

The Fortunes of the Irish Language. Dublin: Three Candles, 1954.
The Hidden Ireland: A Study of Gaelic Munster in the Eighteenth Century. Dublin: Gill, 1925.
Synge and Anglo-Irish Literature: A Study. Dublin: Gill, 1931.

Biography and Criticism

Cullen, L. M. "The Hidden Ireland: Re-Assessment of a Concept." *Studia Hibernica* 9:7–47.
Kiely, Ben. "Chronicle by Rushlight." *Irish Bookman* 2: 23–35.
Larkin, Emmet. "A Reconstruction: Daniel Corkery and His Ideas on Irish Cultural Nationalism." *Éire-Ireland* 8: 35–41.
McCaffrey, Lawrence. "Daniel Corkery and Irish Cultural Nationalism." *Éire-Ireland* 8: 42–51.
O'Connor, Frank. *An Only Child*. New York: Alfred A. Knopf, 1961; Dublin: Pan Books, 1970.

O'Faoláin, Seán. "Daniel Corkery." *Dublin Magazine* 11: 49–61.

———. *Vive Moi*, pp. 168–73. Boston: Little, Brown and Co., 1964.

Ó Tuama, Seán. "Dónal Ó Corcora agus Filíocht na Gaeilge." *Studia Hibernica* 5: 29–41.

Saul, George Brandon. *Daniel Corkery.* Lewisburg. Pa.: Bucknell University Press, 1973.

SEÁN O'FAOLÁIN
(b. 1900)

Though best known as one of his country's premier short-story writers, Seán O'Faoláin has been a writer of many parts in a career that has spanned more than sixty years. Born John Whelan, O'Faoláin took the Irish form of his name in response to the Easter Rising of 1916; it is pronounced "oh fwa-LOIN." Often, he has written as if he were the spokesman for the soul of modern Ireland. This was especially so during his six-year tenure as editor of the influential quarterly, *The Bell,* beginning in 1940, as he fought censorship and provincialism, championed higher critical standards, and furthered the careers of a number of younger writers. His short book, *The Irish* (1947), continues to be one of the most widely read introductions to the national culture. O'Faoláin's deep knowledge of Irish history and politics has also been demonstrated in his five biographies, including those of Eamon de Valera, Countess Markievicz, Daniel O'Connell, and the sixteenth century leader Hugh O'Neill. O'Faoláin has produced distinguished literary criticism, including *The Short Story* (1948) and *The Vanishing Hero* (1956), in addition to travel literature, autobiography, translations, plays, and poetry. Success with the novel has eluded him, however, as he has published only four of the eight he has written, and none of these to either critical or popular acclaim.

At once nationalist and cosmopolitan, O'Faoláin's career embraces many contrasts. In the course of one year in his twenties, for instance, he both served as a private in the Irish Republican Army and was introduced to a member of the British royal family as a Commonwealth scholarship winner! He studied the Irish language among peasants in the *Gaeltacht* (Irish-speaking areas), yet always

254

acknowledged his debt to the Russian writers Turgenev and Chekhov and the French novelist Stendhal. Although O'Faoláin earned a degree at Harvard University, he spent more of his adult career in Ireland than did many of his contemporaries. And while O'Faoláin led the quiet private life of a good Catholic layman, he was published frequently in *Playboy* magazine while in his seventies and eighties.

The story "A Broken World" comes from his second collection, *A Purse of Coppers* (1937). Outwardly plotless, the story is in stark, anti-romantic contrast to the author's first collection, *Midsummer Night Madness* (1932). Additionally, as several critics have noted, the story appears to be an answer to James Joyce's famous novella, "The Dead," from *Dubliners* (1914).

A BROKEN WORLD

1

"That's a lonely place!" said the priest suddenly. He was rubbing the carriage-window with his little finger. He pointed with the stem of his pipe through the window, and the flutter of snow and the blown steam of the engine, at the mountainy farm to his right. He might have been talking to himself, for he did not stir his head or remove his elbow from its rest. He was a skeleton of a man, and the veins of his temples bulged out like nerves. Peering I could barely see, below the pine-forest of "The Department," through the fog of the storm, a lone chapel and a farm-house, now a tangle of black and white. Although it was the middle of the day a light shone yellow in a byre. Then the buildings swivelled and were left behind. The land was blinding.

"Aye!" I said. "It is lonely. But," I said easily, "sure every parish is a world in itself."

He grunted and pulled at his cherrywood pipe and kept looking out the window at the whirling dots of white.

Then, without looking at me—looking down at the flap of my trousers, instead—he leaned forward, one bony hand gripping his left knee, and his elbow resting on the other knee so that he might still hold and smoke his pipe in comfort. I could see that he spoke less for the sake of conversation than from a desire to instruct me, for he seemed to get no other pleasure out of his talk.

"That used to be a credo with me, too," he said, "that every parish is a world in itself. But where there is no moral unity there is no life."

"Moral unity?"

There were ten notes in the wind, boom and whistle and groan and sigh. Listening to them I hardly heard him. The snow had stopped.

"Yes." He was cock-assuredly positive. "Life is a moral unity with a common thought. The *compositum* of one's being, emerging from the Divine Essence, which is harmony itself, cannot, unless it abdicates its own intelligence and lives in chaos, that is to say, in sin, be in disunity with itself. Since society, however, is an entity composed of many members, life becomes a moral unity with a common thought. You can see that?"

"Yes."

He went on, while I wondered if he was a professor in some seminary trying out something he had been studying. He enunciated his ideas with indrawn lips. That gave him a hellish, pedagogic look. The glare outside turned him into marble.

"In places like that—you have a broken world, and there is no unity."

In spite of this abstract way of talk the next thing he said showed me that he was not a professor.

"Let me give you an example of what life is like in those isolated places," jerking his head. "When I was ordained my first parish was a lonely parish in the County Wicklow. From my presbytery window I could see the entire coast, a long straight beach, miles to the north, miles to the south, with a headland at each end stuck out into the sea. By the sea it is marsh. Then comes the first wave of high land around villages like Newtownmountkennedy. The land isn't bad on those hills, though it isn't what you would call really good land. They grow good turnips and potatoes and mangolds; the greens are not bad; but they cannot grow wheat. You need a good marl bottom for wheat. I was a young man then, and keen, so I studied these questions."

(Whatever else you were, I said to myself, you must have been a bloody bore.)

"Look!" he said, pointing through the opposite window.

A vast, white plain, level as a sea, mapped with black hedgerows, all diminishing in size, spread away and away, maybe twenty miles, to a much lower range of mountains.

"My parish was in the same relation to that good land as these mountains here (nodding over his shoulder) in relation to that plain.

That is to say, it was mountain bog, reclaimed by much labour, but always badly drained. Last of all, beyond me, was the utterly, miserably,"—his voice was almost oratorical here—"wretched moor. Miles and miles of it on the plateau of the mountain-tops. The native tribes lived as freebooters up there as late as the end of the eighteenth century. It was wooded then, and untouched by any road. Then, in Ninety-eight, two so-called Military Roads cut it across and across like a scissors. They were fifty miles long, and straight as rulers. By the way," he asked suddenly, catching me looking idly out through the window, "were you ever in County Wicklow?"

"Oh, no, father," I replied, as suddenly. I forced myself to attend. Just then my eyes caught the eye of an old farmer seated opposite me in the carriage; he was midway on the same seat as the priest, and, so, near enough to hear everything. A pool of water had gathered around each boot. Spits starred the dry patch between. Seeing me look at him he took from his mouth, with his entire fist, a bit of a cigarette he was smoking, and winked at me. Then he put back the cigarette and contemplated the priest's face with an air of childlike wonderment. At that wink I began to listen more carefully. Evidently my priest was a local "character."

"They are remarkable roads," went on the priest. "Well, the people of my parish were all poor. The interesting thing about them is that there were two sets of names—either the old tribal names, like O'Toole or O'Byrne or Doyle, or foreign names like Ryder, Nash, Greene, Pugh, Spink, Empie, Gascon, Latour."

A little smile took the corners of his mouth as he said those names; but he never raised his eyes.

"The Greenes and Ryders and Pughs, and the rest of them, were soldiers who long ago trickled down into the houses of the poor, intermarried there, and became poor themselves as a result. However, they brought the people respect for law and order. Or; if you like, they knocked the last bit of rebel spirit out of them."

"Interesting!" I said, politely. I was beginning to enjoy the joke, for I could see the old farmer getting cross, and at the end of that last bit he had spat out his butt-end of cigarette.

"But the middle land, the good land, remained in the possession of the big people who never intermarried. When I went there to take over my duties I looked up the history of those wealthy people in *Debrett* and *Who's Who*, and *Burke's Landed Gentry*."

His palm became an imaginary book, and with his pipe-stem he followed the lines and pretended to read:

"'Lord Blank, family name of Baron Blank. Fifth baron. Created in eighteen hundred and one. Lieutenant of the Seventeenth Hussars. Married Dorothy, oldest daughter of, let's say something like James Whipple Teaman of Grange House, Dilworth, Dorsetshire, you know the kind of thing. Succeeded his father in nineteen-eighteen. Educated at Eton and Sandhurst. Address, Grosvenor Square, London. Club—Travellers' or Brooks's. Recreations? Oh, as usual, hunting, shooting, fishing, racquets, riding.'"

Again the thin smile. The farmer was gob-open.

"My parishioners were their stable-boys, gate-lodge keepers, woodmen, beaters, farmhands, lady's-maids, etcetera. *They* were always intermarrying. *Their* bits of farms, reclaimed from the furze, were always being divided. I've seen people live on a bit of land about twice the size of this carriage."

The farmer leaned forward, listening now with great interest. Our three heads nodded with the jolt of the train.

"Then there was emigration. In the five years I spent there I had one solitary marriage. I had sixty schoolchildren on roll when I went there. I had thirty-five when I left. Last year I heard they were reduced to eleven, and five of those were all one family. No wonder the county is full of ruins. You come on them in scores on scores, with, maybe, a tree growing out of the hearth, and the marks of the ridges they ploughed, still there, now smooth with grass."

"Begobs, then, they're here too, father," said the old farmer. The priest nodded sideways to him and proceeded:

"I like the people. They were clean; hard-working; respectful. Too respectful—tipping their hats to everybody. They were always making what we call the poor mouth—a mendicant habit of centuries, I suppose. They gave me no trouble, except for two things. They had a habit of writing anonymous letters, and I couldn't stop it. They were at it all the time. They wrote them to one another."

He paused. I prompted him. The farmer leaned closer and closer.

"The other thing?" I asked.

"The other thing?" he said irritably to his pipe-bowl. "In every one of these cabins they earned money by taking in boarded-out children—children unwanted by poor parents, or simply illegitimates. There was hardly a cottage without one, two, or three of these stranger children. They were well looked after, and the people often grew so fond of them they wouldn't part with them; and, I suppose, that was a nice trait too. But the point is that the only fresh blood coming into the county was . . . Well . . . a curious county, as you can see, and the morals were a bit curious too. However, that's enough about them."

And he had at least enough sense to go no further with that.

"Well, there you are. That was my parish, and you can't say it was a world in itself. It was too incomplete. Too many things left out. The human dignity of men is always impaired when, like that, they're depending on other people who can make or break them. They weren't men. They were servants. That's the whole of it."

"But did that make their lives lonely? You said they were lonely?"

For the first time he looked up at me. The veins on his temples, swollen from holding his head down, throbbed with relief.

"I didn't say *they* were lonely."

His eyes wavered sideways to the farmer. I easily followed him over the hiatus when he jumped to—

"One day, after three years without stepping out of the parish, I decided to see if the neighbouring parish was any better." (When I heard the personal note come into his voice I wished the farmer was not there; as it was he kept to his cold, factual description.)

"Do you know, the contrast was amazing! When I climbed down to the valley and the good land! And it was the trees that made me realize it. Beeches instead of pines. Great, old beeches with roots like claws on the double ditches. The farm-houses, too. They were large and prosperous with everything you might expect to find in a sturdy English farm—barns, ducks in the pond, thick-packed granaries, airy lofts, a pigeon-croft, a seat under an arbour, fruit-gardens.

"All that was good. But it was those beeches that really impressed me. They were so clean and old, not like the quick-growing pines of the mountains—dirty trees that scatter their needles into the shoots of the houses and block them up three times every winter."

"Oh, they're buggurs, father!" agreed the farmer earnestly.

"I climbed lower still and came to the gates of the houses where the gentry used to live."

"Used to?"

"Used to. I should have expected it, but somehow it hadn't occurred to me. It's funny how we all forget how time passes. But there they were—the gate posts falling. The lodges boarded up. Notices, *For Sale*. Fifteen years of grass on the avenues. You see? Owns ten thousand acres in Ireland. Address, Grosvenor Square, London.'"

The pipe-stem travelled across the palm.

"I met an old man who took me down one of those avenues to see the ruins of a big house burned out during the troubled times. It was a lovely spring evening. The sky was like milk. The rooks were cawing about the roofless chimneys just like the flakes of soot come to life again. I spotted a queer little building at the end of a cypress avenue. The old man called it the oftaphone. He meant octagon. It was a kind of peristyle. He said, "The Lord"—just like that, "The Lord used to have tea-parties and dances there long ago." I went into it and it had a magnificent view, a powerful view, across the valley over at my mountainy parish, yes, and beyond it to the ridges of the mountains, and even beyond that again to the very moors behind with their last little flecks and drifts of snow. They could have sat there and drunk their tea and seen my people—the poor Ryders, and Greenes, and O'Tooles, making little brown lines in the far-off fields in the plough-ing time."

"They could! Oh, begobs, father, so they could!"—and a mighty spit.

"Or at night, of summer evenings, they could have sipped their brandy and coffee and seen the little yellow lights of our cabin windows, and said, How pretty it is!'"

"Begobs, yes! That's true!"

If anyone entered the carriage then he would have taken us for three friends, we were huddled together so eagerly. The priest went on:

"'They must have had good times here, once?' I said to the man who was with me. 'The best, father!' says he. 'Oh, the best out. The best while they lasted. And there were never any times like the old times. But they're scattered now, father, says he, 'to the four winds. And they'll never come back.' 'Who owns the land, now?' I asked him. 'They own it always, but who wants it?' says he. 'The people here don't want it. They'd rather live in the towns and cities and work for wages.'"

"That's right," said the farmer, as if we were really discussing his own county. "Begobs, you're talking sense now, father!"

"'The land was kept from them too long,' says he. 'And now they have lost the knack of it. I have two grown sons of my own, says he, 'and they're after joining the British Army.'"

"Begobs, yes!" said the farmer, leaning to catch every word; but the priest stopped and leaned back.

The white, cold fields were singing by us. The cabins so still they might be rocks clung to the earth. The priest was looking at them and we were all looking at them, and at the flooded and frozen pools of water divided by the hedgerows. By his talk he had evoked a most powerful sense of comradeship in that carriage, whether he meant to or not: we felt one. Then, as quickly, he proceeded to break it.

"Well!" I asked eagerly. "Well?"

"Why, that's all!" said the priest. "I came back from my voyage of exploration, much refreshed. Much improved in spirits. You see, I had extended the pattern of life of my own poor parish. I saw how, how—I mean, how the whole thing had worked, hung together, made up a real unity. It was like putting two halves of a broken plate together. As I walked up another one of those hill-roads on my way home I passed more prosperous houses—smaller houses this time, what you would call private houses. They had neat, green curtains with fine, polished brassware inside on the polished mahogany. And through another window three aluminium hot-water bottles shining on a dark hall-table, signs of comfort as you might say. . . . Yes! I had completed the pattern. That parish and my parish made up a world, as neither did by itself, rich and poor, culture and . . ."

"But," I cried angrily, "where's your moral unity? Your common thought? it's absurd."

"Oh, yes! I realized that even before I got home. I just tell you the thing as it happened. But they in their octagon and we in our lighted cabins, I mean to say, it was two halves of a world . . ."

The farmer was looking at us both with dull, stupid eyes. He had lost the thread of the talk.

"Yes, I suppose so," I agreed, just as lightly. "But now that the gentry are gone, won't the people, the mountainy people, and so on, begin to make a complete world of their own?"

He shook his head. The farmer listened again.

"I refuse to believe they won't," I said.

He shrugged his shoulders.

"And is there no possible solution then?" I asked him.

He was looking out of the window, his poll to the farmer. He rolled up his eyes under his brows—a warning look, and faintly indicated the man behind him. Then he actually began to laugh, a cold, cackling laugh, an extraordinary, inhuman, kind of laugh that ended in a noise like a little groan.

The train slowed up, and we were in a station, and he was gathering his bags. He got out without even saying "Good day" to us, and his face was coldly composed. A manservant, touching his cap, took the bags. The station-master touched his cap to him. The porter receiving the tickets touched his cap to him. The jarvey, who was waiting for him, bowed as he received the bags from the manservant.

Black, tall, thin, and straight as a lamp-post, he left the lit, snow-bright station with every down-looking lounger there bowing and hat-touching as he passed. When I turned away the train was moving out, and the old farmer, in his own place, had lit another cigarette.

2

"Do you know his reverence?' I asked—as irritated as somebody from whom a book has been snatched before the end of the tale.

"Oh, aye!" said the old man, and he added, without interest: "He's silenced."

There was a touch of dread in that word, "silenced."

"What did they silence him for?"

"Politics."

"Oh? He was too extreme?"

"Aye!" Still without interest.

"A clever man?"

No answer. His mind had gone to sleep. I looked at him in annoyance.

"What kind of ideas had he? I mean, what did he want?"

"Begobs, I dunno."

Then he added, as if it was a matter of no importance—

"He wanted the people to have the land."

"What land?"

"The land. The gentry's land."

I leaned to him eagerly—

"But isn't that what ye want? Isn't that what the whole trouble is? Isn't that what the Government wants?"

"Aye. I suppose it is, you know? But he wanted it to be a sudden business."

"They didn't silence him for that?"

"Maybe they didn't. Ach, he's odd. Sure, he took ten or twenty foolish young lads and, one night, he thrun down the walls of Lord Milltown's estate. He started some sort of a League, too. He's odd. God help him."

"What did he want to do with this League of his?"

"I dunno. It was some kind of faddy business. He wanted halls . . . and . . . some kind of halls he wanted. Halls. I dunno what he wanted 'em for. Ah, he's a decent poor man."

I tried another line.

"I suppose it's true for his reverence—ye have a hard time of it up here on the poor land?"

Puffing at his ease he was looking idly at the passing fields. A woman and two small boys, crushed into the doorway of a cabin, waved to us. He looked, and when they were gone his eyes were still fixed, seeing whatever passed beneath them with equal interest—or disinterest?

He tilted his head, but he said nothing. I made one last effort to shake him from his lethargic mood—possibly, most likely indeed, the mood in which he spent the greater part of his life.

"You know," I said, warmly, "I think I'd die in this lonely place. That priest is right!"

He looked at it, and scratched his ear, and said:

"Aye!" And then, suddenly, he added a second "Aye!"—and then, when I thought he was finished, he actually added—"I suppose 'tis quiet," and relapsed into indifference.

Angrily I burst out at him—

"But damn it all, don't you mind, or is it that ye don't want to stir, ye're too damn lazy to stir?"

He took the butt-end from his mouth, and he looked at me, and by the way he looked up and down at me, I was hoping he would say something bitter and strong. But his stare was childish, and the eyes wavered, as if he was very tired. He just dropped one last, vast spit on the wet floor, snuggled into his corner, and went to sleep under his hat.

In his sleep he was as motionless as a rock; but you could not say he was "like a rock" because he was like nothing on earth but himself, everything about him was so personal to him. Unless, because he was so much a random accumulation of work and season and all that belongs to the first human that was ever made, I chose to say, as I glared at him snoring in his corner, that time and nature had engendered something no more human than a rock. So I thought, as the dusk drew down, and the wind moaned in many keys, and the snow blew horizontally and stuck to the edges of the window. It was as if we two might have been jolting into a blank beyond either sleep or night, and I wanted to get up and kick him. I felt that if I did he would only moo.

We halted at several stations, with their one or two silent white-shouldered figures. He slept on. I was just wondering if I should wake him when suddenly, at a station, identical with every other station, as if some animal magnetism in the place stirred him, he rose and stumbled out. He did not speak. He did not raise his head to see if it was his station. He saluted no one. Anyway, there was no one there but a muffled porter who silently waved a lantern over his head. As we moved off he was trudging in the middle of a road that glimmered with its own strange afterglow, passing between a row of pines whose sheltered sides were red and raw as with the cold. He was exactly like an old black mongrel loping home.

3

So I was left with the pool of water on the floor, dark under the carriage-light, and the snow crumbling into the corners of the windows outside, and beyond that only the light leaping and falling along the hedges. And in another two hours or so, when I got out, the carriage would be racing along, empty, through the night—three bits of separateness, the priest and the farmer and myself, flung off it like bits of the *disjecta membra* of the wheel of life.

For those two hours I tried to refute the talk of that priest, thinking that he had merely spoken out of the snowy landscape, which above all other conditions of nature is so powerful to make life seem lonely, and all work futile, and time itself a form of decay; or thinking that, had it been the green-dripping spring or the hot summer, we might all have shown different and more happy sides of our worlds; or thinking that the thin cheeks and the throbbing nerve of the man were nothing but the sign of twenty years of self-corrosion, and that even when he was a young man in his first parish, his heart must have been so bitter and vain that, like a leech, it began to destroy everything to preserve itself; or thinking that because of it he had joined us for a few moments until we seemed to crouch over a fire, and then deliberately scattered us and left us with his pox. But, though that might be all true, I could not deny to the wintry moment its own truth, and that under that white shroud, covering the whole of Ireland, life was lying broken and hardly breathing. His impress remained even when the train swished slowly into the city, where the arc-lamps sizzled in the snow, and the sounds were muffled, and through every street a sharp, pure wind blew down from the Wicklow hills. Once their distant convex gleamed, far away, beyond the vista of a street. There were few people abroad, and as they walked against the wind with huddled backs they, too, seemed to be shrouding something within them that slept, and barely palpitated, and was hurt by the cold. What image, I wondered, as I passed through them, could warm them as the Wicklow priest had warmed us for a few minutes in that carriage now chugging around the edge of the city to the sea? What image of life that would fire and fuse us all, what music bursting like the spring, what triumph, what engendering love, so that those breasting mountains that now looked cold should appear brilliant and gay, the white land that seemed to sleep should appear to smile, and these people who huddled over the embers of their lives should become like the peasants who held the hand of Faust with their singing one Easter morning? Perhaps it was foolish to wish for such an image—so magnificent that it would have the power of a resurrection call? Yet, there are times, as when we hear the percussion of some great music, or when we feel the shrivelling effect of the cold wind and snow, that leave us no other choice but to live splendidly, or gather up at least enough grace for a quick remove.

The train could be heard easily, in the rarefied air, chugging across the bridges that span the city, bearing with it an empty coach. In the morning, Ireland, under its snow, would be silent as a perpetual dawn.

Further Readings on Seán O'Faoláin

Selected Works

The Collected Short Stories of Sean O'Faolain. 3 vols. London: Constable, 1980–83; Boston: Little Brown, 1983.

Constance Markievicz: or, The Average Revolutionary. London and Toronto: Cape, 1934; rev. ed., London: Sphere Books, 1968.

De Valera. Harmondsworth: Penguin, 1939.

The Great O'Neill: A Biography of Hugh O'Neill, Earl of Tyrone, 1550–1616. London: Longmans; New York: Duell, Sloan, Pearce, 1942.

The Irish. West Drayton: Penguin, 1947. Under the title *The Irish: A Character Study.* New York: Devin-Adair, 1949; rev, ed, Harmondsworth: Penguin, 1969.

King of Beggars: A Life of Daniel O'Connell, The Irish Liberator. London: Nelson; New York: Viking, 1938. Reprinted, Dublin: Allen Figgis, 1970.

Midsummer Night Madness. London and Toronto: Cape; New York: Viking, 1932.

A Purse of Coppers. London and Toronto: Cape, 1937; Viking, 1938.

Selected Stories. Boston: Little Brown, 1978.

Short Stories: A Study in Pleasure. Boston: Little, Brown, 1961.

The Short Story. London and Toronto: Collins, 1948; New York: Devin-Adair, 1951.

The Vanishing Hero: Studies in the Novelists of the Twenties. London: Eyre and Spottiswoode, 1956; Boston and Toronto: Little Brown, 1957.

Biography and Criticism

Bonaccorso, Richard. *Sean O'Faolain's Irish Vision.* Albany: State University of New York Press, 1987.

Doyle, Paul A. *Seán O'Faoláin.* New York: Twayne, 1968.

Harmon, Maurice. *Seán O'Faoláin: A Critical Introduction.* South Bend, Ind.: University of Notre Dame Press, 1967.

Irish University Review. Seán O'Faoláin number 6.

Rippier, Joseph Storey. *The Short Stories of Seán O'Faoláin: A Study in Descriptive Technique.* Gerrards Cross, England: Colin Smythe, 1976.

FRANK O'CONNOR
(1903–66)

Although born in poverty and self-educated, Frank O'Connor became one of the most accomplished short-story writers in Ireland, as well as a gifted translator and discerning critic. (Born Michael O'Donovan, he used the pseudonym Frank O'Connor throughout his career.) Critical recognition came immediately and persisted through his thirty-year-long career. The success of his first collection, *Guests of the Nation* (1931), helped to win the position of artistic director of the Abbey Theatre and a working relationship with Yeats from 1935–39. In his last years, his stories appeared regularly in *The New Yorker*, America's most prestigious short-story journal.

O'Connor did less well with the novel, as his two efforts, *The Saint and Mary Kate* (1932) and *Dutch Interior* (1940), are usually ranked among his lesser works. More impressive are his various books dealing with Irish tradition and Old Irish literature. His *Irish Miles* (1947) is both a personal travelogue and an argument for the preservation of early buildings and monuments. A series of lively translations from the Irish (or Gaelic) helped to introduce that literature to a wide international readership; among the most important of these are *The Midnight Court* (1946), from the 18th century poet Brian Merriman; *Kings, Lords, & Commons* (1959); and *The Golden Treasury of Irish Poetry* (1967). O'Connor wrote extensively on literature, and some of his studies have been much admired, especially *Mirror on the Roadway* (1956) on the art of the novel and *The Loneley Voice* (1962) on the art of the short story. In the years before his death he wrote a personalized history of Irish literature, *The Backward Look* (1967)—the only work of its kind ever attempted by a significant Irish writer. Finally, his two volumes of autobiography, *An*

Only Child (1961) and *My Father's Son* (1968), are often ranked with the finest work produced by any Irish writer in this century.

During most of his career O'Connor was a scourge of Irish provincialism and puritanism, a fact that caused some of his books to be banned. Ireland remained his principal concern, however, although he did not always wish to live there. He was affiliated with the British Broadcasting Corporation in the 1940s before emigrating to the United States in 1951, where he lectured at several universities, including Harvard and Stanford. One of his many students in America was Ken Kesey, author of *One Flew Over the Cuckoo's Nest* (1962). After suffering a stroke in 1961, O'Connor returned to Ireland.

"The Long Road to Ummera" (1940), one of O'Connor's best-known stories, first appeared in *The Bell*, edited by his friend and fellow Corkman, Seán O'Faoláin.

THE LONG ROAD TO UMMERA

Stay for me there. I will not fail
To meet thee in that hollow vale.

Always in the evenings you saw her shuffle up the road to Miss O.'s for her little jug of porter, a shapeless lump of an old woman in a plaid shawl, faded to the color of snuff, that dragged her head down on to her bosom where she clutched its folds in one hand; a canvas apron and a pair of men's boots without laces. Her eyes were puffy and screwed up in tight little buds of flesh and her rosy old face that might have been carved out of a turnip was all crumpled with blindness. The old heart was failing her, and several times she would have to rest, put down the jug, lean against the wall, and lift the weight of the shawl off her head. People passed; she stared at them humbly; they saluted her; she turned her head and peered after them for minutes on end. The rhythm of life had slowed down in her till you could scarcely detect its faint and sluggish beat. Sometimes from some queer instinct of shyness she turned to the wall, took a snuffbox from her bosom, and shook out a pinch on the back of her swollen hand. When she sniffed it it smeared her nose and upper lip and spilled all over her old black blouse. She raised the hand to her eyes and looked at it closely and reproachfully, as though astonished that it no longer served her properly. Then she dusted herself, picked up the old jug again, scratched herself against her clothes, and shuffled along close by the wall, groaning aloud.

When she reached her own house, which was a little cottage in a terrace, she took off her boots, and herself and the old cobbler who lodged with her turned out a pot of potatoes on the table, stripping them with their fingers and dipping them in the little mound of salt while they took turn and turn about with the porter jug. He was a lively and philosophic old man called Johnny Thornton.

After their supper they sat in the firelight, talking about old times in the country and long-dead neighbors, ghosts, fairies, spells, and charms. It always depressed her son, finding them together like that when he called with her monthly allowance. He was a well-to-do businessman with a little grocery shop in the South Main Street and a little house in Sunday's Well, and nothing would have pleased him better than that his mother should share all the grandeur with him, the carpets and the china and the chiming clocks. He sat moodily between them, stroking his long jaw, and wondering why they talked so much about death in the old-fashioned way, as if it was something that made no difference at all.

"Wisha, what pleasure do ye get out of old talk like that?" he asked one night.

"Like what, Pat?" his mother asked with her timid smile.

"My goodness," he said, "ye're always at it. Corpses and graves and people that are dead and gone."

"Arrah, why wouldn't we?" she replied, looking down stiffly as she tried to button the open-necked blouse that revealed her old breast. "Isn't there more of us there than here?"

"Much difference 'twill make to you when you won't know them or see them!" he exclaimed.

"Oye, why wouldn't I know them?" she cried angrily. "Is it the Twomeys of Lackroe and the Driscolls of Ummera?"

"How sure you are we'll take you to Ummera!" he said mockingly.

"Och aye, Pat," she asked, shaking herself against her clothes with her humble stupid wondering smile, "and where else would you take me?"

"Isn't our own plot good enough for you?" he asked. "Your own son and your grandchildren?"

"Musha, indeed, is it in the town you want to bury me?" she shrugged herself and blinked into the fire, her face growing sour and obstinate. "I'll go back to Ummera, the place I came from."

"Back to the hunger and misery we came from," Pat said scornfully.

"Back to your father, boy."

"Ay, to be sure, where else? But my father or grandfather never did for you what I did. Often and often I scoured the streets of Cork for a few ha'pence for you."

"You did, amossa, you did, you did," she admitted, looking into the fire and shaking herself. "You were a good son to me."

"And often I did it and the belly falling out of me with hunger," Pat went on, full of self-pity.

" 'Tis true for you," she mumbled, " 'tis, 'tis, 'tis true. 'Twas often and often you had to go without it. What else could you do and the way we were left?"

"And now our grave isn't good enough for you," he complained. There was real bitterness in his tone. He was an insignificant little man and jealous of the power the dead had over her.

She looked at him with the same abject, half-imbecile smile, the wrinkled old eyes almost shut above the Mongolian cheekbones, while with a swollen old hand, like a pot-stick, it had so little life in it, she smoothed a few locks of yellow-white hair across her temples—a trick she had when troubled.

"Musha, take me back to Ummera, Pat," she whined. "Take me back to my own. I'd never rest among strangers. I'd be rising and drifting."

"Ah, foolishness, woman!" he said with an indignant look. "That sort of thing is gone out of fashion."

"I won't stop here for you," she shouted hoarsely in sudden, impotent fury, and she rose and grasped the mantelpiece for support.

"You won't be asked," he said shortly.

"I'll haunt you," she whispered tensely, holding on to the mantelpiece and bending down over him with a horrible grin.

"And that's only more of the foolishness," he said with a nod of contempt. "Haunts and fairies and spells."

She took one step towards him and stood, plastering down the two little locks of yellowing hair, the half-dead eyes twitching and blinking in the candlelight, and the swollen crumpled face with the cheeks like cracked enamel.

"Pat," she said, "the day we left Ummera you promised to bring me back. You were only a little gorsoon that time. The neighbors gathered round me and the last word I said to them and I going down the road was: 'Neighbors, my son Pat is after giving me his word and he'll bring me back to ye when my time comes.' . . . That's as true as the Almighty God is over me this night. I have everything ready." She went to the shelf under the stairs and took out two parcels. She seemed to be speaking to herself as she opened them gloatingly, bending down her head in the feeble light of the candle. "There's the two brass candlesticks and the blessed candles alongside them. And there's my shroud aired regular on the line."

"Ah, you're mad, woman," he said angrily. "Forty miles! Forty miles into the heart of the mountains!"

She suddenly shuffled towards him on her bare feet, her hand raised clawing the air, her body like her face blind with age. Her harsh croaking old voice rose to a shout.

"I brought you from it, boy, and you must bring me back. If 'twas the last shilling you had and you and your children to go to the poorhouse after, you must bring me back to Ummera. And not by the short road either! Mind what I say now! The long road! The long road to Ummera round the lake, the way I brought you from it. I lay a heavy curse on you this night if your bring me the short road over the hill. And ye must stop by the ash tree at the foot of the boreen where ye can see my little house and say a prayer for all that were ever old in it and all that played on the floor. And then—Pat! Pat Driscoll! Are you listening? Are you listening to me, I say?"

She shook him by the shoulder, peering down into his long miserable face to see how was he taking it.

"I'm listening," he said with a shrug.

"Then"—her voice dropped to a whisper—"you must stand up overright the neighbors and say—remember now what I'm telling you!—'Neighbors, this is Abby, Batty Heige's daughter, that kept her promise to ye at the end of all.'"

She said it lovingly, smiling to herself, as if it were a bit of an old song, something she went over and over in the long night. All West Cork was in it: the bleak road over the moors to Ummera, the smooth gray pelts of the hills with the long spider's web of the fences ridging them, drawing the scarecrow fields awry, and the whitewashed cottages, poker-faced between their little scraps of holly bushes looking this way and that out of the wind.

"Well, I'll make a fair bargain with you," said Pat as he rose. Without seeming to listen she screwed up her eyes and studied his weak melancholy face. "This house is a great expense to me. Do what I'm always asking you. Live with me and I'll promise I'll take you back to Ummera."

"Oye, I will not," she replied sullenly, shrugging her shoulders helplessly, an old sack of a woman with all the life gone out of her.

"All right," said Pat. "'Tis your own choice. That's my last word;

take it or leave it. Live with me and Ummera for your grave, or stop here and a plot in the Botanics."

She watched him out the door with shoulders hunched about her ears. Then she shrugged herself, took out her snuffbox and took a pinch.

"Arrah, I wouldn't mind what he'd say," said Johnny. "A fellow like that would change his mind tomorrow."

"He might and he mightn't," she said heavily, and opened the back door to go out to the yard. It was a starry night and they could hear the noise of the city below them in the valley. She raised her eyes to the bright sky over the back wall and suddenly broke into a cry of loneliness and helplessness.

"Oh, oh, oh, 'tis far away from me Ummera is tonight above any other night, and I'll die and be buried here, far from all I ever knew and the long roads between us."

Of course old Johnny should have known damn well what she was up to the night she made her way down to the cross, creeping along beside the railings. By the blank wall opposite the lighted pub Dan Regan, the jarvey, was standing by his old box of a covered car with his pipe in his gob. He was the jarvey all the old neighbors went to. Abby beckoned to him and he followed her into the shadow of a gateway overhung with ivy. He listened gravely to what she had to say, sniffing and nodding, wiping his nose in his sleeve, or crossing the pavement to hawk his nose and spit in the channel, while his face with its drooping mustaches never relaxed its discreet and doleful expression.

Johnny should have known what that meant and why old Abby, who had always been so open-handed, sat before an empty grate sooner than light a fire, and came after him on Fridays for the rent, whether he had it or not, and even begrudged him the little drop of porter which had always been give and take between them. He knew himself it was a change before death and that it all went into the wallet in her bosom. At night in her attic she counted it by the light of her candle and when the coins dropped from her lifeless fingers he heard her roaring like an old cow as she crawled along the naked boards, sweeping them blindly with her palms. Then he heard the bed creak as she tossed about in it, and the rosary being taken from the bedhead, and the old voice rising and falling in prayer; and sometimes when a high wind blowing up the river roused him before dawn he could hear her muttering: a mutter and then a yawn; the scrape of a match as she peered at the alarm clock—the endless nights of the old—and then the mutter of prayer again.

But Johnny in some ways was very dense, and he guessed nothing till the night she called him and, going to the foot of the stairs with a candle in his hand, he saw her on the landing in her flour-bag shift, one hand clutching the jamb of the door while the other clawed wildly at her few straggly hairs.

"Johnny!" she screeched down at him, beside herself with excitement. "He was here."

"Who was there?" he snarled back, still cross with sleep.

"Michael Driscoll, Pat's father."

"Ah, you were dreaming, woman," he said in disgust. "Go back to your bed in God's holy name."

"I was not dreaming," she cried. "I was lying broad awake, saying my beads, when he come in the door, beckoning me. Go down to Dan Regan's for me, Johnny."

"I will not, indeed, go down to Dan Regan's for you. Do you know what hour of night it is?"

" 'Tis morning."

" 'Tis. Four o'clock! What a thing I'd do! . . . Is it the way you're feeling bad?" he added with more consideration as he mounted the stairs. "Do you want him to take you to hospital?"

"Oye, I'm going to no hospital," she replied sullenly, turning her back on him and thumping into the room again. She opened an old chest of drawers and began fumbling in it for her best clothes, her bonnet and cloak.

"Then what the blazes do you want Dan Regan for?" he snarled in exasperation.

"What matter to you what I want him for?" she retorted with senile suspicion. "I have a journey to go, never you mind where."

"Ach, you old oinseach, your mind is wandering," he cried. "There's a divil of a wind blowing up the river. The whole house is shaking. That's what you heard. Make your mind easy now and go back to bed."

"My mind is not wandering," she shouted. "Thanks be to the Almighty God I have my senses as good as you. My plans are made. I'm going back now where I came from. Back to Ummera."

"Back to where?" Johnny asked in stupefaction.

"Back to Ummera."

"You're madder than I thought. And do you think or imagine Dan Regan will drive you?"

"He will drive me then," she said, shrugging herself as she held an old petticoat to the light. "He's booked for it any hour of the day or night."

"Then Dan Regan is madder still."

"Leave me alone now," she muttered stubbornly, blinking and shrugging. "I'm going back to Ummera and that was why my old comrade came for me. All night and every night I have my beads wore out, praying the Almighty God and His Blessed Mother not to leave me die among strangers. And now I'll leave my old bones on a high hilltop in Ummera."

Johnny was easily persuaded. It promised to be a fine day's outing and a story that would delight a pub, so he made tea for her and after that went down to Dan Regan's little cottage, and before smoke showed from any chimney on the road they were away. Johnny was hopping about the car in his excitement, leaning out, shouting through the window of the car to Dan and identifying big estates that he hadn't seen for years. When they were well outside the town, himself and Dan went in for a drink, and while they were inside the old woman dozed. Dan Regan roused her to ask if she wouldn't take a drop of something and at first she didn't know who he was and then she asked where they were and peered out at the public-house and the old dog sprawled asleep in the sunlight before the door. But when next they halted she had fallen asleep again, her mouth hanging open and her breath coming in noisy gusts. Dan's face grew gloomier. He looked hard at her and spat. Then he took a few turns about the road, lit his pipe and put on the lid.

"I don't like her looks at all, Johnny," he said gravely. "I done wrong. I see that now. I done wrong."

After that, he halted every couple of miles to see how she was and Johnny, threatened with the loss of his treat, shook her and shouted at her. Each time Dan's face grew graver. He walked gloomily about the road, clearing his nose and spitting in the ditch. "God direct me!" he said solemnly. "'Twon't be wishing to me. Her son is a powerful man. He'll break me yet. A man should never interfere between families. Blood is thicker than water. The Regans were always unlucky."

When they reached the first town he drove straight to the police barrack and told them the story in his own peculiar way.

"Ye can tell the judge I gave ye every assistance," he said in a reasonable brokenhearted tone. "I was always a friend of the law. I'll keep nothing back—a pound was the price agreed. I suppose if she dies 'twill be manslaughter. I never had hand, act or part in politics. Sergeant Daly at the Cross knows me well."

When Abby came to herself she was in a bed in the hospital. She began to fumble for her belongings and her shrieks brought a crowd of unfortunate old women about her.

"Whisht, whisht, whisht!" they said. "They're all in safe-keeping. You'll get them back."

"I want them now," she shouted, struggling to get out of bed while they held her down. "Leave me go, ye robbers of hell! Ye night-walking rogues, leave me go. Oh, murder, murder! Ye're killing me."

At last an old Irish-speaking priest came and comforted her. He left her quietly saying her beads, secure in the promise to see that she was buried in Ummera no matter what anyone said. As darkness fell, the beads dropped from her swollen hands and she began to mutter to herself in Irish. Sitting about the fire, the ragged old women whispered and groaned in sympathy. The Angelus rang out from a nearby church. Suddenly Abby's voice rose to a shout and she tried to lift herself on her elbow.

"Ah, Michael Driscoll, my friend, my kind comrade, you didn't forget me after all the long years. I'm a long time away from you but I'm coming at last. They tried to keep me away, to make me stop among foreigners in the town, but where would I be at all without you and all the old friends? Stay for me, my treasure! Stop and show me the way. . . . Neighbors," she shouted, pointing into the shadows, "that man there is my own husband, Michael Driscoll. Let ye see he won't leave me to find my way alone. Gather round me with yeer lanterns, neighbors, till I see who I have. I know ye all. 'Tis only the sight that's weak on me. Be easy now, my brightness, my own kind loving comrade. I'm coming. After all the long years I'm on the road to you at last. . . ."

It was a spring day full of wandering sunlight when they brought her the long road to Ummera, the way she had come from it forty years before. The lake was like a dazzle of midges; the shafts of the sun revolving like a great millwheel poured their cascades of milky sunlight over the hills and the little whitewashed cottages and the little black mountain cattle among the scarecrow fields. The hearse stopped at the foot of the lane that led to the roofless cabin just as she had pictured it to herself in the long nights, and Pat, looking more melancholy than ever, turned to the waiting neighbors and said:

"Neighbors, this is Abby, Batty Heige's daughter, that kept her promise to ye at the end of all."

Further Readings on Frank O'Connor

Bibliography

Sheehy, Maurice. "Towards a Bibliography of Frank O'Connor's Writing." In *Michael/Frank: Studies on Frank O'Connor,* ed. M. Sheehy. pp. 168–99. Dublin: Gill and Macmillan; New York: Knopf, 1969.

Selected Works

The Backward Look: A Survey of Irish Literature. London: Macmillan, 1967. Under the title *A Short History of Irish Literature: A Backward Look.* New York: Putnam, 1967.
Collected Stories. New York: Knopf, 1981.
Dutch Interior. New York and London: Macmillan, 1940. Reprinted, Dublin: Millington, 1973.
The Golden Treasury of Irish Poetry. Edited, with David Greene. London: Macmillan, 1967.
Guests of the Nation. London and New York: Macmillan, 1931. Reprinted, Swords, Republic of Ire.: Poolbeg, 1979.
Irish Miles. London: Macmillan, 1947.
Kings, Lords, & Commons. New York: Knopf, 1959; London: Macmillan, 1961.
The Lonely Voice. Cleveland, Ohio: World, 1962; London: Macmillan, 1963.
The Midnight Court. A Rhythmical Bacchanalia from the Irish of Bryan Merriman. Dublin: Fridberg, 1947.
The Mirror in the Roadway. New York: Knopf, 1956; London: Hamish Hamilton, 1957.
My Father's Son. London: Macmillan, 1968; New York: Knopf, 1969.
An Only Child. New York: Knopf, 1961; London: Macmillan, 1962.
The Saint and Mary Kate. London: Macmillan, 1932, 1936; New York: Macmillan, 1932.

Biography and Criticism

Matthews, James H. *Frank O'Connor.* Lewisburg, Pa.: Bucknell University Press, 1976.
———. *Voices: A Life of Frank O'Connor.* New York: Atheneum, 1983.
Sheehy, Maurice, ed. *Michael/Frank: Studies on Frank O'Connor.* Dublin. Gill and Macmillan; New York: Knopf, 1969.
Tomory, William M. *Frank O'Connor.* Boston: Twayne, 1980.
Wohlgelernter, Maurice. *Frank O'Connor: An Introduction.* New York: Columbia University Press, 1977.

LIAM O'FLAHERTY
(1896–1984)

Liam O'Flaherty's best-known work is *The Informer* (1925), a novel about betrayal set in Dublin during the 1920s. John Ford made it into a film and Victor McLaglen won an Academy Award for his role as Gypo Nolan. It is Irish rural life, however, especially life on the Aran Islands where he was born, that provides the theme and setting for most of O'Flaherty's fiction—stories of islanders and their creatures, stories set in a grim world of rock, sea, and sky and told with simplicity and dignity.

O'Flaherty's own story would provide the plot for several novels. By his account, he studied to be a priest, served in the Irish Guards in World War I, led an army of unemployed into the Rotunda Hospital in Dublin, joined the Republicans during the Civil War, shipped out as a merchant sailor, cut lumber in Canada, intrigued in the Balkans, taught in Rio, and stumped for the Irish Communist Party. He then settled down to a writing career that produced more than a dozen novels and several volumes of short stories, as well as two autobiographies, a biography, social and political commentary, an appreciation of Joseph Conrad, and a play. In 1953, O'Flaherty published *Dúil,* a collection of stories that first appeared in English. It was praised by a number of Irish critics, including Seán Ó Riordáin, who wrote in his diary that reading the stories was like holding a live robin in his hands.

"Going into Exile" describes the poignant leave-taking of two Aran teenagers who are going to America. Here the writer may have drawn on the departure of his own brother, since Tom Flaherty's autobiography tells a similar story, although one focused on the restrained but deeply felt relationship between father and son.

277

GOING INTO EXILE

Patrick Feeney's cabin was crowded with people. In the large kitchen men, women, and children lined the walls, three deep in places, sitting on forms, chairs, stools, and on one another's knees. On the cement floor three couples were dancing a jig and raising a quantity of dust, which was, however, soon sucked up the chimney by the huge turf fire that blazed on the hearth. The only clear space in the kitchen was the corner to the left of the fireplace, where Pat Mullaney sat on a yellow chair, with his right ankle resting on his left knee, a spotted red handkerchief on his head that reeked with perspiration, and his red face contorting as he played a tattered old accordion. One door was shut and the tins hanging on it gleamed in the firelight. The opposite door was open and over the heads of the small boys that crowded in it and outside it, peering in at the dancing couples in the kitchen, a starry June sky was visible and, beneath the sky, shadowy grey crags and misty, whitish fields lay motionless, still and sombre. There was a deep, calm silence outside the cabin and within the cabin, in spite of the music and dancing in the kitchen and the singing in the little room to the left, where Patrick Fenney's eldest son Michael sat on the bed with three other young men, there was a haunting melancholy in the air.

The people were dancing, laughing and singing with a certain forced and boisterous gaiety that failed to hide from them the real cause of their being there, dancing, singing and laughing. For the dance was on account of Patrick Feeney's two children, Mary and Michael, who were going to the United States on the following morning.

Feeney himself, a black-bearded, red-faced, middle-aged peasant, with white ivory buttons on his blue frieze shirt and his hands stuck in his leather waist belt, wandered restlessly about the kitchen, urging the people to sing and dance, while his mind was in agony all the time, thinking that on the following day he would lose his two eldest children, never to see them again perhaps. He kept talking to everybody about amusing things, shouted at the dancers and behaved in a boisterous and abandoned manner. But every now and then he had to leave the kitchen, under the pretence of going to the pigsty to look at a young pig that was supposed to be ill. He would stand, however, upright against his gable and look gloomily at some star or other, while his mind struggled with vague and peculiar ideas that wandered about in it. He could make nothing at all of his thoughts, but a lump always came up his throat, and he shivered, although the night was warm.

Then he would sigh and say with a contraction of his neck: "Oh, it's a queer world this and no doubt about it. So it is." Then he would go back to the cabin again and begin to urge on the dance, laughing, shouting and stamping on the floor.

Towards dawn, when the floor was crowded with couples, arranged in fours, stamping on the floor and going to and fro, dancing the "Walls of Limerick," Feeney was going out to the gable when his son Michael followed him out. The two of them walked side by side about the yard over the grey sea pebbles that had been strewn there the previous day. They walked in silence and yawned without need, pretending to be taking the air. But each of them was very excited. Michael was taller than his father and not so thickly built, but the shabby blue serge suit that he had bought for going to America was too narrow for his broad shoulders and the coat was too wide around the waist. He moved clumsily in it and his hands appeared altogether too bony and big and red, and he didn't know what to do with them. During his twenty-one years of life he had never worn anything other than the homespun clothes of Inverara, and the shop-made clothes appeared as strange to him and as uncomfortable as a dress suit worn by a man working in a sewer. His face was flushed a bright red and his blue eyes shone with excitement. Now and again he wiped the perspiration from his forehead with the lining of his grey tweed cap.

At last Patrick Feeney reached his usual position at the gable end. He halted, balanced himself on his heels with his hands in his waist belt, coughed and said, "It's going to be a warm day." The son came up beside him, folded his arms and leaned his right shoulder against the gable.

"It was kind of Uncle Ned to lend the money for the dance, father," he said. "I'd hate to think that we'd have to go without something or other, just the same as everybody else has. I'll send you that money the very first money I earn, father . . . even before I pay Aunt Mary for my passage money. I should have all that money paid off in four months, and then I'll have some more money to send you by Christmas."

And Michael felt very strong and manly recounting what he was going to do when he got to Boston, Massachusetts. He told himself that with his great strength he would earn a great deal of money.

Conscious of his youth and his strength and lusting for adventurous life, for the moment he forgot the ache in his heart that the thought of leaving his father inspired in him.

The father was silent for some time. He was looking at the sky with his lower lip hanging, thinking of nothing. At last he sighed as a memory struck him. "What is it?" said the son. "Don't weaken, for God's sake. You will only make it hard for me." "Fooh!" said the father suddenly with pretended gruffness. "Who is weakening? I'm afraid that your new clothes make you impudent." Then he was silent for a moment and continued in a low voice: "I was thinking of that potato field you sowed alone last spring the time I had the influenza. I never set eyes on that man that could do it better. It's a cruel world that takes you away from the land that God made you for."

Oh, what are you talking about, father? said Michael irritably. "Sure what did anybody ever get ot the land but poverty and hard work and potatoes and salt?"

"Ah, yes," said the father with a sigh, "but it's your own, the land, and over there"—he waved his hand at the western sky—"you'll be giving your sweat to some other man's land, or what's equal to it."

"Indeed," muttered Michael, looking at the ground with a melancholy expression in his eyes, "it's poor encouragement you are giving me."

They stood in silence fully five minutes. Each hungered to embrace the other, to cry, to beat the air, to scream with excess of sorrow. But they stood silent and sombre, like nature about them, hugging their woe. Then they went back to the cabin. Michael went into the little room to the left of the kitchen, to the three young men who fished in the same curragh with him and were his bosom friends. The father walked into the large bedroom to the right of the kitchen.

The large bedroom was also crowded with people. A large table was laid for tea in the centre of the room and about a dozen young men were sitting at it, drinking tea and eating buttered raisin cake. Mrs. Feeney was bustling about the table, serving the food and urging them to eat. She was assisted by her two younger daughters and by another woman, a relative of her own. Her eldest daughter Mary, who was going to the United States that day, was sitting on the edge of the bed with several other young women. The bed was a large four poster bed with a deal canopy over it, painted red, and the young women were huddled together on it. So that there must have been about a dozen of them there. They were Mary Feeney's particular friends, and they stayed with her in that uncomfortable position just to show how much they liked her. It was a custom.

Mary herself sat on the edge of the bed with her legs dangling. She was a pretty, dark-haired girl of nineteen, with dimpled, plump, red cheeks and ruminative brown eyes that seemed to cause little wrinkles to come and go in her little low forehead. Her nose was soft and small and rounded. Her mouth was small and the lips were red and open. Beneath her white blouse that was frilled at the neck and her navy blue skirt that outlined her limbs as she sat on the edge of the bed, her body was plump, soft, well-moulded and in some manner exuded a feeling of freshness and innocence. So that she seemed to have been born to be fondled and admired in luxurious surroundings instead of having been born a peasant's daughter, who had to go to the United States that day to work as a servant or maybe in a factory.

And as she sat on the edge of the bed crushing her little handkerchief between her palms, she kept thinking feverishly of the United States, at one moment with fear and loathing, at the next with desire and longing. Unlike her brother she did not think of the work she was going to do or the money that she was going to earn. Other things troubled her, things of which she was half ashamed, half afraid, thoughts of love and of foreign men and of clothes and of houses where there were more than three rooms and where people ate meat every day. She was fond of life, and several young men among the local gentry had admired her in Inverara. But . . .

She happened to look up and she caught her father's eyes as he stood silently by the window with his hands stuck in his waist belt. His eyes rested on hers for a moment and then he dropped them without smiling, and with his lips compressed he walked down into the kitchen. She shuddered slightly. She was a little afraid of her father, although she knew that he loved her very much and he was very kind to her. But the winter before he had whipped her with a dried willow rod, when he caught her one evening behind Tim Hernon's cabin after nightfall, with Tim Hernon's son Bartly's arms around her waist and he kissing her. Ever since, she always shivered slightly when her father touched her or spoke to her.

"Oho!" said an old peasant who sat at the table with a saucer full of tea in his hand and his grey flannel shirt open at his thin, hairy, wrinkled neck. "Oho! indeed, but it's a disgrace to the island of Inverara to let such a beautiful woman as your daughter go away, Mrs. Feeney. If I were a young man, I'll be flayed alive if I'd let her go."

There was a laugh and some of the women on the bed said: "Bad cess to you, Patsy Coyne, if you haven't too much impudence, it's a caution." But the laugh soon died. The young men sitting at the table felt embarrassed and kept looking at one another sheepishly, as if each tried to find out if the others were in love with Mary Feeney.

"Oh, well, God is good," said Mrs. Feeney, as she wiped her lips with the tip of her bright, clean, check apron. "What will be must be, and sure there is hope from the sea, but there is no hope from the grave. It is sad and the poor have to suffer, but . . ." Mrs. Feeney stopped suddenly, aware that all these platitudes meant nothing whatsoever. Like her husband she was unable to think intelligently about her two children going away. Whenever the reality of their going away, maybe for ever, three thousand miles into a vast unknown world, came before her mind, it seemed that a thin bar of some hard metal thrust itself forward from her brain and rested behind the wall of her forehead. So that almost immediately she became stupidly conscious of the pain caused by the imaginary bar of metal and she forgot the dread prospect of her children going away. But her mind grappled with the things about her busily and efficiently, with the preparation of food, with the entertaining of her guests, with the numerous little things that have to be done in a house where there is a party and which only a woman can do properly. These little things, in a manner, saved her, for the moment at least, from bursting into tears whenever she looked at her daughter and whenever she thought of her son, whom she loved most of all her children, because perhaps she nearly died giving birth to him and he had been very delicate until he was twelve years old. So she laughed down in her breast a funny laugh she had that made her heave where her check apron rose out from the waist band in a deep curve. "A person begins to talk," she said with a shrug of her shoulders sideways, "and then a person says foolish things."

"That's true," said the old peasant, noisily pouring more tea from his cup to his saucer.

But Mary knew by her mother laughing that way that she was very near being hysterical. She always laughed that way before she had one of her fits of hysterics. And Mary's heart stopped beating suddenly and then began again at an awful rate as her eyes became acutely conscious of her mother's body, the rotund, short body with the wonderful mass of fair hair growing grey at the temples and the fair face with the soft liquid brown eyes, that grew hard and piercing for a moment as they looked at a thing and then grew soft and liquid again, and the thin-lipped small mouth with the beautiful white teeth and the deep perpendicular grooves in the upper lip and the tremor that always came in the corner of the mouth, with love, when she looked at her children. Mary became acutely conscious of all these little points, as well as of the little black spot that was on her left breast below the nipple and the swelling that came now and again in her legs and caused her to have hysterics and would one day cause her death. And she was stricken with horror at the thought of leaving her mother and at the selfishness of her thoughts. She had never been prone to thinking of anything important but now, somehow for a moment, she had a glimpse of her mother's life that made her shiver and hate herself as a cruel, heartless, lazy, selfish wretch. Her mother's life loomed up before her eyes, a life of continual misery and suffering, hard work, birth pangs, sickness and again hard work and hunger and anxiety. It loomed up and then it fled again, a little mist came before her eyes and she jumped down from the bed, with the jaunty twirl of her head that was her habit when she set her body in motion.

"Sit down for a while, mother," she whispered, toying with one of the black ivory buttons on her mother's brown bodice. "I'll look after the table." "No, no," murmured the mother with a shake of her whole body, "I'm not a bit tired. Sit down, my treasure. You have a long way to travel to-day."

And Mary sighed and went back to the bed again.

At last somebody said: "It's broad daylight." And immediately everybody looked out and said: "So it is, and may God be praised." The change from the starry night to the grey, sharp dawn was hard to notice until it had arrived. People looked out and saw the morning light sneaking over the crags silently, along the ground, pushing the mist banks upwards. The stars were growing dim. A long way off invisible sparrows were chirping in their ivied perch in some distant hill or other. Another day had arrived and even as the people looked at it, yawned and began to search for their hats, caps and shawls preparing to go home, the day grew and spread its light and made things move and give voice. Cocks crew, blackbirds carolled, a dog let loose from a cabin by an early riser chased madly after an imaginary robber, barking as if his tail were on fire. The people said goodbye and began to stream forth from Feeney's cabin. They were going to their homes to see to the morning's work before going to Kilmurrage to see the emigrants off on the steamer to the mainland. Soon the cabin was empty except for the family.

All the family gathered into the kitchen and stood about for some minutes talking sleepily of the dance and of the people who had been present. Mrs. Feeney tried to persuade everybody to go to bed, but everybody refused. It was four o'clock and Michael and Mary would have to set out for Kilmurrage at nine. So tea was made and they all sat about for an hour drinking it and eating raisin cake and talking. They only talked of the dance and of the people who had been present.

There were eight of them there, the father and mother and six children. The youngest child was Thomas, a thin boy of twelve, whose lungs made a singing sound every time he breathed. The next was Bridget, a girl of fourteen, with dancing eyes and a habit of shaking her short golden curls every now and then for no apparent reason. Then there were the twins, Julia and Margaret, quiet, rather stupid, flat-faced girls of sixteen. Both their upper front teeth protruded slightly and they were both great workers and very obedient to their mother. They were all sitting at the table, having just finished a third large pot of tea, when suddenly the mother hastily gulped down the remainder of the tea in her cup, dropped the cup with a clatter to her saucer and sobbed once through her nose.

"Now mother," said Michael sternly, "what's the good of this work?"

"No, you are right, my pulse," she replied quietly. "Only I was just thinking how nice it is to sit here surrounded by all my children, all my little birds in my nest, and then two of them going to fly away made me sad." And she laughed, pretending to treat it as a foolish joke.

"Oh, that be damned for a story," said the father, wiping his mouth on his sleeve; "there's work to be done. You Julia, go and get the horse. Margaret, you milk the cow and see that you give enough milk to the calf this morning." And he ordered everybody about as if it were an ordinary day of work.

But Michael and Mary had nothing to do and they sat about miserably conscious that they had cut adrift from the routine of their home life. They no longer had any place in it. In a few hours they would be homeless wanderers. Now that they were cut adrift from it, the poverty and sordidness of their home life appeared to them under the aspect of comfort and plenty.

So the morning passed until breakfast time at seven o'clock. The morning's work was finished and the family was gathered together again. The meal passed in a dead silence. Drowsy after the sleepless night and conscious that the parting would come in a few hours, nobody wanted to talk. Everybody had an egg for breakfast in honour of the occasion. Mrs. Feeney, after her usual habit, tried to give her egg first to Michael, then to Mary, and as each refused it, she ate a little herself and gave the remainder to little Thomas who had the singing in his chest. Then the breakfast was cleared away. The father went to put the creels on the mare so as to take the luggage into Kilmurrage. Michael and Mary got the luggage ready and began to get dressed. The mother and the other children tidied up the house. People from the village began to come into the kitchen, as was customary, in order to accompany the emigrants from their home to Kilmurrage.

At last everything was ready. Mrs. Feeney had exhausted all excuses for moving about, engaged on trivial tasks. She had to go into the big bedroom where Mary was putting on her new hat. The mother sat on a chair by the window, her face contorting on account of the flood of tears she was keeping back. Michael moved about the room uneasily, his two hands knotting a big red handkerchief behind his back. Mary twisted about in front of the mirror that hung over the black wooden mantelpiece. She was spending a long time with the hat. It was the first one she had ever worn, but it fitted her beautifully, and it was in excellent taste. It was given to her by the schoolmistress, who was very fond of her, and she herself had taken it in a little. She had an instinct for beauty in dress and deportment.

But the mother, looking at how well her daughter wore the cheap navy blue costume and the white frilled blouse, and the little round black hat with a fat, fluffy, glossy curl covering each ear, and the black silk stockings with blue clocks in them, and the little black shoes that had laces of three colours in them, got suddenly enraged with . . . She didn't know with what she got enraged. But for the moment she hated her daughter's beauty, and she remembered all the anguish of giving birth to her and nursing her and toiling for her, for no other purpose than to lose her now and let her go away, maybe to be ravished wantonly because of her beauty and her love of gaiety. A cloud of mad jealousy and hatred against this impersonal beauty that she saw in her daughter almost suffocated the mother, and she stretched out her hands in front of her unconsciously and then just as suddenly her anger vanished like a puff of smoke, and she burst into wild tears, wailing: "My children, oh, my children, far over the sea you will be carried from me, your mother." And she began to rock herself and she threw her apron over her head.

Immediately the cabin was full of the sound of bitter wailing. A dismal cry rose from the women gathered in the kitchen. "Far over the sea they will be carried," began woman after woman, and they all rocked themselves and hid their heads in their aprons. Michael's mongrel dog began to howl on the hearth. Little Thomas sat down on the hearth beside the dog and, putting his arms around him, he began to cry, although he didn't know exactly why he was crying, but he felt melancholy on account of the dog howling and so many people being about.

In the bedroom the son and daughter, on their knees, clung to their mother, who held their heads between her hands and rained kisses on both heads ravenously. After the first wave of tears she had stopped weeping. The tears still ran down her cheeks, but her eyes gleamed and they were dry. There was a fierce look in them as she searched all over the heads of her two children with them, with her brows contracted, searching with a fierce terror-stricken expression, as if by the intensity of her stare she hoped to keep a living photograph of them before her mind. With her quivering lips she made a queer sound like "im-m-m-m" and she kept kissing. Her right hand clutched at Mary's left shoulder and with her left she fondled the back of Michael's neck. The two children were sobbing freely. They must have stayed that way a quarter of an hour.

Then the father came into the room, dressed in his best clothes. He wore a new frieze waistcoat, with a grey and black front and a white back. He held his soft black felt hat in one hand and in the other hand he had a bottle of holy water. He coughed and said in a weak gentle voice that was strange to him, as he touched his son: "Come now, it is time."

Mary and Michael got to their feet. The father sprinkled them with holy water and they crossed themselves. Then, without looking at their mother, who lay in the chair with her hands clasped on her lap, looking at the ground in a silent tearless stupor, they left the room. Each hurriedly kissed little Thomas, who was not going to Kilmurrage, and then, hand in hand, they left the house. As Michael was going out the door he picked a piece of loose whitewash from the wall and put it in his pocket. The people filed out after them, down the yard and on to the road, like a funeral procession. The mother was left in the house with little Thomas and two old peasant women from the village. Nobody spoke in the cabin for a long time.

Then the mother rose and came into the kitchen. She looked at the two women, at her little son and at the hearth, as if she were looking for something she had lost. Then she threw her hands into the air and ran out into the yard.

"Come back," she screamed; "come back to me."

She looked wildly down the road with dilated nostrils, her bosom heaving. But there was nobody in sight. Nobody replied. There was a crooked stretch of limestone road, surrounded by crags grey that were scorched by the sun. The road ended in a hill and then dropped out of sight. The hot June day was silent. Listening foolishly for an answering cry, the mother imagined she could hear the crags simmering under the hot rays of the sun. It was something in her head that was singing.

The two old women led her back into the kitchen. "There is nothing that time will not cure," said one. "Yes. Time and patience," said the other.

Further Readings on Liam O'Flaherty

Bibliography

Doyle, Paul A. *Liam O'Flaherty.* Troy: Whitston Publishing, 1972. "A Liam O'Flaherty Checklist." *Twentieth Century Literature* 13: 49–51.
Zneimer, John. *The Literary Vision of Liam O'Flaherty,* pp. 199–203. Syracuse, N.Y.: Syracuse University Press, 1970.

Selected Works

The Black Soul. Bath: Lythway Press, 1972 (1924).
Dúil. Baile Átha Cliath: Sáirséal agus Dill, 1953.
Famine. London: Landsborough Publications, 1966.
The Informer. New York: Harcourt Brace, 1980 (1925).
Land. London: Victor Gollancz; New York: Random House, 1946.
The Pedlar's Revenge and Other Stories. Dublin: Wolfhound Press, 1976.
Spring Sowing. London: Travellers' Library, 1935 (1924).
The Short Stories of Liam O'Flaherty. London: Four Square Books, 1966.
The Stories of Liam O'Flaherty. Introduction by Vivian Mercier. New York: Devin-Adair, 1956.

Biography and Criticism

de Bhaldraithe, Tomás. "O'Flaherty-Translator." *Comhar* 25: 35–37.
Doyle, Paul. *Liam O'Flaherty.* New York: Twayne Publishers, 1971.
Kelleher, John V. "Irish Literature Today." *Atlantic Monthly* 176: 70–76.
Kelly, A. A. *Liam O'Flaherty The Storyteller.* London: Macmillan, 1976.
Murray, Michael H. "Liam O'Flaherty and the Speaking Voice." *Studies in Short Fiction,* 5:154–62.

O'Brien, James H. *Liam O'Flaherty.* Lewisburg, Pa.: Bucknell University Press, 1973.

O'Faoláin, Seán. "Don Quixote O'Flaherty." *London Mercury* 37:170–75.

Saul, George Brandon. "A Wild Sowing: The Short Stories of Liam O'Flaherty." *A Review of English Literature* 4: 108–13.

Sheeran, Patrick F. *The Novels of Liam O'Flaherty.* A Study in Romantic Realism. Dublin: Wolfhound Press, 1976.

Zneimer, John. *The Literary Vision of Liam O'Flaherty.* Syracuse, N.Y.: Syracuse University Press, 1970.

POETS FROM THE
POST-INDEPENDENCE GENERATION

The Treaty signed with Great Britain in 1922 changed Ireland as had no other document in its history. However, while it ended the Anglo-Irish War, it did not bring peace. Former comrades in arms fought a civil war over the terms of the Treaty, which provide for the division of Ireland into a twenty-six county Free State, with six counties remaining in the United Kingdom.

Despite the bloodshed and attendant economic decline, however, a generation of younger poets found distinctive voices. They were at once more national and less parochial. The great international prestige of William Butler Yeats brought the attention of new readers in distant lands, even as it sometimes proved a burden for younger writers. At the same time, technological and economic transformations that led to a shrinking of distances often placed Irish writers in new environments: John Hewitt lived much of his life in England; Denis Devlin became ambassador to Italy; and W. R. Rodgers ended his days in southern California. Even those writers who "stayed home" sought new meaning from Irish traditions. Austin Clarke, a lapsed Catholic, could write a verse "sermon" on a Protestant Dubliner of the 18th century, Jonathan Swift, while a Catholic like Denis Devlin sought an explanation of the modern spiritual crisis in a place of pilgrimage, Lough Derg.

Forming no discrete school of their own, the poets of this generation often found themselves divided by new definitions of politics and religion. John Hewitt, and W. R. Rodgers became citizens of the six-county province united with Great Britain, while the others were citizens of the Irish Free State. In many cases, though, the poets of this generation made bonds with foreign poets as diverse as Ezra Pound, W. H. Auden, and Robert Penn Warren.

F[rederick] R[obert] Higgins (1896–1941) is probably best remembered today as W. B. Yeats's closest friend among the poets of his generation. The child of a Protestant, Unionist, Ascendancy family, he was nonetheless passionately interested in Irish folk tradition, and became an official of the Irish labor movement. As manager of the Abbey Theatre during the thirties, he encouraged new plays. Higgins also produced five volumes of poetry, of which only *Arable Holdings* (1933) has been reprinted in recent years.

Austin Clarke (1896–1974) published more than thirty works of poetry, drama, fiction, and autobiography in a career that spanned 57 years (minus a 17-year "silence," 1938–1955). Often compared to Yeats in his youth, Clarke lost the older poet's favor and sought new directions, including many experiments with Gaelic prosody in English. Clarke founded a society to promote spoken verse and helped to produce plays at various Dublin theaters as well as programs on Irish radio. In his later years, Clarke saw his critical prestige rise: while receiving an honorary degree in 1966 he heard himself described as "the outstanding literary figure in modern Ireland."

John Hewitt (b. 1907) spent much of his working career in England, where he was the director of the Herbert Art Gallery and Museum in Coventry. He remains nonetheless, closely associated with his native Belfast, and has drawn deeply from the Ulster Protestant experience. Through his association with two journals, *Lagan* and *Threshold*, he helped to foster an Ulster regional literary consciousness that would be continued in the next generation by such poets as Seamus Heaney, Michael Longley, and Derek Mahon.

Denis Devlin (1908–59) was at once one of the most religious and most cosmopolitan of twentieth century poets. Often compared to Ezra Pound, he drew from French and German traditions, and counted among his acquaintances the American writers Katherine Anne Porter and Robert Penn Warren. His much-admired "Lough Derg" (1946) will stand comparison with Wallace Stevens's "Sunday Morning" and T. S. Eliot's "Gerontion." In his last years he worked on a poetic commentary on the Way of the Cross.

W[illiam] R[obert] Rodgers (1909–69) was an Ulster Protestant who took an independent course in his life and work. An ordained Presbyterian minister, he worked as a scriptwriter and producer for the BBC and later migrated to California, where he became writer-in-residence and a popular campus personality at Pitzer College. Rodgers's lively word-play has invited comparison with Gerard Manley Hopkins.

F. R. HIGGINS (1896–1941)

FATHER AND SON

Only last week, walking the hushed fields
Of our most lovely Meath, now thinned by November,
I came to where the road from Laracor leads
To the Boyne river—that seemed more lake than river,
Stretched in uneasy light and stript of reeds.

And walking longside an old weir
Of my people's, where nothing stirs—only the shadowed
Leaden flight of a heron up the lean air—
I went unmanly with grief, knowing how my father,
Happy though captive in years, walked last with me
          there.

Yes, happy in Meath with me for a day
He walked, taking stock of herds hid in their own
          breathing;
And naming colts, gusty as wind, once steered by his
          hand,
Lightnings winked in the eyes that were half shy in
          greeting
Old friends—the wild blades, when he gallivanted the
          land.

For that proud, wayward man now my heart breaks—
Breaks for that man whose mind was a secret eyrie,
Whose kind hand was sole signet of his race,
Who curbed me, scorned my green ways, yet
          increasingly loved me
Till Death drew its grey blind down his face.

And yet I am pleased that even my reckless ways
Are living shades of his rich calms and passions—
Witnesses for him and for those faint namesakes
With whom now he is one, under yew branches,
Yes, one in a graven silence no bird breaks.

PADRAIC O'CONAIRE, GAELIC STORYTELLER

They've paid the last respects in sad tobacco
And silent is this wakehouse in its haze;
They've paid the last respects; and now their whiskey
Flings laughing words on mouths of prayer and praise;
And so young couples huddle by the gables,
O let them grope home through the hedgy night—
Alone I'll mourn my old friend, while the cold dawn
Thins out the holy candlelight.

Respects are paid to one loved by the people;
Ah, was he not—among our mighty poor—
The sudden wealth cast on those pools of darkness,
Those bearing, just, a star's faint signature;
And so he was to me, close friend, near brother,
Dear Padraic of the wide and sea-cold eyes—
So lovable, so courteous and noble,
The very West was in his soft replies.

They'll miss his heavy stick and stride in Wicklow—
His story-talking down Winetavern Street,
Where old men sitting in the wizen daylight
Have kept an edge upon his gentle wit;
While women on the grassy streets of Galway,
Who hearken for his passing—but in vain,
Shall hardly tell his step as shadows vanish
Through archways of forgotten Spain.

Ah, they'll say: Padraic's gone again exploring;
But now down glens of brightness. O he'll find
An alehouse overflowing with wise Gaelic
That's braced in vigour by the bardic mind,
And there his thoughts shall find their own forefathers—
In minds to whom our heights of race belong,
In crafty men, who ribbed a ship or turned
The secret joinery of song.

Alas, death mars the parchment of his forehead;
And yet for him, I know, the earth is mild—
The windy fidgets of September grasses
Can never tease a mind that loved the wild;
So drink his peace—this grey juice of the barley
Runs with a light that ever pleased his eye—
While old flames nod and gossip on the hearthstone
And only the young winds cry.

AUSTIN CLARKE (1896–1974)

AISLING

At morning from the coldness of Mount Brandon,
The sail is blowing half-way to the light:
And islands are so small, a man may carry
Their yellow crop in one cart at low tide.
Sadly in thought, I strayed the mountain grass
To hear the breezes following their young
And by the furrow of a stream, I chanced
To find a woman airing in the sun.

Coil of her hair, in cluster and ringlet,
Had brightened round her forehead and those curls—
Closer than she could bind them on a finger—
Were changing gleam and glitter. O she turned
So gracefully aside, I thought her clothes
Were flame and shadow while she slowly walked,
Or that each breast was proud because it rode
The cold air as the wave stayed by the swan.

But knowing her face was fairer than in thought,
I asked of her was she the Geraldine—
Few horsemen sheltered at the steps of water?
Or that Greek woman, lying in a piled room
On tousled purple, whom the household saved,
When frescoes of strange fire concealed the pillar:
The white coin all could spend? Might it be Niav
And was she over wave or from our hills?

"When shadows in wet grass are heavier
Than hay, beside dim wells the women gossip
And by the paler bushes tell the daylight;
But from what bay, uneasy with a shipping
Breeze, have you come?" I said. "O do you cross
The blue thread and the crimson on the framework,
At darkfall in a house where nobles throng
And the slow oil climbs up into the flame?"

"Black and fair strangers leave upon the oar
And there is peace," she answered. "Companies
Are gathered in the house that I have known;
Claret is on the board and they are pleased
By story-telling. When the turf is redder
And airy packs of wonder have been told,
By women dance to bright steel that is wed,
Starlike, upon the anvil with one stroke."

"Shall I, too, find at dark of rain," I cried,
"Neighbours around a fire cast up by the ocean
And in that shining mansion hear the rise
Of companies, or bide among my own—
Pleasing a noble ear? O must I wander
Without praise, without wine, in rich strange lands?"
But with a smile the secret woman left me,
At morning in the coldness of Mount Brandon.

THE STRAYING STUDENT

On a holy day when sails were blowing southward,
A bishop sang the Mass at Inishmore,
Men took one side, their wives were on the other
But I heard the woman coming from the shore:
And wild in despair my parents cried aloud
For they saw the vision draw me to the doorway.

Long had she lived in Rome when Popes were bad,
The wealth of every age she makes her own,
Yet smiled on me in eager admiration,
And for a summer taught me all I know,

Banishing shame with her great laugh that rang
As if a pillar caught it back alone.

I learned the prouder counsel of her throat,
My mind was growing bold as light in Greece;
And when in sleep her stirring limbs were shown,
I blessed the noonday rock that knew no tree:
And for an hour the mountain was her throne,
Although her eyes were bright with mockery.

They say I was sent back from Salamanca
And failed in logic, but I wrote her praise
Nine times upon a college wall in France.
She laid her hand at darkfall on my page
That I might read the heavens in a glance
And I knew every star the Moors had named.

Awake or in my sleep, I have no peace now,
Before the ball is struck, my breath has gone,
And yet I tremble lest she may deceive me
And leave me in this land, where every woman's son
Must carry his own coffin and believe,
In dread, all that the clergy teach the young.

IRISH-AMERICAN DIGNITARY

Glanced down at Shannon from the sky-way
With his attendant clergy, stayed night
In Dublin, but whole day with us
To find his father's cot, now dust
And rubble, bless new church, school buildings
At Glanworth, drive to Spangle Hill
And cut first sod, hear, answer, fine speeches,
Accept a learned gown, freedom
Of ancient city, so many kissing
His ring—God love him!—almost missed
The waiting liner: that day in Cork
Had scarcely time for knife and fork.

BURIAL OF AN IRISH PRESIDENT
(DR. DOUGLAS HYDE)

The tolling from St. Patrick's
Cathedral was brangled, repeating
Itself in top-back room
And alley of the Coombe,
Crowding the dirty streets,
Upbraiding all our pat tricks
Tricoloured and beflowered,
Coffin of our President,
Where fifty mourners bowed,
Was trestled in the gloom
Of arch and monument,
Beyond the desperate tomb
Of Swift. Imperial flags,
Corunna, Quatre Bras,
Inkermann, Pretoria,
Their pride turning to rags,
Drooped, smoke-thin as the booming
Of cannon. The simple word
From heaven was vaulted, stirred
By candles. At the last bench
Two Catholics, the French
Ambassador and I, knelt down.
The vergers waited. Outside.
The hush of Dublin town,
Professors of cap and gown,
Costello, his Cabinet,
In Government cars, hiding
Around the corner, ready
Tall hat in hand, dreading
Our Father in English. Better
Not hear that "which" for "who"
And risk eternal doom.

A SERMON ON SWIFT

Friday, 11.30 A.M. April 28th, 1967

Gentle of hand, the Dean of St. Patrick's guided
My silence up the steps of the pulpit, put around
My neck the lesser microphone.
                              "I feel
That you are blessing me, Mr. Dean."
                                        Murmur
Was smile.
              In this first lay sermon, must I
Not speak the truth? Known scholars, specialists,
From far and near, were celebrating the third
Centenary of our great satirist.
They spoke of the churchman who kept his solemn
     gown,
Full-bottom, for Sunday and the Evening Lesson,
But hid from lectern the chuckling rhymster who went,
Bald-headed, into the night when modesty
Wantoned with beau and belle, his pen in hand.
Dull morning clapped his oldest wig on. He looked
     from
The Deanery window, spied the washerwomen
Bundling along, the hay carts swaying from
The Coombe, dropping their country smells, the
     hackney—
Clatter on cobbles—ready to share a quip
Or rebus with Sheridan and Tom Delaney,
Read an unfinished chapter to Vanessa
Or Stella, then rid his mind of plaguey curling—
Tongs, farthingales and fal-de-lals. A pox on
Night-hours when wainscot, walls, were dizziness,
Tympana, maddened by inner terror, celled
A man who did not know himself from Cain.
A Tale of a Tub, Gulliver's Travels, fables
And scatological poems, I pennied them on
The Quays, in second-hand book-stalls, when I was
     young,
Soon learned that humour, unlike the wit o' the Coffee
House, the Club, lengthens the features, smile hid by
A frown.

Scarce had I uttered the words,
                    "Dear Friends,
Dear Swiftians"—
            when from the eastern window
The pure clear ray, that Swift had known, entered the
Shady church and touched my brow. So blessed
Again, I gathered 'em up, four-letter words,
Street-cries, from the Liberties.
                            Ascend,
Our Lady of Filth, Cloacina, soiled goddess
Of paven sewers. Let Roman fountains, a-spay
With themselves, scatter again the imperious gift
Of self-in-sight.
                  Celia on a close-stool
Stirs, ready to relace her ribs. Corinna,
Taking herself to pieces at midnight, slips from
The bed at noon, putting together soilures
And soft sores. Strephon half rouses from a dream
Of the flooding Tiber on his marriage-night,
When Chloe stoops out unable to contain her
Twelve cups of tea. Women are unsweet at times,
No doubt, yet how can willynilly resist
The pleasures of defaulting flesh?
                            My Sermon
Waits in the plethora of Rabelais, since
March veered with the rusty vane of Faith. I had
      reached
The house of Aries. Soon in the pure ray,
I am aware of my ancestor, Archbishop
Browne, hastily come from Christ Church, to dispel
Error and Popish superstition. He supped
Last night with Bishop Bale of Ossory,
Robustious as his plays, and, over the talk
And malmsey, forgot the confiscated wealth
Of abbeys.
      In prose, plain as pike, pillory.
In octosyllabic verse turning the two-way
Corner of rhyme, Swift wrote of privy matters
That have to be my text. The Lilliputian
March-by of the crack regiments saluting
On high the double pendulosity

Of Gulliver, glimpsed through a rent in his breeches;
The city square in admiration below. But who
Could blame the Queen when that almighty
Man hosed the private apartments of her palace,
Hissed down the flames of carelessness, leaving
The royal stables unfit for Houynhnms, or tell (in
A coarse aside) what the gigantic maidens
Of Brobdignab did in their playfulness with
The tiny Lemuel when they put him astride
A pap, broader than the mizzen mast of his
Wrecked ship, or hid him in the tangle below?

Reasonable century of Bolingbroke,
Hume, hundred-quilled Voltaire. Satyr and nymph
Disported in the bosk, prim avenues
Let in the classical sky. The ancient temples
Had been restored. Sculptures replaced the painted
Images of the saints. Altars were fuming,
And every capital was amaranthed.
Abstraction ruled the decumana of verse,
Careful caesura kept the middle silence
No syllable dared to cross.
                              Swift gave his savings
To mumbling hand, to tatters. Bare kibes ran after
Hoof as he rode beside the Liffey to sup
At Celbridge, brood with Vanessa in a star-bloomed
Bower on Tory politics, forget
Queen Anne, stride from a coffee-house in Whitehall
And with his pamphlets furrow the battle-fields
Of Europe once more, tear up the blood-signed
       contracts
Of Marlborough, Victualler of Victories;
While in St. Patrick's Cathedral the candling clerk
Shifted the shadows from pillar to pillar, shuffling
His years along the aisles with iron key.
Last gift of an unwilling patriot, Swift willed
To us a mansion of forgetfulness. I lodged
There for a year until Erato led me
Beyond the high-walled garden of Memory,
The Fountain of Hope, to the rewarding Gate,
Reviled but no longer defiled by harpies. And there

In Thomas Street, night to the busy stalls,
Divine Abstraction smiled.
                              My hour, above.
Myself, draws to an end. Satiric rhymes
Are safe in the Deanery. So I must find
A moral, search among my wits.
                              I have
It.
   In his sudden poem *The Day of Judgment*
Swift borrowed the allegoric bolt of Jove,
Damned and forgave the human race, dismissed
The jest of life. Here is his secret belief
For sure: the doctrine of Erigena,
Scribing his way from West to East, from bang
Of monastery door, click o' the latch,
His sandals worn out, unsoled, a voice proclaiming
The World's mad business—Eternal Absolution.

JOHN HEWITT (1907–87)

THE GLENS

Groined by deep glens and walled along the west
by the bare hilltops and the tufted moors,
this rim of arable that ends in foam
has but to drop a leaf or snap a branch
and my hand twitches with the leaping verse
as hazel twig will wrench the straining wrists
for untapped jet that thrusts beneath the sod.

Not these my people, of a vainer faith
and a more violent lineage. My dead
lie in the steepled hillock of Kilmore
in a fat country rich with bloom and fruit.
My days, the busy days I owe the world,
are bound to paved unerring roads and rooms
heavy with talk of politics and art.
I cannot spare more than a common phrase

of crops and weather when I pace these lanes
and pause at hedge gap spying on their skill,
so many fences stretch between our minds.

I fear their creed as we have always feared
the lifted hand against unfettered thought,
I know their savage history of wrong
and would at moments lend an eager voice,
if voice avail, to set that tally straight.

And yet no other corner in this land
offers in shape and colour all I need
for sight to torch the mind with living light.

AN IRISHMAN IN COVENTRY

A full year since, I took this eager city,
the tolerance that laced its blatant roar,
its famous steeples and its web of girders,
as image of the state hope argued for,
and scarcely flung a bitter thought behind me
on all that flaws the glory and the grace
which ribbons through the sick, guilt-clotted legend
of my creed-haunted, Godforsaken race.
My rhetoric swung round from steel's high promise
to the precision of the well-gauged tool,
tracing the logic in the vast glass headlands,
the clockwork horse, the comprehensive school.

Then, sudden, by occasion's chance concerted,
in enclave of my nation, but apart,
the jigging dances and the lilting fiddle
stirred the old rage and pity in my heart.
The faces and the voices blurring round me,
the strong hands long familiar with the spade,
the whiskey-tinctured breath, the pious buttons,
called up a people endlessly betrayed
by our own weakness, by the wrongs we suffered
in that long twilight over bog and glen,

by force, by famine and by glittering fables
which gave us martyrs when we needed men,
by faith which had no charity to offer,
by poisoned memory, and by ready wit,
with poverty corroded into malice,
to hit and run and howl when it is hit.

This is our fate: eight hundred years' disaster,
crazily tangled as the Book of Kells;
the dream's distortion and the land's division,
the midnight raiders and the prison cells.
Yet like Lir's children banished to the waters
our hearts still listen for the landward bells.

DENIS DEVLIN (1908–59)

LOUGH DERG

The poor in spirit on their rosary rounds,
The jobbers with their whiskey-angered eyes,
The pink bank clerks, the tip-hat papal counts,
And drab, kind women their tonsured mockery tries,
Glad invalids on penitential feet
Walk the Lord's majesty like their village street.

With mullioned Europe shattered, this Northwest,
Rude-sainted isle would pray it whole again:
(Peasant Apollo! Troy is worn to rest.)
Europe that humanized the sacred bane
Of God's chance who yet laughed in his mind
And balanced thief and saint: were they this kind?

Low rocks, a few weasels, lake
Like a field of burnt gorse; the rooks caw;
Ours, passive, for man's gradual wisdom take
Firefly instinct dreamed out into law;
The prophets' jeweled kingdom down at heel
Fires no Augustine here. Inert, they kneel;

All is simple and symbol in their world,
The incomprehended rendered fabulous.
Sin teases life whose natural fruits withheld
Sour the deprived nor bloom for timely loss:
Clan Jansen! less what magnanimity leavens
Man's wept-out, fitful, magniloquent heavens

Where prayer was praise, O Lord! the Temple trumpets
Cascaded down Thy sunny pavilions of air,
The scroll-tongued priests, the galvanic strumpets,
All clash and stridency gloomed upon Thy stair;
The pharisees, the exalted boy their power
Sensually psalmed in Thee, their coming hour!

And to the sun, earth turned her flower of sex,
Acanthus in the architects' limpid angles;
Close priests allegorized the Orphic egg's
Brood, and from the Academy, tolerant wranglers
Could hear the contemplatives of the Tragic Choir
Drain off man's sanguine, pastoral death-desire.

It was said stone dreams and animal sleeps and man
Is awake; but sleep with its drama on us bred
Animal articulate, only somnambulist can
Conscience like Cawdor give the blood its head
For the dim moors to reign through druids again.
O first geometer! tangent-feelered brain

Clearing by inches the encircled eyes,
Bolder than the peasant tiger whose autumn beauty
Sags in the expletive kill, or the sacrifice
Of dearth puffed positive in the stance of duty
With which these pilgrims would propitiate
Their fears; no leafy, medieval state

Of paschal cathedrals backed on earthy hooves
Against the craftsmen's primary-coloured skies
Whose gold was Gabriel on the patient roofs,
The parabled windows taught the dead to rise,
And Christ the Centaur in two natures whole,
With fable and proverb joinered body and soul.

Waters withers from the oars. The pilgrims blacken
Out of the boats to masticate their sin
Where Dante smelled among the stones and bracken
The door to Hell (O harder Hell where pain
Is earthed, a casuist sanctuary of guilt!).
Spirit bureaucracy on a bet built

Part by this race when monks in convents of coracles
For the Merovingian centuries left their land,
Belled, fragrant; and honest in their oracles
Bespoke the grace to give without demand,
Martyrs Heaven winged nor tempted with reward.
And not ours, doughed in dogma, who never have
        dared

Will with surrogate palm distribute hope:
No better nor worse than I who, in my books,
Have angered at the stake with Bruno and, by the rope
Watt Tyler swung from, leagued with shifty looks
To fuse the next rebellion with the desperate
Serfs in the same need to eat and get;

Have praised, on its thunderous canvas, the Florentine
        smile
As man took to wearing his death, his own
Sapped crisis through cathedral branches (while
Flesh groped loud round dissenting skeleton)
In soul, reborn as body's appetite:
Now languisht back in body's amber light,

Now is consumed. O earthly paradise!
Hell is to know our natural empire used
Wrong, by mind's moulting, brute divinities.
The vanishing tiger's saved, his blood transfused.
Kent is for Jutes again and Glasgow town
Burns high enough to screen the stars and moon.

Well may they cry who have been robbed, their wasting
Shares in justice legally lowered until
Man his own actor, matrix, mould and casting,
Or man, God's image, sees, his idol spill.

Say it was pride that did it, or virtue's brief:
To them that suffer it is no relief.

All indiscriminate, man, stone, animal
Are woken up in nightmare. What John the Blind
from Patmos saw works and we speak it. Not all
The men of God nor the priests of mankind
Can mend or explain the good and broke, not one
Generous with love prove communion.

Behind the eyes the winged ascension flags,
For want of spirit by the market blurbed,
And if hands touch, such fraternity sags
Frightened this side the dikes of death disturbed
Like Aran Islands' bibulous, unclean seas:
Pieta: but the limbs ache; it is not peace.

Then to see less, look little, let hearts' hunger
Feed on water and berries. The pilgrims sing:
Life will fare well from elder to younger,
Though courage fail in a world-end, rosary ring.
Courage kills its practioners and we live,
Nothing forgotten, nothing to forgive.

We pray to ourself. The metal moon, unspent
Virgin eternity sleeping in mind,
Excites the form of prayer without content;
Whitehorn lightens, delicate and blind,
The negro mountain, and so, knelt on her sod,
This woman beside me murmuring *My God! My God!*

W. R. RODGERS (1909–69)

AN IRISH LAKE

There in the hard light
Dark birds, pink-footed, dab and pick
Among the addery roots and marrowy stones,

And the blown waves blink and hiccup at the lake's
Lip. A late bee blares and drones on inland
Into a cone-point of silence, and I
Lying at the rhododendron's foot
Look through five finger's grille at the lake
Shaking, at the bare and backward plain, and
The running and bending hills that carry
Like a conveyer belt the bright snail-line
Of clouds along the sky all day unendingly.

There, far from the slack noose of rumour
That tightens into choking fact, I relax,
And sounds and sights and scents sail slowly by.
But suddenly, like delicate and tilted italics,
The up-standing birds stretch urgently away
Into the sky as suddenly grown grey.
Night rounds on Europe now. And I must go.
Before its hostile faces peer and pour
Over the mind's rim enveloping me,
And my so-frightened thoughts dart here and there
Like trout among their grim stony gazes.

THE PARTY

So they went, leaving a picnic-litter of talk
And broken glitter of jokes, the burst bags of spite:
In comes Contempt, the caretaker, eye on ceiling,
Broom in armpit, and with one wide careless cast
Sweeps the stuttering rubbish out of memory,
Opens the shutters, puts out the intimate lamp,
And, a moment, gazes on the mute enormities
Of distant dawn. And far doors bang in mind, idly.

Further Readings on Poets from the Post-Independence Generation

Bibliography

MacManus, M. J. "A Bibliography of F. R. Higgins." *Dublin Magazine* 12: 61–67.

Lyne, Gerard. Austin Clarke: A Bibliography." *Irish University Review* 4,: 137–55.
Miller, Liam. "The Books of Austin Clarke. A Checklist." In *A Tribute to Austin Clarke on his Seventieth Birthday, 9 May 1966,* ed. Liam Miller and John Montague. Dublin: Dolmen; Chester Springs, Pa.: Du Four, 1966.

Selected Works

Clarke, Austin. *The Bright Temptation* [prose]. London: Allen and Unwin, 1932. Reprinted, Dublin: Dolmen, 1965.
———. *Collected Poems.* London: Allen and Unwin, 1936.
———. *Poetry in Modern Ireland.* Dublin: Cultural Relations Committee, 1961.
———. *Collected Plays.* Dublin: Dolmen, 1963.
———. *A Sermon on Swift and Other Poems.* Dublin: Bridge, 1968.
———. *Collected Poems.* Dublin: Dolmen, 1974.
Devlin, Denis. *Lough Derg and Other Poems.* New York: Reynal and Hitchcock, 1946.
———. *Collected Poems.* Dublin: Dolmen, 1964.
Hewitt, John. *Collected Poems.* London: MacGibbon & Kee, 1968.
Higgins, F. R. *The Dark Breed.* London: Macmillan, 1927.
———. *Arable Holdings.* Dublin: Cuala, 1933.
———. *The Gap of Brightness.* London and New York: Macmillian, 1940.
Rodgers, W. R. *Collected Poems.* London: Oxford University Press, 1971.
———. *Irish Literary Portraits.* New York: Taplinger, 1973.

Biography and Criticism

Dawe, Gerald, and Longley, Edna, eds. *Across a Roaring Hill: The Protestant Imagination in Modern Ireland: Essays in Honour of John Hewitt.* Belfast and Dover, N.H.: Blackstaff Press, 1985.
Halpern, Susan. *Austin Clarke, His Life and Works.* Dublin: Dolmen, 1974.
Harmon, Maurice, ed. *Irish Poetry After Yeats: Seven Poets.* Boston: Little Brown, 1979.
Heaney, Seamus. "The Poetry of John Hewitt." *Threshold* 22: 73–77.
Irish University Review. Austin Clarke number 4.
Loftus, Richard J. *Nationalism in Modern Anglo-Irish Poetry.* Madison: University of Wisconsin Press, 1964.
Miller, Liam, and Montague, John, eds. *A Tribute to Austin Clarke on his Seventieth Birthday, 9 May 1966.* Dublin: Dolmen; Chester Springs, Pa.: DuFour, 1966.
O'Brien, Darcy. *W. R. Rodgers.* Lewisburg, Pa.: Bucknell University Press, 1971.
Schirmer, Gregory. *The Poetry of Austin Clarke.* Mountrath, Republic of Ireland: Dolmen: South Bend, Ind.: University of Notre Dame Press, 1983.
Tapping, G. Craig. *Austin Clarke: A Study of His Writings.* Totowa, N.J.: Barnes and Noble, 1981.

PATRICK KAVANAGH
(1905–67)

Seamus Heaney has called Patrick Kavanagh the "twice born" poet. The son of a cobbler and small farmer in County Monaghan, Kavanagh worked at farming and poetry until 1939, when he left Inniskeen for a journalist's life in Dublin. There, he wrote and reviewed for *The Irish Times, The Irish Press* and *The Standard*.

The publication of the first part of his long poem, "The Great Hunger," in *Horizon* (1942) caused that magazine to be taken off the stands. (The poem was published the same year by the Cuala Press.) In April 1952, Kavanagh, with his brother's backing, launched his own paper, *Kavanagh's Weekly*, which ran to thirteen issues. Later that year, the poet initiated a libel action against the *The Leader* for an unsigned article titled "Profile: Mr. Patrick Kavanagh." The case went to trial in 1954 and *The Leader* was found not guilty. The decision was appealed, and the matter finally settled out of court.

Kavanagh's early poems, particularly "The Great Hunger" (its title alludes to the famine of a century before), describes the poverty and isolation of rural Ireland in the thirties and forties; other rural poems, such as "In Memory of My Mother," are nostalgic. Kavanagh's rebirth, after surgery for lung cancer in 1955, is celebrated in the sonnet "Canal Bank Walk," with its lyrical opening: "leafy-with-love." The poem, a personal as well as a poetic achievement, marked Kavanagh's last years—years that brought him the happiness of a late marriage, the comforts of a secure reputation, and the satisfaction of knowing he was a major influence on a new generation of Irish poets.

SHANCODUFF

My black hills have never seen the sun rising,
Eternally they look north towards Armagh.
Lot's wife would not be salt if she had been
Incurious as my black hills that are happy
When dawn whitens Glassdrummond chapel.

My hills hoard the bright shillings of March
While the sun searches in every pocket.
They are my Alps and I have climbed the Matterhorn
With a sheaf of hay for three perishing calves
In the field under the Big Forth of Rocksavage.

The sleety winds fondle the rushy beards of Shancoduff
While the cattle-drovers sheltering in the Featherna Bush
Look up and say: "Who owns them hungry hills
That the water-hen and snipe must have forsaken?
A poet? Then by heavens he must be poor."
I hear and is my heart not badly shaken?

EPIC

I have lived in important places, times
When great events were decided, who owned
That half a rood of rock, a no-man's land
Surrounded by our pitchfork-armed claims.
I heard the Duffys shouting "Damn your soul"
And old McCabe stripped to the waist, seen
Step the plot defying blue cast-steel—
"Here is the march along these iron stones"
That was the year of the Munich bother. Which
Was more important? I inclined
To lose my faith in Ballyrush and Gortin
Till Homer's ghost came whispering to my mind
He said: I made the Iliad from such
A local row. Gods make their own importance.

Monaghan 1934

PEGASUS

My soul was an old horse
Offered for sale in twenty fairs.
I offered him to the Church—the buyers
Were little men who feared his unusual airs.
One said: "Let him remain unbid
In the wind and rain and hunger
Of sin and we will get him—
With the winkers thrown in—for nothing."

Then the men of State looked at
What I'd brought for sale.
One minister, wondering if
Another horse-body would fit the tail
That he'd kept for sentiment—
The relic of his own soul—
Said, "I will graze him in lieu of his labour."
I lent him for a week or more
And he came back a hurdle of bones,
Starved, overworked, in despair.
I nursed him on the roadside grass
To shape him for another fair.

I lowered my price. I stood him where
The broken-winded, spavined stand
And crooked shopkeepers said that he
Might do a season on the land—
But not for high-paid work in towns.
He'd do a tinker, possibly.
I begged, "O make some offer now,
A soul is a poor man's tragedy.
He'll draw your dungiest cart," I said,
"Show you short cuts to Mass,
Teach weather lore, at night collect
Bad debts from poor men's grass."
                              And they would not.

        Where the
Tinkers quarrel I went down
With my horse, my soul.

I cried, "Who will bid me half a crown?"
From their rowdy bargaining
Not one turned. "Soul," I prayed,
"I have hawked you through the world
Of Church and State and meanest trade.
But this evening, halter off,
Never again will it go on.
On the south side of ditches
There is grazing of the sun.
No more haggling with the world. . . ."

As I said these words he grew
Wings upon his back. Now I may ride him
Every land my imagination knew.

IN MEMORY OF MY MOTHER

I do not think of you lying in the wet clay
Of a Monaghan graveyard; I see
You walking down a lane among the poplars
On your way to the station, or happily

Going to second Mass on a summer Sunday—
You meet me and you say:
"Don't forget to see about the cattle—"
Among your earthiest words the angels stray.

And I think of you walking along a headland
Of green oats in June,
So full of repose, so rich with life—
And I see us meeting at the end of a town

On a fair day by accident, after
The bargains are all made and we can walk
Together through the shops and stalls and markets
Free in the oriental streets of thought.

O you are not lying in the wet clay,
For it is a harvest evening now and we

Are piling up the ricks against the moonlight
And you smile up at us—eternally.

CANAL BANK WALK

Leafy-with-love banks and the green waters of the canal
Pouring redemption for me, that I do
The will of God, wallow in the habitual, the banal,
Grow with nature again as before I grew.
The bright stick trapped, the breeze adding a third
Party to the couple kissing on an old seat,
And a bird gathering materials for the nest for the
    Word
Eloquently new and abandoned to its delirious beat.
O unworn world enrapture me, enrapture me in a web
Of fabulous grass and eternal voices by a beech,
Feed the gaping need of my senses, give me ad lib
To pray unselfconsciously with overflowing speech
For this soul needs to be honoured with a new dress
    woven
From green and blue things and arguments that cannot
    be proven.

LINES WRITTEN ON A SEAT ON THE GRAND CANAL, DUBLIN, "ERECTED TO THE MEMORY OF MRS DERMOT O'BRIEN"

O commemorate me where there is water,
Canal water preferably, so stilly
Greeny at the heart of summer. Brother
Commemorate me thus beautifully.
Where by a lock Niagariously roars
The falls for those who sit in the tremendous silence
Of mid-July. No one will speak in prose
Who finds his way to these Parnassian islands.
A swan goes by head low with many apologies,
Fantastic light looks through the eyes of bridges—

And look! a barge comes bringing from Athy
And other far-flung towns mythologies.
O commemorate me with no hero-courageous
Tomb—just a canal-bank seat for the passer-by.

Further Readings on Patrick Kavanagh

Bibliography

Kavanagh, Peter. *Garden of the Golden Apples. A Bibliography of Patrick Kavanagh.* New York: Peter Kavanagh Hand Press, 1972.
Nemo, John. "A Bibliography of Writings by and about Patrick Kavanagh." *Irish University Review* 3: 80–106. *Patrick Kavanagh*, pp. 159–61. Boston: Twayne, 1979. (Secondary sources are annotated.)

Selected Works

By Night Unstarred. An Autobiographical Novel by Patrick Kavanagh. Edited by Peter Kavanagh. The Curragh, Republic of Ireland: Goldsmith Press, 1977.
Collected Poems. New York: W. W. Norton and Co., 1973 (1964).
Collected Prose. London: MacGibbon and Kee, 1973 (1967).
Come Dance with Kitty Stobling and Other Poems. Philadelphia: Dufour, 1964 (1960).
The Complete Poems of Patrick Kavanagh. Collected, arranged, and edited by Peter Kavanagh. New York: Peter Kavanagh Hand Press, 1972.
The Great Hunger: Poem. London: MacGibbon and Kee, 1967.
The Green Fool. London: Martin Brian and O'Keefe, 1972 (1938). Early autobiography.
Kavanagh's Weekly. A Journal of Literature and Politics. 7 vols. (12 April–5 July 1952). Dublin: Peter Kavanagh, 1952.
Lapped Furrows: Correspondence 1933–1967 between Patrick and Peter Kavanagh. Edited by Peter Kavanagh. New York: Peter Kavanagh Hand Press, 1969.
Self Portrait. Dublin: The Dolmen Press, 1964.
A Soul for Sale. London: Macmillan and Co., 1947.
Tarry Flynn. Harmondsworth: Penguin, 1978 (1948).

Biography and Criticism

Garratt, Robert F. "Patrick Kavanagh and the Killing of the Irish Revival." *Colby Library Quarterly* 17: 170–83.
Johnston, Dillon. *Irish Poetry after Joyce,* pp. 121–66. Montrath: The Dolmen Press; South Bend, Ind.: University of Notre Dame Press, 1985.

Kavanagh, Peter. *Beyond Affection: An Autobiography.* New York: Peter Kavanagh Hand Press, 1977.

———. *A Guide to Patrick Kavanagh Country.* New York: Peter Kavanagh Hand Press, 1978.

———, ed. *Patrick Kavanagh, Man and Poet.* Orono, Me.: National Poetry Foundation, Inc., 1986.

———. *Sacred Keeper: A Biography of Patrick Kavanagh.* The Curragh, Republic of Ireland: Goldsmith Press, 1979.

Nemo, John. *Patrick Kavanagh.* Boston: Twayne, 1979.

O'Brien, Darcy. *Patrick Kavanagh.* Lewisburg, Pa.: Bucknell University Press; London: Associated University Presses, 1975.

"Poetry Since Yeats: An Exchange of Views" (Stephen Spender, Patrick Kavanagh, Thomas Kinsella, W. D. Snodgrass). *Tri-Quarterly* 4: 100–11.

Warner, Alan. *Clay is the Word: Patrick Kavanagh 1904–1967.* Dublin: Dolmen Press, 1983.

FLANN O'BRIEN
(1911–66)

The novelist usually known as Flann O'Brien was a man of many parts and many names. Born Brian O'Nolan (or Nolan), the writer used a series of pseudonyms in connection with his various literary efforts. Like many of his contemporaries, he sometimes used the Irish (or Gaelic) form of his name, Brían Ó Nualláin. He was best-known in his lifetime as Myles na Gopaleen (or sometimes gCopaleen), the regular if idiosyncratic columnist of "Cruiskeen Lawn" for the *Irish Times*. At other times he appeared as Brother Barnabas, James John Doe, George Knowall, Matt Duffy, and Count O'Blather. But he is best remembered today for the five volumes of fiction he wrote under the name Flann O'Brien.

Despite the prestige he enjoys posthumously, O'Brien's career had longer periods of disappointment than success. A brilliant young linguist and debater, O'Brien published his greatest work, *At Swim-Two-Birds* (1939), when he was only 28. Despite the acclaim from writers as diverse as Graham Greene and Dylan Thomas, *At Swim-Two-Birds* was a commercial failure. O'Brien's next novel, *The Third Policeman*, was rejected by a series of publishers, and did not appear until 1967, after the author's death. Undeterred, O'Brien produced *An Béal Bocht* [The poor mouth, 1941], a unique and brilliant satire of Irishness written in the Irish language. Meanwhile, under the pseudonym Myles na Gopaleen, he had begun writing the "Cruiskeen Lawn" column, which continued for almost twenty-five years until his death.

At different times the author offered jokes in Old Irish, cross-linguistic puns, phonetic transcriptions from Homeric Greek, and a continuing series of shaggy-dog stories about the adventures of

315

Keats and his friend Chapman. O'Brien continued to write stories and plays, but in his view as well as those of later critics, he did not realize his early promise. He loathed his principal occupation as a minor bureaucrat in the Department of Local Government, from which he retired in 1953. Thus, by the early sixties he appeared to many to be an embittered failure who happened to write a curious newspaper column. But then *At Swim-Two-Birds* was rediscovered and republished, bringing a second period of activity that produced the comic novels *The Hard Life* (1961) and *The Dalkey Archive* (1964)—the latter adapted for the the stage by Hugh Leonard as *When the Saints Go Cycling In* (1965).

The action of *At Swim-Two-Birds* begins as an unnamed narrator, a layabout student at University College, Dublin, tells the story of a tenant in the seedy Red Swan Hotel, Dermot Trellis, who has begun to write a novel. Trellis, with a more limited imagination than the student, borrows characters from pulp fiction as well as Old Irish tradition, notably the hero Finn MacCool (Fionn mac Cumhaill). However, Trellis's characters soon tire of his banality and begin to tell a story about him. The passage excerpted here cuts through different levels of narration. At first, the student narrator converses with his friend Brinsley on the art of fiction, voicing the most frequently cited line from the work: ". . . a satisfactory novel should be a self-evident sham." The action then proceeds to the premises of the Red Swan Hotel. At no point in the entire novel does anyone explain the significance of the title "At Swim-Two-Birds," a translation of the medieval Irish placename, *Snámh-dá-éan*, which appears in *Buile Suibhne* [The frenzy (or madness) of Sweeney].

"A Bash in the Tunnel," though written under the name Brian Nolan in 1951, has much of the voice and tone of the Myles na Gopaleen columns. Here the author comes to grip with the troublesome legacy of James Joyce, an author much esteemed by Irishmen but only rarely in the unquestioning way he is worshipped by foreigners.

From AT SWIM-TWO-BIRDS

I withdrew my elbow and fell back again as if exhausted by my effort. My talk had been forced, couched in the accent of the lower or working-classes. Under the cover of the bed-clothes I poked idly with a pencil at my navel. Brinsley was at the window giving chuckles out.

Nature of chuckles: Quiet, private, averted.

What are you laughing at? I said.

You and your book and your porter, he answered.

Did you read that stuff about Finn, I said, that stuff I gave you?

Oh, yes, he said, that was the pig's whiskers. That was funny all right.

This I found a pleasing eulogy. The God-big Finn. Brinsley turned from the window and asked me for a cigarette. I took out my "butt" or half-spent cigarette and showed it in the hollow of my hand.

That is all I have, I said, affecting a pathos in my voice.

By God you're the queer bloody man, he said.

He then brought from his own pocket a box of the twenty denomination, lighting one for each of us.

There are two ways to make big money, he said, to write a book or to make a book.

It happened that this remark provoked between us a discussion on the subject of Literature—great authors living and dead, and character of modern poetry, the predilections of publishers and the importance of being at all times occupied with literary activities of a spare-time or recreative character. My dim room rang with the iron of fine words and the names of great Russian masters were articulated with fastidious intonation. Witticisms were canvassed, depending for their utility on a knowledge of the French language as spoken in the medieval times. Psycho-analysis was mentioned—with, however, a somewhat light touch. I then tendered an explanation spontaneous and unsolicited concerning my own work, affording an insight as to its aesthetic, its daemon, its argument, its sorrow and its joy, its darkness, its sun-twinkle clearness.

Nature of explanation offered: It was stated that while the novel and the play were both pleasing intellectual exercises, the novel was inferior to the play inasmuch as it lacked the outward accidents of illusion, frequently inducing the reader to be outwitted in a shabby fashion and caused to experience a real concern for the fortunes of illusory characters. The play was consumed in wholesome fashion by large masses in places of public resort; the novel was self-administered in private. The novel, in the hands of an unscrupulous writer, could be despotic. In reply to an inquiry, it was explained that a satisfactory novel should be a self-evident sham to which the reader could regulate at will the degree of his credulity. It was undemocratic to compel

characters to be uniformly good or bad or poor or rich. Each should
be allowed a private life, self-determination and a decent standard of
living. This would make for self-respect, contentment and better
service. It would be incorrect to say that it would lead to chaos.
Characters should be interchangeable as between one book and another. The entire corpus of existing literature should be regarded as a
limbo from which discerning authors could draw their characters as
required, creating only when they failed to find a suitable existing
puppet. The modern novel should be largely a work of reference.
Most authors spend their time saying what has been said before—
usually said much better. A wealth of references to existing works
would acquaint the reader instantaneously with the nature of each
character, would obviate tiresome explanations and would effectively
preclude mountebanks, upstarts, thimbleriggers and persons of inferior education from an understanding contemporary literture.
Conclusion of explanation.

   That is all my bum, said Brinsley.

   But taking precise typescript from beneath the book that was at
my side, I explained to him my literary intentions in considerable
detail—now reading, now discoursing, oratio recta and oratio obliqua.
[direct speech and indirect speech]

Extract from Manuscript as to nature Red Swan premises, oratio recta:
The Red Swan premises in Lower Leeson Street are held in fee farm,
the landlord whosoever being pledged to maintain the narrow lane
which marks its eastern boundary unimpeded and free from nuisance
for a distance of seventeen yards, that is, up to the intersection of
Peter Place. New Paragraph. A terminus of the Cornelscourt coach in
the seventeenth century, the hotel was rebuilt in 1712 and afterwards
fired by the yeomanry for reasons which must be sought in the quiet
of its ruined garden, on the three-perch stretch that goes by Croppies'
Acre. Today, it is a large building of four storeys. The title is worked in
snow-white letters along the circumference of the fanlight and the
centre of the circle is concerned with the delicate image of a red swan,
pleasingly conceived and carried out by a casting process in Bir-
mingham delf. Conclusion of the foregoing.

*Further extract descriptive of Dermot Trellis rated occupier of the Red
Swan Hotel, oratio recta:* Dermot Trellis was a man of average stature
but his person was flabby and unattractive, partly a result of his having
remained in bed for a period of twenty years. He was voluntarily

bedridden and suffered from no organic or other illness. He occasionally rose for very brief periods in the evening to pad about the
empty house in his felt slippers or to interview the slavey in the
kitchen on the subject of his food or bedclothes. He had lost all
physical reaction to bad or good weather and was accustomed to trace
the seasonal changes of the year by inactivity or virulence of his
pimples. His legs were puffed and affected with a prickly heat, a result
of wearing his woollen undertrunks in bed. He never went out and
rarely approached the windows.

*Tour de force by Brinsley, vocally interjected, being a comparable de-
scription in the Finn canon:* The neck to Trellis is house-thick and
house-rough and is guarded by night and day against the coming of
enemies by his old watchful boil. His bottom is the stern of a sea-blue
schooner, his stomach is its mainsail wtih a filling of wind. His face is
snowfall on old mountains, the feet are fields.

There was an interruption, I recall, at this stage. My uncle put
his head through the door and looked at me in a severe manner, his
face flushed from walking and an evening paper in his hand. He was
about to address me when he perceived the shadow of Brinsley by the
window.

Well, well, he said. He came in in a genial noisy manner, closed
the door with vigour and peered at the form of Brinsley. Brinsley took
his hands from his pockets and smiled without reason in the twilight.

Good evening to you, gentlemen, said my uncle.

Good evening, said Brinsley.

This is Mr Brinsley, a friend of mine, I said, raising my shoulders
feebly from the bed. I gave a low moan of exhaustion.

My uncle extended an honest hand in the grip of friendship.

Ah, Mr Brinsley, how do you do? he said. How do you do, Sir?
You are a University man, Mr Brinsley?

Oh yes.

Ah, very good, said my uncle. It's a grand thing, that—a thing
that will stand to you. It is certainly. A good degree is a very nice thing
to have. Are the masters hard to please, Mr Brinsley?

Well, no. As a matter of fact they don't care very much.

Do you tell me so! Well it was a different tale in the old days. The
old schoolmasters believed in the big stick. Oh, plenty of that boyo.

He gave a laugh here in which we concurred without emotion.

The stick was mightier than the pen, he added, laughing again
in a louder way and relapsing into a quiet chuckle. He paused for a

brief interval as if examining something hitherto overlooked in the interior of his memory.

And how is our friend? he inquired in the direction of my bed.

Nature of my reply: Civil, perfunctory, uninformative.

My uncle leaned over towards Brinsley and said to him in a low, confidential manner:

Do you know what I am going to tell you, there is a very catching cold going around. Every second man you meet has got a cold. God preserve us, there will be plenty of 'flu before the winter's out, make no mistake about that. You would need to keep yourself well wrapped up.

As a matter of fact, said Brinsley in a crafty way, I have only just recovered from a cold myself.

You would need to keep yourself well wrapped up, rejoined my uncle, you would, faith.

Here there was a pause, each of us searching for a word with which it might be broken.

Tell me this, Mr Brinsley, said my uncle, are you going to be a doctor?

I am not, said Brinsley.

Or a schoolmaster?

Here I interposed a shaft from my bed.

He hopes to get a job from the Christian Brothers, I said, when he gets his B.A.

That would be a great thing, said my uncle. The Brothers, of course, are very particular about the boys they take. You must have a good record, a clean sheet.

Well I have that, said Brinsley.

Of course you have, said my uncle. But doctoring and teaching are two jobs that call for great application and love of God. For what is the love of God but the love of your neighbour?

He sought agreement from each of us in turn, reverting a second to Brinsley with his ocular inquiry.

It is a grand and a noble life, he said, teaching the young and the sick and nursing them back to their God-given health. It is, faith. There is a special crown for those that give themselves up to that work.

It is a hard life, but, said Brinsley.

A hard life? said my uncle. Certainly so, but tell me this: Is it worth your while?

Brinsley gave a nod.

Worth your while and well worth it, said my uncle. A special crown is a thing that is not offered every day of the week. Oh, it's a grand thing, a grand life. Doctoring and teaching, the two of them are marked out for special graces and blessings.

He mused for a while, staring at the smoke of his cigarette. He then looked up and laughed, clapping his hand on the top of the washstand.

But long faces, he said, long faces won't get any of us very far. Eh, Mr Brinsley? I am a great believer in the smile and the happy word.

A sovereign remedy for all our ills, said Brinsley.

A sovereign remedy for all our ills, said my uncle. Very nicely put. Well . . .

He held out a hand in valediction.

Mind yourself now, he said, and mind and keep the coat buttoned up. The 'flu is the boy I'd give the slip to.

He was civilly replied to. He left the room with a pleased smile but was not gone for three seconds till he was back again with a grave look, coming upon us suddenly in the moment of our relaxation and relief.

Oh, that matter of the Brothers, he said in a low tone to Brinsley, would you care for me to put in a word for you?

Thanks very much, said Brinsley, but—

No trouble at all, said my uncle. Brother Hanley, late of Richmond Street, he is a very special friend of mine. No question of pulling strings, you know. Just a private word in his ear. He is a special friend.

Well, that is very good of you, said Brinsley.

Oh, not in the least, said my uncle. There is a way of doing things, you understand. It is a great thing to have a friend in court. And Brother Hanley, I may tell you privately, is one of the best—Oh, one of the very best in the world. It would be a pleasure to work with a man like Brother Hanley. I will have a word with him tomorrow.

The only thing is, but, said Brinsley, it will be some time before I am qualified and get my parchment.

Never mind, said my uncle, it is always well to be in early. First come, first called.

322

At this point he assembled his features into an expression of extreme secrecy and responsibility:

The Order, of course, is always on the look-out for boys of education and character. Tell me this, Mr Brinsley, have you ever .

I never thought of that, said Brinsley in surprise.

Do you think would the religious life appeal to you?

I'm afraid I never thought much about it.

Brinsley's tone was of a forced texture as if he were labouring in the stress of some emotion.

It is a good healthy life and a special crown at the end of it, said my uncle. Every boy should consider it very carefully before he decides to remain out in the world. He should pray to God for a vocation.

Not everybody is called, I ventured from the bed.

A BASH IN THE TUNNEL

James Joyce was an artist. He has said so himself. His was a case of Ars gratia Artis. He declared that he would pursue his artistic mission even if the penalty was as long as eternity itself. This appears to be an affirmation of belief in Hell, therefore of belief in Heaven and in God.

A better title for this article might be: "Was Joyce Mad?" By Hamlet, Prince of Denmark. Yet there is a reason for the present title.

Some thinkers—all Irish, all Catholic, some unlay—have confessed to discerning a resemblance between Joyce and Satan. True, resemblances there are. Both had other names, the one Stephen Dedalus, the other Lucifer; the latter name, meaning "Maker of Light," was to attract later the ironical gloss "Prince of Darkness"! Both started off very well under unfaultable teachers, both were very proud, both had a fall. But they differed on one big, critical issue. Satan never denied the existence of the Almighty; indeed he acknowledged it by challenging merely His primacy. Joyce said there was no God, proving this by uttering various blasphemies and obscenities and not being instantly struck dead.

A man once said to me that he hated blasphemy, but on purely rational grounds. If there is no God, he said, the thing is stupid and unnecessary. If there is, it's dangerous.

Anatole France says this better. He relates how, one morning, a notorious agnostic called on a friend who was a devout Catholic. The devout Catholic was drunk and began to pour forth appalling blasphemies. Pale and shocked, the agnostic rushed from the house. Later, a third party challenged him on this incident.

"You have been saying for years that there is no God. Why then should you be so frightened at somebody else insulting this God who doesn't exist?"

"I still say there is no God. But that fellow thinks there is. Suppose a thunderbolt was sent down to strike him dead. How did I know I wouldn't get killed as well? Wasn't I standing beside him?"

Another blasphemy, perhaps—doubting the Almighty's aim. Yet it is still true that all true blasphemers must be believers.

What is the position of the artist in Ireland?

Shortly before commencing to assemble material for this essay, I went into the Bailey in Dublin to drink a bottle of stout and do some solitary thinking. Before any considerable thought had formed itself, a man—then a complete stranger—came, accompanied by his drink, and stood beside me: addressing me by name, he said he was surprised to see a man like myself drinking in a pub.

My pub radar screen showed up the word "toucher." I was instantly much on my guard.

"And where do you think I should drink?" I asked. "Pay fancy prices in a hotel?"

"Ah, no," he said. "I didn't mean that. But any time I feel like a good bash myself, I have it in the cars. What will you have?"

I said I would have a large one, knowing that his mysterious reply would entail lengthy elucidation.

"I needn't tell you that that crowd is a crowd of bastards," was his prefatory exegesis.

Then he told me all. At one time his father had a pub and grocery business, situated near a large Dublin railway terminus. Every year the railway company invited tenders for the provisioning of its dining cars, and every year the father got the contract. (The narrator said he thought this was due to the territorial proximity of the house, with diminished handling and cartage charges.)

The dining cars (hereinafter known as "the cars") were customarily parked in remote sidings. It was the father's job to load them from time to time with costly victuals—eggs, rashers, cold turkey and whiskey. These cars, bulging in their lonely sidings with such fabulous fare, had special locks. The father had the key, and nobody else in the world had authority to open the doors until the car was part of a train. But my informant had made it his business, he told me, to have a key too.

"At that time," He told me, "I had a bash once a week in the cars."

One must here record two peculiarities of Irish railway practice. The first is a chronic inability to "make up" trains in advance, i.e., to estimate expected passenger traffic accurately. Week after week a long-distance train is scheduled to be five passenger coaches and a car. Perpetually, an extra 150 passengers arrive on the departure platform unexpectedly. This means that the car must be detached, a passenger coach substituted, and the train despatched foodless and drinkless on its way.

The second peculiarity—not exclusively Irish—is the inability of personnel in charge of shunting engines to leave coaches, parked in far sidings, alone. At all costs they must be shifted.

That was the situation as my friend in the Bailey described it. The loaded dining cars never went anywhere, in the long-distance sense. He approved of that. But they were subject to endless enshunt-ment. That, he said, was a bloody scandal and a waste of the taxpayers' money.

When the urge for a "bash" came upon him, his routine was simple. Using his secret key, he secretly got into a parked and laden car very early in the morning, penetrated to the pantry, grabbed a jug of water, a glass and a bottle of whiskey and, with this assortment of material and utensil, locked himself in the lavatory.

Reflect on that locking. So far as the whole world was concerned, the car was utterly empty. It was locked with special, unprecedented locks. Yet this man locked himself securely within those locks.

Came the dawn—and the shunters. They espied, as doth the greyhound the hare, the lonely dining car, mute, immobile, deserted. So they coupled it up and dragged it to another siding at Liffey Junction. It was there for five hours but ("that crowd of bastards," i.e. other shunters) it was discovered and towed over to the yards behind Westland Row Station. Many hours later it was shunted on to the tail of the Wexford Express but later angrily detached owing to the unexpected arrival of extra passengers.

"And are you sitting in the lavatory drinking whiskey all the time?" I asked.

"Certainly I am," he answered, "what the hell do you think

lavatories in trains is for? And with the knees of me trousers wet with me own whiskey from the jerks of them shunter bastards!"

His resentment was enormous. Be it noted that the whiskey was not in fact his own whiskey, that he was that oddity, an unauthorized person.

"How long does a bash in the cars last?" I asked him.

"Ah, that depends on a lot of things," he said. "As you know, I never carry a watch." (Exhibits cuffless, hairy wrist in proof.) "Did I ever tell you about the time I had a bash in the tunnel?"

He had not—for the good reason that I had never met him before.

"I seen meself," he said, "Once upon a time on a three-day bash. The bastards took me out of Liffey Junction down to Hazelhatch. Another crowd shifted me into Harcourt Street yards. I was having a good bash at this time, but I always try to see, for the good of me health, that a bash doesn't last more than a day and night. I know it's night outside when it's dark. If it's bright it's day. Do you follow me?"

"I think I do."

"Well, I was about on the third bottle when this other shunter crowd come along—it was dark, about eight in the evening—and nothing would do them only bring me into the Liffey Tunnel under the Phoenix Park and park me there. As you know I never use a watch. If it's bright, it's day. If it's dark, it's night. Here was meself parked in the tunnel opening bottle after bottle in the dark, thinking the night was a very long one, stuck there in the tunnel. I was three-quarters way into the jigs when they pulled me out of the tunnel into Kingsbridge. I was in bed for a week. Did you ever in your life hear of a greater crowd of bastards?"

"Never."

"That was the first and last time I ever had a bash in the tunnel."

Funny? But surely there you have the Irish artist? Sitting fully dressed, innerly locked in the toilet of a locked coach where he has no right to be, resentfully drinking somebody else's whiskey, being whisked hither and thither by anonymous shunters, keeping fastidiously the while on the outer face of his door the simple word ENGAGED!

I think the image fits Joyce; but particularly in his manifestation of a most Irish characteristic—the transgressor's resentment with the nongressor.

A friend of mine found himself next door at dinner to a well-known savant who appears in *Ulysses*. (He shall be nameless, for he still lives.) My friend, making dutiful conversation, made mention of Joyce. The savant said that Ireland was under a deep obligation to the author of Joyce's *Irish Names of Places*. My friend lengthily explained that his reference had been to a different Joyce. The savant did not quite understand, but ultimately confessed that he had heard certain rumours about the other man. It seemed that he had written some dirty books, published in Paris.

"But you are a character in one of them," my friend incautiously remarked.

The next two hours, to the neglect of wine and cigars, were occupied with a heated statement by the savant that he was by no means a character in fiction, he was a man, furthermore he was alive and he had published books of his own.

"How can I be a character in fiction," he demanded, "if I am here talking to you?"

That incident may be funny, too, but its curiosity is this: Joyce spent a lifetime establishing himself as a character in fiction. Joyce created, in narcissus fascination, the ageless Stephen. Beginning with importing real characters into his books, he achieves the magnificent inversion of making them legendary and fictional. It is quite preposterous. Thousands of people believe that there once lived a man named Sherlock Holmes.

Joyce went further than Satan in rebellion.

Two characters who confess themselves based on Aquinas: Joyce and Maritain.

In *Finnegans Wake*, Joyce appears to favour the Vico theory of inevitable human and recurring evolution-theocracy: aristocracy: democracy: chaos.

"A.E." referred to the chaos of Joyce's mind.

That was wrong, for Joyce's mind was indeed very orderly. In composition he used coloured pencils to keep himself right. All his works, not excluding *Finnegans Wake*, have a rigid classic pattern. His personal moral and family behaviours were impeccable. He seems to have deserved equally with George Moore the sneer about the latter— he never kissed, but told.

What was really abnormal about Joyce? At Clongowes he had his dose of Jesuit casuistry. Why did he substitute his home-made chaosistry?

It seems to me that Joyce emerges, through curtains of salacity and blasphemy, as a truly fear-shaken Irish Catholic, rebelling not so much against the Church but against its near-schism Irish eccentricities, its pretence that there is only one Commandment, the vulgarity of its edifices, the shallowness and stupidity of many of its ministers. His revolt, noble in itself, carried him away. He could not see the tree for the woods. But I think he meant well. We all do, anyway.

What is *Finnegans Wake?* A treatise on the incommunicable night-mind? Or merely an example of silence, exile and punning?

Some think that Joyce was at heart an Irish dawn-bursting romantic, an admirer of de Valera, and one who dearly wished to be recalled to Dublin as an ageing man to be crowned with a D. Litt. from the national and priest-haunted university. This is at least possible, if only because it explains the preposterous "aesthetic" affectations of his youth, which included the necessity for being rude to his dying mother. The theme here is that a heart of gold was beating under the artificial waistcoat. Amen.

Humour, the handmaid of sorrow and fear, creeps out endlessly in all Joyce's works. He uses the thing in the same way as Shakespeare does but less formally, to attenuate the fear of those who have belief and who genuinely think that they will be in hell or in heaven shortly, and possibly very shortly. With laughs he palliates the sense of doom that is the heritage of the Irish Catholic. True humour needs this background urgency: Rabelais is funny, but his stuff cloys. His stuff lacks tragedy.

Perhaps the true fascination of Joyce lies in his secretiveness, his ambiguity (his polyguity, perhaps?), his leg-pulling, his dishonesties, his technical skill, his attraction for Americans, His works are a garden in which some of us may play. All that we can claim to know is merely a small bit of that garden.

But at the end, Joyce will still be in his tunnel, unabashed.

Further Readings on Flann O' Brien

Bibliography

Powell, David. "A Checklist of Brian O'Nolan." *Journal of Irish Literature* 3: 104–12.

Selected Works

As Flann O'Brien:
At Swim-Two-Birds. London: Longmans, Green, 1939. Reprinted, New York: Pantheon, 1951; London: MacGibbon & Kee, 1960; London: Four Square Books, 1962; New York: Walker, 1966; Harmondsworth: Penguin, 1967; New York: Viking, 1967.
The Dalkey Archive. London: MacGibbon & Kee, 1964; New York: Macmillan, 1965.
The Hard Life. London: MacGibbon & Kee, 1961; New York: Pantheon, 1962.
Stories and Plays by Flann O'Brien. London: Hart-Davis MacGibbon, 1974; New York: Viking, 1974; Harmondsworth: Penguin, 1977.
The Third Policeman. London: MacGibbon & Kee, New York: Walker, 1967; New York: Lancer Books, 1970; London: Picador, 1974.
As Myles na Gopaleen:
An Béal Bocht. Dublin: An Press Náisiunta, 1941. Reprinted, Dublin: Dolmen, 1964. Translated by Patrick C. Power as *The Poor Mouth*. London: Hart-Davis MacGibbon, 1973; New York: Viking, 1974: London: Picador, 1975.
The Best of Myles. London: MacGibbon & Kee; New York: Viking, 1968; London: Picador, 1977.
Cruiskeen Lawn. Dublin: Cahill, 1943.
Faustus Kelly: A Play in Three Acts. Dublin: Cahill, 1943.

Biography and Criticism

Clissmann, Anne. *Flann O'Brien: A Critical Introduction to His Writing*. Dublin: Gill and Macmillan, 1975.
Imhof, Rüdiger. *Alive Alive O! Flann O'Brien's At Swim-Two-Birds*, Dublin: Wolfhound Press; Totowa, N.J.: Barnes & Noble, 1986.
Journal of Irish Literature. Flann O'Brien number, 3.
O'Keefe, Timothy, ed. *Myles: Portraits of Brian O'Nolan*. London: Martin Brian & O'Keefe, 1973.
Wäppling, Eva. *Four Irish Legendary Figures in At Swim-Two-Birds*. Uppsala: Academia Upsaliensis, 1984.

MARY LAVIN
(b.1912)

For more than forty years, Mary Lavin's fiction has appeared on both sides of the Atlantic, a phenomenon that mirrors her own Irish and American roots. Massachusetts-born, her parents moved back to Ireland when she was ten. After earning her B.A. and M.A. degrees at University College, Dublin, she abandoned an academic career to write. Since "Miss Holland" (1939), she has produced eleven collections of short stories and two novels, as well as children's books and even a couple of poems. She has been honored with prizes and fellowships, including an honorary D.Litt. from the National University of Ireland in 1972.

A.A. Kelly called Lavin the "quiet rebel," a reference perhaps to the way that Lavin has been able to develop her own voice while accommodating Irish middle-class sensibility. "Happiness" is one of a series of autobiographical stories. Like the protagonist Vera Traske, Lavin was widowed with three young daughters, was responsible for an elderly mother, and was tireless in her efforts to keep a Dublin house going as well as a working farm near Bective Abbey, County Meath. Vera's celebration of those who joyously respond to life in contrast to those who deny life by being narrow, selfish, and demanding is a favorite Lavin theme in such stories as "Frail Vessel" and "A Happy Death."

HAPPINESS

Mother had a lot to say. This does not mean she was always talking but that we children felt the wells she drew upon were deep, deep, deep.

Her theme was happiness; what it was, what it was not; where we might find it, where not; and how, if found, it must be guarded. Never must we confound it with pleasure. Nor think sorrow its exact opposite.

"Take Father Hugh," Mother's eyes flashed as she looked at him. "According to him, sorrow is an ingredient of happiness—a *necessary* ingredient, if you please!" And when he tried to protest she put up her hand. "There may be a freakish truth in the theory—for some people. But not for me. And not, I hope, for my children." She looked severely at us three girls. We laughed. None of us had had much experience with sorrow. Bea and I were children and Linda only a year old when our father died suddenly after a short illness that had not at first seemed serious. "I've known people to make sorrow a *substitute* for happiness," Mother said.

Father Hugh protested again. "You're not putting me in that class, I hope?"

Father Hugh, ever since our father died, had been the closest of anyone to us as a family, without being close to any one of us in particular—even to Mother. He lived in a monastery near our farm in County Meath, and he had been one of the celebrants at the Requiem High Mass our father's political importance had demanded. He met us that day for the first time, but he took to dropping in to see us, with the idea of filling the crater of loneliness left at our centre. He did not know that there was a cavity in his own life, much less that we would fill it. He and Mother were both young in those days, and perhaps it gave scandal to some that he was so often in our house, staying till late into the night and, indeed, thinking nothing of stopping all night if there was any special reason, such as one of us being sick. He had even on occasion slept there if the night was too wet for tramping home across the fields.

When we girls were young, we were so used to having Father Hugh around that we never stood on ceremony with him but in his presence dried our hair and pared our nails and never minded what garments were strewn about. As for Mother—she thought nothing of running out of the bathroom in her slip, brushing her teeth or combing her hair, if she wanted to tell him something she might otherwise forget. And she brooked no criticism of her behaviour. "Celibacy was never meant to take all the warmth and homeliness out of their lives," she said.

On this point, too, Bea was adamant. Bea, the middle sister, was our oracle. "I'm so glad he *has* Mother," she said, "as well as her having him, because it must be awful the way most women treat them—priests, I mean—as if they were pariahs. Mother treats him like a human being—that's all."

And when it came to Mother's ears that there had been gossip about her making free with Father Hugh, she opened her eyes wide in astonishment." But he's only a priest!" she said.

Bea giggled. "It's a good job he didn't hear *that*," she said to me afterwards." It would undo the good she's done him. You'd think he was a eunuch."

"Bea!" I said. "Do you think he's in love with her?"

"If so, he doesn't know it," Bea said firmly. "It's her soul he's after! Maye he wants to make sure of her in the next world!"

But thoughts of the world to come never troubled Mother. "If anything ever happens to me, children," she said, "suddenly, I mean, or when you are not near me, or I cannot speak to you, I want you to promise you won't feel bad. There's no need! Just remember that I had a happy life—and that if I had to choose my kind of heaven I'd take it on this earth with you again, no matter how much you might annoy me!"

You see, annoyance and fatigue, according to Mother, and even illness and pain, could coexist with happiness. She had a habit of asking people if they were happy at times and in places that—to say the least of it—seemed to us inappropriate. "But are you happy?" she'd probe as one lay sick and bathed in sweat, or in the throes of a jumping toothache. And once in our presence she made the inquiry of an old friend as he lay upon his deathbed.

"Why not?" she said when we took her to task for it later. "Isn't it more important than ever to be happy when you're dying? Take my own father! You know what he said in his last moments? On his deathbed, he defied me to name a man who had enjoyed a better life. In spite of dreadful pain, his face *radiated* happiness!" Mother nodded her head comfortably. "Happiness drives out pain, as fire burns out fire."

Having no knowledge of our own to pit against hers, we thirstily drank in her rhetoric. Only Bea was sceptical. "Perhaps you *got* it from him, like spots, or fever," she said. "Or something that could at least be slipped from hand to hand."

"Do you think I'd have taken it if that were the case!" Mother cried. "Then, when he needed it most?"

"Not there and then!" Bea said stubbornly. "I meant as a sort legacy."

"Don't you think in *that* case," mother said, exasperated, "he would have felt obliged to leave it to your grandmother?"

Certainly we knew that in spite of his lavish heart our grandfather had failed to provide our grandmother with enduring happiness. He had passed that job on to Mother. And Mother had not made too good a fist of it, even when Father was living and she had him—and later, us children—to help.

As for Father Hugh, he had given our grandmother up early in the game. "God Almighty couldn't make that woman happy," he said one day, seeing Mother's face, drawn and pale with fatigue, preparing for the nightly run over to her own mother's flat that would exhaust her utterly.

There were evenings after she came home from the library where she worked when we saw her stand with the car keys in her hand, trying to think which would be worse—to slog over there on foot, or take out the car again. And yet the distance was short. It was Mother's day that had been too long.

"Weren't you over to see her this morning?" Father Hugh demanded.

"No matter!" said Mother. She was no doubt thinking of the forlorn face our grandmother always put on when she was leaving. ("Don't say good night, Vera," Grandmother would plead. "It makes me feel too lonely. And you never can tell—you might slip over again before you go to bed!")

"Do you know the time?" Bea would say impatiently, if she happened to be with Mother. Not indeed that the lateness of the hour counted for anything, because in all likelihood Mother *would* go back, if only to pass by under the window and see that the lights were out, or stand and listen and make sure that as far as she could tell all was well.

"I wouldn't mind if she was happy," Mother said.

"And how do you know she's not?" we'd ask.

"When people are happy, I can feel it. Can't you?"

We were not sure. Most people thought our grandmother was a gay creature, a small birdy being who even at a great age laughed like a girl, and—more remarkably—sang like one, as she went about her day. But beak and claw were of steel. She'd think nothing of sending Mother back to a shop three times if her errands were not exactly right. "Not sugar like that—that's *too* fine; it's not castor sugar I want. But *not* as coarse as *that,* either. I want an in-between kind."

Provoked one day, my youngest sister, Linda, turned and gave battle. "You're mean!" she cried. "You love ordering people about!"

Grandmother preened, as if Linda had acclaimed an attribute. "I was always hard to please," she said. "As a girl, I used to be called Miss Imperious."

And Miss Imperious she remained as long as she lived, even when she was a great age. Her orders were then given a wry twist by the fact that as she advanced in age she took to calling her daughter Mother, as we did.

There was one great phrase with which our grandmother opened every sentence: "if only." "If only," she'd say, when we came to visit her—"if only you'd come earlier, before I was worn out expecting you!" Or if we were early, then if only it was later, after she'd had a rest and could enjoy us, be *able* for us. And if we brought her flowers, she'd sigh to think that if only we'd brought them the previous day she'd have had a visitor to appreciate them, or say it was a pity the stems weren't longer. If only we'd picked a few green leaves, or included some buds, because, she said disparagingly, the poor flowers we'd brought were already wilting. We might just as well not have brought them! As the years went on, Grandmother had a new bead to add to her rosary: if only her friends were not all dead! By their absence, they reduced to nil all *real* enjoyment in anything. Our own father—her son-in-law—was the one person who had ever gone close to pleasing her. But even here there had been a snag. "If only he was my real son!" she used to say with a sigh.

Mother's mother lived on through our childhood and into our early maturity (though she outlived the money our grandfather left her), and in our minds she was a complicated mixture of valiance and defeat. Courageous and generous within the limits of her own life, her simplest demand was yet enormous in the larger frame of Mother's life, and so we never could see her with the same clarity of vision with which we saw our grandfather, or our own father. Them we saw only through Mother's eyes.

"Take your grandfather!" she'd cry, and instantly we'd see him, his eyes burning upon us—yes, upon *us*, although in his day only one of us had been born: me. At another time, Mother would cry, "Take your own father!" and instantly we'd see *him*—tall, handsome, young, and much more suited to marry one of us than poor bedraggled Mother.

Most fascinating of all were the times Mother would say "Take me!" By magic then, staring down the years, we'd see blazingly clear a small girl with black hair and buttoned boots, who, though plain and pouting, burned bright, like a star. "I was happy, you see," Mother said. And we'd strain hard to try and understand the mystery of the light that still radiated from her. "I used to lean along a tree that grew out over the river," she said, "and look down through the grey leaves at the water flowing past below, and I used to think it was not the stream that flowed but me, spread-eagled over it, who flew through the air! Like a bird! That I'd found the secret!" She made it seem there might *be* such a secret, just waiting to be found. Another time she'd dream that she'd be a great singer.

"We didn't know you sang, Mother!"

She had to laugh. "Like a crow," she said.

Sometimes she used to think she'd swim the Channel.

"Did you swim *that* well, Mother?"

"Oh, not really—just the breast stroke," she said. "And then only by the aid of two pig bladders blown up by my father and tied around my middle. But I used to throb—yes, throb—with happiness."

Behind Mother's back, Bea raised her eyebrows.

What was it, we used to ask ourselves—that quality that she, we felt sure, misnamed? Was it courage? Was it strength, health, or high spirits? Something you could not give or take—a conundrum? A game of catch-as-you-can?

"I know," cried Bea. "A sham!"

Whatever it was, we knew that Mother would let no wind of violence from within or without tear it from her. Although, one evening when Father Hugh was with us, our astonished ears heard her proclaim that there might be a time when one had to slacken hold on it—let go—to catch at it again with a surer hand. In the way, we supposed, that the high-wire walker up among the painted stars of his canvas sky must wait to fling himself through the air until the bar he catches at has started to sway perversely from him. Oh no, no! That downward drag at our innards we could not bear, the belly swelling to the shape of a pear. Let happiness go by the board. "After all, lots of people seem to make out without it," Bea cried. It was too tricky a business. And might it not be that one had to be born with a flair for it?

"A flair would not be enough," Mother answered. "Take Father Hugh. He, if anyone, had a flair for it—a natural capacity! You've only to look at him when he's off guard, with you children, or helping me in the garden. But he rejects happiness! He casts it from him."

"That is simply not true, Vera" cried Father Hugh, overhearing her. "It's just that I don't place an inordinate value on it like you. I don't think it's enough to carry one all the way. To the end, I mean—and after."

"Oh, don't talk about the end when we're only in the middle," cried Mother. And, indeed at that moment her own face shone with such happiness it was hard to believe that earth was not her heaven. Certainly it was her constant contention that of happiness she had had a lion's share. This, however, we, in private, doubted. Perhaps there were times when she had had a surplus of it—when she was young, say, with her redoubtable father, whose love blazed circles around her, making winter into summer and ice into fire. Perhaps she did have a brimming measure in her early married years. By straining hard, we could find traces left in our minds from those days of milk and honey. Our father, while he lived, had cast a magic over everything, for us as well as for her. He held his love up over us like an umbrella and kept off the troubles that afterwards came down on us, pouring cats and dogs!

But if she did have more than the common lot of happiness in those early days, what use was that when we could remember so clearly how our father's death had ravaged her? And how could we forget the distress it brought on us when, afraid to let her out of our sight, Bea and I stumbled after her everywhere, through the woods and along the bank of the river, where, in the weeks that followed, she tried vainly to find peace.

The summer after Father died, we were invited to France to stay with friends, and when she went walking on the cliffs at Fécamp our fears for her grew frenzied, so that we hung on to her arm and dragged at her skirt, hoping that like leaded weights we'd pin her down if she went too near to the edge. But at night we had to abandon our watch, being forced to follow the conventions of a family still whole—a home still intact—and go to bed at the same time as the other children. It was at that hour, when the coast guard was gone from his rowing boat offshore and the sand was as cold and grey as the sea, that Mother liked to swim. And when she had washed, kissed, and left us, our hearts almost died inside us and we'd creep out of bed again to stand in our bare feet at the mansard and watch as she ran down the shingle, striking out when she reached the water where, far out, wave and sky and mist were one, and the greyness closed over her. If we took our eyes off her for an instant, it was impossible to find her again.

"Oh, make her turn back, God, please!" I prayed out loud one night.

Startled, Bea turned away from the window, "She'll *have* to turn back sometime, won't she? Unless . . . ?"

Locking our damp hands together, we stared out again. "She

wouldn't!" I whispered. "It would be a sin!"

Secure in the deterring power of sin, we let out our breath. Then Bea's breath caught again. "What if she went out so far she used up all her strength? She couldn't swim back! It wouldn't be a sin then!"

"It's the intention that counts," I whispered.

A second later, we could see an arm lift heavily up and wearily cleave down, and at last Mother was in the shallows, wading back to shore.

"Don't let her see us!" cried Bea. As if our chattering teeth would not give us away when she looked in at us before she went to her own room on the other side of the corridor, where, later in the night, sometimes the sound of crying would reach us.

What was it worth—a happiness bought that dearly.

Mother had never questioned it. And once she told us, "On a wintry day, I brought my own mother a snowdrop. It was the first one of the year—a bleak bud that had come up stunted before its time— and I meant it for a sign. But do you know what your grandmother said? 'What good are snowdrops to me now?' Such a thing to say! What good is a snowdrop at all if it doesn't hold its value always, and never lose it! Isn't that the whole point of a snowdrop? And that is the whole point of happiness, too! What good would it be if it could be erased without trace? Take me and those daffodils!" Stooping, she buried her face in a bunch that lay on the table waiting to be put in vases. "If they didn't hold their beauty absolute and inviolable, do you think I could bear the sight of them after what happened when your father was in hospital?"

It was a fair question. When Father went to hospital, Mother went with him and stayed in a small hotel across the street so she could be with him all day from early to late. "Because it was so awful for him—being in Dublin!" she said. "You have no idea how he hated it."

That he was dying neither of them realized. How could they know, as it rushed through the sky, that their star was a falling star! But one evening when she'd left him asleep Mother came home for a few hours to see how we were faring, and it broke her heart to see the daffodils out all over the place—in the woods, under the trees, and along the sides of the avenue. There had never been so many, and she thought how awful it was that Father was missing them. "You sent up little bunches to him, you poor dears!" she said. "Sweet little bunches, too—squeezed tight as posies by your little fists! But stuffed into vases they couldn't really make up to him for not being able to see them growing!"

So on the way back to the hospital she stopped her car and pulled a great bunch—the full of her arms. "They took up the whole back seat," she said, "and I was so excited at the thought of walking into his room and dumping them on his bed—you know—just plomping them down so he could smell them, and feel them, and look and look! I didn't mean them to be put in vases, or anything ridiculous like that—it would have taken a rainwater barrel to hold them. Why, I could hardly see over them as I came up the steps; I kept tripping. But when I came into the hall, that nun—I told you about her—that nun came up to me, sprang out of nowhere it seemed, although I know now that she was waiting for me, knowing that somebody had to bring me to my senses. But the way she did it! Reached out and grabbed the flowers, letting lots of them fall—I remember them getting stood on. 'Where are you going with those foolish flowers, you foolish woman?' she said. 'Don't you know your husband is dying? Your prayers are all you can give him now!'

"She was right. I *was* foolish. But I wasn't cured. Afterwards, it was nothing but foolishness the way I dragged you children after me all over Europe. As if any one place was going to be different from another, any better, any less desolate. But there was great satisfaction in bringing you places your father and I had planned to bring you— although in fairness to him I must say that he would not perhaps have brought you so young. And he would not have had an ulterior motive. But above all, he would not have attempted those trips in such a dilapidated car."

Oh, that car! It was a battered and dilapidated red sports car, so depleted of accessories that when, eventually, we got a new car Mother still stuck out her hand on bends, and in wet weather jumped out to wipe the windscreen with her sleeve. And if fussed, she'd let down the window and shout at people, forgetting she now had a horn. How we had ever fitted into it with all our luggage was a miracle.

"You were never lumpish—any of you!" Mother said proudly. "But you were very healthy and very strong." She turned to me. "Think of how you got that car up the hill in Switzerland!"

"The Alps are not hills, Mother!" I pointed out coldly, as I had done at the time, when, as actually happened, the car failed to make it on one of the inclines. Mother let it run back until it wedged against the rock face, and I had to get out and push till she got going again in first gear. But when it got started it couldn't be stopped to pick me up until it got to the top, where they had to wait for me, and for a very long time.

"Ah, well," she said, sighing wistfully at the thought of those trips. "You got something out of them, I hope. All that travelling must have helped you with your geography and your history."

We looked at each other and smiled, and then Mother herself laughed. "Remember the time," she said, "when we were in Italy, and it was Easter, and all the shops were chock-full of food? The butchers' shops had poultry and game hanging up outside the doors, fully feathered, and with their poor heads dripping blood, and in the windows they had poor little lambs and suckling pigs and young goats, all skinned and hanging by their hindfeet." Mother shuddered. "They think so much about food. I found it revolting. I had to hurry past. But Linda, who must have been only four then, dragged at me and stared and stared. You know how children are at that age; they have a morbid fascination for what is cruel and bloody. Her face was flushed and her eyes were wide. I hurried her back to the hotel. But next morning she crept into my room. She crept up to me and pressed against me. 'Can't we go back, just once, and look again at that shop?' she whispered. 'The shop where they have the little children hanging up for Easter!' It was the young goats, of course, but I'd said 'kids,' I suppose. How we laughed." But her face was grave. "You were *so* good on those trips, all of you," she said. "You were really very good children in general. Otherwise I would never have put so much effort into rearing you, because I wasn't a bit maternal. You brought out the best in me! I put an unnatural effort into you, of course, because I was taking my standards from your father, forgetting that his might not have remained so inflexible if he had lived to middle age and was beset by life, like other parents."

"Well, the job is nearly over now, Vera," said Father Hugh. "And you didn't do so badly."

"That's right, Hugh," said Mother, and she straightened up, and put her hand to her back the way she sometimes did in the garden when she got up from her knees after weeding. "I didn't go over to the enemy anyway! We survived!" Then a flash of defiance came into her eyes. "And we were happy. That's the main thing!"

Father Hugh frowned. "There you go again!" he said.

Mother turned on him. "I don't think you realize the onslaughts that were made upon our happiness! The minute Robert died, they came down on me—cohorts of relatives, friends, even strangers, all draped in black, opening their arms like bats to let me pass into their company. 'Life is a vale of tears,' they said. 'You are privileged to find it out so young!' Ugh! After I staggered on to my feet and began to take hold of life once more, they fell back defeated. And the first day I gave a laugh—pouff, they were blown out like candles. They weren't living in a real world at all; they belonged to a ghostly world where life was easy: all one had to do was sit and weep. It takes effort to push back the stone from the mouth of the tomb and walk out."

Effort. Effort. Ah, but that strange-sounding word could invoke little sympathy from those who had not learned yet what it meant. Life must have been hardest for Mother in those years when we older ones were at college—no longer children, and still dependent on her. Indeed, we made more demands on her than ever then, being moved into new areas of activity and emotion. And our friends! Our friends came and went as freely as we did ourselves, so that the house was often like a café—and one where pets were not prohibited but took their places on our chairs and beds, as regardless as the people. And anyway it was hard to have sympathy for someone who got things into such a state as Mother. All over the house there was clutter. Her study was like the returned-letter department of a post-office, with stacks of paper everywhere, bills paid and unpaid, letters answered and un-answered, tax returns, pamphlets, leaflets. If by mistake we left the door open on a windy day, we came back to find papers flapping through the air like frightened birds. Efficient only in that she man-aged eventually to conclude every task she began, it never seemed possible to outsiders that by Mother's methods anything whatever could be accomplished. In an attempt to keep order elsewhere, she made her own room the clearing house into which the rest of us put everything: things to be given away, things to be mended, things to be stored, things to be treasured, things to be returned—even things to be thrown out! By the end of the year, the room resembled an obsolescence dump. And no one could help her; the chaos of her life was as personal as an act of creation—one might as well try to finish another person's poem.

As the years passed, Mother rushed around more hectically. And although Bea and I had married and were not at home any more, except at holiday time and for occasional weekends, Linda was noisier than the two of us put together had been, and for every follower we had brought home she brought twenty. The house was never still. Now that we were reduced to being visitors, we watched Mother's tension mount to vertigo, knowing that, like a spinning top, she could not rest till she fell. But now at the smallest pretext Father Hugh would call in the doctor and Mother would be put on the mail boat and dispatched for London. For it was essential that she get far enough away to make phoning home every night prohibitively costly.

Unfortunately, the thought of departure often drove a spur into her and she redoubled her effort to achieve order in her affairs. She would be up until the early hours ransacking her desk. To her, as always, the shortest parting entailed a preparation as for death. And as it were her end that was at hand, we would all be summoned, although she had no time to speak a word to us, because five minutes before departure she would still be attempting to reply to letters that were the acquisition of weeks and would have taken whole days to dispatch.

"Don't you know the taxi is at the door, Vera?" Father Hugh would say, running his hand through his grey hair and looking very dishevelled himself. She had him at times as distracted as herself. "You can't do any more. You'll have to leave the rest till you come back."

"I can't, I can't!" Mother would cry. "I'll have to cancel my plans."

One day, Father Hugh opened the lid of her case, which was strapped up in the hall, and with a swipe of his arm he cleared all the papers on the top of the desk pell-mell into the suitcase. "You can sort them on the boat," he said, "or the train to London."

Thereafter, Mother's luggage always included an empty case to hold the unfinished papers on her desk. And years afterwards a steward on the Irish Mail told us she was a familiar figure, working away at letters and bills nearly all the way from Holyhead to Euston. "She gave it up about Rugby or Crewe," he said. "She'd get talking to someone in the compartment." He smiled. "There was one time coming down the train I was just in time to see her close up the window with a guilty look. I didn't say anything, but I think she'd emptied those paper of hers out the window!"

Quite likely. When we were children, even a few hours away from us gave her composure. And in two weeks or less, when she'd come home, the well of her spirit would be freshened. We'd hardly know her—her step so light, her eyes so bright, and her love and patience once more freely flowing. But in no time at all the house would fill up once more with the noise and confusion of too many people and too many animals, and again we'd be fighting our corner with cats and dogs, bats, mice, bees and even wasps. "Don't kill it!" Mother would cry if we raised a hand to an angry wasp. "Just catch it, dear, and put it outside. Open the window and let it fly away!" But even this treatment could at times be deemed too harsh. "Wait a minute. Close the window!" she'd cry. "It's too cold outside. It will die. That's why it came in, I suppose! Oh dear, what will we do?" Life would be going full blast again.

There was only one place Mother found rest. When she was at breaking point and fit to fall, she'd go out into the garden—not to sit or stroll around but to dig, to drag up weeds, to move great clumps of corms or rhizomes, or indeed quite frequently to haul huge rocks from one place to another. She was always laying down a path, building a dry wall, or making compost heaps as high as hills. However jaded she might be going out, when dark forced her in at last her step had the spring of a daisy. So if she did not succeed in defining happiness to our understanding, we could see that whatever it was, she possessed it to the full when she was in her garden.

One of us said as much one Sunday when Bea and I had dropped round for the afternoon. Father Hugh was with us again. "It's an unthinking happiness, though," he cavilled. We were standing at the drawing-room window, looking out to where in the fading light we could see Mother on her knees weeding, in the long border that stretched from the house right down to the woods. "I wonder how she'd take it if she were stricken down and had to give up that heavy work!" he said. Was he perhaps a little jealous of how she could stoop and bend? He himself had begun to use a stick. I was often a little jealous of her myself, because although I was married and had children of my own, I had married young and felt the weight of living as heavy as a weight of years. "She doesn't take enough care of herself," Father Hugh said sadly. "Look at her out there with nothing under her knees to protect her from the damp ground." It was almost too dim for us to see her, but even in the drawing-room it was chilly. "She should not be let stay out there after the sun goes down."

"Just you try to get her in then!" said Linda, who had come into the room in time to hear him. "Don't you know by now anyway that what would kill another person only seems to make Mother thrive?"

Father Hugh shook his head again. "You seem to forget it's not younger she's getting!" He fidgeted and fussed, and several times went to the window to stare out apprehensively. He was really getting quite elderly.

"Come and sit down, Father Hugh," Bea said, and to take his mind off Mother she turned on the light and blotted out the garden. Instead of seeing through the window, we saw into it as into a mirror, and there between the flower-laden tables and lamps it was ourselves we saw moving vaguely. Like Father Hugh, we, too, were waiting for her to come in before we called an end to the day.

"Oh, this is ridiculous!" Father Hugh cried at last. "She'll have to listen to reason." And going back to the window he threw it open.

"Vera!" he called. "Vera!"—sternly, so sternly that, more intimate than an endearment, his tone shocked us. "She didn't hear me," he said, turning back blinking at us in the lighted room. "I'm going out to get her." And in a minute he was gone from the room. As he ran down the garden path, we stared at each other, astonished; his step, like his voice, was the step of a lover. "I'm coming, Vera!" he cried.

Although she was never stubborn except in things that mattered, Mother had not moved. In the wholehearted way she did everything, she was bent down close to the ground. It wasn't the light only that was dimming; her eyesight also was failing, I thought, as instinctively I followed Father Hugh.

But halfway down the path I stopped. I had seen something he had not: Mother's hand that appeared to support itself in a forked branch of an old tree peony she had planted as a bride was not in fact gripping it but impaled upon it. And the hand that appeared to be grubbing in the clay in fact was sunk into the soft mould. "Mother!" I screamed, and I ran forward, but when I reached her I covered my face with my hands. "Oh Father Hugh!" I cried. "Is she dead?"

It was Bea who answered hysterical. "She is! She is!" she cried, and she began to pound Father Hugh on the back with her fists, as if his pessimistic words had made this happen.

But Mother was not dead. And at first the doctor even offered hope of her pulling through. But from the moment Father Hugh lifted her up to carry her into the house we ourselves had no hope, seeing how effortlessly he, who was not strong, could carry her. When he put her down on her bed, her head hardly creased the pillow. Mother lived for four more hours.

Like the days of her life, those four hours that Mother lived were packed tight with concern and anxiety. Partly conscious, partly delirious, she seemed to think the counterpane was her desk, and she scrabbled her fingers upon it as if trying to sort out a muddle of bills and correspondence. No longer indifferent now, we listened, anguished, to the distracted cries that had for all our lifetime been so familiar to us. "Oh, where is it? Where is it? I had a minute ago! Where on earth did I put it?"

"Vera, Vera, stop worrying," Father Hugh pleaded, but she waved him away and went on sifting through the sheets as if they were sheets of paper. "Oh, Vera!" he begged. "Listen to me. Do you not know—"

"Bea pushed between them. "You're not to tell her!" she commanded. "Why frighten her?"

"But it ought not to frighten her," said Father Hugh. "This is what I was always afraid would happen—that she'd be frightened when it came to the end."

At that moment, as if to vindicate him, Mother's hands fell idle on the coverlet, palm upward and empty. And turning her head she stared at each of us in turn, beseechingly. "I cannot face it," she whispered. "I can't! I can't! I can't!"

"Oh, my God!" Bea said, and she started to cry.;

"Vera. For God's sake listen to me," Father Hugh cried, and pressing his face to hers, as close as a kiss, he kept whispering to her, trying to cast into the dark tunnel before her the light of his own faith.

But it seemed to us that Mother must already be looking into God's exigent eyes. "I can't!" she cried. "I can't!"

Then her mind came back from the stark world of the spirit to the world where her body was still detained, but even that world was now a whirling kaleidoscope of things which only she could see. Suddenly her eyes focussed, and, catching at Father Hugh, she pulled herself up a little and pointed to something we could not see. "What will be done with them?" Her voice was anxious. "They ought to be put in water anyway," she said, and leaning over the edge of the bed, she pointed to the floor. "Don't step on that one!" she said sharply. Then more sharply still, she addressed us all. "Have them sent to the public ward," she said peremptorily. "Don't let that nun take them; she'll only put them on the altar. And God doesn't want them! He made them for *us*—not for Himself!"

It was the familiar rhetoric that all her life had characterized her utterances. For a moment we were mystified. Then Bea gasped. "The daffodils!" she cried. "The day Father died!" And over her face came the light that had so often blazed over Mother's. Leaning across the bed, she pushed Father Hugh aside. And, putting out her hands, she held Mother's face between her palms as tenderly as if it were the face of a child. "It's all right, Mother. You don't *have* to face it! It's over!" Then she who had so fiercely forbade Father Hugh to do so blurted out the truth. "You've finished with this world, Mother," she said, and, confident that her tidings were joyous, her voice was strong.

Mother made the last effort of her life and grasped at Bea's meaning. She let out a sigh, and, closing her eyes, she sank back, and this time her head sank so deeply into the pillow that it would have been dented had it been a pillow of stone.

344

Further Readings on Mary Lavin

Bibliography

Doyle, Paul A. "Mary Lavin: a Checklist." *Papers of the Bibliographical Society of America* 63: 317–21.
Krawchak, Ruth and Mahlke, Regina. *Mary Lavin: A Checklist.* Berlin: Hildebrand, 1979.

Selected Works

The Becker Wives and Other Stories. New York: New American Library, 1971 (1946).
Collected Stories. Introduction by V. S. Pritchett. Boston: Houghton Mifflin, 1971.
In the Middle of the Field and Other Stories. New York: Macmillan, 1969 (1967).
Mary O'Grady. London: Michael Joseph; New York: Little, Brown, 1950.
A Memory and Other Stories. London: Constable; Boston: Houghton Mifflin, 1973.
Selected Stories. Introduction by the author. London and New York: Macmillan, 1959.
Selected Stories. Harmondsworth: Penguin, 1984 (1981).
The Shrine and Other Stories. London: Constable: Boston: Houghton Mifflin, 1977.
The Stories of Mary Lavin: I. London: Constable; New York: Longmans, Green, 1970 (1964).
The Stories of Mary Lavin: II. London: Constable, 1974.
Tales from Bective Bridge. Introduction by Lord Dunsany. Boston: Little, Brown, 1942.

Biography and Criticism

Bowen, Zack. *Mary Lavin.* Lewisburg, Pa.: Bucknell University Press, 1975.
Chauvire, Roger. "The Art of Mary Lavin." *The Bell* 11: 600–609.
Dunleavy, Janet E. "The Fiction of Mary Lavin: Universal Sensibility in a Particular Milieu." *Irish University Review* 7: 222–36.
———. "The Making of Mary Lavin's *A Memory*." *Eire-Ireland* 12: 90–99.
Harmon, Maurice. "The Landscape of Mary Lavin." *Ireland of the Welcomes* 18: 34–37.
Kelly, A. A. *Mary Lavin: Quiet Rebel: A Study of Her Short Stories.* Dublin: Wolfhound Press, 1980.
Kiely, Benedict. "Green Island, Red South." *Kilkenny Magazine,* 18: 18–39.
Martin, Augustine. "A Skeleton Key to the Stories of Mary Lavin." *Studies* 52: 393–406.
Meszaros, Patricia K. "Woman as Artist: The Fiction of Mary Lavin." *Critique: Studies in Modern Fiction* 24: 39–54.

Murphy, Catherine A. "The Ironic Vision of Mary Lavin." *Mosaic* 12: 69–79.
O'Connor, Frank. "The Girl at the Gaol Gate." *A Review of English Literature* 1: 25–33.
Peterson, Richard F. *Mary Lavin.* Boston: Twayne Publisher, 1978.
Reynolds, Lorna. "Mary Lavin: An Appreciation." *Hibernia* 34: 14.

BRENDAN BEHAN
(1923–64)

The most successful Dublin playwright since Sean O'Casey, Brendan Behan was during his lifetime an embarrassment to his
middle-class countrymen. More of a public figure than any Irish
writer since Shaw, Behan often appeared to be little more than a
riotous if witty drunk. Today, however, more than two decades after
his death, his surviving writings portray quite a different character:
ironic, complex, and often exacting and careful in his craft.

Arrested at age sixteen for I.R.A. activities, Behan spent almost
seven years in jail, first in Britain's Borstal (i.e., reform) school and
later in prisons in the Irish Republic. The combined experience
proved to have been a remarkable school. The young Behan read
widely and, in prisons in his own country, became an apt student of
the Irish language. He also took the time to begin his writing career,
having his first story accepted by Seán O'Faoláin in *The Bell* when he
was only nineteen. Behan had published verse and prose fiction in
both Irish and English when he came to be known as a playwright.
He had two short plays produced on radio before the Pike Theatre in
Dublin performed his prison drama, *The Quare Fellow*, in 1954. This
English-language play was based on an Irish-language draft, *Casadh
an tSúgáin Eile* [the twisting of another rope], that Behan had begun
before leaving prison in 1946.

After a highly successful London production of *The Quare
Fellow* in 1956, Behan was spurred to complete a second play, *The
Hostage*, also based on a version the author wrote first in Irish, *An
Giall*. Both were performed in 1958. In this same year, Behan pub-
lished his finest work, the prison autobiography, *Borstal Boy*, on
which he had been working for more than a decade. The interna-

tional acclaim and notoriety that followed led Behan to dissipate his
energies, and little written after 1958 matches the quality of what had
preceded it. He dictated into a tape recorder what he would not take
the time to put on paper. Thus, his *Confessions of an Irish Rebel*
(1965), though purported to be a sequel to *Borstal Boy*, lacks the
power of the earlier book. A novel of Dublin life, *The Catacombs*,
and a play, *Richard's Cork Leg*, did not progress beyond drafts.
Throughout, however, Behan remained a great talker: some of his
quips and witticisms, even from the later years, are still quoted
favorably by writers on Irish literature. His funeral in March, 1964,
drew the biggest crowds Dublin had seen in more than forty years.

   "The Confirmation Suit" (1953), published before Behan's rising
interest in the theater, has something in common with his two best-
known plays—a paradoxical gaity in the treatment of the grimmest of
subjects.

THE CONFIRMATION SUIT

For weeks it was nothing but simony and sacrilege, and the sins crying
to heaven for vengeance, the big green Catechism in our hands,
walking home along the North Circular Road. And after tea, at the
back of the brewery wall, with a butt too to help our wits, what is a
pure spirit, and don't kill that, Billser has to get a drag out of it yet,
what do I mean by apostate, and hell and heaven and despair and
presumption and hope. The big fellows, who were now thirteen and
the veterans of last year's Confirmation, frightened us, and said the
Bishop would fire us out of the Chapel if we didn't answer his
questions, and we'd be left wandering around the streets, in a new suit
and top-coat with nothing to show for it, all dressed up and nowhere
to go. The big people said not to mind them; they were only getting it
up for us, jealous because they were over their Confirmation, and
could never make it again. At school we were in a special room to
ourselves, for the last few days, and went round, a special class of
people. There were worrying times too, that the Bishop would light
on you, and you wouldn't be able to answer his questions. Or you
might hear the women complaining about the price of boys' clothes.

   "Twenty-two and sixpence for tweed, I'd expect a share in the
shop for that. I"ve a good mind to let him go in jersey and pants for
that."

   "Quite right, ma'am," says one to another, backing one another up, "I always say what matter if they are good and pure." What had that got to do with it, if you had to go into the Chapel in a jersey and pants, and every other kid in a new suit, kid gloves and tan shoes and a *scoil* cap. The Cowan brothers were terrified. They were twins, and twelve years old, and every old one in the street seemed to be wishing a jersey and pants on them, and saying their poor mother couldn't be expected to do for two in the one year, and she ought to go down to Sister Monica and tell her to put one back. If it came to that, the Cowans agreed to fight it out, at the back of the brewery wall; whoever got best, the other would be put back.

I wasn't so worried abut this. My old fellow was a tradesman, and made money most of the time. Besides, my grandmother, who lived at the top of the next house, was a lady of capernosity and function. She had money and lay in bed all day, drinking porter or malt, and taking pinches of snuff, and talking to the neighbours that would call up to tell her the news of the day. She only left her bed to go down one flight of stairs and visit the lady in the back drawing room, Miss McCann.

Miss McCann worked a sewing-machine, making habits for the dead. Sometimes girls from our quarter got her to make dresses and costumes, but mostly she stuck to the habits. They were a steady line, she said, and you didn't have to be always buying patterns, for the fashions didn't change, not even from summer to winter. They were like a long brown shirt, and a hood attached, that was closed over the person's face before the coffin lid was screwn down. A sort of little banner hung out of one arm, made of the same material, and four silk rosettes in each corner, and in the middle, the letters I.H.S., which mean, Miss McCann said. "I Have Suffered."

My grandmother and Miss McCann liked me more than any other kid they knew. I like being liked, and could only admire their taste.

My Aunt Jack, who was my father's aunt as well as mine, sometimes came down from where she lived, up near the Basin, where the water came from before they started getting it from Wicklow. My Aunt Jack said it was much better water, at that. Miss McCann said she ought to be a good judge. For Aunt Jack was funny. She didn't drink porter or malt, or take snuff, and my father said she never thought much about men either. She was also very strict about washing yourself very often. My grandmother took a bath every year, whether she was dirty or not, but she was in no way bigoted in the washing line in between times.

Aunt Jack made terrible raids on us now and again, to stop snuff and drink, and make my grandmother get up in the morning, and wash herself, and cook meals and take food with them. My grandmother was a gilder by trade, and served her time in one of the best shops in the city, and was getting a man's wages at sixteen. She liked stuff out of the pork butchers, and out of cans, but didn't like boiling potatoes, for she said she was no skivvy, and the chip man was better at it. When she was left alone it was a pleasure to eat with her. She always had cans of lovely things and spicy meat and brawn, and plenty of seasoning, fresh out of the German man's shop up the road. But after a visit from Aunt Jack, she would have to get up and wash for a week, and she would have to go and make stews and boil cabbage and pig's cheeks. Aunt Jack was very much up for sheep's heads too. They were so cheap and nourishing. •

But my grandmother only tried it once. She had been a first-class gilder in Eustace Street, but never had anything to do with sheep's heads before. When she took it out of the pot, and laid it on the plate, she and I sat looking at it, in fear and trembling. It was bad enough going into the pot, but with the soup streaming from its eyes, and its big teeth clenched in a very bad temper, it would put the heart crossways in you. My grandmother asked me, in a whisper, if I ever thought sheep could look so vindictive, but that it was more like the head of an old man, and would I for God's sake take it up and throw it out of the window. The sheep kept glaring at us, but I came the far side of it, and rushed over to the window and threw it out in a flash. My grandmother had to drink a Baby Power whiskey, for she wasn't the better of herself.

Afterwards she kept what she called her stock-pot on the gas. A heap of bones and, as she said herself, any old muck that would come in handy, to have boiling there, night and day, on a glimmer. She and I ate happily of cooked ham and California pineapple and sock-eyed salmon, and the pot of good nourishing soup was always on the gas even if Aunt Jack came down the chimney, like the Holy Souls at midnight. My grandmother said she didn't begrudge the money for the gas. Not when she remembered the looks that sheep's head was giving her. And all she had to do with the stock-pot was throw in another sup of water, now and again, and a handful of old rubbish the pork butcher would send over, in the way of lights or bones. My Aunt Jack thought a lot about barley, too, so we had a package of that lying beside the gas, and threw a sprinkle in any time her foot was heard on the stairs. The stock-pot bubbled away on the gas for years after, and only when my grandmother was dead did someone notice it. They tasted it, and spat it out just as quick, and wondered what it was. Some said it was paste, and more that it was gold size, and there were other people and they maintained that it was glue. They all agreed on one thing, that it was dangerous tack to leave lying around where there might be young children, and in the heel of the reel, it went out the same window as the sheep's head.

Miss McCann told my grandmother not to mind Aunt Jack but to sleep as long as she liked in the morning. They came to an arrangement that Miss McCann would cover the landing and keep an eye out. She would call Aunt Jack in for a minute, and give the signal by banging the grate, letting on to poke the fire, and have a bit of a conversation with Aunt Jack about dresses and costumes, and hats and habits. One of these mornings, and Miss McCann delaying a fighting action, to give my grandmother time to hurl herself out of bed and into her clothes and give her face the rub of a towel, the chat between Miss McCann and Aunt Jack came to my confirmation suit.

When I made my first Communion, my grandmother dug deep under the mattress, and myself and Aunt Jack were sent round expensive shops, and I came back with a rig that would take the sight of your eye. This time, however, Miss McCann said there wasn't much stirring in the habit line, on account of the mild winter, and she would be delighted to make the suit, if Aunt Jack would get the material. I nearly wept, for terror of what these old women would have me got up in, but I had to let on to be delighted, Miss McCann was so set on it. She asked Aunt Jack did she remember my father's Confirmation suit. *He* did. He said he would never forget it. They sent him out in a velvet suit, of plum colour, with a lace collar. My blood ran cold when he told me.

The stuff they got for my suit was blue serge, and that was not so bad. They got as far as the pants, and that passed off very civil. You can't do much to a boy's pants, one pair is like the next, though I had to ask them not to trouble themselves putting three little buttons on either side of the legs. The waistcoat was all right, and anyway the coat would cover it. But the coat itself, that was where Aughrim was lost.

The lapels were little wee things, like what you'd see in pictures like Ring magazine of John L. Sullivan, or Gentleman Jim, and the buttons were the size of saucers, or within the bawl of an ass of it, and I nearly cried when I saw them being put on, and ran down to my mother, and begged her to get me any sort of a suit, even a jersey and pants, than have me set up before the people in this get-up. My mother said it was very kind of Aunt Jack and Miss McCann to go to all this trouble and expense, and I was very ungrateful not to appreciate it. My father said that Miss McCann was such a good tailor that people were dying to get into her creations, and her handiwork was to be found in all the best cemeteries. He laughed himself sick at this, and said if it was good enough for him to be sent down to North William Street in plum-coloured velvet and lace, I needn't be getting the needle over a couple of big buttons and little lapels. He asked me not to forget to get up early the morning of my Confirmation, and let him see me, before he went to work: a bit of a laugh started the day well. My mother told him to give over and let me alone, and said she was sure it would be a lovely suit, and that Aunt Jack would never buy poor material, but stuff that would last forever. That nearly finished me altogether, and I ran through the hall up to the corner, fit to cry my eyes out, only I wasn't much of a hand at crying. I went more for cursing, and I cursed all belonging to me, and was hard at it on my father, and wondering why his lace collar hadn't choked him, when I remembered that it was a sin to go on like that, and I going up for Confirmation, and I had to simmer down, and live in fear of the day I'd put on that jacket.

The days passed, and I was fitted and refitted, and every old one in the house came up to look at the suit, and took a pinch of snuff, and a sup out of the jug, and wished me long life and the health to wear and tear it, and they spent that much time viewing it round, back, belly and sides, that Miss McCann hadn't time to make the overcoat, and like an answer to a prayer, I was brought down to Talbot Street, and dressed out in a dinging overcoat, belted, like a grown-up man's. And my shoes and gloves were dear and dandy, and I said to myself that there was no need to let anyone see the suit with its little lapels and big buttons. I could keep the topcoat on all day, in the chapel and going round afterwards.

The night before Confirmation day, Miss McCann handed over the suit to my mother, and kissed me, and said not to bother thanking her. She would do more than that for me, and she and my grandmother cried and had a drink on the strength of my having grown to be a big fellow, in the space of twelve years, which they didn't seem to consider a great deal of time. My father said to my mother, and I getting bathed before the fire, that since I was born Miss McCann thought the world of me. When my mother was in hospital, she took me into her place till my mother came out, and it near broke her heart to give me back.

In the morning I got up, and Mrs. Rooney in the next room shouted in to my mother that her Liam was still stalling, and not making any move to get out of it, and she thought she was cursed; Christmas or Easter, Communion or Confirmation, it would drive a body into Riddleys, which is the mad part of Grangegorman, and she wondered she wasn't driven out of her mind, and above in the puzzle factory years ago. So she shouted again at Liam to get up and washed and dressed. And my mother shouted at me, though I was already knotting my tie, but you might as well be out of the world as out of fashion, and they kept it up like a pair of mad women, until at last Liam and I were ready and he came in to show my mother his clothes. She hanselled him a tanner which he put in his pocket and Mrs. Rooney called me in to show her my clothes. I just stood at her door, and didn't open my coat, but just grabbed the sixpence out of her hand, and ran up the stairs like the hammers of hell. She shouted at me to hold on a minute, she hadn't seen my suit, but I muttered something about it not being lucky to keep a Bishop waiting, and ran on.

The Church was crowded, boys on one side and the girls on the other, and the altar ablaze with lights and flowers, and a throne for the Bishop to sit on when he wasn't confirming. There was a cheering crowd outside, drums rolled, trumpeters from Jim Larkin's band sounded the Salute. The Bishop came in and the doors were shut. In short order I joined the queue to the rails, knelt and was whispered over, and touched on the cheek. I had my overcoat on the whole time, though it was warm, and I was in a lather of sweat waiting for the hymns and the sermon.

The lights grew brighter and I got warmer, was carried out fainting. But though I didn't mind them loosening my tie, I clenched firmly my overcoat, and nobody saw the jacket with the big buttons and the little lapels. When I went home I got into bed, and my father said I went into a sickness just as the Bishop was giving us the pledge. He said this was a master stroke and showed real presence of mind.

Sunday after Sunday, my mother fought over the suit. She said I was a liar and a hypocrite, putting it on for a few minutes every week, and running into Miss McCann's and out again, letting her think I wore it every week-end. In a passionate temper my mother said she would show me up, and tell Miss McCann, and up like a shot with her, for my mother was always slim and light on her feet as a feather, and in next door. When she came back she said nothing, but sat at the fire looking into it. I didn't really believe she would tell Miss McCann.

And I put on the suit and thought I would go in and tell her I was wearing it this week-night, because I was going to the Queen's with my brothers. I ran next door and upstairs, and every step was more certain and easy that my mother hadn't told her. I ran, shoved in the door, saying: "Miss Mc., Miss Mc., Rory and Sean and I are going to the Queen's . . ." She was bent over the sewing-machine and all I could see was the top of her old grey head, and the rest of her shaking with crying, and her arms folded under her head, on a bit of habit where she had been finishing the I.H.S. I ran down the stairs and back into our place, and my mother was sitting at the fire, sad and sorry, but saying nothing.

I needn't have worried about the suit lasting forever. Miss Mc-Cann didn't. The next winter was not so mild, and she was whipped before the year was out. At her wake people said how she was in a habit of her own making, and my father said she would look queer in anything else, seeing as she supplied the dead of the whole quarter for forty years, without one complaint from a customer.

At the funeral, I left my topcoat in the carriage and got out and walked in the spills of rain after her coffin. People said I would get my end, but I went on till we reached the graveside, and I stood in my Confirmation suit drenched to the skin. I thought this was the least I could do.

Further Readings on Brendan Behan

Bibliography

Mikhail, E. H. "Behan Checklist." In *The Complete Plays of Brendan Behan*, pp. 28–34. New York: Grove, 1978.
———. *Brendan Behan: An Annotated Bibliography of Criticism.* New York: Barnes and Noble, 1980.

Selected Works

After the Wake [collected stories]. Edited by Peter Fallon. Dublin: O'Brien Press, 1981.
An Giall. Dublin: An Chomhairle Náisiúnta Drámaíochta, c. 1954.
Borstal Boy. London: Hutchinson, 1958; New York: Knopf, 1959.
Brendan Behan's Borstal Boy. Stage adaptation by Frank McMahon. New York: Random House, 1971.
Brendan Behan's Island. London: Hutchinson, 1962.
Complete Plays. London: Eyre Methuen; New York: Grove, 1978.

Interviews and Recollections. Edited by E. H. Mikhail. Totowa, N.J.: Barnes and Noble, 1982.

Life Styles: Poems. Translated by Ulick O'Connor, Dublin: Dolmen, 1973. Translations of Behan's Irish-language poems.

The Scarperer [novel]. Garden City, N. Y.: Doubleday, 1964; London: Hutchinson, 1965. Originally serialized in *The Irish Times* (1953).

The Wit of Brendan Behan. Edited by Sean McCann. London: Leslie Frewin, 1968.

Biography and Criticism

Behan, Beatrice, with Hickey, Des, and Smith, Gus. *My Life With Brendan Behan.* London: Leslie Frewin, 1973.

Behan, Dominic. *My Brother Brendan.* London: Leslie Frewin, 1965.

Boyle, Ted E. *Brendan Behan.* New York: Twayne, 1969.

de Búrca, Seamus. *Brendan Behan: A Memoir.* Newark, Del.: Proscenium, 1971.

Jeffs, Rae. *Brendan Behan: Man and Showman.* London: Hutchinson, 1966; Cleveland, O.: World, 1968.

Kearney, Colbert. *The Writings of Brendan Behan.* Dublin: Gill and Macmillan, 1977.

McCann, Sean, ed. *The World of Brendan Behan.* London: New English Library, 1965.

O'Connor, Ulick *Brendan.* London: Hamish Hamilton; Englewood Cliffs, N.J.: Prentice-Hall, 1970.

Porter, Raymond. *Brendan Behan.* New York: Columbia University Press, 1973.

Simpson, Alan *Beckett and Behan and a Theatre in Dublin.* London: Routledge, 1962.

CONTEMPORARY POETS IN IRISH AND ENGLISH

MÁIRTÍN Ó DIREÁIN (1910–88)

The most prolific poet writing in the Irish language is Máirtín Ó Direáin, whose first book of lyrics, *Coinnle Geala* (1942), played a pioneering role in the development of Modern Irish poetry. His autobiographical *Feamainn Bhealtaine* (1961) describes his boyhood on Aran, a life he abandoned at eighteen when he went to work in Galway.

While Ó Direáin has spent his entire adult life away from Aran, it is a major theme in his poetry. "Honesty" speaks not only to the integrity of landscape, but also to that intensity of feeling that is essential to lyric poetry. "The Dignity of Sorrow" reveals the depth of his feeling about exile; however, it is borne with the stoicism one finds in other Aran Islands literature: Synge's "Riders to the Sea" and O'Flaherty's "Going into Exile," for example. The poem illustrates the association of emigration with death that was so common in the Irish countryside where the ritual of departure parodied the ritual of death. An emigrant from Aran, he has observed with sadness, sometimes even with bitterness, the changes in traditional life.

HONESTY

A great poet once said
an island and a woman's love

are the matter and reason for my poems.
It is truth you speak, my brother.

I'll keep the island
another while in my poem
because of the integrity
that is in stone, rock and strand.

trans. Maureen Murphy

THE DIGNITY OF SORROW

Once I was shown
The great dignity of sorrow
On seeing two women
Walk out from the crowd.
In their clothes of mourning
Not speaking a word,
Dignity went with them
In the murmur of the crowd.

There was a tender at quayside
From the liner in the bay,
And everyone was busy
With noise and loud talk,
But two there were quiet,
Who walked out by themselves;
In their clothes of mourning,
Dignity went with them.

trans. Maureen Murphy

MEMORIES

Their memory lives in my mind
White flannel and bright shirts
Blue shirts and grey vests
Trousers' tweed of homespun frieze
Worn by men of venerable age

On Sunday morning going to mass
Travelling the long way by foot
That in my youth inspired thoughts
Of purity, freshness—
Always of blessedness.

Their memory lives in my mind
Long Sunday skirts of crimson hue
Blue skirts dyed with indigo
Heavy handsome Galway shawls
On comely women, tidy, trim
Going to mass as they've always done
And though they're going out of fashion
Their memory lives in my mind
It will live there surely—
Till I'm in the ground.

trans. Maureen Murphy

Further Readings on Máirtín Ó Direáin

Bibliography

Prút, Liam. "Saothar le Máirtín Ó Direáin," *Máirtín Ó Direáin. File Tréadúil.*
Maigh Nuad: An Sagart Maigh Nuad, 1982, pp. 119–21.

Selected Works

Dánta 1939–1979. Baile Átha Cliath: Clóchomhar, 1980.
Feamainn Bhealtaine. Baile Átha Cliath: An Clóchomhar, 1961.
Selected Poems. Tacar Dánta. Translated by Tomás mac Síomóin and Douglas
Sealy. Newbridge, County Kildare: The Goldsmith Press, 1984.

Biography and Criticism

MacConghail, Muiris. "Ré Dhearóil Mháirtín Ui Dhireáin." *Feasta* 19:13–20.
Murphy, Maureen. "Elegy for Aran: The Poetry of Máirtín Ó Direáin." In
Contemporary Irish Writing, eds. James D. Brophy and Raymond J. Porter,
pp. 143–56. Boston: Iona College Press, Twayne Publishers, 1983.
O'Brien, Frank. *Filíocht Ghaeilge na Linne Seo.* Baile Átha Cliath: An
Clóchomhar, 1968.
Ó hUanacháin, Mícheál. "Máirtín O'Direáin." In *The Pleasure of Gaelic Poetry,*
ed. Sean MacRéamoinn. London: Allen Lane, Penguin Books, 1982.

Prút, Liam. *Máirtín Ó Direáin. File Treadúil.* Maigh Nuad: An Sagart Maigh Nuad, 1982.

SEÁN Ó RÍORDÁIN (1916–77)

Uncertainty Ó Ríordáin's life. He left the West Cork Gaeltacht of Baile Bhúirne (Ballyvorney) where he had been born upon the death of his Irish-speaking father in 1926. His family settled outside Cork city, where he was educated and where he worked as a local government clerk from 1937 to 1965. He spent seven of the thirteen years between 1938 and 1951 in a tuberculosis sanatorium, and for the rest of his life he was haunted by the spectre of that dread illness. Another blow was the death of his mother in 1945, an experience he nevertheless turned into his first important poem, "Adhlacadh mo Mháthar" [My mother's burying].

Ó Ríordáin spent his last years teaching at University College, Cork, and writing a weekly column for *The Irish Times.* An honorary degree from the National University of Ireland formally recognized his influence as a shaping force in modern Irish poetry, His diary, sections of which have been published posthumously, may well provide a similar direction for Irish prose.

This selection of poems offers a contrast between the happiness and innocence of "Cúl an Tí" [Back of the house], a poem which may recall the early years in Baile Bhúirne, and the loneliness and death of "Reo" [Frozen] and "Adhlacadh mo Mháthar" [My mother's burying].

THE BACK OF THE HOUSE

At the back of the house is the Land of Youth,
a beautiful, untidy land,
where four-footed folk wend their way,
without shoes or shirt,
without English or Irish.

But a cloak grows on every back
in this untidy land,

and a language is spoken at the back of the house,
that no man knew but Aesop,
and he is in the clay now.

There are hens there and a clutch of chickens,
and a sluggish unsophisticated duck
and a great black dog like a foe in the land,
snarling at everybody,
and a cat milking the sun.

At the western corner is a bank of refuse,
containing the wonders of the world,
a chandelier, buckles, an old straw hat,
a trumpet dumb but elegant,
and a white goose-like kettle.

It is hither the tinkers come,
saintly and untidy,
they are germane to the back of the house,
and they are accustomed to beg
at the back of every house in Ireland.

I would wish to be at the back of the house,
when it is dark and late,
that I might see on a moonlight visit
the tiny professor Aesop,
that scholarly fairy.

trans. Seán Ó Ríordáin

FROZEN

On a frosty morning I went out
And a handkerchief faced me on a bush.
I reached to put it in my pocket
But it slid from me for it was frozen.
No living cloth jumped from my grasp
But a thing that died last night on a bush
And I went searching in my mind

Till I found the occasion's equivalent—
The day I kissed a woman of my kindred
And she in the coffin, frozen, stretched.

trans. Valentin Iremonger

MY MOTHER'S BURYING

A June sun in an orchard,
    A rustle in the silk of afternoon,
The droning of an ill-natured bee
    Loudly ripping the film of evening.

Reading an old dog-eared letter,
    With every tearful word I drank in
A raging pain stabbed my side.
    Every word forced out its own tear.

I remembered the hand that did the writing
    A hand as familiar as a face,
A hand that dispersed kindness like an old Bible,
    A hand that was like the balsam and you ill.

And June toppled backwards into Winter.
    The orchard became a white graveyard by a river.
In the midst of the dumb whiteness all around me,
    The dark hole screamed loudly in the snow.

The white of a young girl the day of her First
        Communion,
    The white of the holy water Sunday on the altar,
The white of milk slowly issuing from the breasts:
    When they buried my mother—the white of the
        sward.

My mind was screwing itself endeavouring
    To comprehend the interment to the full
When through the white tranquility gently flew
    A robin, unconfused and unafraid.

It waited over the grave as though it knew
    That the reason why it came was unknown to all
Save the person who was waiting in the coffin
    And I was jealous of the unusual affinity.

The air of Heaven descended on that graveside,
    A marvellous holy joy possessed the bird.
I was outside the mystery, a layman.
    The grave before me in the distance.

My debauched soul was bathed in the waters of sorrow,
    A snow of purity fell on my heart.
Now I will bury my heart so made clean
    The memory of the woman who carried me three
        seasons in her womb.

The gravediggers came with the rough noises of shovels
    And vigorously swept the clay into the grave.
I looked the other way, a man was brushing his knees.
    I looked at the priest, in his face was worldliness.

A June sun in an orchard,
    A rustle in the silk of afternoon.
The droning of an ill-natured bee
    Loudly ripping the film of evening.

Lame little verses being written by me.
    I would like to catch a robin's tail.
I would like to rout the spirit of those knee-brushers.
    I would like to journey sorrowfully to the day's end.

trans. Valentin Iremonger

Further Readings on Seán Ó Ríordáin

Bibliography

Ó Coileáin, Seán. *Seán Ó Ríordáin. Beatha agus Saothar.* Dublin: An
    Clóchomhar, 1982.

Selected Works

Brosna. Dublin: Sáirséal agus Dill, 1964.
Eireball Spideoige. Dublin: Sáirséal agus Dill, 1952.
Línte Liombó. Dublin: Sáirséal agus Dill, 1971.
Tar éis mo Bháis. Dublin: Sáirséal agus Dill, 1978.

Biography and Criticism

MacCana, Proinseas. *Literature in Irish*. Dublin: Department of Foreign Affairs," 1980. pp. 60–61.
O'Brien, Frank. *Filíocht Ghaeilge na Linne Seo*. Dublin: An Clóchomhar, 1968. pp. 301–35.
Ó Tuama, Seán. "Seán Ó Ríordáin." In *Filí faoi Screimhle*. Dublin: Oifig an tSolathair, 1978. pp. 1–80.
———. "Seán Ó Ríordáin." In *The Pleasures of Gaelic Poetry*, ed. Seán MacRéamoinn. London: Allen Lane, 1982. pp. 129–41.
Scríobh 3. edited by Seán Ó Mordha. Dublin: An Clóchomar,1978.

Máire Mhac an tSaoi (b. 1922)

Máire Mhac an tSaoi (pronounced Maurya WOK an Tee) was born in Dublin; however, she spent much of her childhood in Dunquin in the Kerry Gaeltacht. Her father, Seán MacEntee, was Tánaiste or deputy prime minister, in the de Valera and Lemass governments. After she completed her degree from University College, Dublin, Mhac an tSaoi studied in Paris, returned to the Dublin Institute for Advanced Studies for further work in Celtic Studies, trained for the Irish Bar, and finally entered the foreign service. She is married to the diplomat and journalist Conor Cruise O'Brien, who served as Minister for Post and Telegraph during the Cosgrave government (1973–1977).

A scholar as well as a poet, Mhac an tSaoi's authoritative essays and reviews provide lucid commentary on poetry in Irish from Gaelic society to the present day. *Margadh na Saoirse* [market of freedom], a collection of poems written over the course of twenty years, has been praised for its sense of craft, its command of Munster Irish, and its erudition. Like the best examples of Early Irish lyrics, Mhac an tSaoi's poetry is spare and compressed. She frequently speaks of loss in her poems: both historical loss, which observes the passing of traditional life, and personal loss—especially lost or hopeless love. "Inquisitio 1584" probably refers to the Desmond Rising in Munster that was suppressed in 1583; the plantation of the province followed and the Irish lands were confiscated. Séamus Ennis, subject of the "Lament for Séamus Ennis," was Ireland's premier piper until his death in 1984.

INQUISITIO 1584

In that year of the age of Our Lord
Fifteen hundred and eighty
Or some few short years after
Sean MacEdmund MacUlick
Hard by Shannon was hanged.

Hard by the shoals of Shannon
In Limerick, history's city,
Sean MacEdmund MacUlick
Come west from the parish of Marrhan
Who was chieftain of Balleneenig.

Treason his crime, his lands
Were given in hand of the stranger
And now around Mount Marrhan
His name is not even remembered
Nor is his kindred known there.

Undisturbed be your sleep
Sean MacEdmund MacUlick
On the banks of the mighty Shannon
When the wind blows in from the sea
From the west and from your own country.

FOR SHEILA

I remember a room on the seaward side—
The squall caught it from the south-west—
And the rain a tattoo on the window
Unslackening since the fall of night,
And I remember that you were there, Sheila,

Sitting low by the fire,
The gold ring on your childlike finger.
You gave us a heartbroken song,
And your voice was the music of flutes,
Love's catalogue brought here from France—
The fairness of your head was like the meadowsweet
Under the light of the lamp set on the table. . . .

What do they matter more, little dear one, between us,
Separation of years and aversions bred of friendship?
It was my lot to know you at that time.

FINIT

By chance I learned from them the marriage-contract
And wondered at this check on the wind's lightness;
You were so unpredictable, spontaneous,
Untamed like it, and lonely, I remember.

Know now the lot of all is yours henceforward,
Hardship and commonplace each following season,
Slipping from memory as turns the quarter—
We doubt you or your like ever existed.

But that there will be tunes I'll not hear ever
Without your being again there in the corner,
Waiting, "music" to hand, before the dancing,
Your eyes the mystery of the night outside.

LAMENT FOR SÉAMUS ENNIS, LATE CHAMPION PIPER OF IRELAND (SLOW AIR)

Shee-people wheening, wintry their wail;
Fairy wives keening near and away
West to the dune's edge:
Donn,* spread the tale.

Make the drum's roar a flail—
    Lay on great strokes,

*"Donn of the dune" was the Old Irish god of death.

Redoubling each in train,
    Hammers of woe;
This prince, the music waned,
    Seeks his clay home.

Wizards of liss and fort, hosts of the air,
Panicked and routed go, each from his lair;
Boyne's† airy pleasure-dome, rainstorm lays bare.

Desert and harpless,
    Tara is grass;
Yet we had argued
    Even such pass
No mortal harm meant—
    No more, alas!

White flowers of repentance the barren staff knew;
The pillar-stones danced to hear Orpheus' tunes;
But, King-piper of Ireland, voice is withheld from you—Ever!

trans. and elaborated by Máire Mhac an tSaoi
from a first draft by Canon Coslett Quinn

Further Readings on Máire Mhac an tSoi

Selected Works

Poetry

Codhladh an Ghaiscígh. Dublin: Sáirséal agus Dill, 1973.
An Galar Dubhach. Dublin: Sáirséal agus Dill, 1980.
A Heart Full of Thought. Translations from the Irish. Dublin: Dolmen Press, 1959.
Margadh na Saoire. Dublin: Sáirséal agus Dill, 1956, 1971.

Studies

[as O'Brien, Máire Cruise]. "The Female Principle in Gaelic Poetry." *Canadian Journal of Irish Studies* 8: 26–37.
"An t-Oileánach." in *The Pleasures of Gaelic Literature,* edited by John Jordan. Dublin: Mercier Press, 1977. pp. 25–38.
"The Role of the Poet in Gaelic Society." In *The Celtic Consciousness,* edited by Robert O'Driscoll. New York: Braziller, 1982.

†Prehistoric tombs on the Boyne were believed to be the palaces of the old god.

Biography and Criticism

Davitt, Michael. "Comhrá le Máire Mhac an tSaoi," *Innti* 8: 38–59.
O'Brien, Frank. *Filíocht Ghaeilge na Línne Seo*. Dublin: An Clochomhar, 1968.
    pp. 163–201.

RICHARD MURPHY (b. 1927)

Richard Murphy was born into an Anglo-Irish family in County Galway but raised in Ceylon, where his father was an officer in the British Colonial Service. After his education at English public schools and at Magdalen College, Oxford, Murphy returned to the west of Ireland, to the island of Inishbofin, to live and to write. He bought a hooker, the one-masted fishing boat used along the Galway coast. On it, he absorbed the knowledge of traditional fishing life that informs many of the poems in his first collection, *Sailing to an Island* (1963).

Murphy's account of a local fishing tragedy, "The Cleggan Disaster," revealed a gift for narration, a quality he developed further in *The Battle of Aughrim* (1968), a long poem commissioned by the BBC. It considers the history and folklore surrounding the famous battle fought in 1691—the last major encounter between the armies of James II, who supported the Catholic cause, and William III (or William of Orange), who led the Protestants to victory at the Boyne as well as at Aughrim. The Irish Jacobite soldier who speaks in the selection says that history—the outcome of the battle—will not change the quality of his life. Poems from The Price of Stone (1985) criticize Murphy's obsession with building: the main beam of his house is the voice in "Roof Tree."

SEALS AT HIGH ISLAND

The calamity of seals begins with jaws.
Born in caverns that reverberate
With endless malice of the sea's tongue
Clacking on shingle, they learn to bark back
In fear and sadness and celebration.
The ocean's mouth opens forty feet wide
And closes on a morsel of their rock.

Swayed by the thrust and backfall of the tide,
A dappled grey bull and a brindled cow

Copulate in the green water of a cove.
I watch from a cliff-top, trying not to move.
Sometimes they sink and merge into black shoals;
Then rise for air, his muzzle on her neck,
Their winged feet intertwined as a fishtail.

She opens her fierce mouth like a scarlet flower
Full of white seeds; she holds it open long
At the sunburst in the music of their loving;
And cries a little. But I must remember
How far their feelings are from mine marooned.
If there are tears at this holy ceremony
Theirs are caused by brine and mine by breeze.

When the great bull withdraws his rod, it glows
Like a carnelian candle set in jade.
The cow ripples ashore to feed her calf;
While an old rival, eyeing the deed with hate,
Swims to attack the tired triumphant god.
They rear their heads above the boiling surf,
Their terrible jaw open, jetting blood.

At nightfall they haul out, and mourn the drowned,
Playing to the sea sadly their last quartet,
An improvised requiem that ravishes
Reason, while ripping scale up like a net:
Brings pity trembling down the rocky spine
Of headlands, till the bitter ocean's tongue
Swells in their cove, and smothers their sweet song.

From "THE BATTLE OF AUGHRIM"

"They pick us for our looks
To line up with matchlocks,
Face shot like sand-bags,
Fall, and manure the grass
Where we wouldn't be let trespass
Alive, but to do their work
Till we dropped in muck.

"Who cares which foreign king
Governs, we'll still fork dung,
No one lets *us* grab soil:
Roman or English school
Insists it is God
Who must lighten our burden
Digging someone else's garden."

ROOF-TREE

After you brought her home with your first child
How did you celebrate? Not with a poem
She might have loved, but orders to rebuild
The house. Men tore me open, room by room.

Your daughter's cries were answered by loud cracks
Of hammers stripping slates; the clawing down
Of dozed rafters; dull, stupefying knocks
On walls. Proudly your hackwork made me groan.

Your greed for kiln-dried oak that could outlast
Seven generations broke her heart. My mind
You filled with rot-proof hemlock at a cost
That killed her love. The dust spread unrefined.

To renovate my structure, which survives,
You flawed the tenderest movement of three lives.

Further Readings on Richard Murphy

Selected Works

The Battle of Aughrim and the God who Eats the Corn. London: Faber and Faber;
    New York: Alfred Knopf, 1968.
High Island: New and Selected Poems. New York: Harper and Row, 1974.
The Price of Stone. London and Boston: Faber and Faber, 1985.
Sailing to an Island: Poems. New York: Chilmark Press, 1963.
Selected Poems. London: Faber and Faber, 1979.

Biography and Criticism

Bowers, Neal. "Richard Murphy: The Landscape of the Mind." *Journal of Irish Literature* 11: 33–41.

Harmon, Maurice, ed. *Richard Murphy: Poet of Two Traditions*, Dublin: Wolfbound, 1978.

Irish University Review, Richard Murphy Special Issue. 7.

Kilroy, Mark. "Richard Murphy's Connemara Locale." *Eire-Ireland* 15: 127–34.

Longley, Edna. "Searching the Darkness: Richard Murphy, Thomas Kinsella, John Montague and James Simmons." In *Two Deacades of Irish Writing: A Critical Survey*, ed. Douglas Dunn, pp. 118–53. Cheadle, Cheshire: Carcanet Press, 1975.

Moynahan, Julian. "The Battle of Aughrim: A Commentary." *Irish University Review* 13: 103–13.

Sendry, Joseph. "The Poet as Builder: Richard Murphy's *The Price of Stone*." *Irish University Review* 15: 38–49.

THOMAS KINSELLA (b.1928)

A major Irish poet with the publication of *Another September* (1958), Thomas Kinsella is at once the most serious and the most experimental of the contemporary Irish poets. His lyrical, formally structured early work, with its debt to such modern poets as Auden, contrasts with the dense, difficult poetry of his later phase—a poetry marked by fragmentation, absorption with a private world, and a dark, brooding tone. It is a poetry that reflects the philosophy expressed in his prose preface to *Wormwood* (1966): "Maturity and peace are to be sought through ordeal after ordeal."

Born to a working-class Dublin family, Kinsella attended the Inchicore Model School and studied science at University College, Dublin, before entering the Civil Service in 1946 as a clerk for the Congested District Board. In 1965 he resigned from his post as a senior officer in the Department of Finance to teach in America—first at Southern Illinois University and later at Temple University, where he now directs their spring program in Dublin. Long associated with the Dolmen Press, Kinsella now has his own publishing company, called Peppercanister.

Kinsella is well known for his translations from the Irish as well as for his own poetry. His highly praised *The Táin* [The cattle raid of Cooley, 1969] was followed in 1981 by translations for *An Duanaire* [An

Irish anthology], a collection of Modern Irish poetry edited by
Seán Ó Tuama. "The Poet Egan O'Rahilly, Homesick in Old Age,"
Kinsella's tribute to one of the most distinguished poets in the
collection, observes O'Rahilly [Aogán Ó Rathaille] the artist who
nourished the spirit of his starving countrymen, the poet in a hostile
landscape. "Sisters" refers to the suicide of two Irish women: De-
irdre, who kills herself at the end of "The Fate of the Children of
Usnach" when Conchobar gives her to Eogan son of Durthacht; and
Sybil Ferriter, who, according to tradition, killed herself after her
poet husband was hanged in Killarney in 1653 for his support of the
Irish cause in the 1641 rising. Another rising, the 1798 rebellion in
Wicklow, provides the setting—Vinegar Hill, the Slaney—for "In the
Ringwood," Kinsella's version of an Irish street ballad in which the
poet's bride is transformed into "Sorrow's daughter."

IN THE RINGWOOD

As I roved out impatiently
Good Friday with my bride
To drink in the rivered Ringwood
The draughty season's pride
A fell dismay held suddenly
Our feet on the green hill-side.

The yellow Spring on Vinegar Hill,
The smile of Slaney water,
The wind that swept the Ringwood,
Grew dark with ancient slaughter.
My love cried out and I beheld her
Change to Sorrow's daughter.

"Ravenhair, what rending
Set those red lips a-shriek,
And dealt those locks in black lament
Like blows on your white cheek,
That in your looks outlandishly
Both woe and fury speak?"

As sharp a lance as the fatal heron
There on the sunken tree

Will strike in the stones of the river
Was the gaze she bent on me.
O her robe into her right hand
She gathered grievously.

"Many times the civil lover
Climbed that pleasant place,
Many times despairing
Died in his love's face,
His spittle turned to vinegar,
Blood in his embrace.

"Love that is every miracle
Is torn apart and rent.
The human turns awry
The poles of the firmament.
The fish's bright side is pierced
And good again is spent.

"Though every stem on Vinegar Hill
And stone on the Slaney's bed
And every leaf in the living Ringwood
Builds till it is dead
Yet heart and hand, accomplished,
Destroy until they dread.

"Dread, a grey devourer,
Stalks in the shade of love.
The dark that dogs our feet
Eats what is sickened of.
The End that stalks Beginning
Hurries home its drove."

I kissed three times her shivering lips.
I drank their naked chill.
I watched the river shining
Where the heron wiped his bill.
I took my love in my icy arms
In the Spring on Ringwood Hill.

HANDCLASP AT EUSTON

The engine screams and Murphy, isolate
—Chalk-white, comedian—in the smoky glare,
Dwindles among the churns and tenders. Weight,
Person, race, the human, dwindle there.
I bow to the cases cluttering the rack,
Their handles black with sweat of exile. Wales,
Wave and home; I close my eyes. The track
Swerves to a greener world: sea-rock, thigh-scales.

SISTERS

Grim Deirdre sought the stony fist, her grief
Capped at last by insult. Pierce's bride,
Sybil Ferriter, fluttered like a leaf
And fell in courtly love to stain the tide.
Each for a murdered husband—hanged in silk
Or speared in harness—threw her body wide,
And offered treachery a bloody milk;
Each cast the other's shadow when she died.

THE POET EGAN O'RAHILLY, HOMESICK IN OLD AGE

He climbed to his feet in the cold light, and began
The decrepit progress again, blown along the cliff road,
Bent with curses above the shrew his stomach.

The salt abyss poured through him, more raw
With every laboured, stony crash of the waves:
His teeth bared at their voices, that incessant dying.

Iris leaves bent on the ditch, unbent,
Shivering in the wind: leaf-like spirits
Chattered at his death-mark as he passed.

He pressed red eyelids; aliens crawled
Breaking princely houses in their jaws;
Their metal faces reared up, chewing at light.

"Princes overseas, who slipped away
In your extremity, no matter where I travel
I find your great houses like stopped hearts.

"Likewise your starving children—though I nourish
Their spirit, and my own, on the lists of praises
I make for you still in the cooling den of my craft.

"Our enemies multiply. They have recruited the sea:
Last night, the West's rhythmless waves destroyed my
    sleep;
This morning, winkle and dogfish persisting in the
    stomach . . ."

Further Readings on Thomas Kinsella

Bibliography

Woodbridge, Hensley C. "Thomas Kinsella. A Bibliography." *Eire-Ireland*,
    122–33.

Selected Works

Another September. Dublin: The Dolmen Press, 1958.
Downstream. Dublin: The Dolmen Press; London: Oxford University Press,
    1962.
Fifteen Dead. Dublin: The Dolmen Press; London: Oxford University Press,
    1979.
New Poems, 1973. Dublin: The Dolmen Press, 1973.
Nightwalker and Other Poems. New York: Alfred Knopf, 1968.
Peppercanister Poems (1972–1978). Winston-Salem, N.C.: Wake Forest Univer-
    sity Press, 1979.
Poems 1956–1973. Winston-Salem, N.C.: Wake Forest University Press, 1979.
Poems and Translations. New York: Atheneum, 1961.

Translations

An Duanaire. An Irish Anthology. 1600–1900: *Poems of the Dispossessed*. ed.
    Seán Ó Tuama. Philadelphia: University of Pennsylvania Press, 1981.

The Táin. Illustrated by Louis le Brocquy. New York: Oxford University Press, 1970 (1969).

Biography and Criticism

Bendient, Calvin. "Thomas Kinsella." In *Eight Contemporary Poets,* pp. 119–38. London and New York: Oxford University Press, 1974.

Garratt, Robert F. "Fragilities and Structures: Poetic Strategy in Thomas Kinsella's 'Night Walker' and 'Phoenix Park.'" *Irish University Review.* 13:88–102.

Harmon, Maurice. *The Poetry of Thomas Kinsella.* Dublin: Wolfhound Press, 1974; Lewisburg, Pa: Bucknell University Press, 1975.

———. "The Poetry of Thomas Kinsella (1972–1983)." *Studies* 72:57–66.

Johnston, Dillon. *Irish Poetry after Joyce.* Mountrath: The Dolmen Press; South Bend, Ind.: University of Notre Dame Press, 1985.

Longley, Edna. "Searching the Darkness: Richard Murphy, Thomas Kinsella, John Montague and James Simmons." In *Two Decades of Irish Writing: A Critical Survey,* ed. Douglas Dunn, pp. 118–53. Cheadle, Cheshire: Carcanet Press, 1975.

O'Hara, Daniel. "An Interview with Thomas Kinsella." *Contemporary Poetry: A Journal of Criticism* 4:1–18.

"Poetry Since Yeats: An Exchange of Views—Stephen Spender, Patrick Kavanagh, Thomas Kinsella, W. D. Snodgrass." *Tri-Quarterly* 4:100–11.

JOHN MONTAGUE (b. 1929)

John Montague was born in Brooklyn, New York, but he was raised in Garvaghey (Irish *garbh acaidh,* rough field, pronounced GAREV-ah-he), County Tyrone, by a pair of maiden aunts. After taking his degree at University College, Dublin, he became a journalist before devoting himself to writing and teaching. He is a member of the English faculty at University College, Cork; however, he is equally at home at colleges and universities in France and in the United States.

Concerned, from his first collection, *Poisoned Lands* (1961), with Ireland past and present—or, as Montague puts it, "Ireland's past in present"—his poem "Like Dolmens Round my Childhood the Old People" explores the mythic qualities of those who represent a vanishing rural Ireland to him. Many of Montague's early poems have been included in his long poem, *The Rough Field* (1972, rev. ed.), an ambitious meditation on Ulster history that combines archaeology, biography, history, literature, and mythology in a format that includes documents, letters, religious tracts, riddles, rhymes, and reproductions of old woodcuts. "Lament for the O'Neills" links the loss of Ulster's Gaelic language and culture with the dispossession and exile of the O'Neills, one of the great Northern families. Finally, "A Grafted Tongue," a poem about the imposition of English on the Irish-speaking countryside, recalls Montague's own humiliation as a stammering child.

LIKE DOLMENS ROUND MY CHILDHOOD, THE OLD PEOPLE

Like dolmens round my childhood, the old people.

I

Jamie MacCrystal sang to himself,
A broken song without tune, without words;
He tipped me a penny every pension day,
Fed kindly crusts to winter birds.
When he died, his cottage was robbed,
Mattress and money box torn and searched,
Only the corpse they didn't disturb.

II

Maggie Owens was surrounded by animals,
A mongrel bitch and shivering pups,
Even in her bedroom a she-goat cried.
She was a well of gossip defiled,
Fanged chronicler of a whole countryside;
Reputed a witch, all I could find
Was her ravening need to deride.

III

The Nialls lived along a mountain lane
Where heather bells bloomed, clumps of foxglove.
All were blind, with Blind Pension and Wireless,
Dead eyes serpent-flicked as one entered
To shelter from a downpour of mountain rain.
Crickets chirped under the rocking hearthstone
Until the muddy sun shone out again.

IV

Mary Moore lived in a crumbling gatehouse,
Famous as Pisa for its leaning gable.
Bag apron and boots, she tramped the fields
Driving lean cattle from a miry stable.
A by-word for fierceness, she fell asleep
Over love stories, Red Star and Red Circle,
Dreamed of gypsy love rites, by firelight sealed.

V

Wild Billy Harbison married a Catholic servant girl
When all his Loyal family passed on:
We danced round him shouting "To Hell with King
    Billy,"
And dodged from the arc of his flailing blackthorn.
Forsaken by both creeds, he showed little concern
Until the Orange drums banged past in the summer
And bowler and sash aggressively shone.

VI

Curate and doctor trudged to attend them,
Through knee-deep snow, through summer heat,
From main road to lane to broken path,
Gulping the mountain air with painful breath.
Sometimes they were found by neighbours,
Silent keepers of a smokeless hearth,
Suddenly cast in the mould of death.

VII

Ancient Ireland, indeed! I was reared by her bedside,
The rune and the chant, evil eye and averted head,
Formorian fierceness of family and local feud.
Gaunt figures of fear and of friendliness,
For years they trespassed on my dreams,
Until once, in a standing circle of stones,
I felt their shadows pass

Into that dark permanence of ancient forms.

A GRAFTED TONGUE

(Dumb,
bloodied, the severed
head now chokes to
speak another tongue:—

As in
a long suppressed dream,
some stuttering garb-
led ordeal of my own)

An Irish
child weeps at school
repeating its English.
After each mistake

The master
gouges another mark
on the tally stick
hung about its neck

Like a bell
on a cow, a hobble
on a straying goat.
To slur and stumble

In shame
the altered syllables
of your own name;
to stray sadly home

and find
the turf cured width
of your parent's hearth
growing slowly alien:

In cabin
and field, they still
speak the old tongue.
You may greet no one.

To grow
a second tongue, as
harsh a humiliation
as twice to be born.

Decades later
that child's grandchild's
speech stumbles over lost
syllables of an old order.

LAMENT FOR THE O'NEILLS

The fiddler settles in
to his playing so easily;
rosewood box tucked under chin,
saw of rosined bow
& angle of elbow

that the mind elides
for a while what he plays:
hornpipe or reel to warm
us up well, heel or toecap
twitching in tune

till the sound expands
in the slow climb of a lament.
As by some forest campfire
listeners draw near, to honour
a communal loss

& a shattered procession
of anonymous suffering
files through the brain:
burnt houses, pillaged farms,
a province in flames.

This was a distinguished
crew for one ship; for it
is indeed certain that the
sea had not supported,
and the winds had not
wafted from Ireland, in
modern times, a party of
one ship who would have
been more illustrious, or
noble in point of
genealogy, or more
renowned for deeds,
valour or high
achievements. . . .

Annals of the Four Masters

We have killed, burnt
and despoiled all along
the Lough to within four
miles of Dungannon . . .
in which journeys we
have killed above a
hundred of all sorts,
besides such as we have
burned, how many I
know not. We spare
none, of what quality or
sex soever, and it had
bred much terror in the

With an intricate
& mournful mastery
the thin bow glides & slides,
assuaging like a bardic poem,
our tribal pain—

Disappearance & death
of a world, as down Lough Swilly
the great ship, encumbered with nobles,
swells its sails for Europe:
The Flight of the Earls.

people who heard not a
drum nor saw not a fire
of long time.

Chichester to Mountjoy,
Spring 1701

Is uaigneach Éire

Further Readings on John Montague

Selected Works

A Chosen Light. Chicago: Swallow, 1969 (1967).
The Dead Kingdom. Winston-Salem, N.C.: Wake Forest University Press, 1984.
Death of a Chieftain and Other Stories. Chester Spring, Pa: Dufour, 1977 (1967).
The Faber Book of Irish Verse. (ed.) London: Faber and Faber, 1974.
Forms of Exile. Poems. Dublin: The Dolmen Press, 1958.
The Great Cloak. Dublin: The Dolmen Press, 1978.
Patriotic Suite. Dublin: The Dolmen Press, 1966.
Poisoned Lands and Other Poems. London: Oxford University Press, 1977
        (1961).
The Rough Field, 1961–1971. Dublin: The Dolmen Press, 1972.
Selected Poems. Winston-Salem, N.C.: Wake Forest University Press, 1982.
A Slow Dance. London: Oxford University Press, 1975.

Biography and Criticism

Frazier, Adrian. "Pilgrim Haunts: Montague's *The Dead Kingdom* and Heaney's
        Station Island." *Éire-Ireland*, 20: 134–43.
Johnston, Dillon. *Irish Poetry after Yeats.* Mountrath, Republic of Ireland: The
        Dolmen Press; South Bend, Ind.: University of Notre Dame Press,
        1985.
Kersnowski, Frank. *John Montague.* Lewisburg, Pa.: Bucknell University Press,
        1975.

SEAMUS HEANEY (b. 1939)

The most widely-acclaimed poet of his generation, Seamus Heaney was born on a farm in Mossbawn, County Derry, a place he has described as "fifty acres between bog and big house." He was educated at St. Columb's College in Derry, Queen's University, Belfast, and at St. Joseph's College of Education. A popular lecturer and gifted teacher, Heaney taught in secondary school and at colleges and universities in both Ireland and America before accepting the Boylston Chair at Harvard University in 1981.

Heaney's poems about his childhood, among them "Digging" and "Mossbawn: Two Poems in Dedication," pay careful attention to folkways, describing traditional skills and naming the tools for cutting turf, smithing, bread-making, and preparing seed. In the concluding stanza of "Digging," Heaney addresses his own trade with the same sense of craftsmanship, and in doing so reconciles the distance that education and his own vocation have interposed between his rural roots and himself.

Heaney's major poetic theme has been history. As he said in a 1972 *Irish Times* interview: "I have been writing poems out of history. It is the hump we live off. I have my tap root in personal and racial memory. The Famine, the '98 Rebellion, things like that have surfaced in my imagination and they are a living language here. . . ." One aspect of history as language—the relationship between Irish and English—is the subject of "Traditions."

Many of the poems in *North* (1975) are informed by Heaney's interest in the perfectly preserved bodies of ancient people found in the bogs of northern Denmark. The collection expands on the concept of the bog as the "memory of landscape" that he explored in "Bogland" (*Death of a Naturalist*, 1966). In "Punishment," the body of a young woman hanged in Jutland for adultery inspires a meditation on tribal justice: the poet sees its modern counterpart in the shaved and tarred heads of the young women in Northern Ireland humiliated for fraternizing with British soldiers. In "Exposure," the last poem in *North*, Heaney broods about living away from his troubled native province. *Station Island* (1985) marked a new development: a long poem on the penitential pilgrimage to Lough Derg, County Donegal, that is much favored by Northern Catholics. Like Dante, the poet meets the dead: family, friends, and such literary forebears as Carleton, Kavanagh, and Joyce.

DIGGING

Between my finger and my thumb
The squat pen rests; snug as a gun.

Under my window, a clean rasping sound
When the spade sinks into gravelly ground:
My father, digging. I look down

Till his straining rump among the flowerbeds
Bends low, comes up twenty years away
Stooping in rhythm through potato drills
Where he was digging.

The coarse boot nestled on the lug, the shaft
Against the inside knee was levered firmly.
He rooted out tall tops, buried the bright edge deep
To scatter new potatoes that we picked
Loving their cool hardness in our hands.

By God, the old man could handle a spade.
Just like his old man.

My grandfather cut more turf in a day
Than any other man on Toner's bog.
Once I carried him milk in a bottle
Corked sloppily with paper. He straightened up
To drink it, then fell to right away

Nicking and slicing neatly, heaving sods
Over his shoulder, going down and down
For the good turf. Digging.

The cold smell of potato mould, the squelch and slap
Of soggy peat, the curt cuts of an edge
Through living roots awaken in my head.
But I've no spade to follow men like them.

Between my finger and my thumb
The squat pen rests.
I'll dig with it.

TRADITIONS

for Tom Flanagan

I

Our guttural muse
was bulled long ago
by the alliterative tradition,
her uvula grows

vestigial, forgotten
like the coccyx
or a Brigid's Cross
yellowing in some outhouse

while custom, that "most
sovereign mistress,"
beds us down into
the British isles.

II

We are to be proud
of our Elizabethan English:
"varsity," for example,
is grass-roots stuff with us;

we "deem" or we "allow"
when we suppose
and some cherished archaisms
are correct Shakespearean.

Not to speak of the furled
consonants of lowlanders
shuttling obstinately
between bawn and mossland.

III

MacMorris, gallivanting
round the Globe, whinged

to courtier and groundling
who had heard tell of us

as going very bare
of learning, as wild hares,
as anatomies of death:
"What ish my nation?"

And sensibly, though so much
later, the wandering Bloom
replied, "Ireland," said Bloom,
"I was born here. Ireland."

MOSSBAWN: TWO POEMS IN DEDICATION

for Mary Heaney

1. SUNLIGHT

There was a sunlit absence.
The helmeted pump in the yard
heated its iron,
water honeyed

in the slung bucket
and the sun stood
like a griddle cooling
against the wall

of each long afternoon.
So, her hands scuffled
over the bakeboard,
the reddening stove

sent its plaque of heat
against her where she stood
in a floury apron
by the window.

Now she dusts the board
with a goose's wing,
now sits, broad-lapped,
with whitened nails

and measling shins:
here is a space
again, the scone rising
to the tick of two clocks.

And here is love
like a tinsmith's scoop
sunk past its gleam
in the meal-bin.

2. THE SEED CUTTERS

They seem hundreds of years away. Breughel,
You'll know them if I can get them true.
They kneel under the hedge in a half-circle
Behind a windbreak wind is breaking through.
They are the seed cutters. The tuck and frill
Of leaf-sprout is on the seed potatoes
Buried under that straw. With time to kill
They are taking their time. Each sharp knife goes
Lazily halving each root that falls apart
In the palm of the hand: a milky gleam,
And, at the centre, a dark watermark.
O calendar customs! Under the broom
Yellowing over them, compose the frieze
With all of us there, our anonymities.

EXPOSURE

It is December in Wicklow:
Alders dripping, birches
Inheriting the last light,
The ash tree cold to look at.

A comet that was lost
Should be visible at sunset,
Those million tons of light
Like a glimmer of haws and rose-hips,

And I sometimes see a falling star.
If I could come on meteorite!
Instead I walk through damp leaves,
Husks, the spent flukes of autumn,

Imagining a hero
On some muddy compound,
His gift like a slingstone
Whirled for the desperate.

How did I end up like this?
I often think of my friends'
Beautiful prismatic counselling
And the anvil brains of some who hate me

As I sit weighing and weighing
My responsible *tristia*.
For what? For the ear? For the people?
For what is said behind-backs?

Rain comes down through the alders,
Its low conducive voices
Mutter about let-downs and erosions
And yet each drop recalls

The diamond absolutes.
I am neither internee nor informer;
An inner émigré, grown long-haired
And thoughtful; a wood-kerne

Escaped from the massacre,
Taking protective colouring
From bole and bark, feeling
Every wind that blows;

Who, blowing up these sparks
For their meagre heat, have missed

The once-in-a-lifetime portent,
The comet's pulsing rose.

PUNISHMENT

I can feel the tug
of the halter at the nape
of her neck, the wind
on her naked front.

It blows her nipples
to amber beads,
it shakes the frail rigging
of her ribs.

I can see her drowned
body in the bog,
the weighing stone,
the floating rods and boughs.

Under which at first
she was a barked sapling
that is dug up
oak-bone, brain-firkin:

her shaved head
like a stubble of black corn,
her blindfold a soiled bandage,
her noose a ring

to store
the memories of love.
Little adulteress,
before they punished you

you were flaxen-haired,
undernourished, and your
tar-black face was beautiful.
My poor scapegoat,

I almost love you
but would have cast, I know,
the stones of silence.
I am the artful voyeur

of your brain's exposed
and darkened combs,
your muscles' webbing
and all your numbered bones:

I who have stood dumb
when your betraying sisters,
cauled in tar,
wept by the railings,

who would connive
in civilized outrage
yet understand the exact
and tribal, intimate revenge.

Further Readings on Seamus Heaney

Bibliography

Durkan, Michael J. "Seamus Heaney: A Checklist for a Bibliography." *Irish University Review* 16: 48–76.
Pearson, Henry. "Seamus Heaney: A Bibliographical Checklist." *American Book Collector* 3: 31–42.

Selected Works

Death of a Naturalist. London: Faber and Faber; New York: Oxford University Press, 1966.
Door into the Dark. London: Faber and Faber; New York: Oxford University Press, 1969.
Field Work. London and Boston: Faber and Faber, 1979.
North. London: Faber and Faber, 1975; New York: Oxford University Press, 1976.
Preoccupations: Selected Prose, 1968–1978. New York: Farrar, Straus and Giroux, 1980.
The Rattle Bag. An Anthology of Poetry. Edited, with Ted Hughes. London: Faber and Faber, 1982.

Selected Poems 1965–1975. New York: Farrar, Straus and Giroux, 1980.
Station Island. New York: Farrar, Straus and Giroux, 1985.
Sweeney Astray. A Version from the Irish. (trans.) New York: Farrar, Straus and Giroux, 1984.
Wintering Out. New York: Oxford University Press, 1972.

Biography and Criticism

Broadbridge, Edward, ed. *Seamus Heaney.* Copenhagen: Danmarks Radio, 1977.
Brown, Terence. "Four New Voices: Poets of the Present," *Northern Voices: Poets from Ulster.* Dublin: Gill and Macmillan, 1975. Pp. 171–213.
Buttel, Robert. *Seamus Heaney.* Lewisburg, Pa.: Bucknell University Press, 1975.
Deane, Seamus. "Unhappy and at Home: Interview with Seamus Heaney." *The Crane Bag* 1: 61–67.
Foster, John Wilson. "The Poetry of Seamus Heaney." *Critical Quarterly* 16: 35–48.
Haffenden, John. "Interview," *Viewpoints: Poets in Conversation.* London: Faber and Faber, 1981.
Longley, Edna. "Stars and Horses. Pigs and Trees." *The Crane Bag* 3: 54–60.
Morrison, Blake. *Seamus Heaney.* London and New York: Methuen, 1982.
Parini, Jay. "Seamus Heaney: The Ground Possessed." *Southern Review* 16: 100–23.
Randall, James. "An Interview with Seamus Heaney." *Ploughshares.* 5:7–22.
Stallworthy, Jon. "The Poet as Archaeologist: W. B. Yeats and Seamus Heaney." *Review of English Studies* 33: 158–74.
Vendler, Helen. "The Music of What Happens," *New Yorker.* 57: 155–57.

MICHAEL LONGLEY (b. 1939)

A Trinity-trained classicist, Michael Longley taught school before settling in his native Belfast to work for the Arts Council of Northern Ireland, which he now serves as associate director. The author of five volumes of poetry, his *Collected Poems* appeared in 1985.

Longley's lyrics reveal his concern for form—for the way that experience shapes syntax and stanza. His economy of form, his striking imagery, and his frequent themes—the natural world; love— are qualities he shares with the poet Emily Dickinson. "In Memoriam" describes Longley's father as a young soldier in a Scottish regiment on the Western Front. A classical love poem, "The Linen Industry" sets love in the landscape of Northern Ireland.

EMILY DICKINSON

Emily Dickinson, I think of you
Wakening early each morning to write,
Dressing with care for the act of poetry.
Yours is always a perfect progress through
Such cluttered rooms to eloquence, delight,
To words—your window on the mystery.

In your house in Amherst Massachusetts,
Though like love letters you lock them away,
The poems are ubiquitous as dust.
You sit there writing while the light permits—
While you grow older they increase each day,
Gradual as flowers, gradual as rust.

THE LINEN INDUSTRY

Pulling up flax after the blue flowers have fallen
And laying our handfuls in the peaty water
To rot those grasses to the bone, or building stooks
That recall the skirts of an invisible dancer,

We become a part of the linen industry
And follow its processes to the grubby town
Where fields are compacted into window-boxes
And there is little room among the big machines.

But even in our attic under the skylight
We make love on a bleach green, the whole meadow
Draped with material turning white in the sun
As though snow reluctant to melt were our attire.

What's passion but a battering of stubborn stalks,
Then a gentle combing out of fibres like hair
And a weaving of these into christening robes,
Into garments for a marriage or funeral?

Since it's like a bereavement once the labour's done
To find ourselves last workers in a dying trade,

Let flax be our matchmaker, our undertaker,
The provider of sheets for whatever the bed—

And be shy of your breasts in the presence of death,
Say that you look more beautiful in linen
Wearing white petticoats, the bow on your bodice
A butterfly attending the embroidered flowers.

IN MEMORIAM

My father, let no similes eclipse
Where crosses like some forest simplified
Sink roots into my mind; the slow sands
Of your history delay till through your eyes
I read you like a book. Before you died,
Re-enlisting with all the broken soldiers
You bent beneath your rucksack, near collapse,
In anecdote rehearsed and summarised
These words I write in memory. Let yours
And other heartbreaks play into my hands.

Now I see in close-up, in my mind's eye,
The cracked and splintered dead for pity's sake.
Each dismal evening predecease the sun,
You, looking death and nightmare in the face
With your kilt, harmonica and gun,
Grow older in a flash, but none the wiser
(Who, following the wrong queue at The Palace,
Having joined the London Scottish by mistake),
Your nineteen years uncertain if and why
Belgium put the kibosh on the Kaiser.

Between the corpses and the soup canteens
You swooned away, watching your future spill.
But, as it was, your proper funeral urn
Had mercifully smashed to smithereens,
To shrapnel shards that sliced your testicle.
That instant I, your most unlikely son,
In No Man's Land was surely left for dead,

Blotted out from your far horizon.
As your voice now is locked inside my head,
I yet was held secure, waiting my turn.

Finally, that lousy war was over.
Stranded in France and in need of proof
You hunted down experimental lovers,
Persuading chorus girls and countesses:
This, father, the last confidence you spoke.
In my twentieth year your old wounds woke
As cancer. Lodging under the same roof
Death was a visitor who hung about,
Strewing the house with pills and bandages,
Till he chose to put your spirit out.

Though they overslept the sequence of events
Which ended with the ambulance outside,
You lingering in the hall, your bowels on fire,
Tears in your eyes, and all your medals spent,
I summon girls who packed at last and went
Underground with you. Their souls again on hire,
Now those lost wives as recreated brides
Take shape before me, materialise.
On the verge of light and happy legend
They lift their skirts like blinds across your eyes.

Further Readings on Michael Longley

Selected Works

ed., *Causeway*. The Arts in Ulster. Belfast: Arts Council; Dublin: Gill and
    Macmillan, 1971.
No Continuing City. Poems 1963–1968. Dublin: Gill and Macmillan; London:
    Macmillan, 1969.
The Echo Gate. London: Secker and Warburg, 1979.
An Exploded View. Poems 1968–1972. London: Victor Gollancz, 1973.
Man Lying on a Wall. London: Victor Gollancz, 1976.
Poems. Dublin: The Gallery Press; Edinburgh: The Salamander Press, 1985.
Selected Poems. 1963–1980. Winston-Salem, N.C.: Wake Forest University
    Press, 1981.

Biography and Criticism

Johnston, Dillon. "Interview with Michael Longley." *Irish Literary Supplement* 5:2.

"Michael Longley." *Contemporary Literary Criticism.* 29: 291–97.

Storey, Mark. "Michael Longley: A Precarious Act of Balancing." *Fortnight* 194: 21–22.

DEREK MAHON (b. 1941)

Derek Mahon started writing poetry as a schoolboy. He won the Eric Gregory Prize for Poetry while an undergraduate at Trinity College, Dublin, for poems which would become part of *Night-Crossing* (1968). Five collections followed, with *Poems 1962–1978* appearing in 1979. Translator as well as poet, Mahon has published versions of Nerval's *Les Chimères* and Molière's *The School for Husbands*. He also adapted Turgenev's *First Love* for Radio Teléfis Éireann.

One of the most elegant poets of his generation, Mahon's poems have been praised for their wit and polish. Critics have described the mood of much of Mahon's poetry as "detached," noting that he often uses images of windows as distancing devices, as in "The Snow Party," where the falling snow silences the sounds of the violent world beyond. Similarly, "A Disused Shed in Co. Wexford" speaks for those silenced. Referring to the image of the mushrooms straining through the darkness toward the shaft of light coming through the keyhole, another poet, Seamus Heaney, has written: "It is about the need to love and be known, the need for selfhood, recognition in the eye of God and the eye of the world."

A DISUSED SHED IN CO. WEXFORD

Let them not forget us, the weak souls among the asphodels.
                                        Seferis, *Mythistorema*
            for J. G. Farrell

Even now there are places where a thought might grow—
Peruvian mines, worked out and abandoned
To a slow clock of condensation,
An echo trapped for ever, and a flutter of
Wildflowers in the lift-shaft,

Indian compounds where the wind dances
And a door bangs with diminished confidence,
Lime crevices behind rippling rainbarrels,
Dog corners for shit burials;
And in a disused shed in Co. Wexford,

Deep in the grounds of a burnt-out hotel,
Among the bathtubs and the washbasins
A thousand mushrooms crowd to a keyhole.
This is the one star in their firmament
Or frames a star within a star.
What should they do there but desire?
So many days beyond the rhododendrons
With the world waltzing in its bowl of cloud,
They have learnt patience and silence
Listening to the crows querulous in the high wood.

They have been waiting for us in a foetor of
Vegetable sweat since civil war days,
Since the gravel-crunching, interminable departure
Of the expropriated mycologist.
He never came back, and light since then
Is a keyhole rusting gently after rain.
Spiders have spun, flies dusted to mildew,
And once a day, perhaps, they have heard something—
A trickle of masonry, a shout from the blue
Or a lorry changing gear at the end of the lane.

There have been deaths, the pale flesh flaking
Into the earth that nourished it;
And nightmares born of these and the grim
Dominion of stale air and rank moisture.
Those nearest the door grow strong—
Elbow room! Elbow room!
The rest, dim in a twilight of crumbling
Utensils and broken pitchers, groaning
For their deliverance, have been so long
Expectant that there is left only the posture.

A half century, without visitors, in the dark—
Poor preparation for the cracking lock

And creak of hinges, Magi, moonmen,
Powdery prisoners of the old regime,
Web-throated, stalked like triffids, racked by drouth
And insomnia, only the ghost of a scream
At the flash-bulb firing squad we wake them with
Shows there is life yet in their feverish forms.
Grown beyond nature now, soft food for worms,
They lift frail heads in gravity and good faith.

They are begging us, you see, in their wordless way,
To do something, to speak on their behalf
Or at least not to close the door again.
Lost people of Treblinka and Pompeii!
Save us, save us, they seem to say,
Let the god not abandon us
Who have come so far in darkness and in pain.
We too had our lives to live.
You with your light meter and relaxed itinerary,
Let not our naive labours have been in vain!

THE SNOW PARTY

for Louis Asekoff

Basho, coming
To the city of Nagoya,
Is asked to a snow party.

There is a tinkling of china
And tea into china,
There are introductions.

Then everyone
Crowds to the window
To watch the falling snow.

Snow is falling on Nagoya
And farther south
On the tiles of Kyoto.

Eastward, beyond Irago,
It is falling
Like leaves on the cold sea.

Elsewhere they are burning
Witches and heretics
In the boiling squares,

Thousands have died since dawn
In the service
Of barbarous kings—

But there is silence
In the houses of Nagoya
And the hills of Ise.

Further Readings on Derek Mahon

Selected Works

Antarctica. Dublin: Gallery Press, 1985.
Courtyards in Delft. Dublin: Gallery Press, 1981.
The Hunt by Night. Winston-Salem, N.C.: Wake Forest University Press, 1972.
Lives. New York: Oxford University Press, 1972.
Night-Crossing. London: Oxford University Press, 1968.
Poems 1962–1978. London: Oxford University Press, 1979.
The Snow Party. London and New York: Oxford University Press, 1975.
The Sphere Book of Modern Irish Poetry. (ed.) London: Sphere, 1972.

Biography and Criticism

Brown, Terence. "An Interview with Derek Mahon." *Poetry Ireland Review* 14:11–19.
Byrne, John. "Derek Mahon: A Commitment to Change." *The Crane Bag* 6:62–72.
"Derek Mahon." *Contemporary Literary Criticism* 27: 286–93.
Johnston, Dillon. *Irish Poetry after Joyce.* South Bend, Ind.: University of Notre Dame Press, 1985. pp. 224–46. "Unaccommodated Mahon: An Ulster Poet." *The Hollins Critic* 17:1–16.
Kelly, Willie. "Each Poem for Me a New Beginning." Interview in *Cork Review* 2:10–12.

EILÉAN NÍ CHUILLEANÁIN (b. 1942)

Eiléan ní Chuilleanáin's first formal recognition as a poet was the *Irish Times* Award for Poetry, which she received in 1966 while a graduate student at Lady Margaret Hall, Oxford, on a travelling studentship from the National University of Ireland. An English Renaissance scholar, she has lectured in English at Trinity since 1966. She is also a founding editor of *Cyphers*.

The scholar-poet role rests easily with ní Chuilleanáin, since she grew up the daughter of the professor of Irish at University College, Cork, and the novelist Éilis Dillon. She is married to Macdara Woods, a poet and another *Cyphers* editor.

Her work has been praised for its sense of history, and the poet for the quality of her imagination, her clarity of image, and her precise diction. The O'Rourke betrayed in "Waterfall" is an allusion to Brian na Múrtha or Brian of the Ramparts, who was hanged as felon in London in 1591 for having aided the shipwrecked survivors of the Spanish Armada.

THE SECOND VOYAGE

Odysseus rested on his oar and saw
The ruffled foreheads of the waves
Crocodiling and mincing past: he rammed
The oar between their jaws and looked down
In the simmering sea where scribbles of weed defined
Uncertain depth, and the slim fishes progressed
In fatal formation, and thought
                    If there was a single
Streak of decency in these waves now, they'd be ridged
Pocked and dented with the battering they've had
And we could name them as Adam named the beasts,
Saluting a new one with dismay, or a notorious one
With admiration; they'd notice us passing
And rejoice at our shipwreck, but these
Have less character than sheep and need more patience.

I know what I'll do he said;
I'll park my ship in the crook of a long pier

(And I'll take you with me he said to the oar)
I'll face the rising ground and walk away
From tidal waters, up riverbeds
Where herons parcel out the miles of stream,
Over gaps in the hills, through warm
Silent valleys, and when I meet a farmer
Bold enough to look me in the eye
With "where are you off to with that long
Winnowing fan over your shoulder?"
There I will stand still
And I'll plant you for a gatepost or a hitching-post
And leave you as a tidemark. I can go back
And organise my house then.
                                    But the profound
Unfenced valleys of the ocean still held him;
He had only the oar to make them keep their distance;
The sea was still frying under the ship's side.

He considered the water-lilies, and thought about
        fountains
Spraying as wide as willows in empty squares,
The sugarstick of water clattering into the kettle,
The flat lakes bisecting the rushes. He remembered
        spiders and frogs
Housekeeping at the roadside in brown trickles floored
        with mud,
Horsetroughs, the black canal, pale swans at dark:
His face grew damp with tears that tasted
Like his own sweat or the insults of the sea.

WATERFALL

    This airy afternoon, warm and free,
    My head lies against the bridge,
    The vibrant coping-stones
    Arching the green insistent waterfall;
    My cheek feels the cold
    Bricks of the cistern where Vercingetorix

Died in Rome, the dark earth of London
Where blood fell from O'Rourke betrayed
1591,
The cool grass of White Island
Monastic, long ruined and freshly springing
In between broken walls,
Carved and scattered stones.

OLD ROADS

Missing from the map, the abandoned roads
Reach across the mountain, threading into
Clefts and valleys, shuffle between thick
Hedges of flowery thorn.
The grass flows into tracks of wheels,
Mowed evenly by the careful sheep;
Drenched, it guards the gaps of silence
Only trampled on the pattern day.

And if, an odd time, late
At night, a cart passes
Splashing in a burst stream, crunching bones,
The wavering candle hung by the shaft
Slaps light against a single gable
Catches a flat tombstone
Shaking a nervous beam in a white face

Their arthritic fingers
Their stiffening grasp cannot
Hold long on the hillside—
Slowly the old roads lose their grip.

Further Readings on Eiléan ní Chuilleanáin

Selected Works

Acts and Monuments. Dublin: Gallery Press, 1972.
The Rose Geranium. Dublin: Gallery Press, 1980.

The Second Voyage. Dublin: Gallery Books, 1977.
Site of Ambush. Dublin: Gallery Books, 1975.

Studies

"Gaelic Ireland Rediscovered: Courtly and Country Poetry." In *Irish Poets in English, The Pleasures of Gaelic Poetry,* ed. Sean Lucy. Cork and Dublin: Mercier Press, 1973.
Irish Women: Image and Achievement. Dublin: Arlen House, 1985.
"Love and Friendship." In *The Pleasures of Gaelic Poetry,* ed. Sean MacReamoinn. London: Allen, Lane, 1982.

Biography and Criticism

Browne, Joseph. "Eiléan ní Chuilleanáin." In *Dictionary of Literary Biography, 40: Poets of Great Britain and Ireland Since 1960.* Detroit: Gale, 1985.

EAVAN BOLAND (b. 1944)

Eavan Boland, the youngest child of diplomat Frederick Boland and painter Frances Kelly, was educated in Dublin, London, and New York. (Her poem "After a Childhood Away from Ireland" speaks to that temporary exile.) After a brilliant undergraduate career at Trinity, she returned there to lecture in 1967–1968. Boland has won a number of awards, including the Irish-American Cultural Institute's prize.

Many of her early poems, such as "The Winning of Etain," are rooted in Irish tradition; others, like "Athene's Song," draw from other mythologies. Marriage to novelist Kevin Casey and the birth of children brought poems about domesticity and motherhood—poems that extend her range from the wit of "The New Pastoral" to the passionate restraint of "Child of Our Time," her moving elegy for her child.

ATHENE'S SONG

(for my father)

From my father's head I sprung
Goddess of the war, created
Partisan and soldiers' physic—

My symbols boast and brazen gong—
Until I made in Athens wood
Upon my knees a new music.

When I played my pipe of bone,
Robbed and whittled from a stag,
Every bird became a lover
Every lover to its tone
Found the truth of song and brag;
Fish sprung in the full river.

Peace became the toy of power
When other noises broke my sleep.
Like dreams I saw the hot ranks
And heroes in another flower
Than any there; I dropped my pipe
Remembering their shouts, their thanks.

Beside the water, lost and mute,
Lies my pipe and like my mind
Remains unknown, remains unknown
And in some hollow taking part
With my heart against my hand
Hold its peace and holds its own.

REQUIEM FOR A PERSONAL FRIEND
(ON A HALF-EATEN BLACKBIRD)

A striped philistine with quick
Sight, quiet paws, today—
In gorging on a feathered prey—
Filleted our garden's music.

Such robbery in such a mouthful!
Here rests, shovelled under simple
Vegetables, my good example—
Singing daily, daily faithful.

No conceit and not contrary—
My best colleague, worst of all,

Was half-digested, his sweet whistle
Swallowed like a dictionary.

Little victim, song for song—
Who share a trade must share a threat—
So I write to cheat the cat
Who got your body, of my tongue.

AFTER A CHILDHOOD AWAY FROM IRELAND

One summer
we slipped in at dawn
on plum-coloured water
in the sloppy quiet.
The engines
of the ship stopped.
There was an eerie
drawing near,
a noiseless, coming head-on
of red roofs, walls,
dogs, barley stooks.
Then we were there.
Cobh.

Coming home.
I had heard of this:
the ground the emigrants
resistless, weeping
laid their cheeks to,
put their lips to kiss.
Love is also memory.
I only stared.
What I had lost
was not land
but the habit
of land,
whether of growing out of

or settling back on
or being defined by.

I climb
to your nursery.
I stand listening
to the dissonances

of the summer's day ending.
I bend to kiss you.
Your cheeks are brick pink.
They store warmth like clay.

CHILD OF OUR TIME

for Aengus

Yesterday I knew no lullaby
But you have taught me overnight to order
This song, which takes from your final cry
Its tune, from your unreasoned end its reason;
Its rhythm from the discord of your murder
Its motive from the fact you cannot listen.

We who should have known how to instruct
With rhymes for your waking, rhythms for your sleep,
Names for the animals you took to bed,
Tales to distract, legends to protect,
Later an idiom for you to keep
And living, learn, must learn from you, dead.

To make our broken images rebuild
Themselves around your limbs, your broken
Image, find for your sake whose life our idle
Talk has cost, a new language. Child
Of our time, our times have robbed your cradle.
Sleep in a world your final sleep has woken.

Further Readings on Eavan Boland

Selected Works

In her Own Image. Dublin: Arlen House, 1980.
New Territory. Dublin: Allen Figgis, 1967.

Night Feed. Dublin: Arlen House, 1982.
The War Horse. London: Victor Gollancz, 1975.
The Younger Irish Poets. Belfast: Blackstaff Press, 1982.

Biography and Criticism

Browne, Joseph. "Eavan Boland." In *Dictionary of Literary Biography 40: Poets of Great Britain and Ireland Since 1960. pp. 36–41.* Detroit: Gale, 1985.
Introducing Eavan Boland: Poems. Princeton, Ont.: Ontario Review Press, 1981.
Kennelly, Brendan. "Eavan Boland." In *Dictionary of Irish Literature,* ed. Robert Hogan, pp. 112–14. Westport, Conn.: Greenwood Press, 1979.

MEDBH MCGUCKIAN (b.1950)

Medbh McGuckian studied English at Queen's University, Belfast. She won the Poetry Society competition in 1979 for "The Flitting," and the following year received an Eric Gregory Award. McGuckian is the author of two collections: *The Flower Master* (1982), which won both the Rooney Prize and the Alice Hunt Barlett Award, and *Venus and the Rain* (1984).

Known for her stunning and often startling imagery and sensual language, two of the poems from *The Flower Master* (1982) treat two quintessential McGuckian subjects: the natural landscape and sexuality. "The Mast Year" describes a stand of trees, a beechwood whose deeply shaded floor allows but little growth with the result that it produces a rich leaf mold. (Lammas, the Anglo-Saxon name for August 1, is still used in the north of Ireland; however, it sometimes refers to Lughnasa, the Celtic harvest festival.) The erotic "Soil Map" suggests a reading of Kinsella's translation of *The Táin* in its two allusions to Maeve of Connacht: she was said never to have been "without one man in the shadow of another," and it was she who offered the "friendship of her thighs" to Dáire mac Fiachna if he would lend her the Brown Bull of Cuailnge.

THE MAST YEAR

Some kinds of trees seem ever eager
To populate new ground, the oak or pine.
Though beech can thrive on many soils
And carve itself an empire, its vocation

Is gentler; it casts a shade for wildflowers
Adapted to the gloom, which feed
Like fungus on its rot of bedstraw leaves.

It makes an awkward neighbour, as the birch
Does, that lashes out in gales, and fosters
Intimacy with toadstools, till they sleep
In the benevolence of each other's smells,
Never occupying many sites for long:
The thin red roots of alder vein
The crumbled bank, the otter's ruptured door.

Bee-keepers love the windbreak sycamore,
The twill of hanging flowers that the beech
Denies the yew—its waking life so long
It lets the stylish beechwood
Have its day, as winded oaks
Lay store upon their Lammas growth,
The thickening of their dreams.

THE SOIL-MAP

I am not a woman's man, but I can tell,
By the swinging of your two-leaf door,
You are never without one man in the shadow
Of another; and because the mind
Of a woman between two men is lighter
Than a spark, the petalled steps to your porch
Feel frigid with a lost warmth. I will not
Take you in hardness, for all the dark cage
Of my dreaming over your splendid fenestration,
Your moulded sills, your slender purlins,

The secret woe of your gutters. I will do it
Without niggardliness, like food with one
Generous; a moment as auspicious
And dangerous as the christening of a ship,
My going in to find the settlement
Of every floor, the hump of water

Following the moon, and her discolouring,
The saddling derangement of a roof
That might collapse its steepness
Under the sudden strain of clearing its name.

For anyone with patience can divine
How your plasterwork has lost key, the rendering
About to come away. So like a rainbird,
Challenged by a charm of goldfinch,
I appeal to the god who fashions edges
Whether such turning-points exist
As these saltings we believe we move
Away from, as if by simply shaking
A cloak we could disbud ourselves,
Dry out, and cease to live there?

I have found the places on the soil-map,
Proving it possible once more to call
Houses by their names, Annsgift or Mavisbank,
Mount Juliet or Bettysgrove; they should not
Lie with the gloom of disputes to interrupt them
Every other year, like some disease
Of language making humorous the friendship
Of the thighs. I drink to you as Hymenstown,
(My touch of fantasy) or First Fruits,
Impatient for my power as a bride.

Further Readings on Medbh McGuckian

Selected Works

The Flower Master. London: Oxford University Press, 1982.
Portrait of Joanna. Belfast: Ulsterman, 1980.
Trio 2: Damian Gorman, Medbh McGuckian, Douglas Marshall. Belfast: Blackstaff
    Press, 1980.
Venus and the Rain. Oxford and New York: Oxford University Press, 1984.
The Younger Irish Poets. Belfast: Blackstaff Press, 1982.

Biography and Criticism

Henigan, Robert. "Contemporary Woman Poets in Ireland" *Concerning Poetry*
    18: 103–15.

PAUL MULDOON (b. 1951)

Any mention of Paul Muldoon usually includes a comment about his precociousness for he was only twenty-one when he published *New Weather* (1973), his stylish first book of lyrics. Born in south Armagh and educated in Belfast, he is sometimes called the youngest of that generation of Queen's University, Belfast, poets of whom Seamus Heaney is preeminent. For a number of years, Muldoon was a producer for BBC in Belfast.

Muldoon has often gone to Old Irish sources. His narrative poem, the mock-heroic "Immran," is a search for a lost father written in the language of Raymond Chandler. It is based on *Imran Mael Dúin* [The voyage of Mael Dúin], an early Irish tale of a son's journey to avenge his father. "Neither one thing or the other," a line from the title poem "Mules," speaks to all mixed marriages in that volume. "The Boundary Commission," an allusion to the commission set up after the Treaty to set the geographical boundary between Northern Ireland and the Republic, also speaks to the problem of identity in Northern Ireland.

MULES

Should they not have the best of both worlds?

Her feet of clay gave the lie
To the star burned in our mare's brow.
Would Parsons' jackass not rest more assured
That cross wrenched from his shoulders?

We had loosed them into one field.
I watched Sam Parsons and my quick father
Tense for the punch below their belts,
For what was neither one thing or the other.

It was as though they had shuddered
To think of their gaunt, sexless foal
Dropped tonight in the cowshed.

We might yet claim that it sprang from earth
Were it not for the afterbirth

Trailed like some fine, silk parachute,
That we would know from what heights it fell.

THE BOUNDARY COMMISSION

You remember that village where the border ran
Down the middle of the street,
With the butcher and baker in different states?
Today he remarked how a shower of rain

Had stopped so cleanly across Golightly's lane
It might have been a wall of glass
That had toppled over. He stood there, for ages,
To wonder which side, if any, he should be on.

Further Readings on Paul Muldoon

Selected Works

The Faber Book of Contemporary Irish Poetry. London: Faber and Faber, 1985.
Mules. Winston-Salem, N.C.: Wake Forest University Press, 1977.
Mules and Earlier Poems. Winston-Salem, N.C.: Wake Forest University Press, 1985.
New Weather. Winston-Salem, N.C.: Wake Forest University Press, 1973.
Quoof. Winston-Salem, N.C.: Wake Forest University Press, 1983.
Why Brownlee Left. Winston-Salem, N.C.: Wake Forest University Press, 1980.

Biography and Criticism

Frazier, Adrian. "Juniper, Otherwise Known: Poems by Pauliñ and Muldoon."
    Eire-Ireland 19: 123–33.
Johnston, Dillon. *Irish Poetry after Joyce*, pp. 263–72. South Bend, Ind.: University of Notre Dame Press, 1975.

NUALA NÍ DHOMHNAILL (b. 1952)

Born in England to Irish parents, Nuala ní Dhomhnaill was fostered at five to her aunt's household in Cahiratrant, a village in the Corca

Dhuibhne Gaeltacht near Ventry, County Kerry. After taking her B.A. at University College, Cork, she married a Turkish geologist and lived abroad. She returned to Ireland in 1980 to locate herself and her art in the place that nourishes both, for she finds the source for much of her powerful imagery in Irish folklore and mythology.

DEEPFREEZE

Cornucopia of the age, the magic casket
from which we draw the best of food and drink,
every delicacy that your mouth might water after
and no two mouthfuls of quite the same taste.

Miscellany of household needs, healing well
of our ancestral hungers which neither increase nor
go away.
We adore its cairn of plenty.
There are no limits to its icy
streams of milk and honey, peaches, apples,
Irish stews, french fries,
quarters of beef already minced,
desserts, sweet cakes, two whole sheep.

There are five loaves here and two fishes
to feed the multitude of neighbours (if they ever
come).
And who chucked this dead cat in amongst the
spinach?
—Jimín Mháire Thadhg, I'll complain you to your
Mam!

Seated victorious in the heart of every kitchen
is this basic metaphor of our civilisation.
The faerie music of the world ringing in our ears
is reduced to its contented hum, high velocity purr of
electricity

A *memento mori*, par excellence, if I
ever saw one, awesome reminder of the ditch

we come from and to which we are going,
graven images everything we hamster there
—dead and hard and as cold as the grave.

INSIDE OUT

Like the full moon
in grand array
you sail
into the room to me.
Master indeed
of all you survey,—
the shine on the furniture, the swellbeat
of my trembling, apprehensive heart.

Let's say you are "well on,"
your head is in a spin,
your gestures and your jests
grandiloquent
you don't even notice
that your white jersey
is crumpled
and inside out on you.

You are so careful
of your waistline,
so dapper and so nifty
in your dressing,—
what else is left for me
to do but go out in the garden
and sit on the lawn
and howl my anguish at the moon.

Because, *ochón*, my sorrow,
but there is truth in the old saw
that there are three smiles
more bitter than death itself:
the grin of a treacherous hound,

the beam of melting snow,
and the smirk of your lover
who has just slept with another woman.

trans. Nuala ní Dhombnaill

Further Readings on Nuala ní Dhomhnaill

Selected Works

An Dealg Droighin. Cork: Mercier Press, 1981.
Féar Suaithinseach. Maynooth: An Sagart, 1984.
Selected Poems, tr. Michael Hartnett. Dublin: Raven Arts, 1986.

Biography and Criticism

nic Eoin, Máirín. "Agallamh: Nuala Rua." Bilingual interview, *An Droichead* 2:
    2–5.

SELECTED BACKGROUND READINGS

Alspach, Russell K. *Irish Poetry from the Invasion to 1798.* 2d ed. Philadelphia: University of Pennsylvania Press, 1960.

Bell, Sam Hanna. *The Theatre in Ulster.* Dublin: Gill and Macmillan, 1972.

Boyd, Ernest A. *Ireland's Literary Renaissance,* rev. ed. New York: Knopf, 1922. Reprint, New York: Barnes & Noble, 1968.

Boylan, Henry. *A Dictionary of Irish Biography.* Dublin: Gill and Macmillan, 1978.

Brady, Anne M., and Cleeve, Brian. *A Biographical Dictionary of Irish Writers.* New York: St. Martin's Press, 1985.

Brown, Malcolm. *The Politics of Irish Literature: From Thomas Davis to W. B. Yeats.* Seattle: University of Washington Press, 1972.

Brown, Stephen J. *A Guide to Books on Ireland.* Dublin: Hodges Figgis, 1912. Reprint, New York: Lemma, 1970.

Brown, Terence. *Northern Voices: Poets from Ulster.* Totowa, N.J.: Rowman and Littlefield, 1975.

Cahalan, James. *Great Hatred, Little Room. The Irish Historical Novel.* Syracuse, N.Y.: Syracuse University Press, 1983.

Canadian Journal of Irish Studies. Vancouver, B.C.: 1974———.

Carney, James, ed. *Early Irish Poetry.* Cork: Mercier Press, 1965.

———. *Early Irish Literature.* New York: Barnes & Noble, 1966. This is a reprint of Gerard Murphy, *Saga and Myth in Early Ireland* (Dublin: Three Candles, 1955); *The Ossianic Lore and Romantic Tales of Medieval Ireland* (Dublin: Three Candles, 1961); and Eleanor Knott, *Irish Classical Poetry* (Dublin: Three Candles, 1955).

Clark, William S. *The Early Irish Stage. The Beginnings to 1720.* Oxford: Clarendon Press, 1955.

———. *The Irish Stage in Country Towns, 1720–1860.* Oxford: Clarendon Press, 1965.

Clarke, Austin. *Poetry in Modern Ireland*. Dublin: Cultural Relations Committee, 1961.

Cleeve, Brian. *Dictionary of Irish Writers*. 3 vols. Cork: Mercier Press, 1967–1971.

Comhar. Dublin: 1942——.

Connolly, Peter, ed. *Literature and the Changing Ireland*. Gerrards Cross: Colin Smythe; Totowa, N.J.: Barnes & Noble Books, 1982.

Corkery, Daniel. *The Hidden Ireland: a Study of Gaelic Munster in the Eighteenth Century*. Dublin: Gill, 1925.

Costello, Peter. *The Heart Grown Brutal*. Dublin: Gill & Macmillan; Totowa, N.J.: Rowman & Littlefield, 1977.

Crane Bag. Dublin: 1977–85.

Cronin, Anthony. *Heritage Now: Irish Literature in English Language*. Dingle, Ireland: Brandon; New York: St. Martin's, 1982.

Cross, Tom Peete. *Motif-Index of Early Irish Literature*. Bloomington: Indiana University Press, 1952.

Deane, Seamus. *Celtic Revivals: Essays on Modern Irish Literature*. London: Faber and Faber, 1985.

de Blacam, Aodh. *Gaelic Literature Surveyed*. rev. ed. Dublin: Talbot Press, 1974.

Dillon, Myles. *The Cycles of Kings*. London: Oxford University Press, 1946.

——. *Early Irish Literature*. Chicago: University of Chicago Press, 1948.

——, ed. *Irish Sagas*. Cork: Mercier Press, 1968.

Donoghue, Denis. *We Irish: Essays on Irish Literature and Society*. New York: Knopf, 1986.

Duggan, G. C. *The Stage Irishman*. Dublin: Talbot Press, 1937.

Eager, Alan R. *A Guide to Irish Bibliographical Material*. Westport, Conn.: Greenwood Press, 1980.

Éire-Ireland. St. Paul, Minn.: 1966——.

Ellis-Fermor, Una. *The Irish Dramatic Movement*. rev. ed. London: Methuen, 1954.

Fallis, Richard. *The Irish Renaissance*. Syracuse, N.Y.: Syracuse University Press, 1977.

Farren, Robert. *The Course of Irish Verse in English*. New York: Sheed & Ward, 1957.

Fay, Gerard. *The Abbey Theatre, Cradle of Genius*. London: Hollis & Carter, 1958.

Finneran, Richard, ed. *Anglo-Irish Literature, a Review of Research*. New York: Modern Language Association, 1976.

Flanagan, Thomas. *The Irish Novelists, 1800–1850*. New York: Columbia University Press, 1959.

Flower, Robin. *The Irish Tradition*. Oxford: Clarendon Press, 1947.

Foster, John Wilson. *Forces and Themes in Ulster Fiction*. Dublin: Gill and Macmillan; Totowa, N.J.: Rowman & Littlefield, 1974.

Gallagher, S. F., ed. *Woman in Irish Legend, Life and Literature.* Gerrards Cross, England: Colin Smythe; Totowa, N.J.: Barnes & Noble Books, 1983.
Garratt, Robert. *Modern Irish Poetry: Tradition and Continuity from Yeats to Heaney.* Berkeley: University of California Press, 1986.
Greene, David. *The Irish Language.* Dublin: Three Candles, 1966.
Hall, Wayne E. *Shadowy Heroes: Irish Literature of the 1890s.* Syracuse, N.Y.: Syracuse University Press, 1980.
Harmon, Maurice. *Select Bibliography for the Study of Anglo-Irish Literature and Its Backgrounds.* Dublin: Wolfhound; Port Credit, Ont.: P. D. Meany, 1977.
———., ed. *The Irish Writer and the City.* Gerrards Cross: Colin Smythe; Totowa, N.J.: Barnes & Noble Books, 1984.
Hayes, Richard J. *Manuscript Sources for the History of Irish Civilization.* 11 vols. Boston: G. K. Hall, 1970.
———. *Sources for the History of Irish Civilization.* 9 vols. Boston: G. K. Hall, 1965.
Hogan, Robert. *After the Irish Renaissance.* Minneapolis: University of Minnesota Press, 1967; London: Macmillan, 1968.
———, ed. *Dictionary of Irish Literature.* Westport, Conn.: Greenwood Press, 1979; London: Macmillan, 1980 (retitled *Macmillan Dictionary of Irish Literature*).
———, and Kilroy, James. *The Modern Irish Drama.* 3 vols. Dublin: Dolmen, 1975–78.
Holloway, Joseph. *Joseph Holloway's Abbey Theatre.* Carbondale, Ill.: Southern Illinois University Press, 1967.
Honest Ulsterman, The. Portrush, Northern Ireland: 1968——.
Howarth, Herbert. *The Irish Writers.* London: Rockliff; N.Y.: Hill and Wang, 1958.
Irish Literary Supplement. Selden, N.Y.: 1982——.
Irish University Review. Dublin: 1970——.
Jackson, Kenneth H. *Studies in Celtic Nature Poetry.* Cambridge: Cambridge University Press, 1935.
———. *The Oldest Irish Tradition: a Window on the Iron Age.* Cambridge: Cambridge University Press, 1964.
James Joyce Quarterly. Tulsa, Okla.: 1963——.
Johnston, Dillon. *Irish Poetry After Joyce.* Notre Dame, Ind.: Notre Dame University Press, 1985.
Jordan, John, ed. *The Pleasures of Gaelic Literature.* Cork: Mercier Press, 1977.
Journal of Irish Literature. Newark, Del.: 1972——.
Kavanagh, Peter. *The Story of the Abbey Theatre.* New York: Devin-Adair, 1950.
Kersnowski, Frank. *The Outsiders: Poets in Contemporary Ireland.* Fort Worth, Tex.: Texas Christian University Press, 1975.
Kiely, Benedict. *Modern Irish Fiction: A Critique.* Dublin: Golden Eagle Books, 1950.
King, Kimball. *Ten Modern Irish Playwrights: A Comprehensive Annotated Bibliography.* New York: Garland, 1979.

Knott, Eleanor. *Irish Classical Poetry*. Dublin: Cultural Relations Committee, 1955; rpt. in James Carney, *Early Irish Literature* (New York, 1966).

Krause, David. *The Profane Book of Irish Comedy*. Ithaca: Cornell University Press, 1982.

Loftus, Richard J. *Nationalism in Modern Anglo-Irish Poetry*. Madison: University of Milwaukee Press, 1964.

Lucy, Sean. *Irish Poets in English*. Cork: Mercier Press, 1973.

McCann, Sean, ed. *The Story of the Abbey*. London: New English Library, 1967.

McCormack, W. J. *Ascendancy and Tradition in Anglo-Irish Literary History from 1798 to 1939*. London: Oxford University Press, 1985.

McHugh, Roger, and Harmon, Maurice. *Short History of Anglo-Irish Literature: From Its Origin to the Present Day*. Dublin: Wolfhound; New York: Barnes & Noble, 1982.

McKenna, Brian. *Irish Literature, 1800–1875. A Guide to Information Sources*. Detroit: Gale, 1978.

MacKillop, James. *Fionn mac Cumhaill: Celtic Myth in English Literature*. Syracuse, N.Y.: Syracuse University Press, 1986.

MacLiammóir, Micheál. *Theatre in Ireland*. Dublin: Cultural Relations Committee, 1964.

Mac Neill, Máire. *The Festival of Lughnasa. A Study of the Survival of the Celtic Festival of the Beginning of Harvest*, 2 vol. Dublin: Comhairle Béaloideas Éireann, 1982, (1962).

Martin, Augustine. *Anglo-Irish Literature*. Dublin: Department of Foreign Affairs, 1980.

Maxwell, D. E. S. *A Critical History of Modern Irish Drama, 1891–1980*. Cambridge: Cambridge University Press, 1984.

Mercier, Vivian. *The Irish Comic Tradition*. Oxford: Clarendon Press, 1962.

Murphy, Gerard. *Saga and Myth in Ancient Ireland*. Dublin: Cultural Relations Committee, 1955. Reprint, in James Carney, ed., *Early Irish Literature* (New York, 1966).

———. *The Ossianic Lore and Romantic Tales of Medieval Ireland*. Dublin: Cultural Relations Committee, 1961. Reprint, in James Carney, ed., *Early Irish Literature*, New York, 1966.

nic Shiubhlaigh, Máire, and Kenny, Edward. *The Splendid Years*. Dublin: Duffy, 1955.

O'Connor, Frank. *The Backward Look. A Survey of Irish Literature*. London: Macmillan, 1967. Retitled as *A Short History of Irish Literature*. New York: Putnam, 1967.

O'Connor, Ulick. *All the Olympians*. New York: Atheneum, 1984.

O'Donoghue, D. J. *The Poets of Ireland, A Biographical and Bibliographical Dictionary*. Dublin: Hodges Figgis, 1912. Reprint, Detroit: Gale, 1968.

Ó hAodha, Micheál. *Theatre in Ireland*. Totowa, N. J.: Rowman & Littlefield, 1974.

Power, Patrick. *A Literary History of Ireland*. Cork: Mercier, 1969.

———. *The Story of Anglo-Irish Poetry*. Cork: Mercier Press, 1967.

Rafroidi, Patrick, and Harmon, Maurice, eds. *The Irish Novel in Our Time.* Lille: Université de Lille, 1976.

Robinson, Lennox. *Ireland's Abbey Theatre.* London: Sidgewick & Jackson, 1951.

Sloan, Barry. *The Pioneers of Anglo-Irish Fiction, 1800–1850.* Gerrards Cross, England: Colin Smythe: Totowa, N.J.: Barnes & Noble Books, 1984.

Studia Hibernica. Dublin: 1961——.

Studies: an Irish Quarterly Review. Dublin: 1912——.

Threshold. Belfast: 1957——.

Waters, Maureen. *The Comic Irishman.* Albany: State University of New York Press, 1983.

Welch, Robert. *Irish Poetry from Moore to Yeats.* Gerrards Cross, England: Colin Smythe; Totowa, N.J.: Barnes & Noble Books, 1980.

Worth, Katharine. *The Irish Drama of Europe from Yeats to Beckett.* Atlantic Highlands, N.J.: Humanities Press, 1978.

GLOSSARY
Words, Places, Persons, Allusions

a bouchal. (Ir. *a bhuachaill*) boy.

acanthus. Decorative representation of a leaf at the top of a Corinthian column in classical architecture.

a-chuisle. (Lit. "Oh pulse [of my heart]," pron. a-KOOSH-la) Dear one, darling, a conventional term of endearment.

Aeneas. *See* pious Aeneas.

agra. (Ir. *a ghrá,* pron. a-GRAW) My love, my dear.

Ailill. (pron. AL-il) Maeve's husband and king of Connacht.

Ainnle. Brother of Naoise, Deirdre's lover.

aisling. (pron. ASH-ling) A kind of vision poetry that flourished in eighteenth century Munster, usually with political implications. The aisling formula consists of three parts: (1) the poet, out walking, meets a lady; (2) he describes her appearance, often employing rose and lily imagery; (3) the poet begins a conversation with her. (The woman is a personification of Ireland.)

Alanna. (Ir. *a leanbh,* pron. a LAN-e) My child. Term of endearment.

Alban, Alba. Poetic name for Scotland.

Alexander (356–323 B.C.). Commonly called Alexander the Great, Macedonian ruler of Greece who extended his kingdom as far as India.

amadán. See oinseach.

amhrán. (pron. aw-RAWN) Meter, song meter; the meter of Irish poetry from 1600 and after that gave up the strict rules of bardic schools in favor of the natural accent of the vowel and vowel sounds.

Angus, Angus Óg. Pre-Christian god of poetry. G. W. Russell perceived him to be a counterpart of the Greek Eros, god of love.

Anne, Queen. Queen of Great Britain and Ireland, 1702–1714.

Antrim, County. One of the six counties of Northern Ireland still a part of Great Britain. It is situated just north of Belfast.

Aoife. (pron. EE-fa) Name borne by many legendary heroines of early Irish

417

literature. One, the mother of Conlaoch (elsewhere *Connla*), was an Amazonian chieftainness who lived in the Scottish Highlands.

Apollo. Classical god of poetry, music, and the fine arts.

Aran Islands. Chain of small islands at the mouth of Galway Bay, between counties Clare and Galway: Inishmore (or Aranmore), Inishmaan, and Inisheer. As the Islands are still Irish-speaking, many nationalists have felt, perhaps wrongly, that they are the most Irish parts of Ireland.

d'Arbois de Jubainville, Marie-Henri (1827–1910). French Celticist whose many publications were influential in the development of Celtic and Irish studies.

Árd Cuillean. Placename in the *Táin* identified with Crossakeel, County Westmeath.

Ardan. Brother of Naoise, Deirdre's lover.

Aries. Zodiacal sign of the Ram (March 21 to April 20).

arrah. (Ir. *ara*) Well, indeed. An interjection that is often deprecatory.

Ascoli, Graziadio I. (1829–1907). Italian linguist who helped to define the place of Celtic languages within the Indo-European family.

Áth Mór. (Ir. big ford) Placename in the *Táin* identified with the modern town of Athlone, County Westmeath, which controls the Shannon crossing between Leinster and Connacht. Maeve's army crossed the Shannon at Áth Mór on its return.

Athene, Athena. Greek goddess of wisdom.

Athy. Market town in County Kildare on the River Barrow.

Aughrim. (pron. AWK-rim). Village in Galway, site of the decisive defeat of the Jacobite-Williamite War, making it the last time an Irish army opposed English forces in the field, 12 July, 1691.

[Saint] Augustine (A.D. 354–430). Bishop, philosopher, one of the Latin Fathers of the Church and seminal thinker in early Christianity, known especially for his self-searching autobiography, *Confessions*.

avick. (Ir. *a mhic*) My son, my boy.

avourneen. (Ir. *a muirnín*) My darling, my dear.

Baile's Strand. The seashore around Dundalk and the mouth of the Boyne River.

Bailey, the. Well-known pub in downtown Dublin, frequented by writers.

bailiff. An agent of an estate.

Ballyrush. Townland in the parish of Inniskeen, Cavan, Patrick Kavanagh's birthplace.

Ballyvaughan. Fishing village in north Clare.

Bann. River in County Antrim that divides the industrialized east from the rural hinterlands to the west.

bardic session. Public gathering of bardic poets to demonstrate their craft.

Barrow. River in southeastern Ireland that empties into Waterford Harbour.

The Barrow valley was a center for stone carving; the high crosses of Castledermot and Moone are among this group.

bawn. Protective walls within which settlers made their homes during the British plantation of Ulster.

Beare. Peninsula in southwest Ireland, between Bantry Bay and the Kenmare River estuary in counties Cork and Kerry Haunt of the Old Woman of Beare, a personification of Ireland.

Beaumont, Francis (1584–1616). English dramatist.

bedad. Disguised oath, comparable to "by gosh," for "by God"; *cf.* begobs.

Beg-Innish. Transliteration of the Irish for Little Island (Ir. *beag inis*). Synge's citation may refer to what is now called Beginish in Valentia Harbour, Kerry.

begobs. A disguised oath, comparable to "by gosh," for "by God"; *cf.* bedad.

Bert, the big-foot. Hungarian princess who became the mother of Charlemagne (eighth century). Subject of romantic legends in France as Berthe au Grand Pied. So named for her club foot.

Binn os Gaoith. (pron. binn os GEE) Placename meaning cliff or peak above the wind.

Bloom. Leopold Bloom, hero of James Joyce's *Ulysses* (1922).

bohereen, boreen. (Ir. *bóithrín*, small road) Narrow country road or lane, especially in hilly country.

Bolingbroke, [Viscount]Henry St. John (1678–1751). Conservative rationalist English statesman and historian.

Book of Kells. Most famous of all early Irish illuminated manuscripts, an illustrated text of the Gospels named for the town of Kells, where it was found.

boreen. *See* bohereen.

bouchal. *See* a bouchal.

Boyne. Most important river of eastern Ireland. Seventy miles long, it empties into the Irish Sea near Drogheda. Site of William of Orange's important defeat of James II and the Catholic cause, 1 July, 1690.

Brandon, Mount. Peak 2764 feet high on the north coast of the Dingle Peninsula, Kerry.

Breagh. Variant spelling for the Latin *Bregia. See* following entry.

Bregia. Placename in the *Táin*. A plain in eastern Ireland between the Liffey and Boyne Rivers, County Meath. Ir. *Mag Breg:* Plain of Bray.

Breughel, Pieter (1520?–1569). Flemish painter know for his depictions of peasant life and landscapes.

Brian Boru. Irish historical king, who defeated the Norse at the Battle of Clontarf in A.D. 1014.

Brigid's Cross. A cross woven of rushes and considered to be a protective charm for a house.

Brobdignab. Kingdom of the giants in Swift's *Gulliver's Travels* (1726).

Bruno, Giordano (*c.* 1548–1600), Italian philosopher burned at the stake for heresy.

bulled. Reference to Adrian IV's papal bull, *Laudabiliter,* which provided the authorization for Henry II's invasion of Ireland in 1171.

Burke, William (1792–1829). The "bodysnatcher." Worked with William Hare murdering by suffocation, in order to sell victims' bodies to scientists for dissection. Burke was hanged after Hare turned King's evidence.

Burns, Robert (1759–1796). Lowland Scottish poet who often wrote in dialect. First poet born of the peasantry in the British Isles to achieve wide acclaim.

Caesar, Gaius Julius (100–44 B.C.) Roman general and statesman. Cleopatra, Caesar's mistress, bore him a son, Cesarion.

Cairbré. (Normative Cairbre) Name borne by many figures of early Irish history and legend, notably Cairbre Lifechair ("of the Liffey," "Liffey-Lover"), a king in the Fenian Cycle.

cairn. (Ir. *carn*) Pile of stones used as a marker, often a memorial.

caoine. (pron. KEEN) Cry for the dead, often, an extempory elegy. *See also* keen.

capernosity. Peevishness, ill-temperedness.

Carbery, Muskerry, Iveleary, etc. The names of baronies, administrative units in the province of Munster.

Carlow, County. A southern, rural county of Leinster, almost midway between Dublin and Cork.

Carrick. (Ir. *carraig*) Rock. Common in place names.

Casement, Sir Roger (1864–1916). Irish patriot, captured while smuggling German arms into Ireland and executed, August 3, 1916.

Cassandra. Princess and prophetess of Troy, seized by the Greeks after the fall of her city.

Castle, the. *See* Dublin Castle.

Cathbad. (pron. KATH-vadh, KAFF-a) Chief druid of Ulster and a leading figure of the Ulster Cycle; among many distinctions, he foretells the fate of Deirdre and serves as a teacher to Cuchulainn.

Cathleen ní Houlihan. *See* Kathleen ní Houlihan.

Cavan, County. Rural, dominantly Roman Catholic southern county of the province of Ulster, about 80 miles southwest of Belfast It is today a part of the Republic of Ireland.

Cawdor. Macbeth was prophesied to be the Thane of Cawdor in Shakespeare's play.

ceangal. (pron. CAN-gul) Tie or binding, as in prosody. Name given to a stanza that serves a postscript to a poem.

Ceannt, Eamonn (1881–1916). (pron. CANT) Revolutionary, athlete, and musician who participated in the Howth gun running, July 1914 and commanded the South Dublin Union during Easter week, 1916. Executed 8 May, 1916.

Celbridge. Village in Kildare, about ten miles west of Dublin. A favorite retreat of Jonathan Swift.

Celia. An idealization of feminine beauty, especially as immortalized in the poetry of Ben Jonson (1572–1637).

Cervantes, Miguel de (1547–1616). Spanish novelist, author of *Don Quixote.*

chip man. Man who cooks fish and *chips,* i.e., deep-fried potatoes.

Chloe. Stock name for a shepherdess in pastoral romances.

Clan Colam, Conaill, Creide. Rolleston's variant spellings for several heroic families of Ireland. The Clan Conaill (or *Cenél* Conaill) occupied Tirconnnel in what is now Donegal.

Clan Jansen. *See* Jansen.

Clare, County. A Munster county north of the Shannon estuary on the west coast. Anciently called Thomond, it is associated with the O'Brien family.

Clarke, Thomas J. (1857–1916). Fenian, revolutionary leader, and publisher of the anti-English journal, *Irish Freedom.* At the request of the other leaders, he was the first signer of the Proclamation of the Republic. Executed 3 May, 1916.

Cloacina. Ironic feminine personification of a sewer or drain (Latin: *cloaca*).

Clongowes Wood. Jesuit boarding school for boys in Kildare, attended by James Joyce from 1888 to 1891.

Clonmacnois, Clonmacnoise. Important monastic site, now a ruin, on the east bank of the Shannon, four miles north of Shannonbridge, Offaly. Founded by St. Ciarán (or Kieran) A.D. 545, the monastery is perhaps best known for the compilation of the great codex of early Irish literature, *Leabhar na hUidre:* The Book of the Dun Cow.

Clontarf. Site of battle where the Irish under Brian Boru defeated the Norse A.D. 1014. It is north of the modern city of Dublin.

Cnogba na Rig. Place name in the *Táin* identified with Knowth, County Meath, the site of an important megalithic tomb.

Cobh. (pron. COVE) Southern port near Cork city. Formerly called Queenstown, it was the major embarcation point for those emigrating to America.

Colam. *See* Clan Colam.

"Colleen dhas crotha na mbo." (Ir. *cailín deas crúite na mbó,* pron. COLL-een DYASS CRU-te na MO) Literally, "A pretty girl milking her cow." Irish folk song thought to be unlucky since it had once distracted a priest on his way to a sick call, causing him to arrive too late.

Collins, Michael (1890–1922). Revolutionary leader and one of the originators of modern guerrilla warfare, using a system of cadres he called "Flying Columns." Killed in ambush, August 22, 1922.

Combe, The. A back street near St. Patrick's Cathedral, Dublin.

compositum. Latin: Something made of parts joined together.

Conaill, Clan. People of Donegal, western Ulster.

Conall. A leading Ulster hero, foster-brother of Cuchulainn and avenger of his death. His name often carries the cognomen *Cernach,* or "of the victories."

Conchobar mac Nessa, Conchubar, Conor MacNessa (pron. KON-or). Legendary king of Ulster throughout much of the Ulster cycle. Although usually a heroic figure, he is less attractive when he appears as the lover of Deirdre.

Conn "the Hundred-Fighter," or **"of the Hundred Battles"** (Ir. Cetchathach). Legendary ancestor of the kings of Ireland, and of many important families.

Connacht, Connaught. The most westerly of the four ancient provinces of Ireland, running roughly from the Shannon Valley to the west coast of the island.

Connolly, James (1868–1916). Labor leader, political theorist, and a leader in the seizure of the General Post Office in Easter Week, 1916. Executed 12 May, 1916.

Cootehill. Market town in County Cavan that takes its name from the Coote family who settled there in the seventeenth century.

Corinna. An idealization of feminine beauty, specifically: (1) a Greek poetess who gave instruction to Pindar (522–442 B.C.); (2) a character in the poetry of Robert Herrick (1591–1674).

Cormac Conloingeas. Ulster warrior, son of Conchobar.

Corunna [La Caruna]. Site of an important British imperial battle (1809). Others cited by Austin Clarke evoke the Crimean War (Inkermann, 1854) and the Boer War (Pretoria), etc.

Costello, John A. (1891–1976). Prime Minister (*Taoiseach*) of the Republic of Ireland, 1948–1951 and 1954–1957.

Coventry. English industrial city. To be "put in Coventry" is to be shunned by one's fellow workers.

Crashaw, Richard (c.1612–1649). English poet known for religious works showing devotional ecstasy.

crathur. Pronounced as in the Irish, *créatúr* (Cray-toor). Creature. Usually an expression of sympathy, as "the poor crathur," though occasionally used contemptuously. Also used to mean a drop of whiskey.

creels. Wicker baskets.

Creide. *See* Clan Creide.

Cromwell, Oliver (1599–1658). English general and statesman. While Lord Lieutenant of Ireland, Cromwell arrived in 1649 to begin a campaign to subdue the Irish. His massacres at Drogheda and Wexford established a reputation for cruelty that continues to smolder in folk memory.

Cruachan. Royal seat of Maeve/Medb, warrior queen of Connacht; the site, three miles from Tulsk, Roscommon, is known today at Rathcroghan.

Cruithne. Irish name for the Picts, aboriginal inhabitants of the British Isles. The Picts are of disputed cultural originals, probably non-Indo-European.

Cuchulainn, Cúchulain, Cú Chulainn, etc. (pron. koo-KHULL-in) Hero of the Old Irish Ulster Cycle and principal figure of the epic *Táin Bó Cuailnge* [Cattle raid of Cooley]. His name means "Hound of Culann."

Cúil Silinni. Placename in the *Táin,* near Tulsk, Roscommon.

Dál nAraide. In *The Madness of Suibhne,* Suibhne's home in southern Antrim, near Lough Neagh.

Dana. Great mother goddess of pre-Christian Ireland, patroness of the Tuatha Dé Danann. Also spelled Ana.

Dante Alighieri (1265–1321). Italian poet and author of the *Divine Comedy,* which includes an oft-cited vision of the afterlife.

decumana. A large portion, literally—the largest from among ten.

Debrett's Peerage & Baronetage. Guide to the history of noble and landowning families.

Deirdre. Tragic lover of the Ulster Cycle, whose story is one of the "Three Sorrows of Storytelling." Betrothed to Conchobar, she eloped with Naoise and his three brothers, all of whom were eventually betrayed and killed. In Yeats's play, Deirdre committed suicide rather than marry Conchobar.

Derg. *See* Lough Derg.

Derry. Modern city in Derry, Northern Ireland, founded on the site of a monastery established by St. Columcille in A.D. 546. Also called Doire Choluim Cille (Columcille's Oak Grove) and Londonderry by Unionists.

de Valera, Éamon (1882–1975). American-born leader of the 1916 Uprising who escaped execution, opposed the 1922 Treaty, founded the Fianna Fáil Party, and served as prime minister and later president of Ireland.

Diana. Roman deity identified with the Greek Artemis. Goddess of the moon, as well as of hunting, archery, and running.

disjecta membra. Latin: scattered fragments.

dolmen. Type of megalithic monument still seen in the Irish countryside. A tripod of stone, its large capstone is sometimes called "the bed of Diarmaid and Gráinne."

Donegal, County. A mountainous and thinly populated county in western Ulster, in the far northwest of Ireland.

Drogheda (pron. DRAW-hed-a). Small port town near the mouth of the Boyne River, 32 miles north of Dublin. The name of the city lives in Irish history as the site of the slaughter of Irish men, women, and children by Cromwellian troops in 1649.

druid. Pre-Christian priestly class among the Celts.

Dublin Castle. Imposing building in downtown Dublin whose foundations date from 13th century. Seat of British government in Ireland before 1922.

Dubthach, Dubhthach. (pron. DUV-thach, DUFF-ach). Ulster warrior noted for his evil disposition.

Dundealgan. Dundalk, coastal town in Louth, midway between Dublin and Belfast.

Dungloe, Donglow. Fishing village in County Donegal.

Dunleary. (Ir. *Dún Laoghaire,* pron. doon-LEARY). Literally, Leary's fort. Formerly, Kingstown. Port city south east of Dublin, embarkation point for Irish leaving by boat train for Britain.

Dunquin. Parish in western Kerry, seven miles west of Dingle.

Dun Scathach. Archaeological site on the Isle of Skye, Scotland.

Dun Sobairche. Placename in the *Táin* identified with Dunseverick, County Antrim.

Durrow. Abbey four miles from Tullamore, Offaly, founded by St. Columcille, A.D. 551. The Book of Durrow, an illuminated manuscript of the Gospels, is in the library of Trinity College, Dublin.

Earls, Flight of. *See* Flight of Earls.

Elmo's Fire, [Saint]. A bright ball of fire, a natural phenomenon formerly seen to play among the masts of ships.

Emain Macha (pron. EV-in MAH-cha). Political center of Ulster in Old Irish literature. Identified with a site known as Navan Fort, near the modern town of Armagh.

Ennis. The principal town in county Clare.

Eochu Feidlech. (pron. OCH-oo FAYTH-lech) Father of Maeve (Medb).

Eogan son of Durthacht. (pron. OWEN) Naoise's killer.

Erato. Muse of erotic poetry in classical mythology.

Erigena, Johannes Scotus (c.810–c.870). Irish-born cleric and philosopher. One of the initiators of Scholastic philosophy, and, by implication, the first Irish intellectual.

Erne. River of northwestern Ireland, emptying into Donegal Bay. Site of many heroic adventures in Old Irish literature.

Étaín (pron. ay-TOYN or ay-TEEN) Name of several romantically beautiful women in Old Irish literature.

Euston. London railroad station, terminus for the Irish boat train.

fal-de-lals. Gaudy or trifling ornaments or trinkets.

fan lights. Distinctive decorative windows found in many Dublin houses, above the doors of both elegant townhouses and tenements. A semicircle of long glass triangles in roughly the shape of a fan.

Fand. Mythic queen of Old Irish literature, closely associated with the powers of the sea.

Fedlimid. (pron. FAYTH-lim-ith or FAY-lim-id) Deirdre's mother.

Fenian Cycle. One of three cycles of Old Irish literature, centering on Fionn mac Cumhaill, Oisín (or Ossian), and Oscar. (The other two cycles are the Ulster and the Mythological.)

Fenians. Alternate name for the Irish Republican Brotherhood in the British Isles and North America, especially during the 1860s. At other times the word Fenian may refer to any Irish nationalist.

Fer Diad. (pron. fer-DEE-adh) Friend of Cuchulainn who fought with the men of Connacht in the *Táin*. Later slain by Cuchulainn in single combat.

Fergus son of Roech. King of Ulster. He took the Connacht side in the *Táin* after learning he had been tricked by Conchobar into betraying the sons of Usnach.

Ferriter, Pierce or **Piaras** (*c.* 1600–1653). Kerry soldier and poet who supported the Irish cause in 1641. Hanged 1653.

Fian, Fians (Ir. pl. of Fianna). Roving bands of hunter-warriors, sometimes but not always identical with the followers of Fionn.

Fianna, Fianna Éireann, Fianna-Finn. Followers of Fionn in the Fenian Cycle.

Finn. *See* Fionn.

Fionn mac Cumhaill, Fin MacCool, etc. Hero of Old Irish Fenian Cycle whose stories have continued in the oral tradition in modern times.

firkin. A small wooden barrel for butter.

Flight of the Earls. After the Irish defeat at the battle of Kinsale (1603), the old Gaelic order was broken. In 1607, the Great Ulster Earls of Tirconnell (O'Donnell) and Tyrone (O'Neill) left for the Continent with their followers. Their departure left Ulster without leadership, facilitating the plantation of that province with Protestant settlers from Scotland and England.

footy. Poor, insignificant.

France, Anatole (1844–1924). French novelist and critic.

frieze coat. A coat made of shaggy, long-haired wool.

Gae Bulg. Spear of Cuchulainn.

Gaeltacht. (pron. GOIL-tahcht) Areas of Ireland, especially along the western coast, where the Irish language (or Gaelic) is still the first language of most of the population.

gaiks. Instrument that mechanically lifts a churn staff.

Gall. Not a Gael, i.e., a foreigner living in Ireland, a Norman, Anglo-Norman, Dane, or Englishman.

Galway. (1) A county in western Ireland, the western portion of which is Connemara. (2) The shire town or county seat of County Galway, a large town (pop. *c.* 35,000) and important port. (3) A bay on the west coast of Ireland, 30 miles long and 23 miles across, adjacent to the Aran Islands.

Gauls. Ancient inhabitants of what is now France, cultural cousins of the Gaelic Irish.

Gaza. An area of ancient Palestine where the blinded Samson went into exile.

geis. (Ir. *geis,* pron. gesh) Taboo or prohibition; binding obligation; magic spells.

Gentleman Jim. Nickname of James J. Corbett (1866–1933), Irish-American heavyweight boxing champion.

Georgian. Pertaining to the reigns of Kings George I, II, III, and IV, 1714–1830, especially as the era is reflected in the urban architecture of Dublin and some other Irish cities.

Geraldine. Conglomerate name for the group of interconnecting Catholic families who led the "Geraldine Rebellion" against English rule, 1565–1583.

Glanworth. A village in County Cork with a small woolen manufacturing industry.

Glen Dubh. Literally, "Dark Glen." A figurative placename.

Glencree. Rivulet and valley in north Wicklow.

Glenmacnass. Valley and waterfall in Wicklow near the monastic site of Glendalough.

glims. Lights.

Glorianna. Poetic name for Elizabeth I (1533–1603).

gob. (Ir. beak or bill) Mouth.

Gonne, Maud (1866–1953). Patriot and revolutionary, remembered today principally for the unrequited love W. B. Yeats bore for her.

gorse. Furze; plant covered with dark-green spines.

gossoon (Ir. *garsún,* a small boy; Fr. *garçon.*) A boy.

Gortin. (Ir. the little field) Townland in Inniskeen parish, County Cavan.

Gortinfliuch. Irish, "the little wet field."

Grangegorman. A Dublin mental hospital.

Granuaile, Gran Uaile. A poetic name for Ireland, cast heroically. Contains an allusion to Gráinne (or Grace) ni Mhaille (or O'Malley), c. 1530–1603, an Irish pirate widely celebrated in story and song. For more information, see Anne Chambers, *Granuaile, the Life and Times of Grace O'Malley.* Dublin: Wolfhound Press, 1983.

Green or **Greene, Robert** (*c.* 1560–1592). Elizabethan wit, poet, playwright, and pamphleteer.

Green, the. *See* St. Stephen's Green.

Griffith, Arthur (1871–1922). Journalist. Founder of the nationalist movement *Sinn Féin,* and first President of the Irish Free State.

Grosvenor Square, London. A fashionable address for wealthy absentee landlords.

Guinea. In Irish and English currency before decimalization (1970), a measurement of one pound and one shilling, or 5% more than a pound. Often used in calculating the price of such luxury items as *objets d'art.*

Gweedore. Village on the west coast of Donegal.

harpies. Monstrous creatures of classical mythology, part bird and part woman, who contaminated what they could not eat.

Hibernia. Roman name for Ireland.

Hibernian. A person from Ireland.

hob. Projection on the far side of a fireplace on which something, such as food, can be kept warm.

Houlihan. *See* Kathleen.

Hound of Cuailnge. Translation of the name Cuchulainn. Sometimes written as Hound of Culann.

House of the Red Branch. Alternative name for the warriors of the Ulster Cycle.

Houynhnms. The horses (and embodiments of rationality) in Book IV of Swift's *Gulliver's Travels* (1726).

Hume, David (1711–1776). Scottish philosopher.

Hungry Grass. (Ir. *féar gortach*) According to Irish folk belief, a field of grass that will induce insatiable hunger in all who walk upon it.

I.H.S. A monogram for the name of Jesus, derived from Greek letters.

Inishmore. Largest of the Aran Islands off Ireland's west coast. Also known as Aranmore.

Inkermann. See Corunna.

Iraird Cuillenn. (pron. IR-erd QUILL-in) Placename in the *Táin*, Crossakeel, County Westmeath.

Irish Volunteers. Name for the military force that seized British buildings in Dublin during Easter week, April 1916. Founded November 1913, by Eoin MacNeill, the Irish Volunteers reached its peak of 200,000 men in August 1914, at which time an ideological split divided the membership, when John Redmond pledged to volunteer for World War I.

Is uaigneach Eire. (pron. iss. WIG-nach AIR-eh) Literally, "It's lonely, Ireland."

Jansen, Clan, Jansenism. A puritanical movement within Roman Catholicism that denied free will. Originating in seventeenth-century Holland and France, the movement persisted in rural Ireland until the twentieth century. Named for Cornelis Jansen (1585–1638).

jarvey. Driver of a horse-drawn hackney or taxi.

jobber. A middleman who deals with stocks and securities among stockbrokers. In Devlin's implication, an affluent businessman.

John the Blind. St. John the apostle and evangelist who, according to tradition, composed the last book of the New Testament, Revelation (Protestant) or Apocalypse (Roman Catholic), while in exile on Patmos.

Joyce, Patrick Weston (1827–1914). Historian, collector of folk music, scholar, and author of *Origin and History of Irish Names of Places* (1869) and other works.

Jubainville. *See* d'Arbois de Jubainville.

Judith. Heroine of the book of the Apocrypha that bears her name. The

Apocrypha was regarded by some to be a part of the Bible, but is rejected by Protestants because it was not first written in Hebrew.

Jutes. Germanic invaders of fifth century Britain, along with the Angles and Saxons. The Jutes settled in the southeastern county of Kent.

Kateen-beug. Little Kate. Synge's name for any Irish peasant girl.

Kathleen ní Houlihan, Cathleen ní Houlihan. A romantic personification of Ireland.

Kead millia Failta ghud. (Ir. *céad míle failte dhuit,* pron. KAYD MEAL-a FALL-te'ud) One hundred thousand welcomes to you (traditional greeting).

keen. (Anglization of *caoine*) A wailing lamentation for the dead.

Kells. *See* Book of Kells.

Kent. Southeastern county of England, settled by Jutes in the fifth century.

kerne. Armed foot soldier: medieval Irish infantryman.

kibosh. (Ir. *caidhp bháis,* pron. KY-bosh) Literally, the cap of death. The expression has come to mean put and end to something, stop it finally.

Kieran, Saint. (Ir. Ciarán) Founder (A.D. 545) of the great monastery at Clonmacnois.

Kilmainham. Jail the junction of South Circular Road and Inchicore Road on the western side of Dublin. Site of the ancient church for which it is named. Used for political prisoners from the eighteenth through the twentieth century, including Parnell, Pearse, Plunkett, and MacDonagh.

Kilmallock. A small market town 20 miles south of Limerick.

Kilmore. (Ir.: big monastic church) Although more than twenty Irish locations bear this name, Hewitt implies the one in County Antrim, four miles from Cushendall.

Kyoto, Nagoya, Irago. Cites on the island of Honshu, Japan.

Laegaire of Victories (elsewhere Loegaire Buadach). (pron. LEER-eh) One of the three most important champions of ancient Ulster.

Land League. Agrarian movement founded by Michael Davitt and others in 1879 to win rights for small farmers, especially tenant farmers. The Land League organized history's first "boycott" by refusing to provide services to the landlord of that name.

Laracor. Village in western Meath, two miles south of Trim. Jonathan Swift once lived here.

Leborcham. (pron. LE-vor-cham) Deidre's guardian, a satirist.

Leinster (pron. LEN-ster). The easternmost of the four ancient provinces of Ireland, running roughly from the Shannon Valley to the eastern coast of the Island.

Leitrim, Country (pron. LEE-trim). A rural county in northernmost Connacht. One of the poorest and least populous of all Irish counties.

Lemuel. First name of Gulliver in Swift's *Gulliver's Travels* (1726).

Liffey. A river, 50 miles long, that flows through Dublin.

Lir. A sea god of old Irish mythology. The exile of his children and their transformation into swans is one of the best-known stories in Old Irish literature. Lir is the father of a greater sea god, Manannán mac Lir.

Liss. (Ir. lios) Ringed-fort or enclosed space. Fairy mound.

Londonderry. *See* Derry.

Longford, County. Rural county in central Ireland on the east bank of the Shannon River.

Lough Carra. Lake in County Mayo seven miles from Balintubber. Moore Hall, George Moore's family home, overlooks Lough Carra, which is described in the opening pages of *The Lake* (1905).

Lough Derg. Place of pilgrimage. Also known as "St. Patrick's Purgatory," since the saint was thought to have fasted and had a vision of the next world there. Known since the Middle Ages; the lough (lake) itself, one of several of this name, is located between counties Fermanagh and Donegal in western Ulster.

Lough Neah. One hundred fifty-three square mile lake in Ulster, northeastern Ireland. The largest body of fresh water in the British Isles.

Lough Swilly. Bay in northern County Donegal. The Earls of Tírconnel and Tyrone left Lough Swilly in 1607, and Wolfe Tone was captured there aboard a French ship, part of the expeditionary force in 1798.

Lyon. Large city in eastern France. France's "second city."

MacCarthy, John G. (1829–1892). Land commissioner, author, and pro-Home Rule Member of Parliament at Westminster.

MacCarthys. Family that ruled Desmond from Cashel after defeating the Anglo-Irish at the Battle of Callan near Kenmare, County Kerry, in 1261.

MacDiarmada, Séan (1884–1916). Revolutionary, organizer for Irish Republican Brotherhood, and despite being crippled by polio participant in the seizing of the General Post Office, Easter Week, 1916. Executed, 12 May, 1916.

Macha, plain of. Area in what is today County Armagh, A home territory of the Ulster warriors. It includes Emain Macha (q.v.).

Macha na Bo. (pron. MACH-ah na BOW) Cow's pasture.

MacMorris, Shakespeare's only Irishman *(Henry V)*.

MacNessa, Conor. *See* Conchobar mac Nessa.

MacSwiney, Terence (1879–1920). Lord Mayor of Cork who died on a hunger strike in Brixton prison protesting British policies.

Maeve. Warrior-queen of Connacht in Old Irish Literature, especially the epic *Táin Bó Cuailnge:* [The Cattle Raid of Cooley]. Also spelled Medb, Medbh, Medhbh, etc.

Mag Ai. Plains around Cruachan, County Roscommon. Placename in the *Táin.*

Maginn, William (1794–1842). Journalist and wit who died after having been imprisoned for debt.

Malin Head. A promontory in southwest County Donegal, one of the westernmost points in Ulster.

malt. Liquor made from malt, including beer or ale.

Mannan mac Lir. *See* Lir.

Maritain, Jacques (1882–1973). French Catholic philosopher, a leading interpreter of St. Thomas Aquinas in the twentieth century.

Marlborough, Duke of (1650–1744). English general and statesman who defeated the French at Blenheim in 1704.

Marot, Clement (1496–1544). French poet, known for his sonnets, pastorals, and translations of the Psalms.

Maurya Jude. Maurya, Daughter of Jude. Synge's name for any Irish peasant girl.

Maynooth. Town in County Kildare 15 miles west of Dublin. Site of St. Patrick's College (founded 1795). The College, usually known as "Maynooth," is the principal seminary of the nation, and has traditionally been associated with political conservatism. The College of St. Patrick is today part of the National University of Ireland.

Mazzini, Giuseppe (1805–1872). Italian nationalist and writer. His movement, Young Italy (1831), sought to unify Italy, and was a model for Irish nationalists.

Meath, County. A flat county north and west of Dublin, containing many of the most important archaeological sites in Ireland, including Tara (q.v.).

Medb. *See* Maeve.

memento mori. Lat.: Remember that you must die.

Merovingian. Dynasty of kings in what is now France, *c.*A.D. 500–751. Associated with the post-Roman spread of Christianity.

Meyer, Kuno (1858–1919). German Celticist who edited and translated many texts. He helped to found the School for Irish Learning, and edited its scholarly journal, *Ériu* (1904).

Milesian. The last in a series of invaders of Ireland, and therefore identical with the early Gaels (according to the *Lebor Gabála* [The Book of Invasions], a legendary history of early Ireland). Also, the early Irish as perceived heroically.

minerals. Carbonated soft drinks; soda pop.

Monna Lisa. J. M. Synge's spelling for Mona Lisa, Leonardo's famous painting.

Morrígu, Morrigan. Goddess of war (perhaps one of a trio of goddesses). She appears in the *Tain.*

mossa. *See* musha.

Mount Jerome. A Protestant cemetery in Dublin.

Mountjoy. A prison, formerly the most famous in Ireland. *See also* Kilmainham.

Muirtheimne, Muirthe   (pron. MUR-hev-na) Homeland or domain of

Cuchulainn in northeast County Louth, a plain north of the mouth of the River Boyne.

Munich bother. Munich was the site of the 1938 meeting between Neville Chamberlain (England), Édouard Daladier (France), Benito Mussolini (Italy) and Adolf Hitler (Germany) that resulted in the partition of Czechoslovakia. The word Munich has come to be a symbol for appeasement.

Munster. Largest and most southerly of the four ancient provinces of Ireland. It stretches from Waterford in the east to Kerry in the west, and includes Cork and the Shannon estuary.

musha, mossa. (Ir. *muise*) An assertive interjection used at the opening of a sentence: well; indeed. A milder form is *wisha*.

Naoise, Naoisi (pron. NEE-sha) Lover of Deirdre, with whom he elopes to Scotland, fleeing Conchobar. Naoise is always accompanied by his brothers, Ainnle and Ardan; together, they are the "Sons of Usnach."

Nash or Nashe, Thomas (1567–1601). Elizabethan satirist and writer who introduced the novel of adventure into England.

Nelson's Pillar. Imposing monument to British Admiral Horatio Nelson that formerly stood on Dublin's O'Connell Street (Sackville Street before 1922). Long resented by Irish nationalists, the Pillar was destroyed by a bomb blast in 1966.

Newtownmountkennedy. Village in northeast County Wicklow, 22 miles south of Dublin.

Niav. Anglicization of the Irish name Niamh, borne by many female figures in Old and Middle Irish—especially the beautiful woman who led Oisín to the land of eternal youth, Tir na nÓg, beyond the waves.

Ninety-eight. 1798, a year of rebellion in Ireland: risings in Leinster and Ulster by the United Irishmen in May and June. A small French force in support of the Irish landed in Connacht in August. All were unsuccessful.

nob. Head.

noggin. Small drinking vessel, less than a pint.

Nore. River that runs through the southeastern lowlands of Ireland past Kilkenny, where it meets the Barrow and empties into Waterford Harbor.

O'Brien, Dermot (1866–1945). President of the Royal Hibernian Academy and grandson of William Smith O'Brien (q.v.).

O'Brien, William Smith (1803–1864). Parliamentarian and later a leader of the Young Ireland rebellion of 1848. After the failure of the rebellion, O'Brien was exiled to Tasmania (1849–1856).

O'Clery, Mícheál [Ó Cléirigh, Micheal] (1575–1643). Franciscan monk who served as the chief compiler of the *Annals of the Four Masters* (1632–1636), a chronicle of Irish history from earliest days down to 1616.

Odi atque amo. Lat.: I hate and I love.

Odysseus. Greek hero of the Trojan War. His adventures en route home provide the subject of Homer's *Odyssey*.

Óg. (pron. Oge) Young.

ogham. A system of reproducing the Irish and Pictish languages dating from about the fourth century and lasting until the early seventh century. It used sets of grooves and notches, usually at the corners of standing stones.

O'Growney, Eugene (1863–1899). Priest and Irish language revival leader. His *Simple Lessons in Irish* (1894) was for many years a standard introductory textbook on the subject.

oinseach (Ir. *óinseach*). Stupid or foolish woman; fool. A male fool is an *amadán*.

Oisín. Son of Fionn mac Cumhaill, and a leading character of the Fenian Cycle.

Old Woman of Beare. (Ir. *Cailleach Bheare*) A sovereignty figure and personification of Ireland, thought to reside on the Beare peninsula, in counties Cork and Kerry, southwestern Ireland.

O'Moore [O'More], Rory (d. *c.* 1652). Leader of an unsuccessful rebellion against the English, 1641–1649.

Orange, Orange Lodge. An organization of Protestant men, largely working-class, who favor union with Great Britain and are therefore anti-nationalist.

oratio obliqua. Lat.: indirect speech; reported speech.

oratio recta. Lat.: direct speech; quoted speech.

Orphic egg. According to the ancient cult of Orphism, contemporary with early Christianty, the world was egg-shaped, and was hatched from an egg made by the Creator.

Oscar. Grandson of Fionn in the Fenian Cycle. An admirable and heroic figure, he is sometimes called the Galahad of the Cycle.

Ossian. Anglicized spelling for Oisín, the son of Fionn mac Cumhaill. In James Macpherson's partially bogus translations, *The Poems of Ossian* (1760–1763), Ossian is the narrator of a heroic Gaelic past.

Ossory. A diocese in County Kilkenny coextensive with the ancient kingdom of Osraighe.

Pan. Greek and Roman god of the countryside, poetry, and music.

Paris. Trojan prince who had to select the fairest from among the Greek goddesses Hera, Aphrodite, and Athena. He chose Aphrodite, thus sowing the first seeds of the Trojan War.

Parnassian Islands. Islands in the Parnassus range, which terminates at the Corinthian Gulf.

Parnell, Charles (1846–1891). Powerful leader of the Irish Party at Westminster. His fall from power with the revelation of his adulterous affair with Kitty O'Shea in 1890 is often perceived as one of the milestones in Irish political and intellectual life in the years preceeding the Irish Renaissance.

Paschal. Easter or Passover season.

Patmos. Island in Aegean Sea, where, according to legend, St. John the Divine wrote the last book of The New Testament—Revelation (Protestant) or Apocalypse (Roman Catholic).

Peelers. Irish constabulary founded by Sir Robert Peel (1788–1850), who also gave his name to London Bobbies.

penal times. Peiod following the Treaty of Limerick (1691) when the rights of the native Irish (as well as those of the Roman Catholic Church) were severely curtailed.

pension day. The pension is an Irish government subsidy to the elderly. For country people, therefore, pension day is a day in town.

pietá (Italian: pity). In painting and sculpture, a representation of the Virgin Mary mourning the body of Christ that she holds in her arms.

pike. Weapon used by Irish rebels in 1798, consisting of a shaft and a steel head. Precursor of the bayonet.

pious Aeneas. Hero of the Roman epic, *The Aeneid*. Called "pious" for his loyalty to his family and to the gods.

Pompeii. City located at the foot of Mr. Vesuvius, destroyed in A.D. 79 by a volcanic eruption.

porter. Dark brown malt liquor, resembling ale, especially popular in Ireland.

potato drills. Potatoes sown in a light furrow or trench.

poteen (pron. puh-TSHEEN) Anglicization of *poitín*: little pot; home-distilled (illegal) whiskey; moonshine.

praskeen. (Ir. *práiscín*) Rag.

Pretoria. *See* Corunna.

Prometheus. Titan of Greek mythology who defied the gods to steal fire for the benefit of mankind.

Quartre Bras. See Corunna.

Quays, The. (pron. KEYS) Commercial streets built on embankments lining the sides of the river Liffey in central Dublin.

Rabelais, Francois (*c*.1494–*c*.1553). French humorist and satirist, known for his bawdy and boisterous novel *Gargantua*.

rasher. A slice of bacon.

Red Branch Cycle. Another name for the Ulster Cycle. (The name is taken from the hall of the Ulstermen.)

Red Dan Sally, Red Dan Philly. Names evocative of the peasantry.

Redmond, John Edward (1856–1918). Political leader and supporter of C. S. Parnell. Redmond headed the pro-Parnell minority in the Irish Party at Westminster after that leader's fall from power in 1890. Redmond supported the British cause in World War I, and was surprised by the Rising of Easter Week 1916.

ricks. Stacks or piles of grain, straw, or hay in the fields.

Ringsend. Working-class neighborhood southeast of Dublin, adjacent to the harbor.

Ronsard, Pierre de (1524–1584). French lyric poet, principal figure of a group of poets known as the Pleiade.

Rossa, Jeremiah O'Donovan (1831–1915). Journalist and leader of the Irish Republican Brotherhood or Fenians. After having been jailed from 1865 to 1871, he spent his later life in the United States, where his many publications counseled violent action in the cause of Irish independence. P. H. Pearse delivered a famous panegyric at Rossa's grave, 1 August, 1915.

The Rosses. Area of rocks and small lakes in western County Donegal.

Sackville Street. former name of Dublin's principal commercial thoroughfare. Now called O'Connell Street.

Saint—. *See* cited name, as Kieran, etc.

Saint Patrick's Cathedral. Largest church ever built in Ireland, serving worshippers from the Church of Ireland, which is comparable to the Anglican (U.K.) or Episcopalian (U.S.A.) faiths.

St. Stephen's Green. One of Dublin's large squares, now a public park.

Salamanca. Spanish university. Irish clerics were trained here when Catholic education was outlawed in the British Isles.

Samhain (pron. SOW-en). Old Irish calendar feast beginning the dark or deathly half of the year. Counterpart of Halloween.

Sartor Resartus. Thomas Carlyle's discussion of philosophical systems, disguised as a philosophy of clothes. Published in *Fraser's Magazine,* 1833–1834.

scoil. (pron. skull). School.

settle. Long wooden bench with a high back.

"Shan Van Vocht." (Ir. *Sean Bhean Bhocht:* poor old woman) Title of a song associated with the rebellion of the United Irishmen in 1798. The Poor Old Woman is a personification of Ireland, and the song named for her is a kind of Irish *Marseillaise.*

Shannon. (1) The principal river of Ireland, following 224 miles though the central and western portions of the island. (2) The principal international airport of Ireland, adjacent to the Shannon River estuary in south County Clare.

Sheba, Queen of. Woman mentioned in the Old Testament as having Solomon (1 Kings 10).

Shee. Anglicization of *sí* or *sidhe*: fairly mound, or creature of the Otherworld.

Shelley, Percy Bysshe (1792–1822). English poet. His works include *Prometheus Unbound* (1818).

Sheridan, Thomas (1719–1788). Irish actor, elocutionist, and lexicographer. He was the godson of Jonathan Swift and the father of playwright Richard Brinsley Sheridan.

shillelagh. An oak stick, named for the place famous for such oak.

Shule Aroon. (Ir. walk, treasure) Familiar from the verse: Walk, walk, walk, treasure! / Walk calmly and walk quietly. / Walk to the door and steal off with me / And may you go safely my darling.

Sigerson, George (1836–1925). Scientist and man of letters who wrote on both medicine and early Irish literature. His translations, *Bards of the Gael and Gall* (1897), were especially influential.

simony. The buying or selling of ecclesiastical offices in the Church—a sin that a child would know of only by studying a catechism.

Sinn Féin. (Irish: we ourselves). A political (non-military) movement founded in 1905 by Arthur Griffith and others to promote non-violent economic independence. Although Sinn Féin did not support the Easter Rising of 1916, the phrase "Sinn Fein" nevertheless denoted all Irish nationalist groups in the popular mind.

skivvy. A scullery maid; an unappreciated female drudge of low social station. A term of derogation.

Slane. Village in County Meath, on the north bank of the Rover Boyne.

sloe. The fruit of the blackthorn.

Smith, Goldwin (1823–1910). English historian and journalist, known for his liberal, anti-imperialistic views.

Smyrna. Former Greek name for a port city on the east shore of the Aegean. (The current Turkish name is Izmir.)

sneezer. Drink.

Sorcha. Mythical land that can be identified with almost any distant place, perhaps Syria.

squeezer. Gallows.

Stella. Nickname given to Esther Johnson (1681–1728) by Jonathan Swift, who addressed love poems to her.

Stephens, James (1825–1901). Political leader who founded the Irish Republican Brotherhood, or Fenians, during the 1850's, but parted company with that body when he failed to lead a rising in 1865. (Note: Should be distinguished from the poet and storyteller of the same name [1880–1950].)

stooks. Shocks of flax. Also, a step in the linen-making process.

storeen. (Ir. *stór:* treasure, riches) Little treasure, dear one—a conventional term of endearment.

stout. A strong, very dark porter or ale.

streels. Strolls, saunters, drags, trails. In Gogarty's "Ringsend," this makes a pun with another word in Irish-English, the noun *streel* (from *sraoilleog:* slattern, slut).

Strephon. A stock name for a rustic lover in pastoral poetry.

Sualtam. (pron. SOOL-tam) Cuchulainn's mortal father.

sugawn. (Ir. *sugán*) Straw rope. Also, a chair with a seat woven of sugawn.

Suir. river that rises in Tipperary and flows southeast, emptying into Waterford Harbor.

Sullivan, John L. (1858–1918) Irish-American heavyweight boxing champion.

Susanna. Beautiful and virtuous woman in the Old Testament, proved innocent of adultery by Daniel.

sweated their duds. Pawned their clothes.

Tandy, (James) Napper (1740–1803). Dublin orator and politician. Instrumental in founding the United Irishmen in Dublin (1791) with Wolfe Tone.

tanner. Sixpence (before Irish and British money was decimalized [1970]).

Tara. Hill in County Meath, about 25 miles northwest of Dublin; site of the ritual coronation of Irish high kings. The nineteenth century assumption that Tara was once a palace is not supported by modern archaeology. Also written *Teamhair, Temair,* etc.

Teffia. Poetic, bogus-historical name for northern Ireland.

Thanam o'n dhoul. (Ir. *D'anam don diabhal,* Pron. HAN-am un DOWL). Go the the devil!

theosophy. Any of several systems of philosophy that seek direct knowledge of the divine through contemplation or spiritual ecstasy.

Thig im thu shinn? Thigum. Thigum. (Ir. *An dtuigeann tú sin?* pron. DIG-in too shin? HIG-im. HIG-im) Do you understand that? I understand. I understand.

Thomond. Former name of north Munster, especially County Clare.

throttler. One who chokes or suffocates another; the hangman.

tinker. Itinerant.

titan. Greek divinity representing an elemental force of nature. (When a titan is referred to as *the* Titan, it is usually Prometheus).

Titian (c.1477–1576). Italian painter.

toucher. Someone likely to ask for a small loan.

trap-case. Coffin.

Treblinka. Major German concentration camp located sixty-two miles northeast of Warsaw, Poland. Treblinka 2, the extermination camp that operated between July 1942 and October 1943, killed an estimated 731,000 Jews.

tricolour. The Irish flag since 1922, of green, white, and orange.

tristia. Sadness; gloom.

"Troubles, the." Colloquial name for the civic unrest in Ireland, 1916–1926. The Easter Rising and the taking of the GPO on Sackville Street occurred in April, 1916; the Anglo-Irish War, or "Black and Tan War," was 1919–1922; the Civil War, between pro-Treaty or Free State Forces and anti-Treaty or Republican forces, was 1922–1923.

Tuam. Small market town in eastern County Galway, seat of both a Roman Catholic archdiocese and a Protestant diocese.

Tubber. (Ir. *tobar:* well, spring, fountain) Name of several Irish hamlets.

turf. Partially carbonized vegetable materials, chiefly mosses, found in bogs in Ireland; although usually saturated with water, it can be cut, dried, and turned into a fuel, one with a distinctive odor. Known as peat in North America.

Turloch Caille Móire. Placename in the *Táin,* north of Knowth.

twenty-two and sixpence. 22 shillings and 6 pence, or 1 pound, 2 1/2 shillings.

Tyler, Watt (d. 1381). Leader of an unsuccessful peasants' revolt in England; killed by the lord mayor of London while speaking with King Richard II.

Tyrone, County. Anciently, the homeland of the O'Neill family, County Tyrone in central Ulster, is one of the six counties still united with Great Britain.

Uch, Uch, Ochone! (Ir. *ochón*) Alas! Cry, wail.

Ulaid. Men of Ulster.

Ulster. The most northeasterly of the four ancient provinces of Ireland. Although comprised of nine counties, Ulster is sometimes wrongly thought to refer only to the six counties still united to Great Britain.

Ulster Cycle. One of the three heroic cycles of Old Irish literature, sometimes described as the most "aristocratic" of the three. Leading figures include Cuchulainn, Deirdre, Conchobar, and Maeve. Also known as the Red Branch Cycle."

Unionist. One who favors or supports the Act of Union (1800), making Ireland a part of the United Kingdom of Great Britain. In much of the twentieth century, "Unionist" has been a political term for a person who supports the union of the six counties of North Ireland with Great Britain. *Cf.* West Briton.

Usnach, sons of. Naoise, the lover of Deirdre, and his brothers Ainnle and Ardan (Usnach is a hill in County Westmeath).

Vanessa. Nickname given to Esther Vanhomrigh (1687–1723) by Jonathan Swift, who wrote poems about her but eventually denied her love.

Vercingetorix. Leader of the rebellion that started the Gallic War.

Vico, Giovanni Battista (1668–1744). Italian philosopher, whose theory of history influenced James Joyce.

Villon, Francois (1431–c.1463). French poet.

Vinegar Hill. Site of the battle between the United Irishmen and the English during the rising of 1798. After a bloody battle, the Irish were defeated. It is near Enniscorthy, County Wexford.

Voltaire. Pseudonym of F. M. Arouet (1694–1778), French wit and philospher.

Volunteers. *See* Irish Volunteers.

West Briton. A disparaging term for an Irishperson who apes British manners and denies Irish identity. *Cf.* Unionist.

"which" for "who." Pronouns used in Protestant and Roman Catholic translations of the Lord's Prayer, the Our Father.

whisht. (Ir. *thoist*) Silence! hush! be quiet!

Whitehall. The former royal palace of English monarchs, near Westminster Abbey, where goverment offices are located.

Wicklow, County. A mountainous county of eastern Leinster, just south of Dublin. J. M. Synge spent much of his childhood here.

Wild Geese. Irish soldiers who fled their native country after the defeats of 1689–1691 to serve in foreign armies.

William, King, William of Orange. Dutch prince who helped to vanquish Irish national aspiration, 1698–1691, and later served as king, first in conjunction with his wife Mary and later as William III. Known derisively as "King Billy" by Irish nationalists.

Williamite. A follower or admirer of William of Orange, King William III. More recently, "Williamite" refers to someone who has come from England or Scotland to exploit Ireland's economic weakness.

Windisch, Ernst (1844–1918). German scholar of Sanskrit and early Celtic languages who compiled an important Old Irish grammar and dictionary, as well as translated many texts.

winkers. Horse's blinders.

wisha. (Ir. *mhiuse*) Well! indeed! An interjection. A milder form of *musha, mossa* (q.v.).

workhouse. Poorhouse, in nineteenth century Ireland.

Wotan. Name used in early England for Odin, old Germanic sky god.

Young Ireland. Nationalist movement led by Thomas Davis. Young Ireland supported the unsuccessful rebellion of 1848 led by William Smith O'Brien and others.

Zeuss, Johann Kaspar (1806–1856). German Celticist whose *Grammatica Celtica* (1853) opened the field of ancient Celtic philology to scientific inquiry.

Zimmer, Heinrich (1851–1910). German Celticist, known for his daring and imaginative theories that sought to explain the early history of Ireland.

INDEX

Woods, Macdara, 396
Woolf, Virginia, 95
Wormwood, 369
Worth, Katharine, 415

Yeats, Jack B., 62
Yeats, William Butler, xvii, 3, 4, 95, 103,
    108, 114, 120, 122, 130, 133, 148,
    164, 165, 173, 174, 191, 204, 267,
    289, 290, 388, 423; "Cuchulain's

Fight with the Sea," 148; *Herne's
    Egg, The,* 120; "The Madness of
    King Goll," 4; *On Baile's Strand,* 120,
    148
"Yellow Bittern, The," 238–39
Young Ireland, 114

Zimmerman, George-Denis, 87
Zneimer, John, 287, 288
Zola, Émile, 191